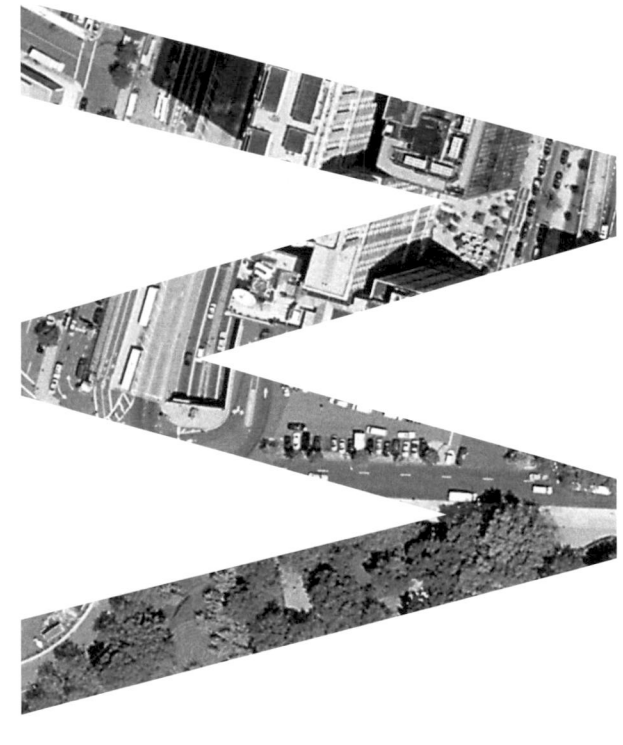

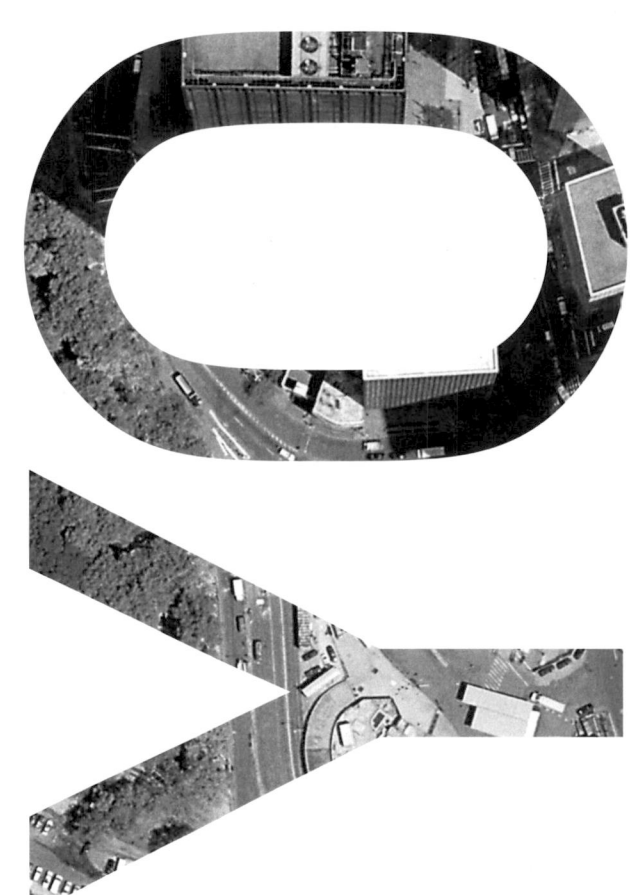

NEW YORK

THE PHOTO ATLAS

AN AERIAL TOUR OF ALL FIVE BOROUGHS AND MORE

HarperResource

An Imprint of HarperCollins *Publishers*

First published in 2004 by
Collins
An imprint of HarperCollinsPublishers
77–85 Fulham Palace Road
London W6 8JB
www.collins.co.uk

Getmapping can produce an individual print of any area shown in this book, or of any area within the United Kingdom. The image can be centered wherever you choose, printed at any size from A6 to 7.5 meters square, and at any scale up to 1:1,000. For further information, please contact Getmapping at www.getmapping.com.

New York: The Photo Atlas.

HarperCollins books may be purchased for educational, business or sales promotional use. For information, please write: Special Markets Department, HarperCollins Publishers Inc., 10 East 53rd Street, New York, NY 10022.

FIRST EDITION

The publisher regrets that it can accept no responsibility for any errors or omissions within this publication, or for any expense or loss thereby caused.

The representation of a road, track or footpath is no evidence of a right of way.

ISBN: 0-06-059499-3

04 05 06 07 08
9 8 7 6 5 4 3 2 1

Photographic image processing by Bluesky plc

Color origination by Radstock Reproductions Ltd., Midsomer Norton
Printed and bound in Great Britain by Butler & Tanner, Frome, Somerset

Designed and produced by Martin Brown
Editorial Direction: Philip Parker
Captions: Ian Harrison
Production: Graham Cook

Index generated by Cartografix. For more information on
all aspects of mapping, design and data manipulation,
contact info@cartografix.com or visit www.cartografix.com

Introduction

We are all familiar with aerial photographs of well-known places, usually taken obliquely from a particular angle and direction to show off a famous landmark to its best effect. This atlas is quite different in concept — it uses vertical aerial photography to create a photographic map of the five boroughs of New York City. This treatment lets you see the city as it really is, not flattering any particular aspect, but revealing each area in its true proportions and each building in its proper place. It is extraordinary how the photography brings the city alive. An ordinary map tells you how to find your way to a place, but it gives you no concept of what the place will look like when you get there. By contrast, this atlas gives you a bird's-eye view of New York as it really is.

If you live in New York, you will already have a personal stake in this book — within its pages you will be able to find your house or apartment block, trace a route around Central Park, visit some of your favorite shops, or find familiar landmarks. Aerial photography is interesting because it shows a familiar environment from an unfamiliar perspective, forcing you, the viewer, to interpret the scene anew. From these photographs you will notice patterns that are invisible from the ground, discover surprising links between unconnected areas, find large areas of greenery you never knew existed, and explore new neighborhoods.

Even if you are not familiar with New York, you will still find this a fascinating book. The window seats on airplanes are always the first to be taken because looking down is so intriguing, whether you know the place below or not. If you do, you seek out familiar landmarks; if not, you imagine what it must be like, and try to reconcile the view with your preconceptions.

Getmapping was founded in 1998 to make a complete and map-accurate photograph, known as the Millennium Map, of the whole of England. In 2000, HarperCollins published LONDON: THE PHOTOGRAPHIC ATLAS, which proved to be such a success that a second edition has already been published to reflect the rapid development of the city. The New York Atlas, as the first companion volume to be published outside Britain, is a real landmark, but we expect to extend the catalog to cover many other major cities over the next few years.

Keystone Aerial Surveys Inc. took the photography for NEW YORK: THE PHOTO ATLAS in the summer of 2003 using a large-format survey camera flown at 5,500 feet in a specialist survey airplane. The camera uses conventional 9-inch film, and each photograph overlaps its neighbor by about 80

percent so that every point on the ground is covered several times. Each negative from the survey was scanned to create digital files, which were then mosaicked together to create a seamless and map-accurate picture of the whole city. In most photographic mosaics, buildings are shown from a slight angle to give an idea of their height and construction. For this atlas the extreme height of the buildings in Manhattan presented us with a particular challenge, as even a modest lean on a skyscraper obscures a considerable area of the street beneath.

For aerial survey work you always need a combination of clear weather and air-traffic-control clearance. In New York this is notoriously difficult to achieve. The weather is often hazy, and the density of air traffic is extremely high. Since 9/11 it has become even more difficult to obtain permission to fly over New York, and Keystone is one of the very few survey companies allowed to do so. Despite these challenges, Keystone managed to capture all the photography of New York in two sorties over a 4-week period.

This photographic atlas is easy to use. The photography and the cartography share the same standard grid system, meaning you can cross-reference quickly between the two elements, and these are supported by a comprehensive index of streets. The extensive scope of the book means that no part of New York City's five boroughs — and slightly beyond — is left unexplored. Manhattan, Brooklyn, Queens, Staten Island, and the Bronx are of course included, but the atlas goes beyond to cover a substantial strip of the New Jersey coastline, and from Yonkers in the north to Long Beach in the south. Once they have it in the hand, many lovers of New York all over the world will be incapable of putting down this extraordinary and compelling book.

The idea of a complete photographic atlas is such a simple one that it is astonishing that it has never been done before. NEW YORK: THE PHOTO ATLAS is a compelling book that brings this complex and vibrant city alive. We hope that you will enjoy exploring the city through these pages.

Tristram Cary
Managing Director, Getmapping plc
April 2004

Key to photography

The corresponding cartography page reference is located at the bottom
left of each photography spread

The approximate grid interval, in yards and (meters), is for each scale;

1:2,400	218.7 yards (200.0 meters) width x 287.4 yards (262.8 meters) height
1:3,200	291.6 yards (266.6 meters) width x 383.2 yards (350.4 meters) height
1:5,000	455.5 yards (416.6 meters) width x 598.7 yards (547.5 metres) height
1:6,400	583.3 yards (533.3 meters) width x 766.4 yards (700.8 meters) height
1:12,800	1157.4 yards (1058.3 meters) width x 1390.7 yards (1390.7 meters) height

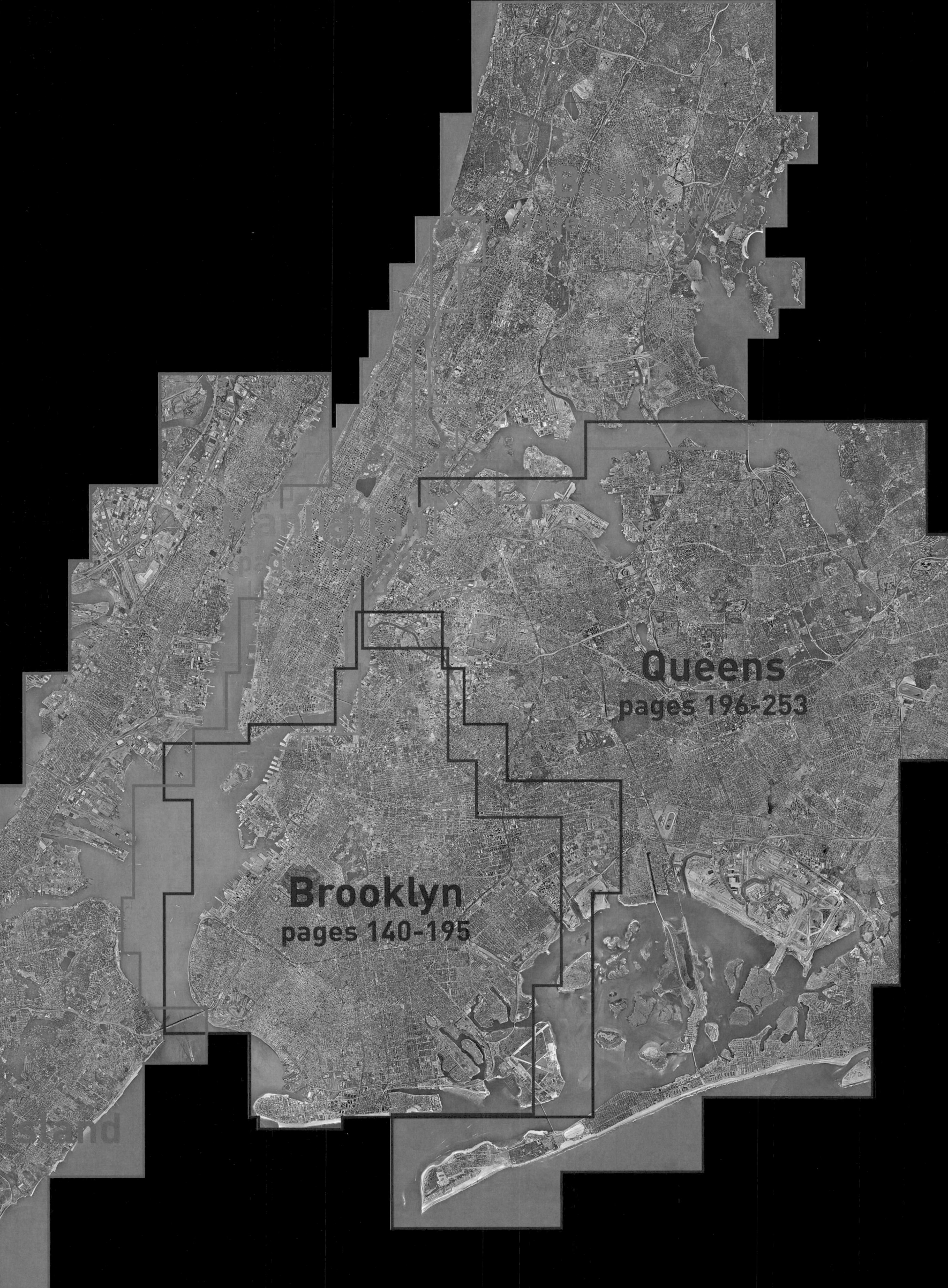

Queens
pages 196-253

Brooklyn
pages 140-195

Manhattan

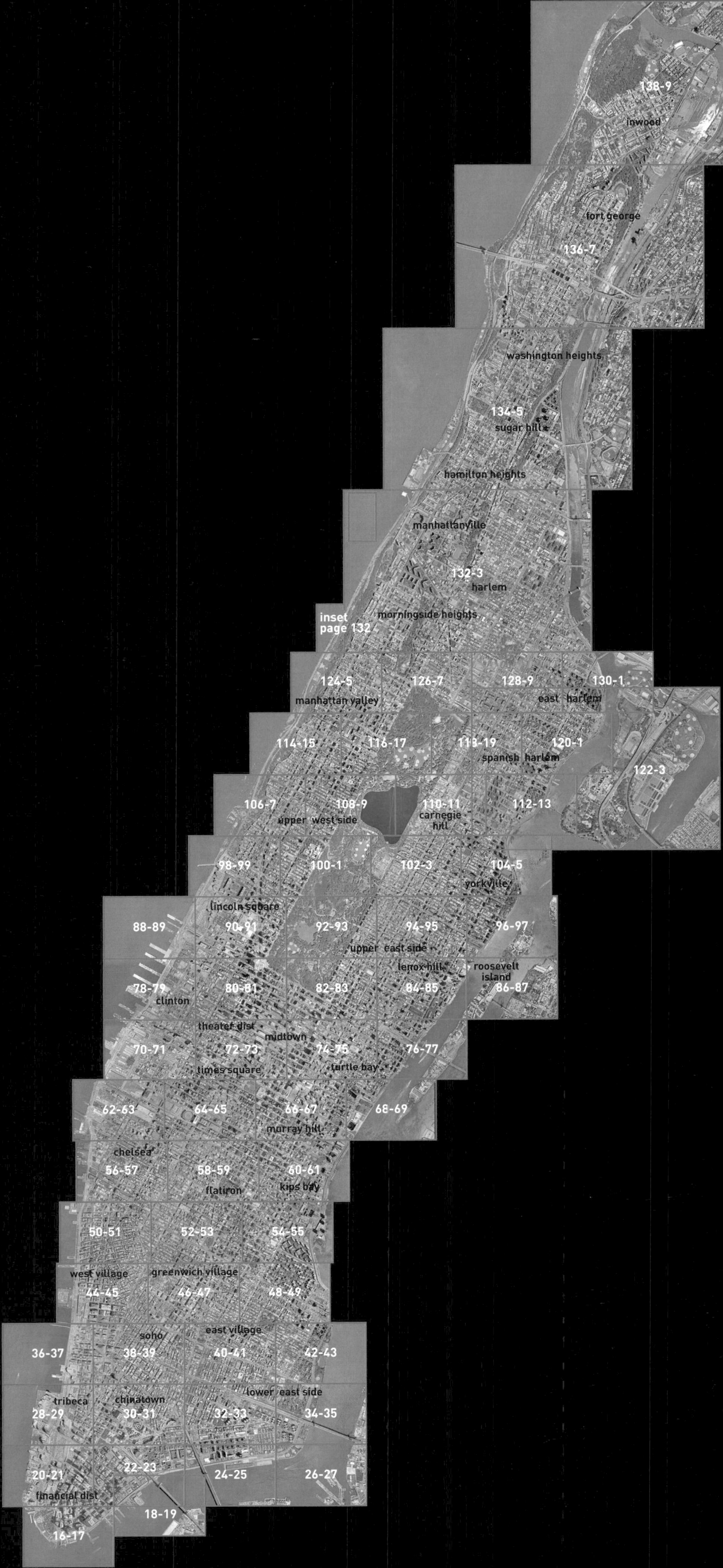

138-9
inwood

fort george

136-7

washington heights

134-5
sugar hill

hamilton heights

manhattanville

132-3
harlem

morningside heights

inset
page 132

124-5   126-7   128-9   130-1
manhattan valley   east harlem

114-15   116-17   118-19   120-1
spanish harlem

122-3

106-7   108-9   110-11   112-13
upper west side   carnegie hill

98-99   100-1   102-3   104-5
yorkville

lincoln square

88-89   90-91   92-93   94-95   96-97
upper east side
lenox hill   roosevelt island

78-79   80-81   82-83   84-85   86-87
clinton

theater dist   midtown
70-71   72-73   74-75   76-77
times square   turtle bay

62-63   64-65   66-67   68-69
murray hill

chelsea
56-57   58-59   60-61
flatiron   kips bay

50-51   52-53   54-55

west village   greenwich village
44-45   46-47   48-49

soho   east village
36-37   38-39   40-41   42-43

lower east side
tribeca   chinatown
28-29   30-31   32-33   34-35

20-21   22-23   24-25   26-27
financial dist

18-19

16-17

22/3

17

scale 1:2,400 see cartography pages 336-7

scale 1:2,400 see cartography pages 336–7

23

scale 1:2,400 see cartography pages 336-7

25

145

37

30

21

39

32

39

23

41

34

43

152

B

27

39

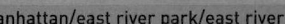

A

B

B

C

47

56

44

59

53

54

47

scale 1:2,400 see cartography pages 338-9

66

scale 1:2,400 see cartography pages 338–9

67

76

206

212

B

C

79
72
64

B

B

71

76

scale 1:2,400 see cartography pages 338–9

206

89

80

71

82

scale 1:2,400 see cartography pages 338–9

325

78

99

92

81

5

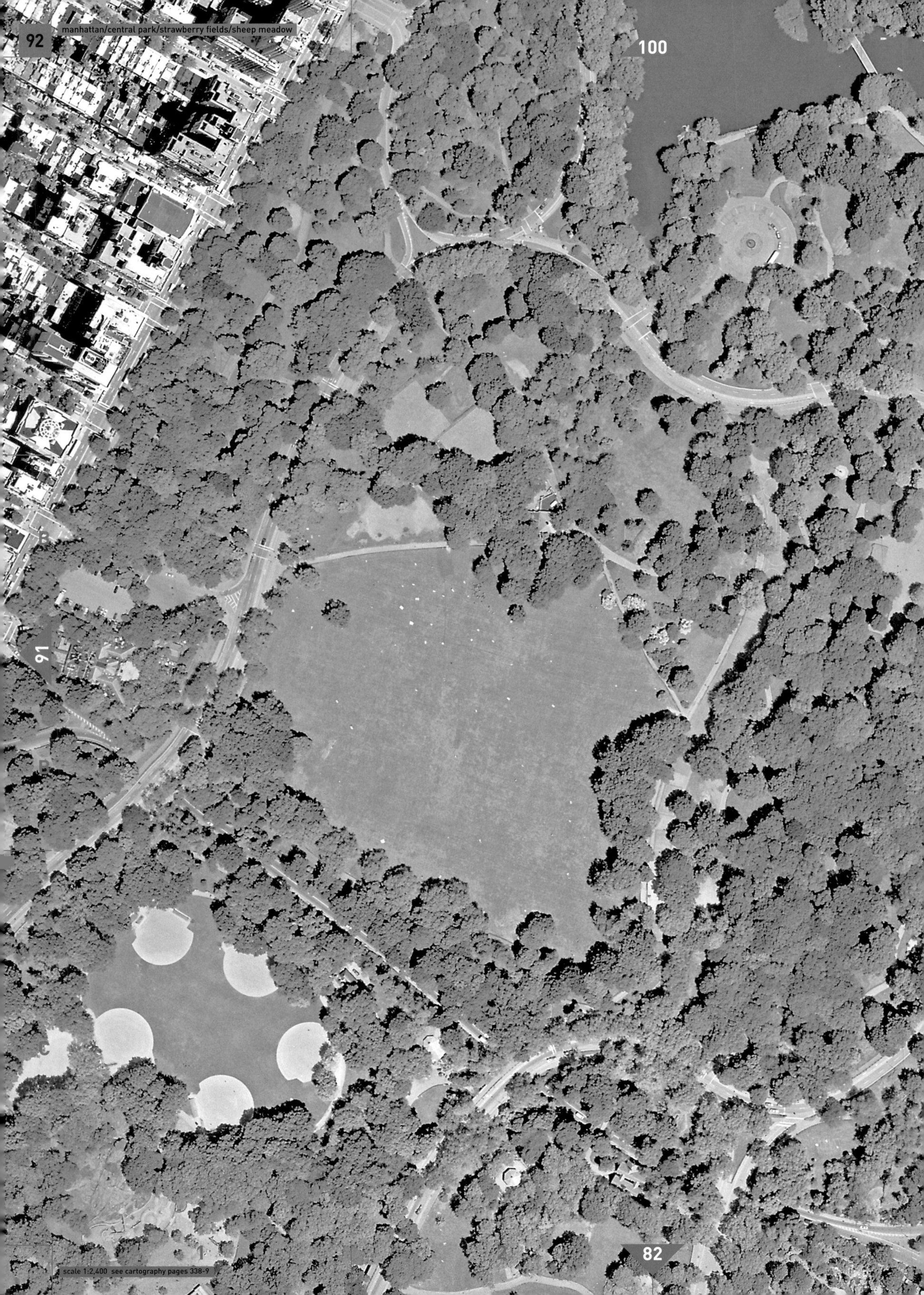

96

95

B

198

106-7

100

91

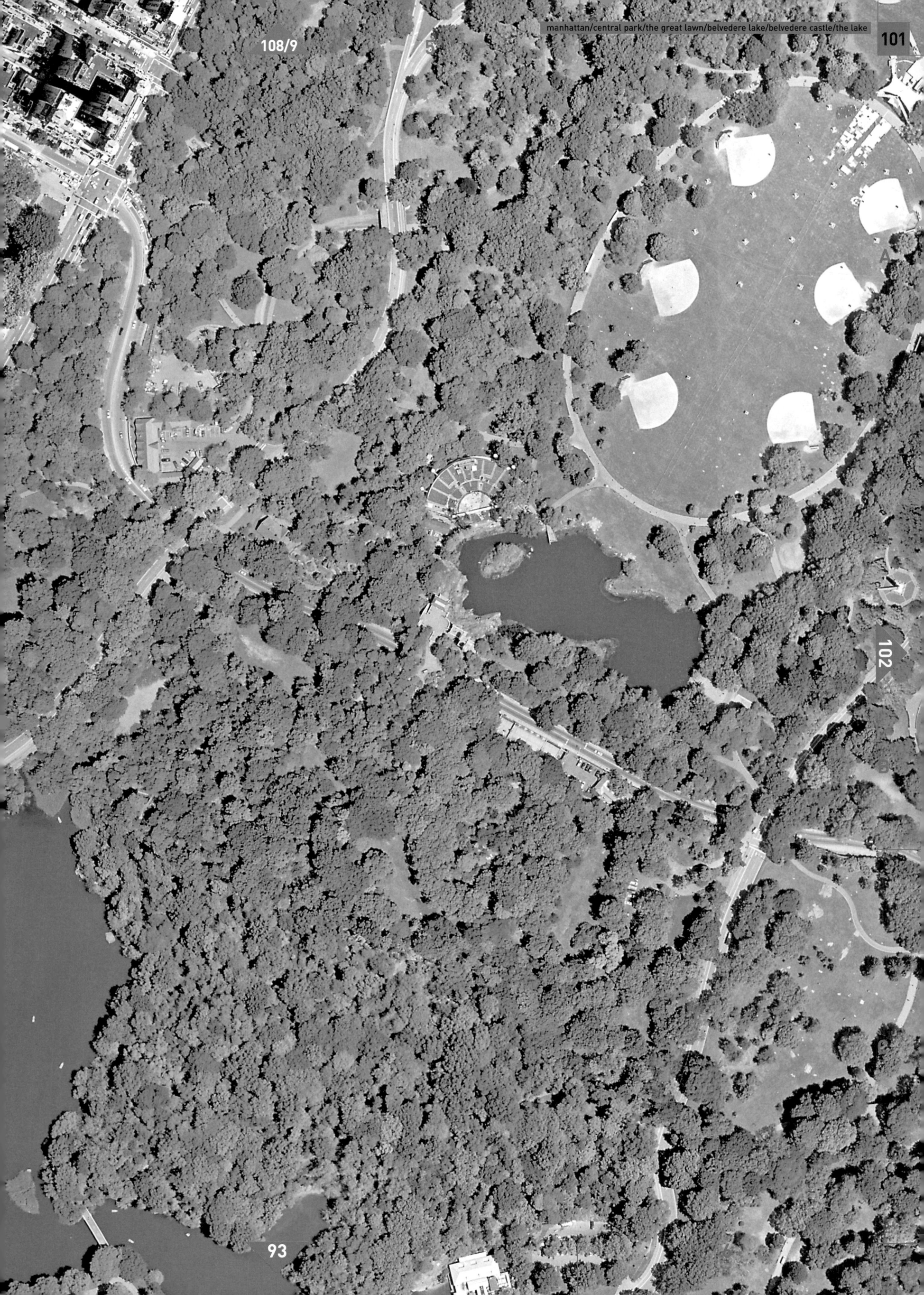

A

110/11

104

95

103

scale 1:2,400 see cartography pages 346-7

112/13

198

97

scale 1:2,400 see cartography pages 346-7

B

110

B

C

109

B

B

C

1

102/3

119

111

104/5

120

122

331

124

116

B

manhattan/central park/the pool/north meadow/ball field/recreation house

B

B

120

B

119

scale 1:2,400 see cartography pages 346-7/348-9

128-30

111/118

104/5

131/258

manhattan/harlem river/randalls island/wards island/water pollution control plant/triborough bridge/hell gate bridge/east river/queens

123

A

B

331

B

C

1

132

126

B

116

132

128

118

133

127

119

133
130
133
120

A

B

scale 1:6,400

331

inset above

scale 1:6,400 see cartography pages 342-3

258

132/3

266

scale 1:6,400 see cartography pages 342-3

manhattan/fort george/high bridge park/washington bridge/alexander hamilton bridge/high bridge/harlem river/bronx/morris heights

138

137

274

manhattan/fort george/high bridge park/washington bridge/alexander hamilton bridge/high bridge/harlem river/bronx/morris heights

274

274

Brooklyn

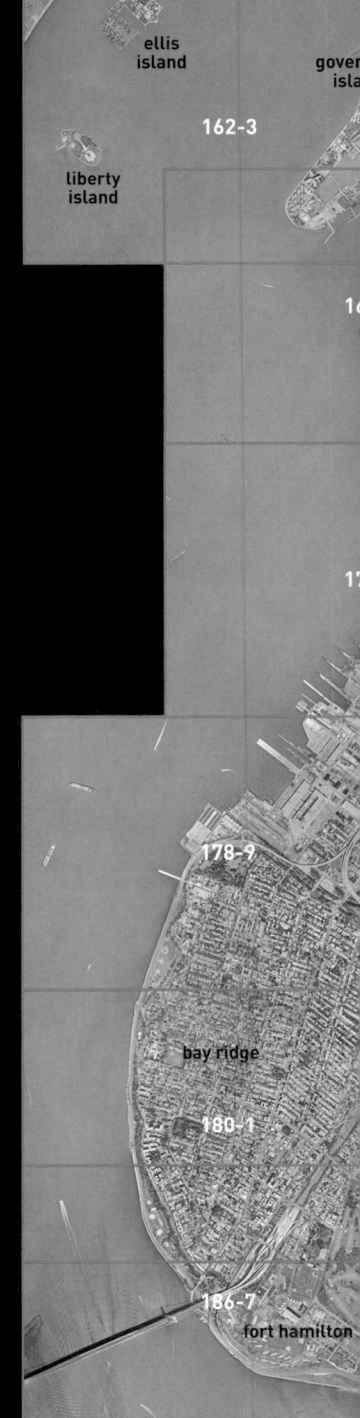

150-1

greenpoint

northside

152-3

156-7

southside

154-5

east
williamsburg

williamsburg

142-3

vinegar hill

144-5

brooklyn
heights

bushwick

160-1

downtown
brooklyn

158-9

146-7

148-9

clinton hill

cobble hill

boerum
hill

stuyvesant
heights

ocean
hill

cyprus hills

carroll
gardens

166-7

prospect
heights

168-9

broadway junction

weeksville

city line

ook

crown
heights

east new york

176-7

brownsville

wingate

172-3

prospect
lefferts
gardens

174-5

spring creek

reenwood
heights

windsor
terrace

rugby

remsen village

set park

kensington

starrett
city

borough
park

canarsie

east flatbush

182-3

flatbush

paerdergat
basin

184-5

r heights

mapleton

midwood

canarsie
pol

new utrecht

flatlands

bergen beach

bensonhust

marine park

mill island

188-9

homecrest

floyd
bennett
field

190-1

gravesend

gerritsen
beach

n beach

sea gate

coney island

brighton beach

manhattan beach

192-3

194-5

21

A

16

C

scale 1:3,200 see cartography pages 352-3/354-5

144

144

brooklyn/east river/manhattan bridge/empire-fulton ferry state park/fulton ferry/brooklyn-queens expressway/brooklyn heights

24

143

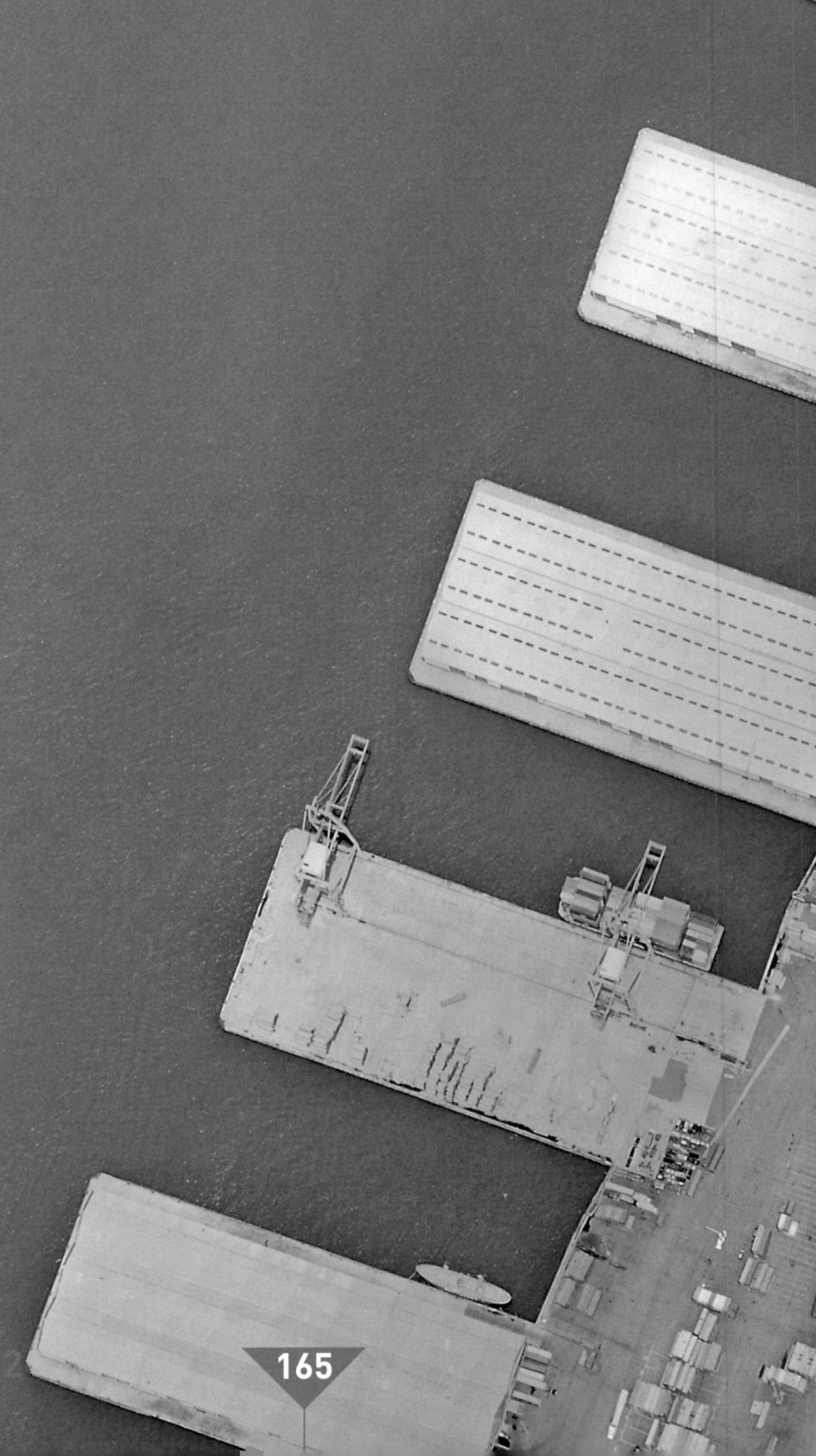

163

148

2

144

3

147

166

A

B

C

1

153/156

214-15

6

A

214/222

B

C

43

scale 1:3,200 see cartography pages 354-5

156

27/35

150/1

scale 1:6,400 see cartography pages 354–5

222

145/149

scale 1:6,400 see cartography pages 354-5

scale 1:6,400 see cartography pages 354–5

1

2

162/3

3

A

B

C

scale 1:6,400 see cartography pages 354-5

167

159-160

176

178/9

A

B

C

178/9

brooklyn/gowanus/greenwood cemetery

scale 1:6,400 see cartography pages 354-5

173

236

A

B

C

186

scale 1:6,400 see cartography pages 360-1

179/181

183

brooklyn/holy cross cemetery/brooklyn terminal market/east flatbush/paedergat basin/georgetown/flatlands/east mill basin

A

B

240

5

182/188

B

C

188

B

3

Queens

scale 1:6,400

A

B

105/122

B

scale 1:6,400 see cartography pages 348-9

A

B

257

202

264/5

4

5

A

204

A

203

B

scale 1:6,400 see cartography pages 348-9

208

207

209

201/2

218

217

B

scale 1:6,400

scale 1:6,400 see cartography pages 348-9

inset
left

214

queens/sunnyside gardens/sunnyside/new calvary cemetery/brooklyn-queens expressway

208

216

queens/jackson heights/elmhurst

210

215

224

217

230

228
234/5

230

queens/forest hills/meadow lake/willow lake/subway yards/van wyck expressway/kew gardens hills/forest park/kew gardens/briarwood

218

225/229

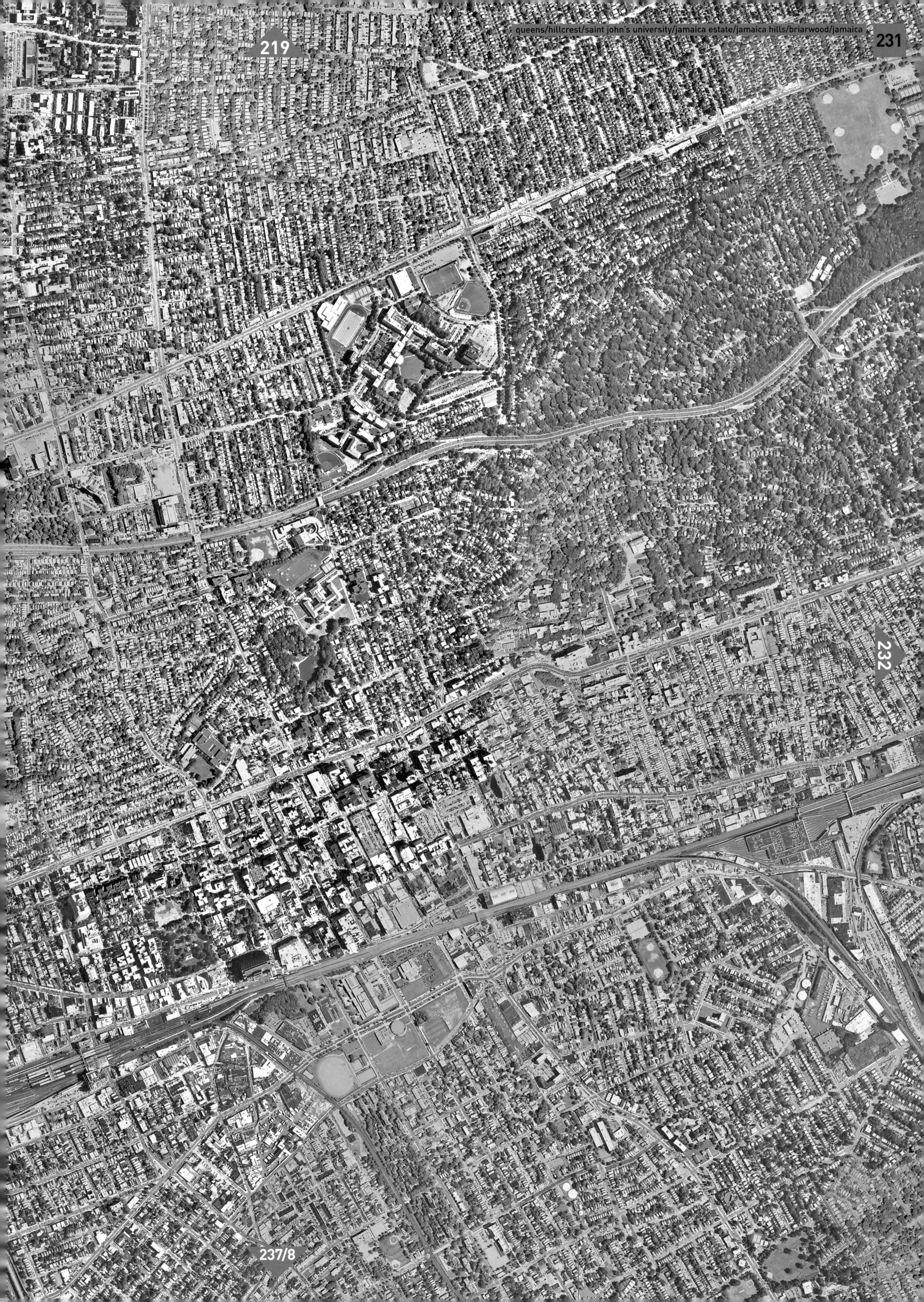
219
232
237/8

227/8

236

177/235

238

232/3

185

scale 1:12,800 see cartography pages 354-5/356-7/362-3/364-5

B

queens/john f. kennedy international airport

A

B

scale 1:12,800 see cartography pages 356-7/364-5

2

A

B

B

C

scale 1:5,000 see cartography pages 364–5

242

242

242

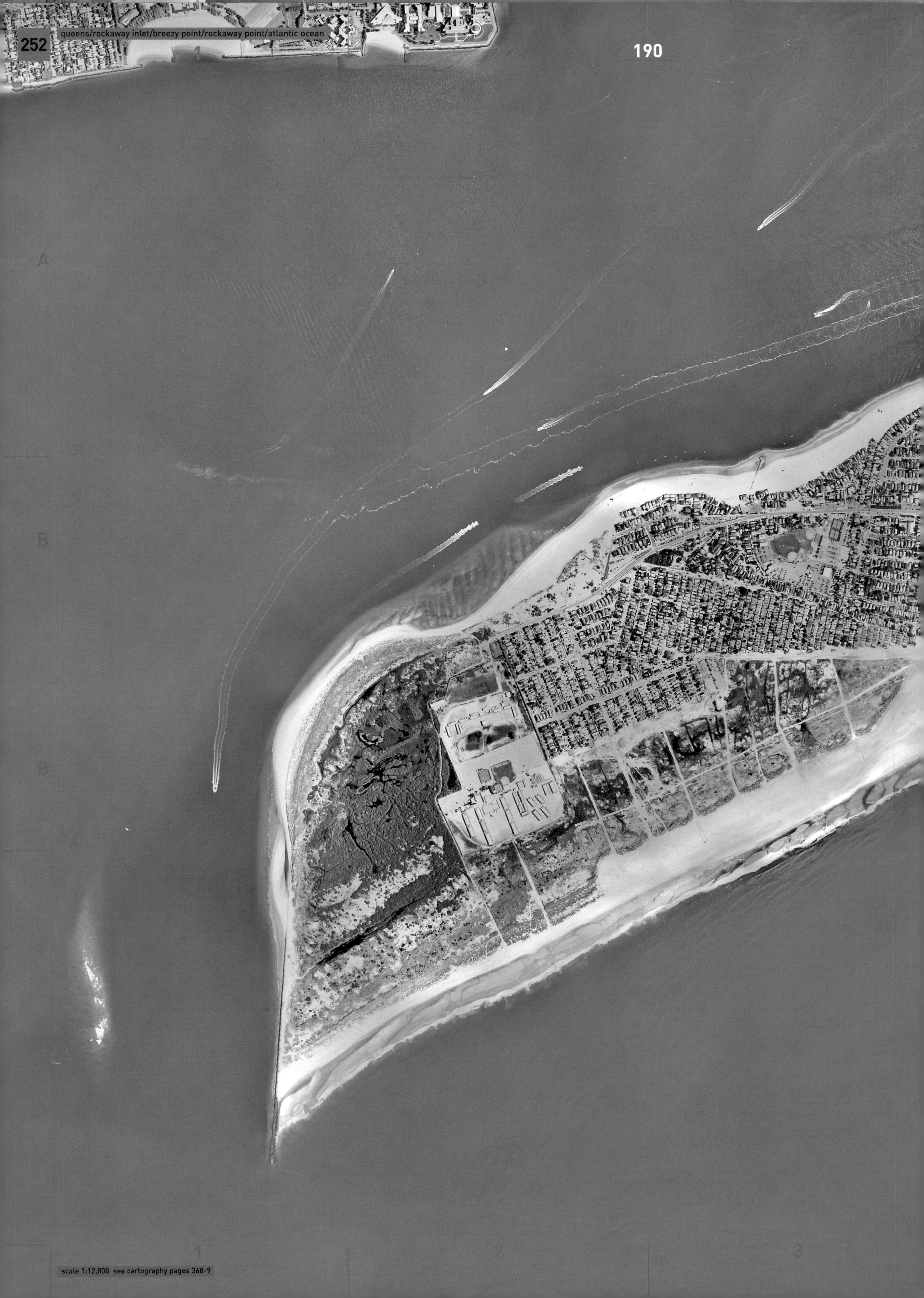

scale 1:12,800 see cartography pages 368-9

inset
262

scale 1:6,400 see cartography pages 348-9

261

5

6

A

201

202

B

C

22

133

B

B

C

scale 1:12,700

scale 1:6,400 see cartography pages 344-5

B

B

C

270

scale 1:6,400 see cartography pages 344-5

265

268/9

275

270/1

bronxville

scale 1:12,800 see cartography pages 340–1

Staten Island

and Bayonne, Jersey City, Hoboken, Union City, Weehawken, West New York (New Jersey)

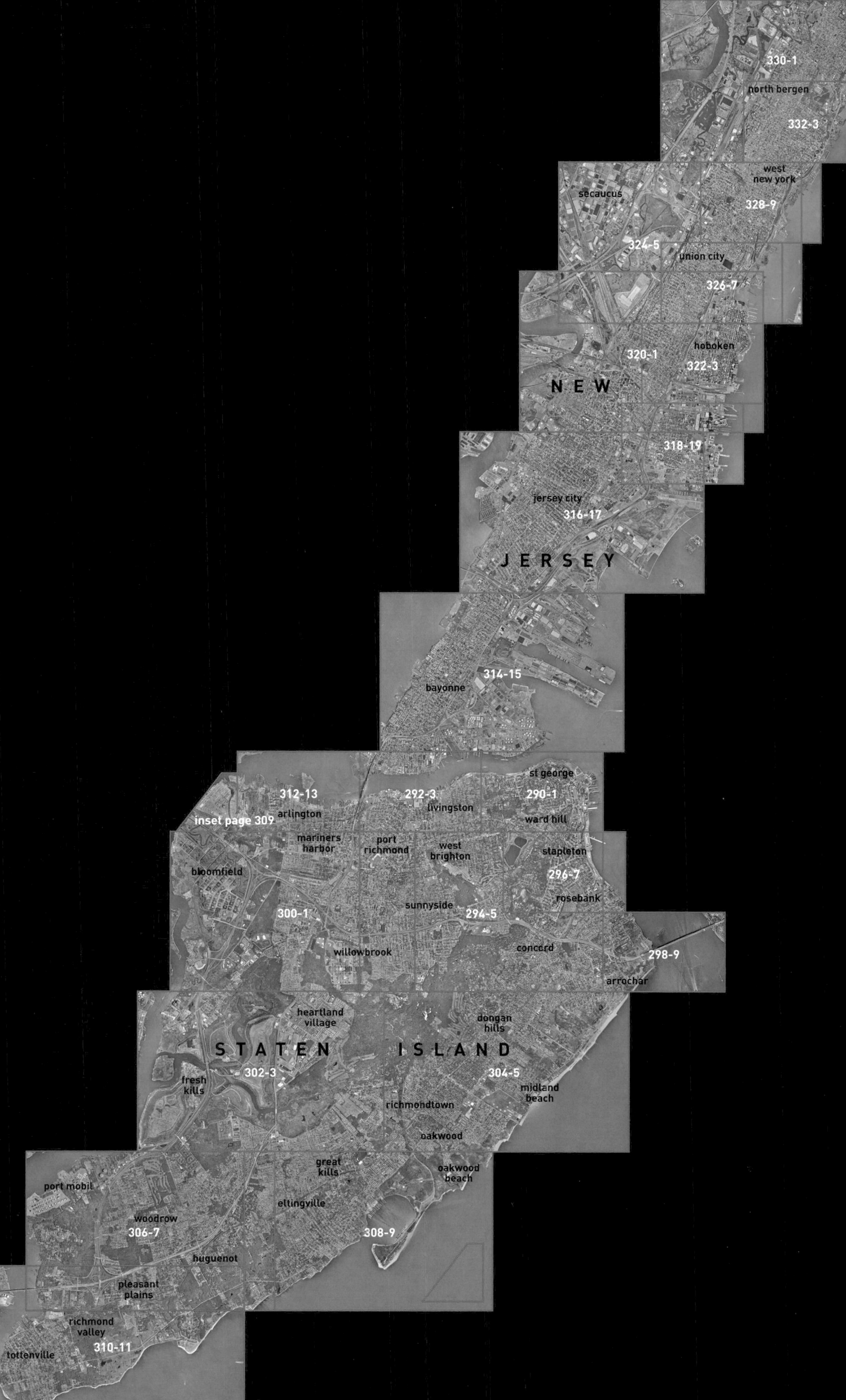

330-1

north bergen

332-3

west
new york

secaucus

328-9

324-5

union city

326-7

hoboken

320-1

322-3

N E W

318-19

jersey city
316-17

J E R S E Y

314-15

bayonne

st george

312-13

292-3

290-1

inset page 309

arlington

livingston

ward hill

mariners
harbor

port
richmond

west
brighton

stapleton

bloomfield

296-7

rosebank

300-1

sunnyside

294-5

willowbrook

concord

298-9

arrochar

heartland
village

dongan
hills

S T A T E N   I S L A N D

fresh
kills

302-3

304-5

midland
beach

richmondtown

oakwood

great
kills

oakwood
beach

port mobil

eltingville

308-9

woodrow

306-7

huguenot

pleasant
plains

richmond
valley

310-11

tottenville

293

A

A

B

313

scale 1:6,400 see cartography pages 358-9

staten island/silver lake park and reservoir/stapleton/rosebank/staten island expressway/emerson hill/grasmere lake/grasmere

295

A

298

B

295

291

295

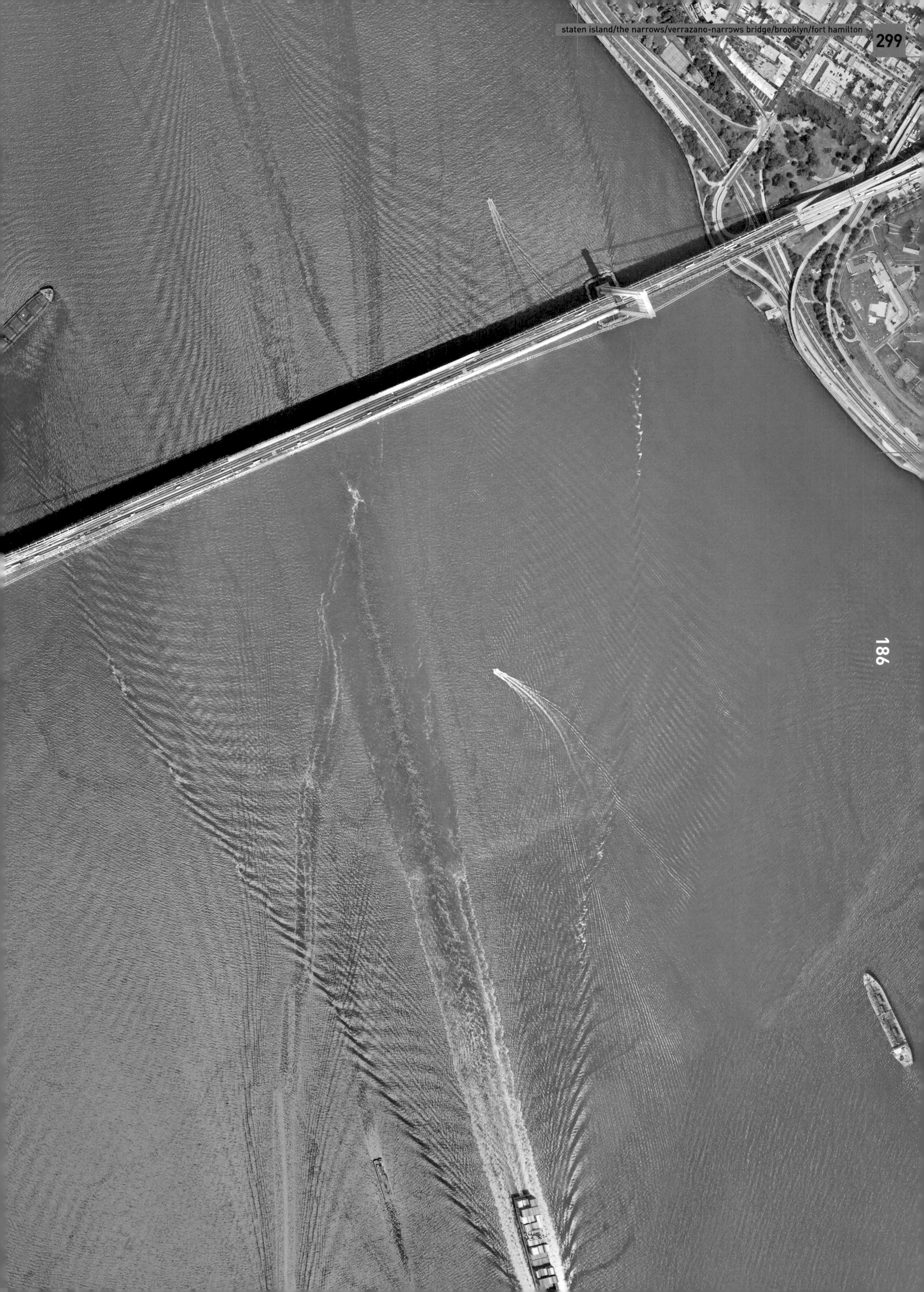

186

scale 1:12,800 see cartography pages 358-9

294

303

scale 1:12,800 see cartography pages 358-9/366-7

A

staten island/bay terrace/great kills park/great kills harbor/oakwood beach/atlantic ocean/howland hook (inset)/goethals bridge (inset)

309

304

309
inset

scale 1:6,400 see cartography pages 358-9

292/314

A

B

292/3

new jersey/jersey city industrial park/port jersey industrial and marine center/military ocean terminal bayonne/constable hook

315

316/17

290/1

B

322

317

A

B

C

6

325

A

B

C

317

320

318

scale 1:12,800 see cartography pages 346-7

324

322

B

C

330/332

325

332

A

B

88

B

C

5

6

B

A

B

132

B

A

B

C

Cartography

The cartography is at 1:12,800 and 1:25,600 scale

The approximate grid interval, in yards/miles and (meters/kilometers), is for each scale;

1:12,800	1157.4 yards (1058.3 meters) width x 1390.7 yards (1390.7 meters) height
1:25,600	1.31 miles (2.11 kilometers) width x 1.58 miles (2.78 kilometers) height

Photography spreads are shown using locators in different colors

Manhattan
Brooklyn
Queens
Bronx
Staten Island

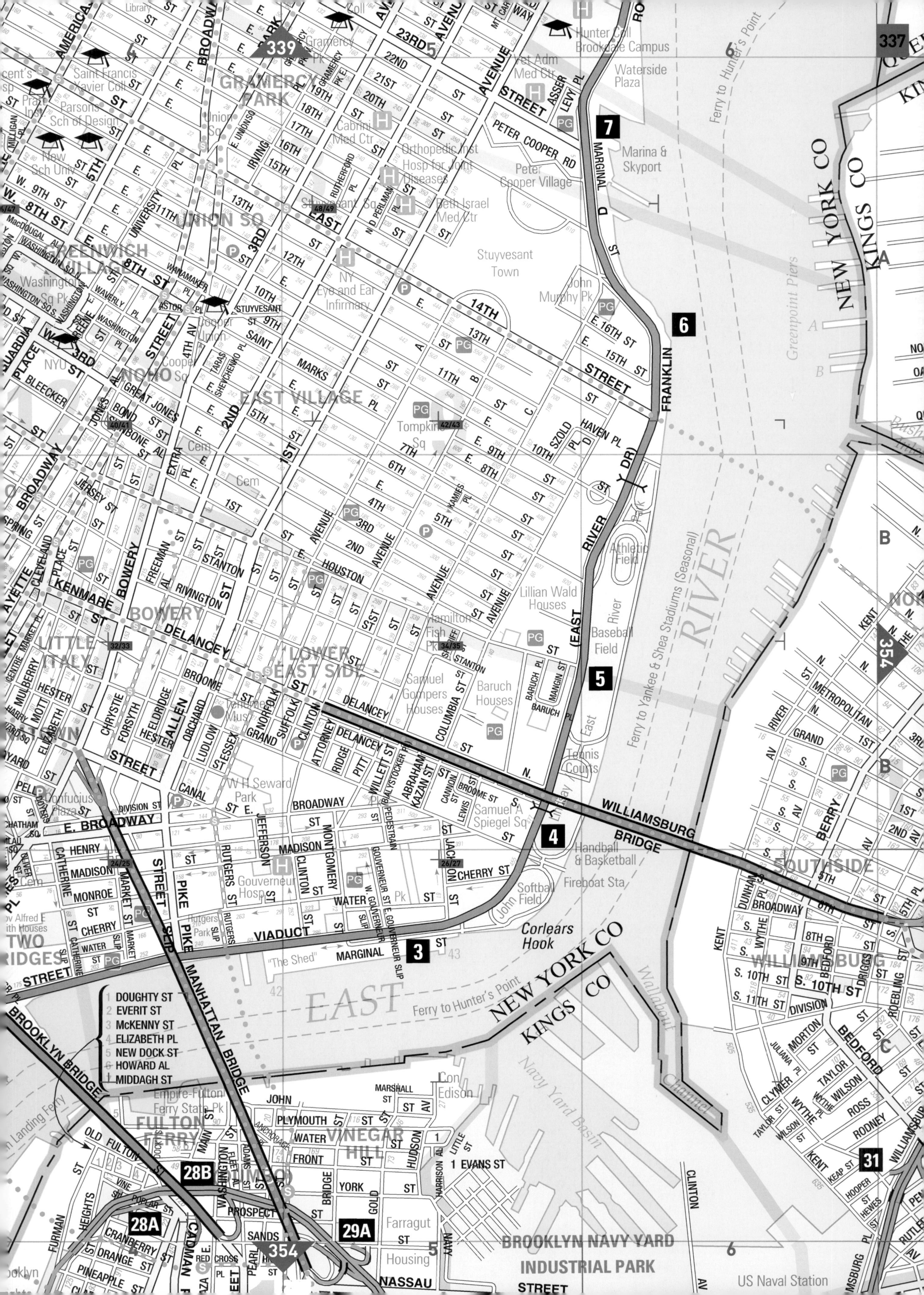

1   2   3

A

B

C

LONG

ECHO BAY

New Rochelle

Pelham CC

Davenport's Neck

NORTH BERGEN TWP

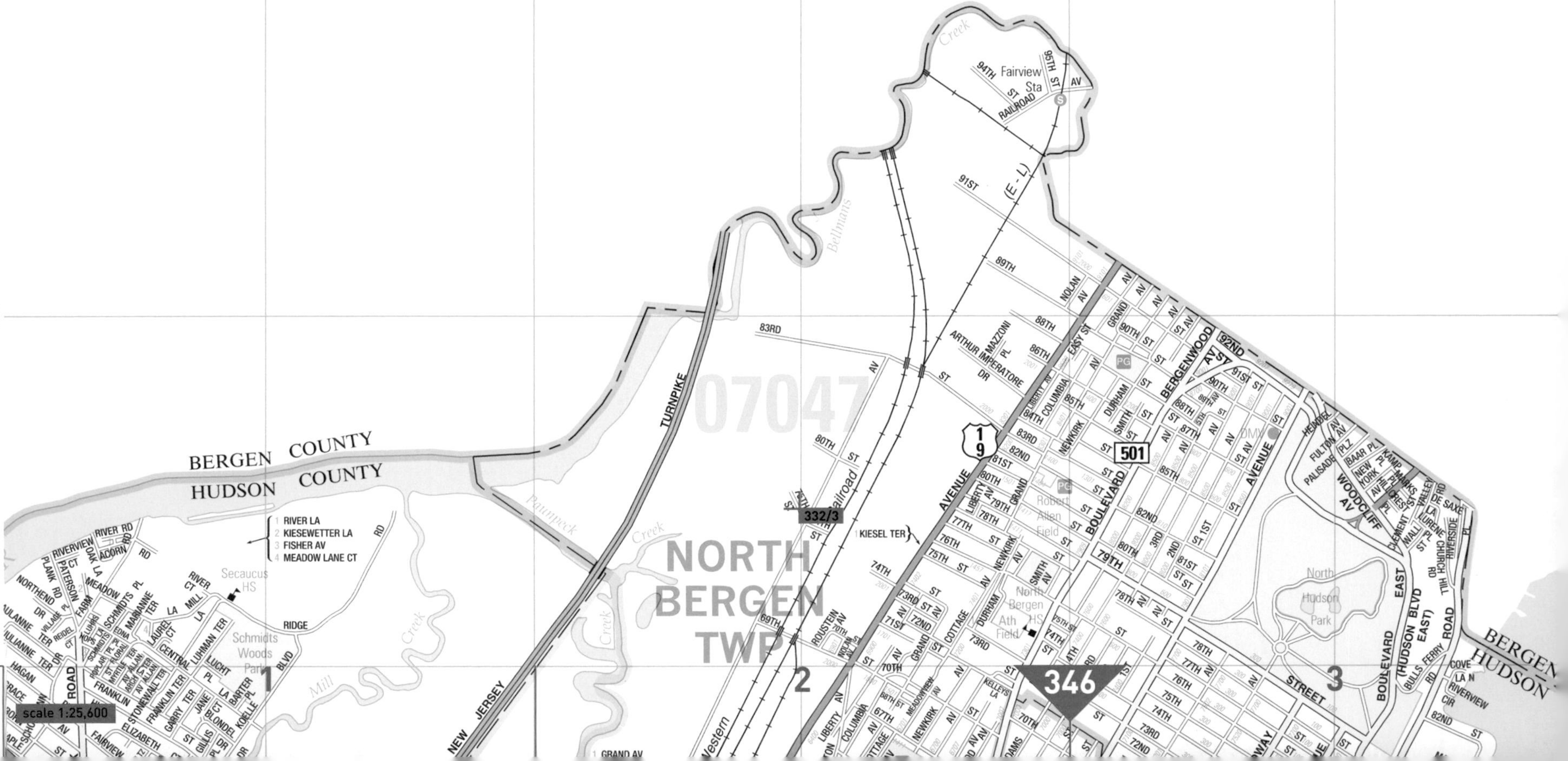

BERGEN COUNTY
HUDSON COUNTY

Secaucus

07047

scale 1:25,600

330/1

332/3

346

501

95

15

16

286/7

111

Central and Lower
Manhattan
Pages 336-339

Queens
Pages 348-349

Brooklyn
Pages 354-355

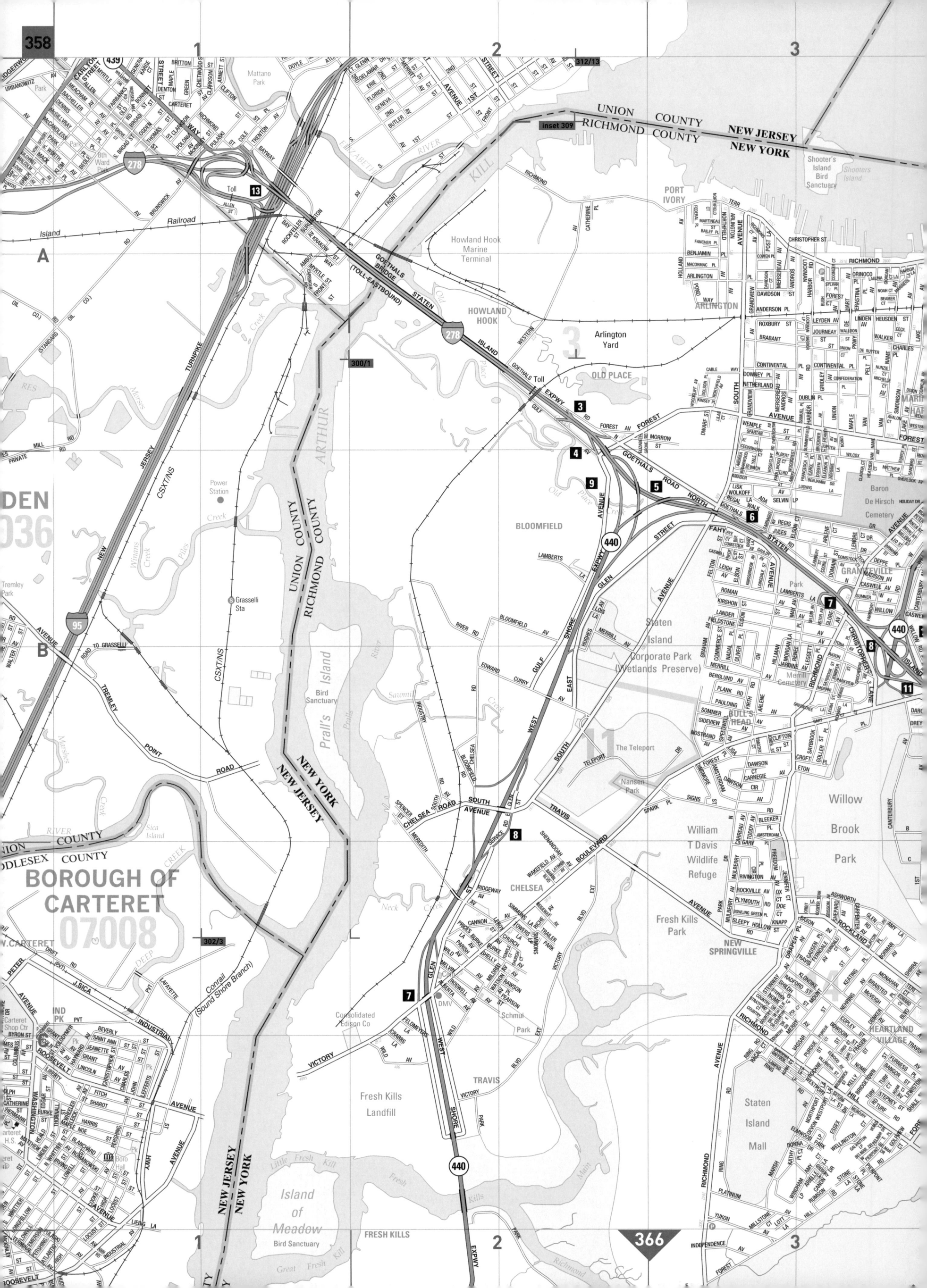

11N
11S

Floyd

Bennett

Field

250/1

US Coast
Guard

Barren Island
Marina

Deep Creek

Dead Horse
Bay

Park Hdq

Unit Hdq

US Navy
Reserve

AVENUE

AVIATION RD

Toll

MARINE PARKWAY - GIL HODGES MEMORIAL

BRIDGE (TOLL)

Ruffle Bar

The Raunt

KINGS COUNTY

QUEENS COUNTY

Little Egg Marsh

Bg

Channel

CHANNEL

BSg

A

Beach

Marine Park

BEACH

Rockaway Park

AVENUE

Channel

BELLE HARBOR

BEACH

Rockaway

BOULEVARD

CRONSTON

Newport

Neponsit

Rockaway

Neponsit

KINGS COUNTY

QUEENS COUNTY

Roxbury

Bayside

Roxbury AV

Hillside AV

ROXBURY

US Coast
Guard

Parking Field

Jacob Riis Park

BOARDWALK

ROAD

STATE

Rockaway
Point
Comm

97

BOULEVARD

DORIS LA

Fort Tilden

95

B 195TH ST

B 169TH ST

BOARDWALK

POINT UNIT

BREEZY

GATEWAY NATIONAL RECREATION AREA

B

C

Index

The index reads in this sequence: street name/postal district or post town/photography page number/cartography page number/grid reference.

General abbreviations used within cartography and index

All	Alley
Allot	Allotments
Amb	Ambulance
App	Approach
Arc	Arcade
Ave	Avenue
Bdy	Broadway
Bldgs	Buildings
Boul	Boulevard
Bowl	Bowling
Bri	Bridge
Bus	Business
C of E	Church of England
Cath	Cathedral
Cem	Cemetery
Cen	Central, Center
Cft	Croft
Cfts	Crofts
Ch	Church
Chyd	Churchyard
Cin	Cinema
Circ	Circus
Clo	Close
Co	County
Coll	College
Comm	Community
Conv	Convent
Cor	Corner
Cors	Corners
Coron	Coroners
Cotts	Cottages
Cov	Covered
Crem	Crematorium
Cres	Crescent
Ct	Court
Ctyd	Courtyard
Dep	Depot
Dr	Drive
Dws	Dwellings
E	East
Ed	Education
Elec	Electricity
Emb	Embankment
Est	Estate
Ex	Exchange
FB	Footbridge
FC	Football Club
Fld	Field
Flds	Fields
Fm	Farm
Gall	Gallery
Gar	Garage
Gdn	Garden
Gdns	Gardens
Govt	Government
Gra	Grange
Grd	Ground
Grds	Grounds
Grn	Green
Grns	Greens
Gro	Grove
Gros	Groves
Ho	House
Hos	Houses
Hosp	Hospital
Ind	Industrial
Junct	Junction
La	Lane
Las	Lanes
Lo	Lodge
Lwr	Lower
Mag	Magistrates
Mans	Mansions
Meml	Memorial
Met	Metropolitan
Mkt	Market
Mkts	Markets
Ms	Mews
Mt	Mount
Mus	Museum
N	North
North	Northern
PH	Public House
Par	Parade
Pas	Passage
Pav	Pavilion
Pia	Piazza
Pk	Park
Pl	Place
Prec	Precinct
Prom	Promenade
Pt	Point
Quad	Quadrant
RC	Roman Catholic
Rd	Road
Rds	Roads
Rec	Recreation
Res	Reservoir
Ri	Rise
S	South
Sch	School
Shop	Shopping
Sq	Square
St	Street
St.	Saint
Sta	Station
Sts	Streets
Sub	Subway
Swim	Swimming
TA	Territorial Army
Tenn	Tennis
Ter	Terrace
Thea	Theater
Trd	Trading
Twr	Tower
Twrs	Towers
Tun	Tunnel
Vill	Villas
Vw	View
W	West
Wd	Wood
Wds	Woods
Wf	Wharf
Wk	Walk
Wks	Walks
Yd	Yard

Abbreviations used for Westchester County

B'ville	Bronxville
Eastch.	Eastchester
Mt V.	Mount Vernon
N. Roch.	New Rochelle
Pel.	Pelham
Pel. M.	Pelham Manor
Tuck.	Tuckahoe
Yonk.	Yonkers

The Bronx

and Southern Westchester County

NEIGHBORHOODS

Allerton	69	275	A6	344	A3
Bathgate	57	274	C3	344	B1
Baychester	69	276	A2	344	A3
Bedford Park	58	275	A4	344	A1
Belmont	58	275	B4	344	A2
Bronx Park S	6	275	C4	344	B2
Bronx River	72	269	B4	344	B2
Bronxdale	67	275	A5	344	A2
Bruckner	72	269	B5	344	B2
Castle Hill	73	270	C1	344	C3
City Island	64	277	C6	345	B5
Claremont	56	267	A5	344	B1
Clason Point	73	262	B1	344	C3
Concourse	52	266	A3	343	B6
Concourse Vill	51	266	C2	343	C6
Co-Op City	75	276	A3	345	A4
Country Club	65	272	A1	345	B4
Crotona Park East	6	268	A3	344	B2
East Tremont	57	275	C4	344	B1
Eastchester	66	280	B2	341	C4
Eastchester Bay	65	272	A2	345	B4
Edenwald	66	280	C1	341	C4
Edgewater Park	65	272	C3	345	C5
Fieldston	71	278	B1	340	C1
Fordham	68	274	A3	344	A1
Harding Park	73	262	A1	344	C3
Hart Island	64	273	Inset	345	A6
High Bridge	52	266	A2	343	B6
Hunts Point	74	260	B2	344	C1
Kingsbridge	63	278	C2	340	C1
Kingsbridge Heights					
	68	274	A3	344	A1
Locust Point	65	265	A4	345	C5
Longwood	59	268	C1	344	C1
Melrose	51	267	C4	343	C6
Middletown	61	276	C2	345	B4
Morris Heights	53	274	B1	343	A6
Morris Park	61	276	C1	344	B3
Morrisania	56	267	C6	344	C1
Mott Haven	54	258	B3	343	C6
Mount Eden	52	274	C2	343	B6
Mount Hope	57	274	C2	344	B1
North Riverdale	71	278	A2	340	B1
Norwood	67	275	A5	344	A2
Olinville	67	279	C5	340	C3
Parkchester	62	270	A1	344	B3
Pelham Bay	61	276	C2	345	B4
Pelham Gdns	69	276	B2	344	A3
Pelham Parkway	62	275	B6	344	A2
Port Morris	54	259	C5	344	C1
Riverdale	71	278	B2	340	C1
Schuylerville	65	271	B6	345	B4
Silver Beach	65	264	B3	345	C5
Soundview	73	269	C5	344	C2
South Riverdale	63	278	C1	340	C1
Spencer Estates	65	276	C3	345	B4
Spuyten Duyvil	63	278	C1	340	C1
Throgs Neck	65	264	A1	345	C4
Tremont	57	274	B3	344	A1
Unionport	62	270	B3	344	B3
University Heights	68	274	B2	344	A1
Van Cortlandt Vill	63	278	C3	340	C2
Van Nest	62	275	C6	344	B2
Wakefield	66	280	B1	341	C4
West Farms	6	275	C5	344	B2
Westchester Square					
	61	276	C2	344	B3
Williamsbridge	67	279	C6	340	C3
Woodlawn	7	279	B5	340	C3
Wykagyl	N. Roch.	285	B5	341	A6

NUMBERED STREETS

1st Av	65	272	C2	345	C4
1st Av	Pel.	285	C4	341	B5
1st St	N. Roch.	286	A1	342	Inset
1st St	Pel.	281	A4	341	B5
1st St	Yonk.	279	A6	340	B3
2nd Av	65	272	C3	345	C5
2nd Av	Pel.	285	C4	341	B5
2nd St	N. Roch.	281	A5	341	B6
2nd St	Pel.	285	C4	341	B5
2nd St	Pel. M.	281	A4	341	B5
3rd Av	65	272	C2	345	C4
3rd Av		258	B1	343	C6
2400-2738 (even)	54	258	B2	343	C6
2401-2773 (odd)	51	258	B2	343	C6
2740-3040 (even)	55	259	A4	343	C6
2775-3045 (odd)	55	259	A4	343	C6
3042-3246 (even)	51	267	C5	344	C1
3047-3249 (odd)	51	267	C5	344	C1
3248-3798 & 3251-3799					
	56	267	B5	344	B1
3800-4422 & 3801-4529					
	57	274	C3	344	B1
4424-OUT & 4531-OUT					
	58	275	B4	344	A1
3rd Av	Pel.	285	C4	341	B5
3rd St	N. Roch.	281	A5	341	B
3rd St	Pel.	285	C4	341	B5
4th Av	65	272	C3	345	C5
4th Av	Mt V.	280	A2	341	B4
4th Av	Pel.	285	C4	341	B5
4th St	N. Roch.	281	A5	341	B6
5th Av	65	272	C3	345	C5
5th Av	N. Roch.	285	C6	341	B6
5th Av	Pel.	285	C4	341	B5
5th St	N. Roch.	281	A5	341	B6
5th St	Pel.	285	C4	341	B5
6th Av	Pel.	285	C4	341	B5
6th St	N. Roch.	281	A5	341	B6
6th St	Pel.	285	C4	341	B5
7th Av	65	272	C2	345	C4
7th Av	Pel.	285	C4	341	B5
7th St	N. Roch.	281	A4	341	B5
7th St	Pel.	285	C4	341	B5
8th Av	Pel.	285	C4	341	B5
8th St	N. Roch.	281	A4	341	B5
9th Av	65	272	C3	345	C5
9th Av	Pel.	285	C4	341	B5
9th St	N. Roch.	281	A4	341	B5
11th Av	65	272	C3	345	C5
Bronx River Pkwy	Yonk.	279	A6	340	B3
Gov E. Thomas Dewey Thruway					
	Yonk.	283	A5	340	A3
Hutchinson River Pkwy					
	Pel.	285	A4	341	A5
I-87		283	A5	340	A3
I-95		281	B5	341	C5
I-278	54	259	C5	344	C1
I-278	73	270	B1	344	B3
I-295	65	265	B5	345	C5
I-678	65	263	B5	345	C4
I-695	65	272	A1	345	B4
I-87	52	266	A2	343	B6
I-87	68	274	A2	344	A1
I-895	59	268	B3	344	B2
I-95	57	274	C3	344	B1
I-95	72	269	A4	344	B2
I-95	75	276	A2	345	A4
New England Thruway					
	N. Roch.	286	B1	342	Inset
NY 9A	71	278	A3	340	B2
NY-100		284	A1	341	A4
NY-22		284	B3	341	A5
NY-9A		282	A3	340	A2
Saw Mill River Pkwy	Yonk.	282	C3	340	B2
Sprain Brook Pkwy		284	A1	341	A4
US 9	63	278	C2	340	C1
US 9	71	278	A3	340	B2
US-1		281	B4	341	B5

NAMED STREETS

Abbott St	7	279	A6	340	B3
Abeel St	Yonk.	282	C1	340	B1
Aberfoyle Rd	N. Roch.	285	B5	341	A6
Abner Pl	Yonk.	283	C5	340	B3
Acacia Ter	N. Roch.	287	A4	342	Inset
Acorn Pl	65	264	B3	345	C5
Acorn Ter	N. Roch.	285	C6	341	B6
Adams Pl		275	B4	344	A1
1-2289	57	275	B4	344	A1
2290-OUT	58	275	B4	344	A1
Adams St	6	275	C5	344	B2
Adams St	Mt V.	280	A2	341	B4
Adams St	N. Roch.	285	C6	341	B6
Adee Av		275	A5	344	A2
1-899	67	275	A5	344	A2
900-OUT	69	275	A6	344	A3
Adele La	Yonk.	284	A1	341	A4
Adler Pl	75	276	A3	345	A4
Admiral La	73	262	C2	344	C3
Aetna Pl	Mt V.	285	C4	341	B5
Agar Pl	65	276	C3	345	B4
Agar St	Yonk.	282	A3	340	A2
Agawam N	Yonk.	279	A4	340	B2
Agawam S	Yonk.	279	A4	340	B2
Alameda Pl	Mt V.	284	B3	341	A5
Alan B. Shepard Jr Pl					
	Yonk.	282	C3	340	B2
Alan Pl	65	265	B4	345	C5
Albany Cres	63	278	C1	340	C1
Albemarle Av	N. Roch.	285	C6	341	B6
Albert Leonard Rd	N. Roch.	285	A6	341	A6
Albert Pl	N. Roch.	285	C5	341	B6
Alcott Pl	75	276	A2	345	A4
Alden Pk	65	265	A4	345	C5
Alden Pl	57	274	B3	344	A1
Alden Pl	B'ville	284	B2	341	A4
Alder La	B'ville	284	A3	341	A5
Alder St	Yonk.	282	B3	340	A2
Alderbrook Rd	71	278	B1	340	C1
Aldrich St	75	276	A2	345	A4
Aldrich St	Yonk.	284	B1	341	A4
Aldus Av	Mt V.	280	A3	341	B5
Aldus St	59	268	C2	344	C1
Alexander Av	54	258	B2	343	C6
Alexander Av	Yonk.	279	A5	340	B3
Alexander Pl	Eastch.	285	B4	341	A5
Alexander Pl	Yonk.	283	C5	340	B3
Alexander St	Yonk.	282	A1	340	A1
Alida St	Yonk.	283	B4	340	B3
Allaire St	Eastch.	285	B4	341	A5
Allard Av	N. Roch.	286	B1	342	Inset
Allen Pl	Eastch.	285	B4	341	A5
Allen St	Yonk.	283	C4	340	B3
Allerton Av		275	A5	344	A2
1-899	67	275	A5	344	A2
900-OUT	69	276	A1	344	A3
Alpha Pl	N. Roch.	287	A4	342	Inset
Alpine Rd	N. Roch.	285	B5	341	A6
Alta Av	Yonk.	282	C2	340	B2
Alta Dr	Mt V.	285	B4	341	A5
Alta Pkwy	Mt V.	285	B4	341	A5
Altamont Pl	Yonk.	279	A6	340	B3
Amadou Diallo Pl (Wheeler Av)					
	72	269	B4	344	B2
Amanda La	N. Roch.	285	A6	341	A6
Amberson Av	Yonk.	282	C1	340	B1
Ambrose Pl	Yonk.	283	B4	340	A3
Amethyst St	62	275	C6	344	B2
Ampere Av	65	276	C3	345	B4
Amsterdam Av	Yonk.	284	A1	341	A4
Amsterdam Pl	Mt V.	280	A2	341	B4
Amundson Av	66	280	B2	341	C4
Amundson Av	Mt V.	280	B1	341	C4
Ancon Av	Pel.	281	A4	341	B5
Anderson Av	52	266	A2	343	B6
Anderson Av	Mt V.	280	B3	341	C5
Anderson St	N. Roch.	286	A2	342	Inset
Andrews Av N		274	B2	344	A1
1-2249	53	274	B2	343	A6
2250-OUT	68	274	B2	344	A1
Andrews Av S	53	274	C1	343	B6
Anita Rd	Yonk.	284	A1	341	A4
Ann St	Yonk.	282	B2	340	A2
Anthony Av	57	274	C3	344	B1
Anthony J Griffin Pl	51	258	A2	343	C6
Antin Pl	62	275	B6	344	A2
Antler Pl	N. Roch.	285	B6	341	A6
Aqueduct Av	Yonk.	279	A5	340	B3
Aqueduct Av E		274	B2	344	A1
1-2257	53	274	B2	343	A6
2276-2353	68	274	B2	344	A1
Aqueduct Av W	68	274	A3	344	A1
Arbor St	Yonk.	282	A3	340	A2
Archer Av	Mt V.	284	C2	341	B4
Archer Dr	Eastch.	285	B4	341	A5
Archer Pl	Eastch.	284	A3	341	A5
Archer Rd	62	275	C6	344	B2
Archer St		275	C6	344	B2
1-1879	6	275	C6	344	B2
1880-OUT	62	275	C6	344	B3
Archer St	Yonk.	282	B3	340	A2
Ardell Rd	Yonk.	284	B1	341	A4
Arden Ter	Mt V.	285	B4	341	A5
Argyle Pl	B'ville	284	B3	341	A5
Argyll Av	N. Roch.	285	B5	341	A6
Arlington Av		278	C1	340	C1
1-3899	63	278	C1	340	C1
3900-OUT	71	278	A1	340	B1
Arlington St	Yonk.	284	A1	341	A4
Armand Pl	63	278	C2	340	C1
Armourvilla Av	Tuck.	284	A2	341	A4
Armstrong Av	Yonk.	283	A4	340	A3
Arnow Av		275	A5	344	A2
600-899	67	275	A5	344	A2
900-OUT	69	276	A1	344	A3
Arnow Pl	61	276	B2	345	A4
Arthur Av		274	C3	344	B1
1700-2299	57	274	C3	344	B1
2300-OUT	58	275	B4	344	A2
Arthur Murphy Sq	57	274	B3	344	A1
Asch Lp	75	276	A2	345	A4
Ash St	Yonk.	282	B2	340	A2
Ashburton Av	Yonk.	282	A2	340	A2
Ashburton Pl	Yonk.	282	A2	340	A2
Ashford Pl	Yonk.	283	A4	340	A3
Ashland St	N. Roch.	285	B6	341	A6
Ashton Rd	Yonk.	282	C1	340	B1
Askins Pl	N. Roch.	285	B4	341	A5
Aster Pl	65	264	A2	345	C4
Astor Av		275	B6	344	A2
700-899	67	275	B6	344	A2
900-OUT	69	276	B1	344	A3
Astor Pl	Yonk.	282	B2	340	A2
Atherton St	Yonk.	282	B1	340	A1
Atlas Pl	Mt V.	285	B4	341	A5
Audobon Av	Mt V.	284	C3	341	B5
Audrey Av	Mt V.	280	A2	341	B4
August Petrillo Plz	Mt V.	284	C2	341	B4
Austin Pl	55	259	B5	344	C1
Av Saint John	55	259	A6	344	C1
Avon Rd	B'ville	284	A2	341	A4
Avon Rd	N. Roch.	285	A5	341	A6
Axminster St	Yonk.	282	A3	340	A2
B St	61	271	A6	345	B4
Babcock Pl	Yonk.	282	A1	340	A1
Badeau Pl	N. Roch.	286	A1	342	Inset
Bailey Av	63	274	A2	344	A1
Bailey Pl	63	278	C2	340	C1
Bailey Pl	N. Roch.	285	B5	341	A6
Bainbridge Av		275	A4	344	A2
1-3029	58	275	A4	344	A1
3030-OUT	67	275	A5	344	A2
Bainton St	Yonk.	283	C4	340	B3
Baisley Av		271	A6	345	B4
1-3099	61	271	A6	345	B4
3100-OUT	65	272	A1	345	B4
Bajart Pl	Yonk.	282	C3	340	B2
Baker Av	6	275	C6	344	B2
Baker Av	62	275	C6	344	B2
Balcom Av		271	B5	345	B4
1-1299	65	271	C6	345	C4
1300-OUT	61	271	A5	345	B4
Baldwin Pl	Yonk.	282	B2	340	A2
Baldwin St	7	279	A6	340	B3
Ball Av	Yonk.	283	A4	340	A3
Bally Pl	N. Roch.	285	C6	341	B6

Balsam Pl	65	264	A2	345	C4
Bancker Pl	N. Roch.	286	B2	342	Inset
Bantam Pl	69	276	A2	344	A3
Banyer Pl	73	269	C5	344	C2
Barbara Pl	Eastch.	285	A4	341	A5
Barberry La	N. Roch.	285	A5	341	A6
Barker Av	67	275	A5	344	A2
Barkley Av	65	271	B6	345	B4
Barlow St	Yonk.	279	A6	340	B3
Barn Hill Sq	68	274	A3	344	A1
Barnard Rd	N. Roch.	285	B6	341	A6
Barnes Av		275	B6	344	A2
1-2199	62	275	B6	344	A2
2200-3899	67	275	A6	344	A2
3900-4599	66	279	B6	340	C3
4600-OUT	7	280	A1	341	B4
Barrett Av	73	262	A2	344	C3
Barrett St	62	275	C6	344	B2
Barretto St		260	A2	344	C1
1-899	74	260	A2	344	C1
900-OUT	59	268	C2	344	C1
Barrington Rd	Yonk.	284	A1	341	A4
Barry St	74	260	B1	344	C1
Bartels Pl	N. Roch.	286	A2	342	Inset
Bartholdi Pl	Yonk.	282	A2	340	A1
Bartholdi St	67	275	A6	344	A2
Barton Rd	Yonk.	283	A4	340	A3
Bartow Av		276	A2	344	A3
1-1999	69	276	A2	344	A3
2000-OUT	75	276	A3	345	A4
Bashford St	Yonk.	282	B1	340	A1
Bassett Av		276	C1	344	B3
1-1699	61	276	C1	344	B3
1700-2099	75	276	B3	345	A4
Bassford Av		275	B4	344	A1
1-2289	57	275	B4	344	A1
2290-OUT	58	275	B4	344	A2
Bateman Pl	Mt V.	284	C3	341	B5
Bathgate Av	57	274	C3	344	B1
Bathgate Av	58	275	B4	344	A1
Bay Park W	75	280	C3	341	C5
Bay St	64	277	C6	345	B5
Bayard St	N. Roch.	286	C1	342	Inset
Bayberry La	N. Roch.	285	A6	341	A6
Bayberry St	Yonk.	284	A1	341	A4
Baychester Av		276	A2	345	A4
1-3200	75	276	A2	345	A4
3201-3499	69	280	C1	341	C4
3500-OUT	66	280	B1	341	C4
Bayeau Rd	N. Roch.	285	A6	341	A6
Bayley Av	Yonk.	282	C1	340	B1
Bayshore Av	65	277	C4	345	B4
Bayview Av	65	277	C4	345	B4
Bayview Av	N. Roch.	286	A3	342	Inset
Beach Av		269	C6	344	C2
1-199	73	269	C6	344	C2
1000-1399	72	269	A6	344	B2
1400-OUT	6	269	A6	344	B2
Beach St	64	277	B6	345	A5
Beach St	Mt V.	279	A6	340	B3
Beachfront La	N. Roch.	285	B5	342	Inset
Beachwood Rd	B'ville	284	B2	341	A4
Beacon St	Yonk.	282	A3	340	A2
Beall Cir	Yonk.	284	A1	341	A4
Beattie La	N. Roch.	286	C1	342	Inset
Beaufort Pl	N. Roch.	285	C6	341	B6
Beaumont Av		275	B4	344	A2
1111-2299	57	275	B4	344	A2
2300-OUT	58	275	B4	344	A2
Beck St		259	A6	344	C1
1-809	55	259	A6	344	C1
810-OUT	59	260	A1	344	C1
Bedford Av	Mt V.	280	A3	341	B5
Bedford Park Blvd		275	A4	344	A1
1-199	68	278	C3	340	C2
200-OUT	58	275	A4	344	A1
Beech Pl	65	264	B3	345	C5
Beech St	Eastch.	285	A4	341	A5
Beech St	Yonk.	282	B2	340	A2
Beech Ter	54	259	B4	343	C6
Beech Ter	Yonk.	282	C2	340	B2
Beech Ter La	Pel. M.	281	C4	341	C5
Beechmont Av	Yonk.	284	A1	341	A4
Beechmont Dr	N. Roch.	285	B6	341	A6
Beechmont Pl	N. Roch.	285	B6	341	A6
Beechtree La	B'ville	284	A2	341	A4
Beechwood Av	Mt V.	280	A3	341	B5
Beechwood Av	N. Roch.	286	B1	342	Inset
Beechwood Ter	Yonk.	282	C1	340	B1
Beekman Av	54	259	B4	343	C6
Beekman Av	Mt V.	280	A2	341	B4
Belden Av	Yonk.	283	C5	340	B3
Belden St	64	277	C6	345	B6
Bell Av	66	280	B2	341	C4
Bell Av	Mt V.	280	B2	341	C4
Bell St	Yonk.	282	B2	340	A2
Bellamy Lp	75	276	A3	345	A4
Belleview Pl	N. Roch.	285	C6	341	B6
Belmont Av		275	C4	344	B1
1-2299	57	275	C4	344	B1
2300-OUT	58	275	B4	344	A2
Belmont Av	Yonk.	283	C4	340	B3
Belmont Pl	57	274	C3	344	B1
Belvedere Dr	Yonk.	282	C1	340	B1
Belvidere Pl	N. Roch.	281	B5	341	C5
Benchley Pl	75	276	A3	345	A4
Benedict Av	62	270	A1	344	B3
Benedict Pl	Pel.	281	A4	341	B5
Bennett Av	Yonk.	283	A4	340	A3
Benson St	61	276	C1	344	B3
Berg St	Mt V.	284	C1	341	B4
Bergen Av	55	259	A4	343	C6
Bergholz Dr	N. Roch.	285	C4	341	B5
Berkeley Av	Yonk.	282	C2	340	B2
Berkley Cir	Eastch.	285	A4	341	A5
Berkwit Ter	63	278	C2	340	C1
Berrian Rd	N. Roch.	285	A4	341	A5
Bertel Av	Mt V.	280	B3	341	C5
Betts Av	73	262	B2	344	C3
Beverly Pl	B'ville	284	A2	341	A4
Beverly Rd	B'ville	284	A2	341	A4
Bevy Pl	65	265	B4	345	C5
Billingsley Ter	53	274	B2	343	A6
Birch Av	Pel.	285	C4	341	B5
Birch Brook Rd	Yonk.	284	A1	341	A4
Birch Rd	Yonk.	282	C3	340	B2
Birch St	Mt V.	284	B2	341	A4
Birch St	N. Roch.	286	B1	342	Inset
Birchall Av	6	275	C5	344	B2
Bishop Wm. J. Walls Dr					
	Yonk.	282	A2	340	A2
Bissel Av E	66	279	B6	340	C3
Bivona St	66	280	C2	341	C4
Black St	Pel. M.	281	B4	341	C5
Blackford Av	Yonk.	279	A6	340	B3

Blackrock Av		270	B2	344	B3
1-2299	72	270	B2	344	B3
2300-OUT	62	270	B3	344	B3
Blackstone Av		278	B2	340	C1
1-3899	63	278	B2	340	C1
3900-OUT	71	278	B2	340	C1
Blackstone Pl	71	278	B2	340	C1
Blair Av	65	272	C3	345	C5
Blair St	Yonk.	284	B1	341	A4
Blondell Av	61	276	C1	344	B3
Bobolink Pl	Yonk.	283	A5	340	A3
Bobolink Rd	Yonk.	283	A5	340	A3
Bogart Av	62	275	B6	344	A2
Bogert Pl	Yonk.	284	A1	341	A4
Boller Av		280	C2	341	C4
1-3499	75	280	C2	341	C4
3500-OUT	66	280	C2	341	C4
Bolton Av	73	270	C1	344	C3
Bolton Gdns	B'ville	284	B2	341	A4
Bolton Rd	Pel. M.	281	B5	341	C6
Bolton St	62	275	B5	344	A2
Bon Air Av	N. Roch.	285	A4	341	A5
Bonita Vista Rd	Mt V.	284	B3	341	A5
Bonmar Rd	Pel. M.	281	B4	341	C5
Bonnefoy Pl	N. Roch.	286	B2	342	Inset
Bonner Pl	56	267	B4	343	B6
Boone Av	6	268	A3	344	B2
Boone St	Yonk.	283	C4	340	B3
Borcher Av	Yonk.	283	C4	340	B3
Borghild Av	Yonk.	283	C4	340	B3
Boscobel Pl	52	274	C1	343	B6
Boston Close	66	280	C2	341	C4
Boston Post Rd	Pel. M.	280	B3	341	C5
Boston Rd		267	B5	344	B1
1-1432	56	267	B5	344	B1
1433-2163	6	268	A2	344	B1
2164-2199	62	275	B5	344	A2
2201-2733 (odd)	67	275	B6	344	A2
2200-2748 (even)	67	275	B6	344	A2
2735-3599 (odd)	69	276	A1	344	A3
2750-3798 (even)	69	276	A1	344	A3
3601-4339 (odd)	66	280	C2	341	C4
3800-4340 (even)	75	280	C2	341	C4
Botanical Sq	58	275	A4	344	A2
Bouck Av	69	276	A1	344	A3
Boulder Pl	Yonk.	282	C3	340	B2
Boulder Tr	Yonk.	284	B1	341	A4
Bowne St	64	277	B6	345	A5
Boyd Av	66	279	B6	340	C3
Boyd Pl	Yonk.	284	A1	341	A4
Boynton Av		269	B4	344	B2
1-999	73	269	C4	344	C2
1000-OUT	72	269	B4	344	B2
Bradford Av	61	271	A5	345	B4
Bradford Rd	Mt V.	280	A3	341	B5
Bradley Av	Mt V.	284	C3	341	B5
Bradley St	7	279	A6	340	B3
Bradley Ter	63	278	C1	340	C1
Brady Av	62	275	B6	344	A2
Brady Av	N. Roch.	286	C1	342	Inset
Braemer Av	N. Roch.	285	B5	341	A6
Brandon Rd	Yonk.	283	C5	340	B3
Brandt Pl	53	274	C2	343	B6
Brassie La	Yonk.	284	A1	341	A4
Breglia St	Yonk.	283	C5	340	B3
Brewster Av	Yonk.	283	B5	340	A3
Brewster Ter	N. Roch.	285	B5	341	A6
Briar Cir	N. Roch.	285	A6	341	A6
Bridge St	64	277	B6	345	A5
Bridge St	N. Roch.	286	A2	342	Inset
Bridge St	Yonk.	282	C1	340	B1
Brier La	Pel. M.	280	B3	341	C5
Briggs Av	58	275	A4	344	A1
Briggs Av	Yonk.	283	A4	340	A3
Bright Pl	Yonk.	282	B2	340	A2
Brinsmade Av	65	271	B5	345	B4
Bristow St	59	268	A1	344	B1
Britton St	67	275	A5	344	A2
Broad St	Mt V.	284	B2	341	B4
Broad St E	Mt V.	284	B2	341	A4
Broad St W	Mt V.	284	B1	341	A4
Broadview Av	N. Roch.	285	B5	341	A6
Broadway		278	C3	340	C2
5171-5970	63	278	C2	340	C1
5971-OUT	71	278	B3	340	C2
Broadway Blvd	Yonk.	283	A5	340	A3
Bronx And Pelham Pkwy					
	61	275	B5	344	A2
Bronx Blvd		279	B6	340	C3
1-3899	67	279	C5	340	C3
3900-4399	66	279	B5	340	C3
4400-OUT	7	279	B6	340	C3
Bronx Park Av	6	275	C5	344	B2
Bronx Park E		275	B5	344	A2
1-2199	62	275	B5	344	A2
2200-OUT	67	275	B5	344	A2
Bronx Park S	6	275	C5	344	B2
Bronx River Av		268	B3	344	B2
1-999	73	268	C3	344	C2
1000-1499	72	268	B3	344	B2
1500-OUT	6	275	C5	344	B2
Bronx River Pkwy	67	279	C5	340	C3
Bronx River Pkwy	6	275	C5	344	B2
Bronx River Pkwy	72	269	A5	344	B2
Bronx River Rd	Yonk.	279	A6	340	B3
Bronx St	Mt V.	284	C1	341	B4
Bronx Ter	Yonk.	283	C5	340	B3
Bronxdale Av	62	275	C6	344	B2
Bronxville La	Yonk.	284	B1	341	A4
Bronxville Rd	Yonk.	284	A1	341	A4
Bronxwood Av		279	C6	340	C3
1-3899	69	275	A6	344	A3
3900-OUT	66	279	B6	340	C3
Brook Av		258	C3	343	C6
1-439	54	258	C3	343	C6
440-738	55	259	A4	343	C6
739-1016	51	267	C5	344	C1
1017-1504	56	267	B5	344	B1
1505-OUT	57	274	C3	344	B1
Brook Av	58	275	B4	344	A1
Brook Rd	Yonk.	284	A1	341	A4
Brook St	N. Roch.	285	C5	341	B6
Brook St	Yonk.	282	B2	340	A2
Brookdale Av	N. Roch.	285	C6	341	B6
Brookdale Cir	N. Roch.	285	C6	341	B6
Brookdale Pl	Mt V.	280	A2	341	B4
Brooke Av	Yonk.	284	A1	341	A4
Brookfield Rd	Mt V.	284	B3	341	A5
Brooklands	Yonk.	284	A1	341	A4
Brookside Av	Mt V.	280	A3	341	B5
Brookside Av	Pel.	281	A4	341	B5
Brookside Cir	Yonk.	284	A1	341	A4
Brookside Pl	N. Roch.	285	C6	341	B6
Brown Pl	54	258	C3	343	C6
Brown Pl	75	276	A3	345	A4

Browning Av	Yonk.	283	B5	340	B3
Browns La	64	277	C6	345	B6
Bruce Av	Mt V.	284	C2	341	B4
Bruce Av	Yonk.	282	C2	340	B2
Bruckner Blvd		269	C6	344	C2
1-419	54	258	B2	343	C6
420-799	55	259	B6	344	C1
800-1408 (even)	74	268	C2	344	C1
801-1409 (odd)	59	268	C2	344	C1
1410-2498 (even)	73	269	C6	344	C2
1411-2499 (odd)	72	269	C5	344	C2
2500-OUT (even)	65	271	B5	345	B4
2501-2899 (odd)	72	270	B2	344	B3
2901OUT (odd)	61	271	A6	345	B4
Bruckner Elevated Expwy					
	55	259	B5	344	C1
Bruckner Expwy	61	276	C3	345	B4
Bruckner Expwy	72	268	C3	344	C2
Bruner Av		276	B2	345	A4
1-3599	69	276	A2	345	A4
3600-OUT	66	280	B1	341	C4
Brush Av	65	271	B4	344	B3
Brust Sq	71	278	B2	340	C1
Bryant Av		268	B2	344	B1
1-949	74	260	B3	344	C2
950-1453	59	268	B2	344	B1
1454-OUT	6	268	A2	344	B1
Bryant Rd	Yonk.	282	B2	340	A2
Bryn Mawr Pl	Yonk.	283	A5	340	A3
Bryn Mawr Ter	Yonk.	283	A5	340	A3
Brynwood Rd	Yonk.	283	A4	340	A3
Bucharan Pl	53	274	B2	344	A1
Buck St	61	276	C1	344	B3
Buckley St	64	277	C6	345	B6
Buena Vista Av	Yonk.	282	B1	340	A1
Buffington Pl	Eastch.	285	B4	341	A5
Buhre Av	61	276	C2	345	B4
Bullard Av		279	B6	340	C3
1-4399	66	279	B6	340	C3
4400-OUT	7	279	A6	340	B3
Burhans Av	Yonk.	282	A3	340	A2
Burke Av		275	A5	344	A2
1-899	67	275	A5	344	A2
900-OUT	69	276	A1	344	A3
Burkewood Rd	Mt V.	284	B2	341	A4
Burling La	N. Roch.	285	C6	341	B6
Burnett Pl	74	260	A2	344	C1
Burnsice Av E		274	B3	344	A1
1-199	53	274	B3	344	A1
200-OUT	57	274	B3	344	A1
Burnside Av W	53	274	B2	343	A6
Burr Av	61	276	B3	345	A4
Burtis Av	Yonk.	283	B4	340	A3
Bush St		274	B3	344	A1
1-199	53	274	B3	344	A1
200-OUT	57	274	B3	344	A1
Bushnell Pl	Mt V.	280	A1	341	B4
Bussing Av	66	279	B6	340	C3
Bussing Pl	66	280	B1	341	C4
Butler Pl		270	A3	344	B3
1-2399	62	270	A3	344	B3
2400-OUT	61	270	A3	344	B3
Buttrick Av	65	271	C6	345	C4
Byron Av	66	279	B6	340	C3
Byron Av	Yonk.	283	C5	340	B3
Byron Pl	Yonk.	283	B5	340	A3
Byworth Rd	N. Roch.	285	A5	341	A6
Caesar Pl	73	262	A2	344	C3
Calhoun Av	65	271	A5	345	B4
Calhoun Av	N. Roch.	285	C5	341	B5
California Rd	Eastch.	285	A4	341	A5
California Rd	Mt V.	284	B3	341	A5
Calmet Pl	Yonk.	283	B4	340	A3
Calton La	N. Roch.	285	B5	341	A6
Calton Rd	N. Roch.	285	B5	341	A6
Calvi La	Yonk.	283	A5	340	A3
Cambreleng Av		275	B4	344	A2
1-2289	57	275	B4	344	A2
2290-OUT	58	275	B4	344	A2
Cambridge Av	63	278	C2	340	C1
Cameron Pl	53	274	B2	344	A1
Cameron Pl	N. Roch.	285	B5	341	A6
Cameron Pl	Tuck.	284	A2	341	A4
Camp St	66	280	A1	341	B4
Campbell Dr	65	277	C4	345	B4
Canal Pl	51	258	B2	343	C6
Canal Rd	Pel M.	280	B3	341	C5
Canal St	Mt V.	280	B3	341	C5
Canal St W	51	258	B2	343	C6
Cannon Pl	63	278	C3	340	C2
Cannons La	Eastch.	284	A3	341	A5
Canterbury Rd	Yonk.	283	C4	340	B3
Canyon Cir	Yonk.	282	C2	340	B2
Capuchin Way	67	275	A6	344	A2
Carleton Av	Mt V.	280	B3	341	C5
Carlisle Pl	67	279	C5	340	C3
Carlisle Pl	Yonk.	282	B2	340	A2
Carlisle Rd	N. Roch.	285	A6	341	A6
Carlton Rd	Yonk.	284	A1	341	A4
Carniato Plz	N. Roch.	281	A5	341	B6
Carol Av	Pel.	280	A3	341	B5
Carol Pl	Pel. M.	280	A3	341	B5
Caroline Av	Yonk.	282	B2	340	A2
Caroline Pl	Yonk.	282	B2	340	A2
Carolyn Pl	Eastch.	284	B3	341	A5
Carpenter Av		279	B5	340	C3
1-3899	67	279	C5	340	C3
3900-4399	66	279	B6	340	C3
4400-OUT	7	279	B6	340	C3
Carpetner Pl	Mt V.	280	A3	341	B5
Carroll Pl	56	266	B3	343	B6
Carroll St	64	277	C6	345	B5
Carroll St	Yonk.	282	C2	340	B2
Carter Av	57	274	C3	344	B1
Carver Lp	75	280	C2	341	C4
Carwall Av	Mt V.	284	B3	341	B5
Caryl Av	Yonk.	278	A3	340	B2
Casals Pl	75	280	C3	341	C5
Casanova St	74	260	B2	344	C1
Casler Pl	65	265	B4	345	C5
Cassillis Av	Yonk.	284	A1	341	A4
Castle Hill Av		270	A2	344	B3
1-999	73	270	C3	344	C3
1000-1105	72	270	B2	344	B3
1106-OUT	62	270	A2	344	B3
Castle Pl	N. Roch.	286	B2	342	Inset
Castle St	Yonk.	284	B1	341	A4
Catalpa Pl	65	264	A2	345	C4
Catskill Av	Yonk.	283	B4	340	A3
Cauldwell Av		267	C5	344	C1
1-736	55	259	A5	344	C1
737-OUT	56	267	C5	344	C1
Cauldwell St	Eastch.	284	A3	341	A5
Cayuga Av	71	278	B3	340	C2
Cedar Av		274	B1	343	A6

1800-2059	53	274	B1	343	A6
2060-OUT	68	274	B2	343	A6
Cedar Av	Mt V.	280	A2	341	B4
Cedar La	51	266	C2	343	C6
Cedar La	Yonk.	284	A1	341	A4
Cedar Pl	65	264	B3	345	C5
Cedar Pl	Yonk.	282	B2	340	A2
Cedar St	B'ville	284	A2	341	A4
Cedar St	Mt V.	284	C2	341	B4
Cedar St	N. Roch.	285	C6	341	B6
Cedar St	Yonk.	282	B3	340	A2
Celli Pl	Yonk.	282	B2	340	A2
Cemetery La	N. Roch.	281	A5	341	B6
Central Av	Pel.	285	C4	341	B5
Central Dr	Eastch.	285	B4	341	A5
Central Park Av N	Yonk.	283	C4	340	B3
Central Park Av S	Yonk.	283	C4	340	B3
Central Pkwy	Mt V.	284	B2	341	A4
Centre Av	N. Roch.	286	A2	342	Inset
Centre Pl	Yonk.	282	B3	340	A2
Centre St	65	272	C3	345	C5
Centre St	Mt V.	284	B2	341	A4
Cerone Av	Yonk.	283	B5	340	A3
Cerrato La	Yonk.	282	B3	340	A2
Chaffee Av	65	264	A3	345	C5
Chamberlain Av	Yonk.	283	C4	340	B3
Chanfrau Pl	Yonk.	282	A3	340	A2
Charles Pl	Eastch.	285	B4	341	A5
Charles Pl	Mt V.	280	B2	341	C4
Charles Pl	Yonk.	284	C1	341	B4
Charles St	N. Roch.	286	A1	342	Inset
Charlotte St	59	268	A1	344	B1
Chatfield Rd	Yonk.	284	A1	341	A4
Chatsworth Pl	N. Roch.	285	B6	341	A6
Chatterton Av		270	B2	344	B3
1-2338	72	270	B2	344	B3
2339-OUT	62	270	B3	344	B3
Chauncey Av	N. Roch.	285	C5	341	B6
Chelsea Rd	N. Roch.	287	B4	342	Inset
Cherwing Rd	Yonk.	283	A5	340	A3
Chesbrough Av	61	276	C1	344	B3
Chester Pl	Eastch.	284	B3	341	A5
Chester Pl	Yonk.	283	C5	340	B3
Chester St	69	280	C1	341	C4
Chester St	Mt V.	284	C2	341	B4
Chesterwood Av	Mt V.	284	C2	341	B4
Chestnut Av	B'ville	284	A2	341	A4
Chestnut Av	Pel.	285	C4	341	B5
Chestnut Dr	67	275	A6	344	A2
Chestnut La	N. Roch.	286	C2	342	Inset
Chestnut Pl	Mt V.	280	A3	341	B5
Chestnut St	67	275	A6	344	A2
Chestnut St	Yonk.	282	B2	340	A2
Chisholm St	59	268	B1	344	B1
Choctaw Pl	61	276	B1	344	A3
Church Sq	72	270	B2	344	B3
Church St	N. Roch.	286	B3	342	Inset
Churchill Av	Yonk.	279	A5	340	B3
Cicero Av	73	262	A2	344	C3
Cincinnatus Av	73	270	C3	344	C3
Circle Hill Rd	Pel. M.	281	B4	341	C5
Circle Rd	Tuck.	284	A3	341	A5
Circuit Rd	N. Roch.	286	C2	342	Inset
City Island Av	64	277	C6	345	B6
City Island Rd	64	277	A4	345	A5
Claflin Av	68	274	A3	344	A1
Claire Av	N. Roch.	285	B6	341	A6
Claremont Av	Mt V.	284	C2	341	B4
Claremont Pkwy	57	274	C3	344	B1
Claremont Pl	Mt V.	280	A2	341	B4
Claremont Ter	Mt V.	280	A2	341	B4
Clarence Av	65	272	A1	345	C4
Clarendon Av	Yonk.	282	A3	340	A2
Clark Pl	Yonk.	284	A1	341	A4
Clark St	Yonk.	283	C4	340	B3
Claudet Way	Eastch.	285	A4	341	A5
Clay Av		267	B4	343	B6
1-1505	56	267	B4	343	B6
1506-OUT	57	274	C3	344	B1
Clay Av	Pel. M.	281	B4	341	
C5Clayton Pl	Yonk.	283	C4	340	B3
Clementine St	66	280	C2	341	C4
Cleveland Av	N. Roch.	281	B5	341	C6
Cleveland Ct	N. Roch.	281	A5	341	B6
Cliff Av	Pel.	281	A4	341	B5
Cliff Av	Yonk.	282	C2	340	B2
Cliff Pl	Pel. M.	281	A4	341	B5
Cliff St	N. Roch.	286	B1	342	Inset
Cliff St	Yonk.	282	B3	340	A2
Clifford Av	Pel.	281	A4	341	B5
Clifford Pl	53	274	C2	344	B1
Clifton Av	Yonk.	282	C1	340	B1
Clinton Av		267	A6	344	B1
1-1499	56	267	A6	344	B1
1500-OUT	57	275	C4	344	B1
Clinton Av	N. Roch.	285	C5	341	B6
Clinton Pl	53	274	B2	344	A1
Clinton Pl	Mt V.	284	C2	341	B4
Clinton Pl	N. Roch.	286	A2	342	Inset
Clinton Pl	Yonk.	282	B1	340	A1
Clinton St	Mt V.	284	B2	341	A4
Clinton St	Yonk.	282	B1	340	A1
Close Av		268	B3	344	B2
1-999	73	268	C3	344	C2
1000-OUT	72	268	B3	344	B2
Clove Rd	N. Roch.	285	B5	341	A6
Clover Pl	N. Roch.	287	C4	342	Inset
Coddington Av	61	271	A5	345	B4
Colden Av		275	B6	344	A3
1-2199	62	275	B6	344	A3
2200-OUT	69	275	A6	344	A3
Cole Ter	N. Roch.	285	C5	341	B6
Coles La	58	275	B4	344	A1
Colgate Av		268	B3	344	B2
1-999	73	269	C4	344	C2
1000-OUT	72	268	B3	344	B2
Coligni Av	N. Roch.	285	C6	341	B6
Colin St	Yonk.	282	A3	340	A2
College Av		258	A3	343	C6
1-927	51	258	A3	343	C6
928-1449	56	267	B4	343	B6
1450-OUT	57	274	C2	344	B1
College Pl	Yonk.	283	B5	340	A3
College Rd	71	278	B2	340	C1
Collins Av	Mt V.	284	B2	341	A4
Collis Pl	65	264	A1	345	C4
Colonel J. Oliver Troster Mall					
	Yonk.	282	C1	340	B1
Colonial Av	61	276	B3	345	A4
Colonial Av	Pel.	281	A4	341	B5
Colonial Pl	Mt V.	280	A3	341	B5
Colonial Pl	N. Roch.	285	C5	341	B6
Colonial Rd	Eastch.	285	B3	341	A5
Columbia Pl	Mt V.	284	B3	341	A5
Columbus Av	N. Roch.	286	A1	342	Inset

Columbus Pl	Yonk.	282	B2	340	A2
Columbus Sq	58	275	B4	344	A1
Commerce Av		271	A4	344	B3
1-1299	62	271	A4	344	B3
1300-OUT	61	271	A4	344	B3
Commonwealth Av		261	A6	344	C2
1-999	73	261	A6	344	C2
1000-1419	72	269	A5	344	B2
1420-OUT	6	269	A5	344	B2
Commonwealth Av	Mt V.	284	C3	341	B5
Compton Av	73	262	B2	344	C3
Concord Av		259	B5	344	C1
1-413	54	259	B5	344	C1
414-OUT	55	259	B5	344	C1
Concordia Pl	B'ville	284	A3	341	A5
Concourse Vill E	51	266	C3	343	C6
Concourse Vill W	51	266	C2	343	C6
Congress St	N. Roch.	285	B6	341	A6
Connell Pl	65	276	C3	345	B4
Conner St		280	C2	341	C4
1-2299	66	280	C2	341	C4
2300-OUT	75	280	C2	341	C4
Continental Av	61	276	B3	345	A4
Convent Av	Yonk.	282	A3	340	A2
Convent Pl	Yonk.	282	A2	340	A2
Cook Av	Yonk.	283	A4	340	A3
Cooley Pl	Mt V.	280	A2	341	B4
Coolidge Av	Yonk.	282	A3	340	A2
Co-Op City Blvd	75	280	C2	341	C4
Cooper Pl	75	280	C2	341	C4
Cooper St	Yonk.	283	C4	340	B3
Copcutt La	Yonk.	282	B2	340	A2
Corlear Av	63	278	C2	340	C1
Corlies Av	Pel.	281	A4	341	B5
Cornell Av	73	262	B2	344	C3
Cornell Av	Yonk.	282	C2	340	B2
Cornell Pl	61	276	C2	345	B4
Cornell Pl	N. Roch.	285	B5	341	A6
Corona Av	Pel.	281	A4	341	B5
Corpl Fischer Sq	52	274	C2	343	B6
Corpl Fufidio Sq	74	260	A2	344	C1
Corsa Av	69	280	C1	341	C4
Cortland St	Mt V.	280	A1	341	B4
Cortlandt Av	N. Roch.	285	B6	341	A5
Cortlandt Ct	N. Roch.	285	B6	341	A5
Cortlandtville La	Yonk.	278	A3	340	B2
Corwood Rd	Eastch.	285	B4	341	A5
Cosma La	Yonk.	279	A4	340	B2
Coster St	74	260	B2	344	C1
Cottage Av	Mt V.	284	C2	341	B4
Cottage Pl	56	267	A6	344	B1
Cottage Pl	N. Roch.	285	C6	341	B6
Cottage Pl	Tuck.	284	A2	341	A4
Cottage Pl	Yonk.	282	B2	340	A2
Country Club Dr	Pel. M.	281	B4	341	C5
Country Club La	Pel. M.	281	B4	341	C5
Country Club Rd	65	276	C3	345	B4
Courseview Rd	B'ville	284	B3	341	A5
Courter Av	Yonk.	278	A3	340	B2
Courtlandt Av	51	267	C4	343	C6
Courtney Pl	Yonk.	279	A6	340	B3
Coventry La	N. Roch.	287	B4	342	Inset
Cowdrey St	Yonk.	283	C4	340	A3
Cowles Av	Yonk.	283	C4	340	B3
Cox Av	Yonk.	279	A5	340	B3
Coyle Pl	Yonk.	278	A3	340	B2
Cramaton Rd	B'ville	284	B3	341	A5
Cramers Sq	59	268	C2	344	C1
Cranford Av		280	A1	341	B4
1-849	7	280	A1	341	B4
850-OUT	66	280	A1	341	B4
Cranston Pl	Yonk.	284	A1	341	A4
Crary Av	Mt V.	284	C2	341	B4
Craven St	74	260	B2	344	C1
Crawford Av	66	280	C1	341	C4
Crawford Pl	Tuck.	284	A3	341	A5
Crawford St	Eastch.	284	A3	341	A5
Crawford St	Yonk.	282	C3	340	B2
Crawford Ter	N. Roch.	285	B6	341	A6
Crescent Av	58	275	B4	344	A1
Crescent Av	N. Roch.	286	A1	342	Inset
Crescent Pl	Yonk.	283	C5	340	B3
Crest Av	Mt V.	284	C2	341	B4
Crest Pl	Yonk.	282	C2	340	B2
Crestmont Av	Yonk.	283	C5	340	B3
Crestor Av		274	B3	344	A1
1-2293	53	274	B3	344	A1
2294-OUT	68	274	B3	344	A1
Crestview St	N. Roch.	285	B6	341	A6
Crestwood La	N. Roch.	285	A6	341	A6
Cricklewood N	Yonk.	279	A4	340	B2
Cricklewood S	Yonk.	279	A4	340	B2
Crimmins Av	54	259	B4	343	C6
Croes Av		269	A5	344	B2
1-999	73	269	C5	344	C2
1000-OUT	72	269	A5	344	B2
Croft Ter	N. Roch.	285	A6	341	A6
Cromwell Av		266	C2	343	C6
1-889	51	266	C2	343	C6
890-OUT	52	266	A3	343	B6
Cromwell Pl	Yonk.	282	B2	340	A2
Crosbeck Rd	Yonk.	283	A5	340	A3
Crosby Av	61	276	C2	345	B4
Crosby Pl	N. Roch.	285	C5	341	B6
Cross Bronx Expwy		274	C1	343	B6
1-100	52	274	C1	343	B6
101-759	57	274	C3	344	B1
760-1199	6	275	C4	344	B1
1200-2498 (even)	72	269	A5	344	B2
1201-1899 (odd)	62	270	A1	344	B3
1901-2499 (odd)	62	270	A1	344	B3
2500-OUT	65	271	B6	345	B4
Cross County Pkwy	Mt V.	284	B2	341	A4
Cross County Pkwy	Yonk.	283	B5	340	A3
Cross St	64	277	B6	345	A5
Cross St	N. Roch.	285	C6	341	B6
Cross St	Yonk.	284	A1	341	A4
Croton Ter	Yonk.	282	B3	340	A2
Crotona Av		268	A1	344	B1
1-1499	56	268	A1	344	B1
1500-2289	57	268	A1	344	B1
2290-OUT	58	275	B4	344	A2
Crotona Park E	6	268	A1	344	B1
Crotona Park N		274	C3	344	B1
1-759	57	274	C3	344	B1
760-OUT	6	275	C4	344	B1
Crotona Park S	56	268	A1	344	B1
Crotona Pkwy	6	275	C4	344	B2
Crotona Pl	56	267	A6	344	B1
Crotty Av	Yonk.	283	C4	340	B3
Crown Cir	B'ville	284	B3	341	A5
Crow's Nest Rd	B'ville	284	B2	341	A4
Cruger Av		275	B6	344	A2
1-2199	62	275	B6	344	A2
2200-OUT	67	275	A6	344	A2

The Bronx

The Bronx

Laurel Dr	62	275	C6	344	B2
Laurel Pl	N. Roch.	286	B2	342	Inset
Laurel Pl	Yonk.	279	A6	340	B3
Laurie Av	61	276	C2	345	B4
Lawn Av	N. Roch.	285	C6	341	B6
Lawrence Park Cres	Yonk.	283	B5	341	A4
Lawrence Park Ter	Yonk.	283	B5	341	A4
Lawrence Pl	N. Roch.	285	B4	341	A5
Lawrence Pl	Pel. M.	280	B3	341	C5
Lawrence Pl	Yonk.	282	B2	340	A2
Lawrence St	Mt V.	284	C3	341	B5
Lawrence St	Yonk.	282	C2	340	B2
Lawton Av	65	264	A1	345	C4
Lawton La	Yonk.	283	B5	340	A3
Lawton St	N. Roch.	286	A2	342	Inset
Lawton St	Yonk.	279	A4	340	B2
Layton Av	65	272	A1	345	B4
Leary St	Eastch.	285	A4	341	A5
Lebanon St	6	275	C5	344	B2
Lecount Pl	N. Roch.	286	B3	342	Inset
Ledgewood Rd	Yonk.	284	B1	341	A4
Lee Av	Yonk.	282	C3	340	B2
Lee Ct	N. Roch.	286	C2	342	Inset
Lee Pl	B'ville	284	B3	341	A5
Lee St	Yonk.	279	A4	340	B2
Lefferts Rd	Yonk.	282	C3	340	B2
Leffingwell Pl	N. Roch.	285	C5	341	B6
Legget Rd	B'ville	284	B2	341	A4
Leggett Av		260	B1	344	C1
1-1079	55	259	A6	344	C1
1080-OUT	74	260	B1	344	C1
Lehman Ter	Yonk.	282	C1	340	B1
Leighton Av	Yonk.	282	C2	340	B2
Leland Av		262	A1	344	C3
1-999	73	262	A1	344	C3
1000-1359	72	269	A6	344	B2
1360-OUT	6	269	A6	344	B2
Leland Av	N. Roch.	286	B3	342	Inset
Lennon Av	Yonk.	282	A3	340	A2
Lenox Av	Mt V.	284	C3	341	B5
Lenox Av	Yonk.	284	A2	341	A4
Leona La	Mt V.	280	B3	341	C5
Leonard Pl	Yonk.	283	C5	340	B3
Leonard Rd	B'ville	284	A2	341	A4
Lepinsky Pl	Yonk.	283	C5	340	B3
Leroy Av	Yonk.	279	A4	340	B2
Leroy Pl	N. Roch.	286	A2	342	Inset
Leroy Pl	Yonk.	282	C3	340	B2
Lester Pl	N. Roch.	285	B6	341	A6
Lester St	67	275	A5	344	A2
Leticia Rd	Eastch.	284	A3	341	A5
Leviness Pl	N. Roch.	285	C5	341	B6
Lewis Av	Yonk.	282	A2	340	A2
Lewis Pkwy	Yonk.	282	C2	340	B2
Lexington Av	Mt V.	284	C3	341	B5
Libby Pl	61	276	C2	345	B4
Liberty Av	N. Roch.	286	B2	342	Inset
Library Av	65	276	C3	345	B4
Library Rd	B'ville	284	B2	341	A4
Lieb Pl	Eastch.	284	A3	341	A5
Liebig Av	71	278	A2	340	B1
Light St	66	280	C2	341	C4
Lincoln Av	54	258	B2	343	C6
Lincoln Av	Pel.	285	C4	341	B5
Lincoln Av	Yonk.	283	C5	340	B3
Lincoln St	N. Roch.	285	C6	341	B6
Lincoln Ter	Yonk.	282	A2	340	A2
Linden Av	65	264	A3	345	C5
Linden Av	Mt V.	284	C1	341	B4
Linden Av	Pel.	285	C4	341	B5
Linden Dr	62	275	C6	344	B3
Linden Pl	N. Roch.	286	B2	342	Inset
Linden St	Yonk.	282	B2	340	A2
Lindsey St	Yonk.	283	B4	340	A3
Linn Av	Yonk.	282	C3	340	B2
Linwick Pl	Yonk.	279	A6	340	B3
Lisbon Pl	58	275	A4	344	A2
Lispenard Av	Eastch.	285	B4	341	A5
Lispenard Av	N. Roch.	285	C6	341	B6
Little John Pl	Yonk.	283	A5	340	A3
Livingston Av	71	278	B2	340	C1
Livingston Av	Yonk.	282	C2	340	B2
Livingston St	Mt V.	284	C2	341	B4
Lockwood Av	Eastch.	285	B4	341	A5
Lockwood Av	N. Roch.	285	C5	341	B6
Lockwood Av	Yonk.	283	A4	340	A3
Lockwood Path	N. Roch.	285	C5	341	B6
Locust Av	54	259	C5	344	C1
Locust Av	N. Roch.	286	A3	342	Inset
Locust Hill Av	Yonk.	282	B2	340	A2
Locust La	B'ville	284	B3	341	A5
Locust Point Dr	65	265	A4	345	C5
Locust St	Mt V.	284	C1	341	B4
Lodovick Av	69	276	B2	345	A4
Loehr Pl	Yonk.	282	A2	340	A2
Logan Av	65	271	A6	345	B4
Lohengrin Pl	65	272	A1	345	B4
Lomond Pl	N. Roch.	285	B5	341	A6
London Ter	N. Roch.	285	A6	341	A6
Long Meadow Rd	Yonk.	279	A4	340	B2
Longfellow Av		260	A3	344	C2
1-999	74	260	A3	344	C2
1000-1454	59	268	B2	344	B1
1455-OUT	6	268	A3	344	B2
Longspur Rd	Yonk.	283	A5	340	A3
Longstreet Av	65	272	C3	345	C5
Longue Vue Av	N. Roch.	285	A6	341	A6
Longvale Rd	Yonk.	284	A1	341	A4
Longwood Av		267	C6	344	C1
1-1050	59	267	C6	344	C1
1051-OUT	74	260	A1	344	C1
Lookout Av	B'ville	284	A2	341	A4
Loomis Av	Yonk.	283	B5	340	A3
Loomis St	61	276	B1	344	A3
Lorenz Av	N. Roch.	285	C6	341	B6
Lorillard Pl	58	275	B4	344	A1
Loring Av	Pel.	281	A4	341	B5
Loring Av	Yonk.	283	C4	340	B3
Loring Pl N		274	B2	344	A1
1-2249	53	274	B2	344	A1
2250-OUT	68	274	B2	344	A1
Loring Pl S	53	274	B2	343	A6
Lorraine Av	Mt V.	284	C3	341	B5
Lorraine Ter	Mt V.	284	C3	341	B5
Lou Auger Sq	63	278	C2	340	C1
Loudoun St	Yonk.	282	C2	340	B2
Louis Nine Blvd	59	268	A1	344	B1
Louisiana Av	Yonk.	284	B1	341	A4
Lovell Rd	N. Roch.	285	A5	341	A6
Lowell St	59	268	B2	344	B1
Lowell St	Yonk.	282	A3	340	A2
Lowerre Pl	66	279	B6	340	C3
Lucerne St	65	276	C3	345	B4
Lucille Pl	Eastch.	284	B3	341	A5
Ludlow St	Yonk.	282	C1	340	B1
Lurting Av		275	A6	344	A3
1-2199	61	276	B1	344	A3
2200-OUT	69	275	A6	344	A3
Lusk Av	Yonk.	283	C5	340	B3
Lustre St	66	280	B2	341	C4
Lydig Av		275	B6	344	A2
1-1023	62	275	B6	344	A3
1024-OUT	61	276	B1	344	A3
Lyman Pl	59	268	B1	344	B1
Lyncroft Rd	N. Roch.	285	A6	341	A6
Lynns Way	N. Roch.	287	B4	342	Inset
Lyon Av	62	270	A2	344	B3
Lyons Pl	Mt V.	280	A2	341	B4
Lyvere St	61	276	C1	344	B3
Mac Questen Pkwy N	Mt V.	284	C1	341	B4
MacCracken Av	53	274	B1	343	A6
MacDonough Pl	65	276	C3	345	B4
Mace Av		275	A5	344	A2
1-899	67	275	A5	344	A2
900-OUT	69	276	A1	344	A3
Maclay Av		276	C1	344	B3
1-2399	62	276	C1	344	B3
2400-OUT	61	276	C1	344	B3
Macombs Rd		274	C2	343	B6
1-1603	52	274	C2	343	B6
1604-OUT	53	274	C2	343	B6
Macy Pl	55	259	A6	344	C1
Madeleine Av	N. Roch.	285	C5	341	B6
Madeleine Pkwy	Yonk.	282	C2	340	B2
Madison Av	Yonk.	282	A2	340	A2
Madison St	Mt V.	280	A2	341	B4
Magenta St		279	C5	340	C3
1-899	67	279	C5	340	C3
900-OUT	69	275	A6	344	A3
Magnolia Av	Mt V.	284	C3	341	B5
Magnolia Pl	65	264	A3	345	C5
Mahan Av	61	276	C3	345	B4
Main St	65	272	C3	345	C5
Main St	Eastch.	284	A3	341	A5
Main St	N. Roch.	286	A2	342	Inset
Main St	Yonk.	282	B1	340	A1
Maitland Av	61	276	C2	345	B4
Major Deegan Expwy	51	258	A1	343	C6
Major Deegan Expwy	52	266	A1	343	B6
Major Deegan Expwy	53	274	B1	343	A6
Major Deegan Expwy	63	274	A2	344	A1
Major Deegan Expwy	68	274	B2	343	A6
Major Deegan Expwy	71	278	B3	340	C2
Manger Cir	Pel. M.	280	B3	341	C5
Mangrove Rd	Yonk.	283	A5	340	A3
Manhattan Av	N. Roch.	285	C6	341	B6
Manhattan College Pkwy	71	278	B2	340	C1
Manida St	74	260	A2	344	C3
Manning Av	Yonk.	283	A4	340	A3
Manning Cir	Pel.	280	A3	341	B5
Manning St	62	270	A2	344	B3
Manor Av	72	269	A4	344	B2
Manor Cir	Pel. M.	281	B5	341	C6
Manor House Sq	Yonk.	282	B2	340	A2
Manor La	Pel. M.	281	B4	341	C5
Manor Pl	N. Roch.	285	C6	341	B6
Manor Ridge Rd	Pel. M.	281	A4	341	B5
Manor Rd	B'ville	284	B3	341	A5
Mansion Av	Yonk.	283	B5	340	A3
Mansion St	6	269	A5	344	B2
Mapes Av	6	275	C4	344	B1
Maple Av	65	264	A3	345	C5
Maple Av	N. Roch.	286	B2	342	Inset
Maple Av	Pel.	285	C4	341	B5
Maple Dr	62	275	C6	344	B3
Maple Pl	Mt V.	284	C2	341	B4
Maple Pl	Yonk.	283	C5	340	B3
Maple St	Yonk.	282	B2	340	A2
Maran Pl	62	275	B5	344	A2
Marcy Pl		267	A4	343	B6
1-199	52	274	C2	343	B6
200-OUT	56	267	A4	343	B6
Marina Dr	65	264	A1	345	C4
Marine Memorial Causeway	N. Roch.	285	B5	341	A6
Marine St	64	277	C6	345	B6
Marion Av	58	275	A4	344	A1
Marion Av	Mt V.	284	C3	341	B5
Marion Pl	Mt V.	284	C3	341	B5
Marion Pl	Yonk.	278	A3	340	B2
Market Pl	Yonk.	282	B1	340	A1
Marmion Av	6	275	C4	344	B1
Marolla Pl	66	280	C1	341	C4
Marquand Av	Yonk.	284	A1	341	A4
Marquand Pl	Pel.	280	A3	341	B5
Marshall Rd	Yonk.	282	C3	340	B2
Marston Pl	Yonk.	283	C5	340	B3
Martens Pl	Mt V.	280	A2	341	B4
Martha Av	7	279	A5	340	B3
Martin Rd	Yonk.	283	A5	340	A3
Marvin Pl	61	276	C1	344	B3
Marvin Pl	N. Roch.	286	B2	342	Inset
Marwood La	Yonk.	283	A4	340	A3
Masterton Rd	B'ville	284	B2	341	A4
Mathews Av	67	275	C6	344	B2
Mathewson Rd	53	274	B1	343	A6
Matilda Av		279	B6	340	C3
1-4399	66	279	B6	340	C3
4400-OUT	7	279	A6	340	B3
Matthews Av		275	B6	344	A2
1-2199	62	275	B6	344	A2
2200-OUT	67	275	A6	344	A2
Maul Pl	N. Roch.	285	C4	341	B5
Maul St	N. Roch.	285	C4	341	B5
May St	N. Roch.	285	C6	341	B6
Maybrook Cir	Eastch.	285	B4	341	A5
Mayflower Av	61	271	A5	345	B4
Mayflower Av	N. Roch.	285	C4	341	B5
Mcclellan Av	Mt V.	280	A3	341	B5
McClellan St		266	A3	343	B6
1-159	52	266	A3	343	B6
160-OUT	56	267	A4	343	B6
Mccollom Pl	Yonk.	279	A5	340	B3
Mccorkle St	Yonk.	284	A2	341	A4
McDonald St	61	276	B1	344	A3
Mcgeory Av	Yonk.	283	B5	340	A3
McGraw Av		269	A6	344	B2
1-1859	72	269	A6	344	B2
1860-OUT	62	270	A1	344	B3
Mcintyre St	Yonk.	284	A1	341	A4
Mckinley Av	Yonk.	283	B5	340	A3
McKinley Sq E	56	267	A6	344	B1
Mckinley St	Tuck.	284	A3	341	A5
Mclean Av	Yonk.	279	A4	340	B2
McOwen Av	66	280	B3	341	C5
Mead St	6	275	C6	344	B2
Mead Way	Yonk.	284	B1	341	A4
Meadow Av	B'ville	284	A2	341	A4
Meadow Av	Yonk.	284	A1	341	A4
Meadow La	N. Roch.	286	B2	342	Inset
Meadowood Path	N. Roch.	285	A6	341	A6
Meagher Av	65	265	A4	345	C5
Mealpin Av	61	276	C1	344	B3
Melrose Av		259	A4	343	C6
1-742	55	259	A4	343	C6
743-OUT	51	267	C4	343	C6
Melrose Av	Mt V.	284	C1	341	B4
Melrose Dr	N. Roch.	285	B6	341	A6
Melville St	6	275	C5	344	B2
Memorial Hwy	N. Roch.	286	A2	342	Inset
Meredith Pl	Eastch.	285	B4	341	A5
Mereland Rd	N. Roch.	285	A5	341	A6
Merriam Av	52	274	C1	343	B6
Merriam Av	Yonk.	284	A1	341	A4
Merriam Pl	Yonk.	284	A1	341	A4
Merrill St	6	269	A6	344	B2
Merritt Av		280	C2	341	C4
1-3599	75	280	C2	341	C4
3600-OUT	66	280	B2	341	C4
Merry Av	61	276	C3	345	B4
Mersereau Av	Mt V.	284	C3	341	B5
Metcalf Av		269	A5	344	B2
1-999	73	269	C5	344	C2
1000-OUT	72	269	A5	344	B2
Metropolitan Av	62	270	A1	344	B3
Metropolitan Oval	62	275	C6	344	B3
Meyer Av	Yonk.	283	C5	340	B3
Meyers St	61	271	A6	345	B4
Mickle Av	69	276	B2	344	A3
Middle Rd	B'ville	284	A3	341	A5
Middle Rd	Eastch.	284	A3	341	A5
Middleton Pl	Eastch.	284	A3	341	A5
Middletown Rd		276	C2	345	B4
1-3149	61	276	C2	345	B4
3150-OUT	65	276	C3	345	B4
Midland Av	B'ville	284	A2	341	A4
Midland Av	Eastch.	284	A3	341	A5
Midland Av	Yonk.	282	C3	340	B2
Midland Pl	Tuck.	284	A3	341	A5
Midland Ter	Yonk.	283	C4	340	B3
Milburn St	B'ville	284	A2	341	A4
Mildred St	Yonk.	283	C5	340	B3
Mile Square Pl	Yonk.	283	C5	340	B3
Mile Square Rd	Yonk.	283	A4	340	A3
Miles Av	65	272	C3	345	C5
Mill St	Yonk.	282	B2	340	A2
Millard Av	Yonk.	284	A1	341	A4
Miller Pl	Mt V.	280	B2	341	C4
Miller Pl	Yonk.	284	A1	341	A4
Millington St	Mt V.	280	A3	341	B5
Millison Cl	Yonk.	284	A1	341	A4
Milton Pl	65	264	A2	345	C4
Minerva Pl	68	275	A4	344	A1
Minford Pl	6	268	A2	344	B1
Minnieford Av	64	277	B6	345	A5
Minturn Rd	Tuck.	284	A2	341	A4
Miriam St	58	275	A4	344	A1
Mitchell Av	Yonk.	283	A4	340	A3
Mitchell Pl	65	265	B4	345	C5
Mitchell Pl	Pel. M.	281	B4	341	C5
Mohegan Av	6	275	C4	344	B1
Monroe Av	57	274	C2	344	B1
Monroe St	64	281	C4	341	C5
Monroe St	Mt V.	280	A2	341	B4
Monroe St	N. Roch.	285	C6	341	B6
Monroe St	Pel. M.	281	B4	341	C5
Monsignor Cahill Pl	69	279	C6	340	C3
Monsignor Halpin Pl	65	264	A2	345	C4
Monterey Av	57	274	C3	344	B1
Monterey Av	Pel. M.	281	A4	341	B5
Monterey Dr	Mt V.	284	B3	341	A5
Montgomery Av	53	274	C1	343	B6
Montgomery Av	Yonk.	283	A4	340	A3
Montgomery Cir	N. Roch.	285	B5	341	A6
Montgomery Pl	61	276	C1	344	B3
Montgomery Pl	N. Roch.	285	B6	341	A6
Monticello Av	66	280	A1	341	B4
Mooney Pl	Yonk.	282	B3	340	A2
Moore Rd	Yonk.	284	A1	341	A4
Moquette N Row	Yonk.	282	A3	340	A2
Moquette S Row	Yonk.	282	A3	340	A2
Moreland St	Yonk.	284	B1	341	A4
Morgan Av	69	276	B1	344	A3
Morgan St	N. Roch.	286	C1	342	Inset
Morgan St	Yonk.	282	B2	340	A2
Morningside Av	Yonk.	282	A2	340	A2
Morningside Cir	B'ville	284	A2	341	A4
Morningside Pl	Yonk.	282	A3	340	A2
Morris Av		258	B2	343	C6
1-928	51	258	B2	343	C6
929-1449	56	267	B4	343	B6
1450-1799	57	274	C2	344	B1
Morris Av	53	274	C2	344	B1
Morris Av	68	274	B3	344	A1
Morris Cir	Yonk.	282	C1	340	B1
Morris Park Av		275	C5	344	B2
1-646	6	275	C5	344	B2
647-1023	62	275	C6	344	B2
1024-OUT	61	276	B1	344	A3
Morris Pl	Yonk.	282	C2	340	B2
Morris St	N. Roch.	285	C6	341	B6
Morris St	Yonk.	282	C2	340	B2
Morrison Av		269	A4	344	B2
1-999	73	269	C5	344	C2
1000-OUT	72	269	A4	344	B2
Morrison Pl	Mt V.	280	A2	341	B4
Mortimer Pl	Eastch.	285	B4	341	A5
Morton Pl	53	274	B2	343	A6
Mosholu Av	71	278	A2	340	B1
Mosholu Golf Course Rd	67	279	B4	340	C2
Mosholu Pkwy	58	279	C4	340	C2
Mosholu Pkwy	71	279	A4	340	B2
Mostyn St	Yonk.	282	A3	340	A2
Mount Carmel Pl	Yonk.	282	B2	340	A2
Mount Eden Av W	52	274	C2	343	B6
Mount Eden Pkwy	57	274	C2	344	B1
Mount Etna Pl	N. Roch.	286	B3	342	Inset
Mount Hope Pl		274	C2	344	B1
1-199	53	274	C2	344	B1
200-OUT	57	274	C3	344	B1
Mount Joy Pl	N. Roch.	285	C5	341	B6
Mount Tom Rd	N. Roch.	286	C1	342	Inset
Mount Tom Rd	Pel. M.	281	B5	341	C6
Mount Vernon Av	Mt V.	280	A1	341	B4
Muir Pl	N. Roch.	285	C5	341	B6
Mulberry St	Yonk.	282	B3	340	A2
Mulford Av	61	276	C2	345	B4
Muliner Av	62	275	B6	344	A3
Mullan Pl	65	264	A3	345	C5
Mulvey Av	66	280	B2	341	C4
Mundy La	66	280	A1	341	B4
Munn Av	62	270	A3	344	B3
Munn Pl	Yonk.	283	C5	340	B3
Murdock Av		280	B1	341	C4
1-4799	66	280	B1	341	C4
4800-OUT	7	280	A1	341	B4
Murray Av	Yonk.	283	B5	340	A3
Murray St	Pel. M.	280	B3	341	C5
Myrtle St	Yonk.	282	A3	340	A2
Nancy Pl	Eastch.	284	B3	341	A5
Napier Av	7	279	B4	340	C2
Naples St	63	278	C2	340	C1
Nardozzi Pl	N. Roch.	281	B5	341	C6
Narragansett Av	61	276	B1	344	A3
Nautilus Pl	N. Roch.	286	C2	342	Inset
Nebraska Av	Yonk.	284	B1	341	A4
Needham Av		279	C6	340	C3
1-1599	69	279	C6	340	C3
1600-2199	66	280	C1	341	C4
Neill Av		275	B6	344	A2
1-1023	62	275	B6	344	A2
1024-OUT	61	276	B1	344	A3
Nelson Av		266	A2	343	B6
1-1599	52	266	A2	343	B6
1600-OUT	53	274	C1	343	B6
Nelson St	Yonk.	283	C5	340	B3
Nepperhan Av	Yonk.	282	B2	340	A1
Nepperhan St	Yonk.	282	B1	340	A1
Neptune Av	N. Roch.	286	C1	342	Inset
Neptune Ct	73	262	C2	344	C3
Neptune Island Rd	N. Roch.	281	B6	341	C5
Neptune La	73	262	B2	344	C3
Nereid Av		279	B6	340	C3
1-699	7	279	B6	340	C3
700-OUT	66	279	B6	340	C3
Netherland Av		278	C1	340	C1
1-3899	63	278	C1	340	C1
3900-OUT	71	278	A2	340	B1
Nevada Pl	Yonk.	284	B1	341	A4
New Av	Yonk.	279	A6	340	B3
New England Thruway	69	276	A2	345	A4
New Haven Railroad St	Mt V.	279	A6	340	B3
New Main St	Yonk.	282	B2	340	A2
New Pl	Yonk.	279	A6	340	B3
New Rochelle Rd	Eastch.	284	B3	341	A5
Newbold Av		270	A3	344	B3
1-1999	72	270	A1	344	B3
2000-OUT	62	270	A3	344	B3
Newell St	67	279	C5	340	C3
Newman Av	73	262	B2	344	C3
Newport Av	61	276	B1	344	A3
Newton Pl	Mt V.	280	B3	341	C5
Nichols Av S	Yonk.	283	A4	340	A3
Nile St	Yonk.	283	C4	340	B3
Noble Av		269	C6	344	C2
1-999	73	269	C6	344	C2
1000-1499	72	269	A5	344	B2
1500-OUT	6	269	A5	344	B2
Noble Av	Yonk.	283	B5	340	A3
Noell Av	66	280	C2	341	C4
Nolan Av	Yonk.	283	C5	340	B3
Norman Rd	N. Roch.	285	B4	341	A5
Normandy Rd	B'ville	284	B2	341	A4
North 2nd Av	Mt V.	284	C2	341	B4
North 3rd Av	Mt V.	284	C2	341	B4
North 5th Av	Mt V.	284	C1	341	B4
North 6th Av	Mt V.	284	C1	341	B4
North 7th Av	Mt V.	284	C1	341	B4
North 8th Av	Mt V.	284	C1	341	B4
North 9th Av	Mt V.	284	C1	341	B4
North 10th Av	Mt V.	284	C1	341	B4
North Av	N. Roch.	286	A2	342	Inset
North Bleeker St	Mt V.	284	C1	341	B4
North Bond St	Mt V.	280	A1	341	B4
North Broadway	Yonk.	282	B2	340	A2
North Columbus Av	Mt V.	284	C3	341	B4
North Dr	Yonk.	283	B5	340	A3
North Fulton Av	Mt V.	284	C2	341	B4
North High St	Mt V.	284	C1	341	B4
North Oak Dr	67	275	A6	344	A2
North Pkwy	7	279	A4	340	B2
North Rd	Eastch.	284	a3	341	A5
North St	68	274	B3	344	A1
North St	Mt V.	284	C1	341	B4
North Terrace Av	Mt V.	284	C1	341	B4
North Way	B'ville	284	B3	341	A5
North Way	Eastch.	284	B3	341	A5
North West St	Mt V.	284	C1	341	B4
North West Way	B'ville	284	B3	341	A5
Northern Av	B'ville	284	A2	341	A4
Northfield Rd	N. Roch.	285	A5	341	A6
Northfield St	Yonk.	283	B4	340	A3
Norton Av	73	262	A2	344	C3
Nostrand Pl	Yonk.	283	A5	340	A3
Nuber Av	Mt V.	280	A3	341	B5
Nuvern Av	66	280	B1	341	C4
Nuvern Av	Mt V.	280	B2	341	C4
Nyac Av	Pel.	281	A4	341	B5
Oak Av	65	264	A3	345	C5
Oak Av	Pel.	285	C4	341	B5
Oak Av	Tuck.	284	A2	341	A4
Oak Bend	Yonk.	284	B1	341	A4
Oak Dr	Mt V.	284	C3	341	B5
Oak La	64	281	B4	341	C5
Oak La	Pel. M.	281	B4	341	C5
Oak Point Av	74	260	B1	344	C1
Oak St	Mt V.	284	C1	341	B4
Oak St	N. Roch.	285	C6	341	B6
Oak St	Yonk.	282	B2	340	A2
Oak Ter	54	259	B4	343	C6
Oak Ter	Tuck.	284	A2	341	A4
Oak Tree Pl	57	275	B4	344	A1
Oakdale Av	N. Roch.	285	C4	341	B5
Oakland Av	Mt V.	284	C3	341	B5
Oakland Pl	57	275	C4	344	B1
Oakledge Rd	B'ville	284	B2	341	A4
Oakley Av	Mt V.	284	C2	341	B4
Oakley Pl	Mt V.	284	C1	341	B4
Oakley St	69	279	C6	340	C3
Oakwood Av	Mt V.	284	C3	341	B5
O'Brien Av	73	262	B2	344	C3
O'Brien Sq	57	274	C3	344	B1
Odell Pl	N. Roch.	286	A2	342	Inset
Odell St	62	276	C1	344	B3
Ogden Av	52	266	A2	343	B6
Ohm Av	65	276	C3	345	B4
Old Jerome Av	Yonk.	279	A5	340	B3
Old Orchard Rd	N. Roch.	285	A5	341	A6
Olinville Av	67	275	B5	344	A2
Oliver Av	Yonk.	282	B3	340	A2
Oliver Pl	58	275	A4	344	A2
Olmstead Av		270	A2	344	B3
1-999	73	270	C2	344	C3
1000-1199	72	270	B2	344	B3
1200-OUT	62	270	A2	344	B3
One Lighting Pl	74	260	C3	344	C2
Oneida Av	7	279	B5	340	C3
Oneida Av	Mt V.	280	A2	341	B4
Oneida St	Yonk.	282	A3	340	A2
O'Neil Pl	69	276	A1	344	A3
Onondaga St	Yonk.	283	B5	340	A3
Orchard Beach Rd	64	277	A4	345	A5
Orchard Pl	B'ville	284	A3	341	A5
Orchard Pl	N. Roch.	285	C6	341	B6
Orchard Pl	Yonk.	282	A3	340	A2
Orchard St	Mt V.	284	B2	341	A4
Orchard St	Yonk.	282	A3	340	A2
Oregon Av	Eastch.	285	B4	341	A5
Orient St	Yonk.	283	C4	340	B3
Oriole Av	B'ville	284	A3	341	A5
Oriole Rd	Yonk.	283	A5	340	A3
Orloff Av	63	278	C3	340	C2
Ormonde Pl	N. Roch.	285	C4	341	B5
Osborne Pl	53	274	B2	343	A6
Osgood St	7	279	A6	340	B3
Osman Pl	7	280	A1	341	B4
Osmun Pl	Yonk.	283	A4	340	A3
Otis Av	65	271	A6	345	B4
Otsego Av	N. Roch.	285	B5	341	A6
Otsego St	Yonk.	283	C5	340	B3
Outlook Av	65	277	C4	345	B4
Oval Ct	B'ville	284	A2	341	A4
Overcliff St	Yonk.	282	C2	340	B2
Overhill Pl	Yonk.	283	C5	340	B3
Overhill Rd	Mt V.	284	B3	341	A5
Overhill Rd	N. Roch.	285	A6	341	A6
Overing St	61	276	C1	344	B3
Overlook Av	Eastch.	284	A3	341	A5
Overlook Cir	N. Roch.	285	B6	341	A6
Overlook Rd	N. Roch.	285	A5	341	A6
Overlook St	Mt V.	284	C2	341	B4
Overlook Ter	Yonk.	282	B2	340	A2
Overman Pl	N. Roch.	285	C4	341	B5
Oxford Av	63	278	C2	340	C1
Oxford La	Yonk.	284	B1	341	A4
Oxford Pl	N. Roch.	285	A5	341	A6
Oxford Rd	N. Roch.	285	A5	341	A6
Packman Av	Mt V.	284	A2	341	A4
Paddington Cir	B'ville	284	B3	341	A5
Paddington Rd	B'ville	284	A3	341	A5
Page Av	Yonk.	283	B5	340	B3
Paine Av	N. Roch.	285	A6	341	A6
Paine St	61	271	A6	345	B4
Palisade Av		278	C1	340	C1
1-3899	63	278	C1	340	C1
3900-OUT	71	278	B2	340	C1
Palisade Av	Yonk.	282	A2	340	A2
Palisade Pl	53	274	B1	343	A6
Palmer Av		280	C1	341	C4
2200-3399	75	280	C2	341	C4
3500-OUT	66	280	C1	341	C4
Palmer Av	B'ville	284	A1	341	A4
Palmer Av	Mt V.	284	B3	341	A5
Palmer Av	N. Roch.	285	C6	341	E6
Palmer Rd	Yonk.	283	A4	340	A3
Palo Alto Pl	Mt V.	284	B3	341	A5
Palumbo Pl	B'ville	284	B2	341	A4
Paradise Rd	B'ville	284	A2	341	A4
Parcot Av	N. Roch.	285	B5	341	A6
Park Av		258	A2	343	C6
2300-3267	51	258	A2	343	C6
3268-3799	56	267	B5	344	B1
3801-4545 & 3800-4552	57	274	C3	344	B1
4547-OUT & 4554-OUT	58	275	B4	344	A1
Park Av	B'ville	284	A2	341	A4
Park Av	Mt V.	284	C2	341	B4
Park Av	N. Roch.	287	A4	342	Inset
Park Av	Yonk.	282	A2	340	A2
Park Dr	64	281	C4	341	C5
Park Hill Av	Yonk.	282	B2	340	A2
Park Hill Pl	Yonk.	282	C2	340	B2
Park Hill Ter	Yonk.	282	C2	340	B2
Park Knoll	Mt V.	284	B2	341	A4
Park La	Mt V.	284	C2	341	B4
Park La	Pel. M.	281	C5	341	C6
Park Pl	B'ville	284	A2	341	A4
Park Pl	Mt V.	284	C2	341	B4
Park Pl	N. Roch.	285	C6	341	B6
Park Pl	Pel.	285	C4	341	B5
Park Ridge Av	N. Roch.	286	C1	342	Inset
Park Rd	Mt V.	284	C3	341	B5
Parkchester Rd	62	270	A1	344	B3
Parker St	62	276	C1	344	B3
Park-Hill Av	Yonk.	282	C2	340	B2
Parkiew Ter	68	274	A3	344	A1
Parkside Pl	67	275	A5	344	A2
Parkview Av	61	276	C3	345	B4
Parkview Av	N. Roch.	286	C2	342	Inset
Parkview Av	Yonk.	284	A1	341	A4
Parkview Dr	Eastch.	285	B4	341	A5
Parkview Ter	68	274	A3	344	A1
Parkway Cir	Mt V.	284	B2	341	A4
Parkway Dr	Pel.	280	A3	341	B5
Parkway E	Mt V.	284	B2	341	A4
Parkway E	Yonk.	283	A5	340	A3
Parkway Plz	Eastch.	285	B4	341	A5
Parkway Rd	B'ville	284	A2	341	A4
Pkwy South	Mt V.	284	C2	341	B4
Parkway W	Mt V.	284	B2	341	A4
Parsifal Pl	65	276	C3	345	B4
Pasadena Pl	Mt V.	284	B3	341	A5
Pasadena Rd	Eastch.	284	B3	341	A5
Patricia Pl	Yonk.	283	C4	340	B3
Patterson Av	73	261	B6	344	C2
Paul Av	68	274	A3	344	A1
Paula Av	Yonk.	284	B1	341	A4
Paulding Av		275	A6	344	A3
1-1549	61	276	C1	344	B3
1550-2199	62	275	B6	344	A3
2200-3899	69	275	A6	344	A3
3900-OUT	66	279	C6	340	C3
Paulis Pl	64	277	C6	345	B5
Pawnee Pl	61	276	B1	344	A3
Paxton Av	B'ville	284	A1	341	A4
Peace St	64	280	C3	341	C5
Peace St	Pel. M.	281	B4	341	C5
Pearl St	Mt V.	279	A6	340	B3
Pearl St	Yonk.	282	A3	340	A2
Pearsall Av	69	276	A1	344	A3
Pearsall Dr	Mt V.	284	C3	341	B5
Peartree Av	66	280	C2	341	C4
Pease St	Mt V.	280	A3	341	B5
Pebble Way	N. Roch.	285	A6	341	A6
Pelham Bridge Rd (Shore Rd)	64	281	C4	341	C5
Pelham Manor Rd	Pel. M.	281	A4	341	B5
Pelham Pkwy	Pel. M.	280	B3	341	C5
Pelham Pkwy N		276	B1	344	A3
1-899 (odd)	67	275	B6	344	A2

901-OUT	67	276	B1	344	A3
Pelham Pkwy S		275	B6	344	A2
2-948 (even)	62	275	B6	344	A2
950-OUT (even)	61	276	B1	344	A3
Pelham Rd	N. Roch.	286	C2	342	Inset
Pelhamdale Av	N. Roch.	285	B6	341	A5
Pelhamdale Av	Pel.	281	A4	341	B5
Pelhamdale Av	Pel. M.	281	B4	341	C5
Pelhamside Dr	N. Roch.	281	A5	341	B6
Pelhamwood Av	Pel.	281	A4	341	B5
Pell Pl	64	277	C6	345	B5
Pell Pl	N. Roch.	285	B6	341	A6
Pell Pl	Pel.	285	C4	341	B5
Pelton St	Yonk.	282	C2	340	B2
Penfield Av	Pel. M.	281	B4	341	C5
Penfield St	7	280	A1	341	B4
Penn Pl	Pel. M.	280	B3	341	C5
Pennsylvania Av	Mt V.	284	C3	341	B5
Pennyfield Av	65	265	A4	345	C5
Perot St	63	278	C2	340	C1
Perry Av		275	A4	344	A2
1-3029	58	275	A4	344	A2
3030-OUT	67	275	A5	344	A2
Perry Pl	Yonk.	284	A1	341	A4
Pershing Av	N. Roch.	285	C4	341	B5
Pershing Av	Yonk.	282	C1	340	B1
Pershing Sq	N. Roch.	285	C6	341	B6
Perth Av	N. Roch.	285	B5	341	A6
Peters Pl	7	279	B5	340	C3
Phelan Pl	53	274	B2	343	A6
Philip Av	65	271	B6	345	B4
Pier St	Yonk.	282	C1	340	B1
Pierce Av		276	C1	344	B3
1-1023	62	276	C1	344	B3
1024-OUT	61	276	C1	344	B3
Pilgrim Av	61	276	C2	345	B4
Pilot St	64	277	C6	345	B6
Pinchot Pl	61	276	B1	344	A3
Pine Brook Blvd	N. Roch.	285	A6	341	A6
Pine Brook Dr	N. Roch.	285	A6	341	A6
Pine Cir	Eastch.	284	A3	341	A5
Pine Ct	N. Roch.	281	A5	341	B6
Pine Dr	62	275	C6	344	B3
Pine St	N. Roch.	286	B1	342	Inset
Pine St	Yonk.	282	A2	340	A2
Pine Ter	B'ville	284	B3	341	A5
Pinkney Av	75	280	C3	341	C5
Pintard Av	N. Roch.	286	B2	342	Inset
Pitman Av	66	279	B6	340	C3
Plateau Cir E	B'ville	284	A2	341	A4
Plateau Cir W	B'ville	284	A2	341	A4
Plaza Pl	65	264	A3	345	C5
Plimpton Av	52	274	C1	343	B6
Ploughman's Bush	71	278	B1	340	C1
Plymouth Av	61	276	C2	345	B4
Plymouth St	Pel. M.	281	B4	341	C5
Poe Pl	58	275	A4	344	A1
Point St	Yonk.	282	A2	340	A2
Polo Pl	65	276	C3	345	B4
Polychrome Pl	Yonk.	282	A1	340	A1
Pond Pl	58	275	A4	344	A1
Pond Rd	Yonk.	282	B3	340	A2
Pondfield Pkwy	Mt V.	284	B2	341	A4
Pondfield Rd	B'ville	284	B2	341	A4
Pondfield Rd W	Yonk.	284	A1	341	A4
Pontiac Pl	55	259	A5	344	C1
Ponton Av	61	276	C1	344	B3
Popham Av	53	274	C1	343	B6
Poplar Av	65	264	B3	345	C5
Poplar Av	Pel.	285	C4	341	B5
Poplar Pl	N. Roch.	286	B2	342	Inset
Poplar St	61	276	C1	344	B3
Poplar St	Yonk.	282	B2	340	A2
Porach St	Yonk.	282	B3	340	A2
Portnellan Av	N. Roch.	285	B5	341	A6
Portugal Pl	Mt V.	284	C2	341	B4
Post Rd	71	278	B3	340	C2
Post St	Yonk.	282	C2	340	B2
Potters La	N. Roch.	287	B4	342	Inset
Powell Av		270	B1	344	B3
1-2139	72	270	B1	344	B3
2140-OUT	62	270	B2	344	B3
Powers Av	54	259	B4	343	C6
Pratt Av	66	280	B2	341	C4
Pratt Av	Mt V.	280	B2	341	C4
Prentiss Av	65	272	C3	345	C5
Prescott Av	B'ville	284	A2	341	A4
Prescott St	Yonk.	282	B3	340	A2
President St	N. Roch.	285	B6	341	A5
Primrose Av	Mt V.	284	C2	341	B4
Prince St	N. Roch.	285	C5	341	B6
Priory La	Pel. M.	281	C5	341	C6
Prospect Av		259	A6	344	C1
1-831	55	259	A6	344	C1
833-1429 & 832-1434	59	268	B1	344	B1
1431-1499 & 1436-1498	56	268	A1	344	B1
1500-2299	57	275	C4	344	B1
2300-OUT	58	275	B4	344	A2
Prospect Av	Eastch.	284	A3	341	A5
Prospect Av	Pel. M.	281	B4	341	C5
Prospect Dr	Yonk.	282	C2	340	B2
Prospect Pl	57	274	C3	344	B1
Prospect St	N. Roch.	286	B2	342	Inset
Prospect St	Yonk.	282	B1	340	A1
Prospect Ter	Yonk.	282	C2	340	B2
Prospect W Av	Mt V.	284	C1	341	B4
Provost Av	66	280	C2	341	C4
Pryer Pl	N. Roch.	285	B6	341	A6
Pryer Ter	N. Roch.	285	B6	341	A6
Pugsley Av		270	A1	344	B3
1-999	73	270	C2	344	C3
1000-1269	72	270	B1	344	B3
1270-OUT	62	270	A1	344	B3
Pulsifer Av	Yonk.	283	A4	340	A3
Purdy St	62	276	C1	344	B3
Puritan Av	61	271	A5	345	B4
Purser Pl	Yonk.	282	C1	340	B1
Putnam Av	Yonk.	282	C3	340	B2
Putnam Av W	63	278	C2	340	C1
Putnam Pl	67	279	C4	340	C2
Putnam Rd	N. Roch.	285	C6	341	B6
Putnam St	Mt V.	284	C1	341	B4
Quaker La	N. Roch.	285	A5	341	A6
Quaker Ridge Rd	N. Roch.	285	A5	341	A6
Quarry Rd	57	275	B4	344	A1
Queens Dr	Yonk.	282	B3	340	A2
Quentin Charlton Ter	Yonk.	282	C3	340	B2
Quimby Av	73	270	B2	344	B3
Quincy Av	65	271	B6	345	B4
Quincy Pl	Yonk.	282	A2	340	A2
Radcliff Av		275	A6	344	A3
1-2199	62	275	B6	344	A3
2200-OUT	69	275	A6	344	A3

Radford Pl	Yonk.	282	B2	340	A2
Radford St	Yonk.	282	C2	340	B2
Radio Dr	65	276	C3	345	B4
Rae St	55	259	A5	344	C1
Ramada Plz	N. Roch.	285	C6	341	B6
Ramsey Av	Yonk.	283	A4	340	A3
Randall Av		260	B2	344	C1
1-1599	74	260	B2	344	C1
1600-2499	73	261	A6	344	C2
2500-OUT	65	272	B1	345	B4
Randall Pl	Pel. M.	281	B4	341	C5
Randolph Pl	65	276	C3	345	B4
Randolph St	Yonk.	282	C2	340	B2
Ranger Pl	N. Roch.	285	A5	341	A6
Ravine Av	Yonk.	282	A2	340	A2
Rawlins Av	65	272	A1	345	B4
Raybrook Pl	Yonk.	279	A6	340	B3
Raybrook Rd	Yonk.	279	A6	340	B3
Raymond Pl	Yonk.	283	C5	340	B3
Raynor Av	Mt V.	284	B2	341	A4
Red Oak Dr	62	275	C6	344	B3
Red Oak Rd	B'ville	284	A2	341	A4
Reed Av	Pel. M.	281	A4	341	B5
Reed Pl	65	276	C3	345	B4
Reeds Mill La	75	280	C2	341	C4
Regina Pl	66	280	C2	341	C4
Reiss Pl	67	275	B5	344	A2
Relyea Pl	N. Roch.	286	A2	342	Inset
Remington Pl	N. Roch.	285	C5	341	B6
Research Av	65	276	C3	345	B4
Reservoir Av	68	274	A3	344	A1
Reservoir Oval E	67	279	C4	340	C2
Reservoir Oval W	67	279	C4	340	C2
Reservoir Pl	67	279	C4	340	C2
Return Bend	Yonk.	284	B1	341	A4
Rev James A Polite Av	59	268	B1	344	B1
Revere Av	65	271	A6	345	B4
Review Pl	63	278	C2	340	C1
Reville St	64	277	C6	345	B6
Rex Pl	Yonk.	279	A5	340	B3
Reyer Av	Yonk.	284	C1	341	B4
Reynold St	64	277	C6	345	B6
Reynolds Av	65	272	C3	345	C5
Rhinelander Av		275	C6	344	B2
1-1023	62	275	C6	344	B2
1024-OUT	61	276	B1	344	A3
Rhodes St	N. Roch.	285	C6	341	B6
Rhynas Dr	Mt V.	284	B2	341	A4
Rich Av	Mt V.	284	B2	341	A4
Richardson Av		279	B6	340	C3
4300-4399	66	279	B6	340	C3
4400-OUT	7	279	B6	340	C3
Richfield Av	Yonk.	283	C5	340	B3
Richmond Plz	53	274	B1	343	A6
Rider Av	51	258	B2	343	C6
Ridge Av	Yonk.	282	A2	340	A2
Ridge Dr	Yonk.	282	C2	340	B2
Ridge Pl	64	281	C4	341	C5
Ridge Pl	Pel. M.	281	B4	341	C5
Ridge Rd	Tuck.	284	A2	341	A4
Ridge Rd	Yonk.	282	C2	340	B2
Ridge St	Eastch.	284	A3	341	A5
Ridgecroft Rd	B'ville	284	A3	341	A5
Ridgeway St	Mt V.	284	B2	341	A4
Ridgewood Av	Yonk.	283	C5	340	B3
Rigby St	Yonk.	283	C5	340	B3
Risley Pl	N. Roch.	285	C5	341	B6
Risse St	68	279	C4	340	C2
Ritchie Dr	Yonk.	282	C3	340	B2
Rittenhouse Rd	Eastch.	285	A4	341	A5
Ritter Pl	59	268	B1	344	B1
Ritters La	Yonk.	282	A2	340	A2
River Av		266	B2	343	B6
1-870	51	266	B2	343	B6
871-OUT	52	266	A3	343	B6
River Av	Pel.	285	C4	341	B5
River Rd	63	278	C1	340	C1
River St	N. Roch.	285	C6	341	B6
River St	Yonk.	282	B1	340	A1
Rivercrest Rd	71	278	A2	340	B1
Riverdale Av		278	A2	340	B1
1-3899	63	278	C2	340	C1
3900-OUT	71	278	A2	340	B1
Riverview Pl	Yonk.	282	B2	340	A2
Robbins Pl	Yonk.	282	B2	340	A2
Roberts Av	61	276	C1	344	B3
Robertson Pl	65	276	C3	345	B4
Robertson St	7	279	A6	340	B3
Robins Cres	N. Roch.	285	B4	341	A5
Robins Rd	N. Roch.	285	B4	341	A5
Robinson Av	65	263	A6	345	C4
Robley St	Yonk.	283	C4	340	B3
Rochambeau Av	67	279	C4	340	C2
Rochelle Pl	N. Roch.	285	C6	341	B6
Rochelle St	64	277	C6	345	B6
Rochelle Ter	Mt V.	284	C1	341	B4
Rock Pl	Yonk.	282	C3	340	B2
Rockdale Av	N. Roch.	281	A5	341	B6
Rockland Av	Yonk.	282	C2	340	B2
Rockland Pl	N. Roch.	285	B6	341	A6
Rockland Pl	Yonk.	282	C3	340	B2
Rockledge Av	Mt V.	280	B2	341	C4
Rockledge Dr	Pel. M.	281	B5	341	C6
Rockledge Pl	N. Roch.	285	B6	341	A6
Rockledge Pl (off Broadway Av)	Yonk.	282	C2	340	B2
Rockledge Pl (off Rockledge Rd)	Yonk.	283	A5	340	A3
Rockledge Rd	Yonk.	284	A1	341	A4
Rockridge Rd	Mt V.	284	B2	341	A4
Rockwood St	52	274	C2	343	B6
Rodman Pl	6	275	C4	344	B2
Roebling Av	61	276	C2	345	B4
Rogers Pl	59	268	C1	344	C1
Rohr Pl	65	271	C4	344	C3
Rollins St	Yonk.	282	C2	340	B2
Romaine Av	Yonk.	282	C2	340	B2
Roman Oval	N. Roch.	287	B4	342	Inset
Romano La	Yonk.	282	B2	340	A2
Rombouts Av		280	C2	341	C4
1-3599	75	280	C2	341	C4
3600-OUT	66	280	C2	341	C4
Ronalds Av	N. Roch.	281	A5	341	B6
Ronalds La	N. Roch.	281	A5	341	B6
Roosevelt Av	65	272	C1	345	C4
Roosevelt Av	Pel. M.	281	C5	341	C6
Roosevelt Pl	Pel. M.	281	C5	341	C6
Roosevelt Sq N	Mt V.	284	C1	341	B4
Roosevelt Sq S	Mt V.	280	A1	341	B4
Roosevelt Sq W	Mt V.	280	A1	341	B4
Roosevelt St	Yonk.	283	A3	340	A2
Ropes Av	66	280	B3	341	C5
Rose Av	Eastch.	284	A3	341	A5
Rose Hill Av	N. Roch.	285	B4	341	A5
Rose La	N. Roch.	285	B4	341	A5

Rose La	Yonk.	282	C2	340	B2
Rosedale Av		269	A5	344	B2
1-999	73	269	C6	344	C2
1000-1419	72	269	A5	344	B2
1420-OUT	6	269	A5	344	B2
Rosedale Av	N. Roch.	285	C4	341	B5
Rosedale St	N. Roch.	285	C4	341	B5
Roselle St	61	276	C1	344	B3
Rosewood St	67	275	A5	344	A2
Roslyn Pl	Mt V.	280	B2	341	C4
Rossmore Av	Yonk.	284	B1	341	A4
Rotunno Pl	N. Roch.	285	C5	341	B6
Rowe St	61	270	A3	344	B3
Rowland St	61	276	C1	344	B3
Royal St	Yonk.	283	C5	340	B3
Rumsey Av	Yonk.	283	B4	340	A3
Rumsey Rd	Yonk.	282	C3	340	B2
Ruppert Pl	51	266	B2	343	B6
Rusciano Blvd	Pel. M.	280	B3	341	C5
Russell Av	N. Roch.	286	B1	342	Inset
Rutland Rd	Yonk.	283	A5	340	A3
Ryawa Av	74	260	C3	344	C2
Ryder Pl	Yonk.	283	C5	340	B3
Ryer Av		274	B3	344	A1
1-2299	57	274	B3	344	A1
2300-OUT	58	274	B3	344	A1
Sacket Av		276	C1	344	B3
1-1023	62	276	C1	344	B3
1024-OUT	61	276	C1	344	B3
Sagamore Rd	B'ville	284	A2	341	A4
Sagamore St	62	275	C5	344	B2
Sageman St	Mt V.	284	C2	341	B4
Saint Andrews Pl	Yonk.	282	C2	340	B2
Saint Ann's Av		259	A4	343	C6
1-439	54	258	C3	343	C6
440-740	55	259	A4	343	C6
741-OUT	56	267	C5	344	C1
Saint Ann's Pl	54	258	C3	343	C6
Saint Barnabas Pl	Yonk.	279	A5	340	B3
Saint Casimir Av	Yonk.	282	B2	340	A2
Saint George's Cres	58	279	C4	340	C2
Saint James Ter	Yonk.	283	C5	340	B3
Saint John's Av	Yonk.	283	C5	340	B3
Saint John's Pl	N. Roch.	281	A5	341	B6
Saint Joseph Av	Yonk.	282	A2	340	A2
Saint Joseph Pl	Yonk.	282	A2	340	A2
Saint Joseph St	N. Roch.	286	C1	342	Inset
Saint Lawrence Av		269	C6	344	C2
1-999	73	269	C6	344	C2
1000-1419	72	269	A6	344	B2
1420-OUT	6	269	A6	344	B2
Saint Marks Pl	Yonk.	279	A5	340	B3
Saint Mary St	Yonk.	282	B1	340	A1
Saint Mary's St	54	259	B5	344	C1
Saint Nicholas Av	Yonk.	284	A2	341	A4
Saint Ouen St	7	280	A1	341	B4
Saint Paul Av	61	276	B3	345	A4
Saint Paul's Pl	56	267	A6	344	B1
Saint Paul's Pl	Mt V.	280	B2	341	C4
Saint Paul's Pl	N. Roch.	285	C5	341	B6
Saint Peter's Av	61	276	C1	344	B3
Saint Raymonds Av		270	A2	344	B3
1-2399	62	270	A2	344	B3
2400-OUT	61	276	C1	344	B3
Saint Theresa Av	61	276	C2	345	B4
Sampson Av	65	272	C1	345	C4
Sandford Blvd E	Mt V.	280	A2	341	C4
Sandford Blvd W	Mt V.	280	B1	341	C4
Sandford St	Yonk.	279	A4	340	B2
Sands Pl	61	276	B3	345	A4
Santa Monica Dr West	Eastch.	285	A4	341	A5
Santo Donato Pl	61	276	B2	345	A4
Saratoga Av	Yonk.	282	C2	340	B2
Sargent Pl	Mt V.	280	B3	341	C5
Saw-Mill River Rd	Yonk.	282	A3	340	A2
Saxon Av	63	278	C3	340	C2
Scenic Pl	63	278	C1	340	C1
Schieffelin Av	66	280	C1	341	C4
Schieffelin Pl	66	280	C1	341	C4
Schley Av	65	272	C1	345	C4
Schley Av	N. Roch.	285	B6	341	A6
Schofield St	64	277	C6	345	B5
School St	Yonk.	282	B2	340	A2
Schorr Pl	65	276	A2	345	A4
Schudy Pl	N. Roch.	285	C5	341	B6
Schurz Av	65	264	A2	345	C4
Schuyler Pl	61	276	B2	345	A4
Schuyler St	N. Roch.	285	C6	341	B6
Schuyler Ter	65	265	B4	345	C5
Scott Av	Yonk.	279	A5	340	B3
Scott Pl	65	272	B1	345	B4
Screvin Av	73	262	A2	344	C3
Seabury Av		271	A4	344	B3
1-1300	62	271	A4	344	B3
1301-OUT	61	271	A4	344	B3
Seabury Pl	6	268	A2	344	B1
Seacord Rd	N. Roch.	285	A5	341	A6
Secor Av	66	280	C2	341	C4
Secor La	Pel. M.	280	B3	341	C5
Secor Pl	Yonk.	283	C5	340	B3
Seddon St	61	276	C1	344	B3
Sedgwick Av		274	C1	343	B6
1-1499	52	274	C1	343	B6
1500-2199	53	274	B1	343	A6
2200-3099	68	274	A3	344	A1
3100-OUT	63	278	C3	340	C2
Sedgwick Av	Yonk.	282	C3	340	B2
Selwyn Av	57	274	C2	344	B1
Seminary Av	Yonk.	283	B4	340	A3
Seminole Av	61	276	B1	344	A3
Seminole St	61	276	B1	344	A3
Semy Av	Yonk.	283	B4	340	B3
Seneca Av	74	268	C2	344	C1
Seneca Av	Mt V.	280	A2	341	B4
Senger Pl	65	271	C4	344	C3
Seton Av	66	280	A1	341	B4
Seward Av	73	270	C2	344	C3
Sexton Pl	69	276	A1	344	A3
Seymour Av	69	276	B1	344	A3
Seymour St	Yonk.	282	B3	340	A2
Shady Glen Ct	N. Roch.	286	C3	342	Inset
Shaefer Av	Yonk.	283	B5	340	B3
Shakespeare Av	52	274	C1	343	B6
Shea Pl	N. Roch.	286	B2	342	Inset
Sheldon Av	N. Roch.	285	B6	341	A6
Sheldon Pl	N. Roch.	285	B6	341	B6
Sheridan Av		266	B3	343	B6
1-939	51	266	B3	343	B6
940-1449	56	267	A4	343	B6
1450-OUT	57	274	C2	344	B1
Sheridan Av	Mt V.	284	C3	341	B5
Sheridan Expwy	6	268	B3	344	B2
Sherman Av		266	B3	343	B6
802-940	51	266	B3	343	B6
941-OUT	56	267	A4	343	B6

Sherman Av	B'ville	284	B3	341	A5
Sherman Av	Mt V.	284	C3	341	B5
Sherman Av	Yonk.	279	A4	340	B2
Sherwood Av	Pel. M.	280	B3	341	C5
Sherwood Av	Yonk.	283	C5	340	B3
Sherwood Ter	Yonk.	283	C5	340	B3
Shipman Av	Yonk.	279	A5	340	B3
Shore Dr	65	272	A2	345	B4
Shore Rd	Pel. M.	281	C5	341	C6
Shore Rd (now Pelham Bridge Rd)	64	281	C4	341	C5
Shoreview Cir	Pel. M.	281	C5	341	C6
Short St	Mt V.	280	A1	341	B4
Shrady Pl	63	278	C2	340	C1
Sicard Av	N. Roch.	285	B5	341	A6
Sickles Av	N. Roch.	285	C5	341	B6
Sickles Pl	N. Roch.	285	C5	341	B6
Sidney St	N. Roch.	285	C6	341	B6
Siebrecht Pl	N. Roch.	285	B5	341	A6
Siegfried Pl	65	276	C3	345	B4
Sigma Pl	71	278	A2	340	B1
Silver Birch Rd	N. Roch.	285	A5	341	A6
Silver St	61	276	C1	344	B3
Silverman Pl	57	274	C2	344	B1
Simpson St	59	268	C1	344	C1
Siwanoy Blvd	Eastch.	284	A3	341	A5
Siwanoy Club Way	Eastch.	284	B3	341	A5
Siwanoy Pl	Pel. M.	281	B4	341	C5
Slocum Av	Yonk.	283	B5	340	A3
Slocum Rd	N. Roch.	285	C6	341	B6
Smart Av	Yonk.	283	B5	340	A3
Smith Pl	Yonk.	284	A1	341	A4
Somerville Pl	Yonk.	282	A3	340	A2
Sommer Pl	65	271	B6	345	B4
Sound View Av		262	A1	344	C3
1-999	73	262	A1	344	C3
1000-OUT	72	269	B5	344	B2
Soundview Av	Yonk.	283	B4	340	A3
Soundview Dr	65	272	B3	345	B5
Soundview St	N. Roch.	286	A3	342	Inset
Soundview Ter	65	265	B4	345	C5
South 1st Av	Mt V.	280	A2	341	B4
South 2nd Av	Mt V.	280	A2	341	B4
South 3rd Av	Mt V.	280	A2	341	B4
South 4th Av	Mt V.	280	A2	341	C4
South 5th Av	Mt V.	280	A2	341	C4
South 6th Av	Mt V.	280	A1	341	B4
South 7th Av	Mt V.	280	A1	341	B4
South 8th Av	Mt V.	280	A1	341	B4
South 9th Av	Mt V.	280	A1	341	B4
South 10th Av	Mt V.	280	A1	341	B4
South 11th Av	Mt V.	280	A1	341	B4
South 12th Av	Mt V.	280	A1	341	B4
South 13th Av	Mt V.	280	A1	341	B4
South 14th Av	Mt V.	280	A1	341	B4
South 15th Av	Mt V.	280	A1	341	B4
South 16th Av	Mt V.	280	A1	341	B4
South Bleeker St	Mt V.	280	A1	341	B4
South Bond St	Mt V.	280	A1	341	B4
South Broadway	Yonk.	282	C2	340	B2
South Columbus Av	Mt V.	280	A3	341	B5
South Devoe Av	Yonk.	278	A3	340	B2
South Dr	Yonk.	283	B5	340	A3
South Fulton Av	Mt V.	280	A2	341	B4
South High St	Mt V.	280	A1	341	B4
South High St	Tuck.	284	A3	341	A5
South Oak Dr	67	275	A6	344	A2
South Path	N. Roch.	285	B5	341	A6
South Rd	B'ville	284	A3	341	A5
S Waverley St	Yonk.	282	B2	340	A2
South Way	Eastch.	284	B3	341	A5
South West St	Mt V.	279	A6	340	B3
Southern Blvd		259	B5	344	C1
1-419	54	259	B5	344	C1
420-799	55	259	B5	344	C1
800-1459	59	268	B2	344	B1
1460-2399	6	275	C4	344	B1
2400-OUT	58	275	B4	344	A2
Southfield Rd	Mt V.	284	B3	341	A5
Spafford Av	Yonk.	283	C5	340	A3
Sparks Av	Pel.	280	A3	341	B5
Spaulding La	71	278	B1	340	C1
Split Rock Rd	Pel. M.	280	B3	341	C5
Spaulding Pl	Yonk.	284	A1	341	A4
Spencer Av	71	278	A3	340	B2
Spencer Dr	65	276	C3	345	B4
Spencer Pl	71	278	A3	340	B2
Spencer Ter	71	278	A3	340	B2
Split Rock Rd	64	280	C3	341	C5
Spofford Av	74	260	A2	344	C1
Spring Rd	Pel. M.	280	B3	341	C5
Spring Rd	Yonk.	282	C3	340	B2
Springer Av	Yonk.	284	C1	341	B4
Spruce St	N. Roch.	286	C1	342	Inset
Spruce St	Yonk.	282	B3	340	A2
Stadium Av	65	276	C3	345	B4
Stanley Av	Yonk.	282	B1	340	A1
Stanley Pl	Yonk.	282	C1	340	B1
Starling Av	62	270	A2	344	B3
Starr Ter	N. Roch.	285	A6	341	A6
State St	N. Roch.	285	B6	341	A6
Station Pl	Mt V.	284	C3	341	B5
Station Plz N	N. Roch.	286	A3	342	Inset
Station Plz S	N. Roch.	286	A2	342	Inset
Staunton St	Yonk.	283	B5	340	A3
Stearns St	62	276	C1	344	B3
Stebbins Av	59	268	A1	344	B1
Stebbins Av	Eastch.	284	A3	341	A5
Stebbins Av	Tuck.	284	A3	341	A5
Stedman Pl	69	276	A1	344	A3
Steenwick Av	66	280	C2	341	C4
Stell Pl	69	275	B6	344	A3
Stellar Av	Pel. M.	281	B4	341	C5
Stellar Pl	Pel. M.	281	B4	341	C5
Stephens Av	73	262	B2	344	C3
Stephenson Blvd	N. Roch.	285	C6	341	B6
Sterling Av	Yonk.	279	A5	340	B3
Steuben Av	67	279	C4	340	C2
Stevens Av	Mt V.	280	A1	341	B4
Stevens Av	Yonk.	279	A6	340	B3
Stevenson Pl	63	278	C3	340	C2
Stewart Pl	Yonk.	282	A2	340	A2
Stickball Blvd	73	270	C1	344	C3
Stickney Pl	69	279	C6	340	C3
Stillwell Av		276	B2	345	A4
1-1699	61	276	B2	344	A3
1700-1999	69	276	B2	345	A4
2000-OUT	75	276	B3	345	A4
Stillwell Av	Yonk.	283	C5	340	B3
Stone Av	Yonk.	283	A4	340	A3
Stone Pl	B'ville	284	A2	341	A4
Stoneleigh Plz	B'ville	284	A2	341	A4
Stony Run	N. Roch.	285	A6	341	A6
Storer Av	N. Roch.	285	C4	341	B5
Storer Av	Pel.	281	A4	341	B5

Story Av	73	268	C3	344	C2
Strang Av	66	280	B1	341	C4
Stratford Av	72	269	A4	344	B2
Stratford Rd	N. Roch.	285	A5	341	A6
Stratton S St	Yonk.	282	A3	340	A2
Stratton St	Yonk.	283	A4	340	A3
Strong St	68	274	A3	344	A1
Studio La	B'ville	284	A2	341	A4
Sturgis Rd	B'ville	284	B3	341	A5
Sturgis St	Mt V.	284	B2	341	A4
Stuyvesant Plz	Mt V.	284	C3	341	B5
Suburban Av	Pel. M.	280	B3	341	C5
Suburban Pl	6	268	A2	344	B1
Sullivan Pl	65	271	B6	345	B4
Summerfield St	Yonk.	283	B4	340	A3
Summit Av	52	266	A1	343	B6
Summit Av	B'ville	284	A3	341	A4
Summit Av	Mt V.	284	C2	341	B4
Summit Av	N. Roch.	285	C5	341	B6
Summit Pl	63	278	C2	340	C1
Summit St	Eastch.	284	A3	341	A5
Summit St	Yonk.	282	A2	340	A2
Sumner Av	Yonk.	283	B4	340	A3
Sunlight Hill	Yonk.	283	C4	340	B3
Sunny Brae Pl	B'ville	284	B3	341	A5
Sunnybrook Rd	Yonk.	284	A1	341	A4
Sunnyside Dr	Yonk.	282	C1	340	B1
Sunset Av	B'ville	284	A2	341	A4
Sunset Blvd	73	262	C2	344	C3
Sunset Dr	Yonk.	282	C3	340	B2
Sunset Indian Tr	65	264	A2	345	C4
Sussex Av	B'ville	284	B3	341	A5
Sussex Pl	Yonk.	283	B5	340	A3
Sutherland St	64	277	B6	345	A5
Sutton Manor La	N. Roch.	287	A4	342	Inset
Sutton Manor Rd	N. Roch.	287	A4	342	Inset
Sutton Oval	Yonk.	282	A3	340	A2
Suydam Pl	Yonk.	282	A3	340	A2
Sweeney Pl	Yonk.	279	A4	340	B2
Sweetfield Cir	Yonk.	283	B4	340	A3
Swinton Av	65	271	B5	345	B4
Sycamore Av	71	278	A1	340	B1
Sycamore Av	Mt V.	284	C3	341	B5
Sycamore Av	N. Roch.	281	A5	341	B6
Sycamore Dr	62	270	A1	344	B3
Sycamore St	B'ville	284	A2	341	A4
Sylvan Av	71	278	A3	340	B2
Sylvan Pl	N. Roch.	285	B6	341	A6
Taft Av	Yonk.	283	B5	340	A3
Tamerton St	Mt V.	284	C3	341	B5
Tanglewylde Av	B'ville	284	A2	341	A4
Tara Way	Tuck.	284	A3	341	A5
Taylor Av		269	C6	344	C2
1-999	73	269	C6	344	C2
1000-1359	72	269	A6	344	B2
1360-OUT	6	269	A6	344	B2
Taymil Rd	N. Roch.	285	A5	341	A6
Tecumseh Av	Mt V.	280	A2	341	B4
Teller Av		267	B4	343	B6
1-955 & 2-932	51	267	B4	343	B6
957-1449 & 934-1448	56	267	B4	343	B6
1450-OUT	57	274	C2	344	B1
Tenbroeck Av		276	A1	344	A3
1-2199	61	276	B1	344	A3
2200-OUT	69	276	A1	344	A3
Tenny Pl	53	274	C1	343	B6
Terace Pl	64	281	C4	341	C5
Terace St	64	277	B6	345	A5
Teresa Av	Yonk.	283	C4	340	B3
Terrace Pl	Pel. M.	281	B4	341	C5
Terrace Pl	Tuck.	284	A2	341	A4
Terrace Pl	Yonk.	282	B2	340	A2
Texas Av	Yonk.	284	B1	341	A4
The Boulevard	N. Roch.	285	C6	341	B6
The Byway	B'ville	284	B2	341	A4
The Circle	N. Roch.	285	C6	341	B6
The Court	N. Roch.	285	C6	341	B6
The Crescent	Yonk.	282	C2	340	B2
The Crossway	Yonk.	283	A4	340	A3
The East Al	B'ville	284	A2	341	A4
The East Blvd	N. Roch.	285	C6	341	B6
The Esplanade	N. Roch.	285	B6	341	A6
The Frank Kelly Field Rd	71	278	A3	340	B2
The High Rd	B'ville	284	B2	341	A4
The Serpentine	N. Roch.	285	C6	341	B6
Thieriot Av		269	C6	344	C2
1-999	73	269	C6	344	C2
1000-1359	72	269	A6	344	B2
1360-OUT	6	269	A6	344	B2
Thomas E. Sharp Blvd	Mt V.	284	C1	341	B4
Thomas Pl	Eastch.	285	B4	341	A5
Thomas Pl	N. Roch.	285	C5	341	B6
Thomas Pl	Yonk.	283	A4	340	A3
Throgmorton Av	65	272	A1	345	B4
Throgs Neck Blvd	65	272	A1	345	B4
Throgs Neck Expwy	65	272	A1	345	B4
Throop Av	69	276	A1	344	A3
Thurman Munson Wy	51	266	C3	343	C6
Thurman St	Yonk.	282	B2	340	A2
Thurton Pl	Yonk.	283	C5	340	B3
Thwaites Pl	67	275	B5	344	A2
Tibbett Av		278	C2	340	C1
1-3999	63	278	C2	340	C1
4000-OUT	71	278	B2	340	C1
Tibbetts Rd	Yonk.	282	C3	340	B2
Tiebout Av		274	B3	344	A1
1-2299	57	274	B3	344	A1
2300-OUT	58	274	B3	344	A1
Tiemann Av	69	280	C1	341	C4
Tier St	64	277	C6	345	B5
Tierney Pl	65	264	B3	345	C5
Tiffany St		260	A2	344	C1
1-849	74	260	A2	344	C1
850-OUT	59	268	C1	344	C1
Tilden St		279	C5	340	C3
1-899	67	279	C5	340	C3
900-OUT	69	279	C6	340	C3
Tillotson Av		280	C1	341	C4
1-1999	69	280	C1	341	C4
2000-OUT	75	280	C2	341	C4
Tim Hendrick Pl	63	278	C2	340	C1
Timpson Pl	55	259	B6	344	C1
Timpson St	Pel. M.	280	B3	341	C5
Tinton Av		259	B5	344	C1
1-743	55	259	B5	344	C1
744-OUT	56	267	C6	344	C1
Tioga Av	Yonk.	283	C5	340	B3
Tocco Pl	Yonk.	283	B5	340	A3
Tomlinson Av	61	276	B1	344	A3
Topping Av	57	274	C2	344	B1
Torry Av	73	262	A3	344	C3
Tower Pl	Mt V.	284	B2	341	A4

The Bronx

Town Dock Rd	N. Roch.	286	C3	342	Inset
Townsend Av		274	C2	343	B6
1-1649	52	274	C2	343	B6
1650-OUT	53	274	C2	343	B6
Townsend Av	Pel. M.	281	B4	341	C5
Trafalgar Pl	6	275	C4	344	B1
Tratman Av	61	270	A3	344	B3
Travers Av	Yonk.	282	C3	340	B2
Tremont Av see East or West		274	B2	344	A1
Trenchard St	Yonk.	283	C5	340	B3
Treno St	N. Roch.	285	C6	341	B6
Trenor Dr	N. Roch.	285	A5	341	A6
Treyon Pl	N. Roch.	285	A5	341	A6
Triangle Pl	Tuck.	284	A2	341	A4
Trinity Av		259	A5	344	C1
1-731 & 2-738	55	259	A5	344	C1
733-OUT & 740-OUT	56	267	C5	344	C1
Trinity Pl	N. Roch.	286	B3	342	Inset
Trinity Pl E	Mt V.	280	A2	341	B4
Trinity Pl N	Mt V.	280	A2	341	B4
Trinity Pl S	Mt V.	280	A2	341	B4
Trinity Pl W	Mt V.	280	A2	341	B4
Trinity St	Yonk.	282	A3	340	A2
Troy La	N. Roch.	285	C5	341	B5
Troy La	Yonk.	282	A3	340	A2
Truesdale Pl	Yonk.	282	B3	340	A2
Truxton St	74	260	B2	344	C1
Tryon Av	67	279	C4	340	C2
Tuckahoe Av	Eastch.	285	A4	341	A5
Tudor La	Yonk.	283	A5	340	A3
Tudor Pl	52	266	A3	343	B6
Tulfan Ter	63	278	C2	340	C1
Tunis Av	Yonk.	283	B5	340	A3
Turnbull Av	73	270	C2	344	C3
Turner St	Yonk.	283	C5	340	B3
Turneur Av	73	262	A3	344	C3
Tyndall Av	71	278	A2	340	B1
Umberto Pl	Yonk.	283	A4	340	A3
Undercliff Av		274	C1	343	B6
1-1499	52	274	C1	343	B6
1500-OUT	53	274	C1	343	B6
Undercliff St	Yonk.	282	C2	340	B2
Underhill Av		270	B1	344	B3
1-999	73	262	A1	344	C3
1000-OUT	72	270	B1	344	B3
Union Av		259	A6	344	C1
1-790	55	259	A6	344	C1
791-OUT	59	267	C6	344	C1
Union Av	Mt V.	280	A2	341	B4
Union Av	N. Roch.	281	A5	341	B6
Union La	Mt V.	280	A2	341	B4
Union Pl	52	266	A2	343	B6
Union Pl	Tuck.	284	A2	341	A4
Union Pl	Yonk.	282	A2	340	A2
Union St	N. Roch.	286	A3	342	Inset
Unionport Rd	62	275	C5	344	B2
University Av	68	274	A3	344	A1
University Av	Yonk.	283	B5	340	A3
Upland Rd	N. Roch.	285	A4	341	A5
Urban St	Mt V.	284	C2	341	B4
Utra Pl	N. Roch.	285	C4	341	B5
Valdale Av	Yonk.	282	C1	340	B1
Valentine Av		274	B3	344	A1
1-2299	57	274	B3	344	A1
2300-OUT	58	274	B3	344	A1
Valentine La	Yonk.	282	C1	340	B1
Valentine St	Mt V.	280	A1	341	B4
Valentine St	Yonk.	283	B4	340	A3
Valhalla Pl	65	276	C3	345	B4
Valles Av	71	278	A2	340	B1
Valley Cl	Yonk.	279	A4	340	B2
Valley Rd	B'ville	284	A2	341	A4
Valley Rd	N. Roch.	285	A5	341	A6
Valley Rd	Yonk.	282	C3	340	B2
Valois Pl	Mt V.	285	B4	341	A5
Van Buren St	6	275	C5	344	B2
Van Buren St	Yonk.	282	B3	340	A2
Van Cortlandt Av E		279	C4	340	C2
1-149	68	279	C4	340	C2
150-199	58	279	C4	340	C2
200-OUT	67	279	C4	340	C2
Van Cortlandt Av W	63	278	C3	340	C2
Van Cortlandt Park Av	Yonk.	282	C2	340	B2
Van Cortlandt Park E	7	279	B4	340	C2
Van Cortlandt Park S	63	278	C3	340	C2
Van Duzen Pl	Tuck.	284	A2	341	A4
Van Guilder Av	N. Roch.	286	A1	342	Inset
Van Hoesen Av	61	276	B1	344	A3
Van Nest Av		275	C5	344	B2
1-646	6	275	C5	344	B2
647-1023	62	275	C6	344	B2
1024-OUT	61	276	C1	344	B3
Vance St	69	276	B2	345	A4
Varian Av	75	280	C2	341	C4
Vark St	Yonk.	282	B1	340	A1
Vaughn Av	N. Roch.	285	C4	341	B5
Veltri La	Yonk.	283	C5	340	B3
Vernon Av	Mt V.	280	A3	341	B5
Vernon Av	Yonk.	283	C5	340	B3
Vernon Pkwy	Mt V.	284	B2	341	A4
Vernon Pl	Mt V.	284	C2	341	B4
Vernon Pl	Yonk.	283	C5	340	B3
Verveleen Pl	63	278	C2	340	C1
Victor St	62	275	C6	344	B2
Victor St	Yonk.	282	B2	340	A2
Victoria La	Yonk.	283	A4	340	A3
Viele Av	74	260	C2	344	C1
View St	Yonk.	282	A2	340	A2
Villa Av	68	275	A4	344	A1
Villa Av	Yonk.	283	C5	340	B3
Villa St	Mt V.	284	C2	341	B4
Village La	B'ville	284	B2	341	A4
Villus Av	N. Roch.	286	B1	342	Inset
Vincent Av	65	272	A1	345	B4
Vincent Rd	Yonk.	284	B1	341	A4
Vine St	B'ville	284	A2	341	A4
Vineyard Av	Yonk.	282	A2	340	A2
Vineyard La	Yonk.	282	A3	340	A2
Vineyard Pl	6	275	C4	344	B1
Vireo Av	7	279	B5	340	C3
Virgil Pl	73	270	C2	344	C3
Virginia Av		270	B1	344	B3
1-1299	72	270	B1	344	B3
1300-OUT	62	270	A1	344	B3
Virginia St	Yonk.	283	C5	340	B3
Vista Pl	Mt V.	280	A1	341	B4
Volz Pl	Yonk.	283	A5	340	A3
Voss Av	Yonk.	282	A3	340	A2
Vredenburgh Av	Yonk.	283	C5	340	B3
Vreeland Av	61	271	A4	344	B3
Vyse Av		268	B2	344	B1
1-1459	59	268	B2	344	B1
1460-OUT	6	268	A2	344	B1
Wade Sq	57	275	B4	344	A1
Wakefield Av	Yonk.	279	A5	340	B3
Waldo Av		278	B2	340	C1
1-3899	63	278	C2	340	C1
3900-OUT	71	278	B2	340	C1
Wales Av		259	B5	344	C1
1-415	54	259	B5	344	C1
416-OUT	55	259	B5	344	C1
Wales Pl	Mt V.	284	C2	341	B4
Wallace Av		275	B6	344	A2
1-2199	62	275	B6	344	A2
2200-3299	67	275	A6	344	A2
Wallace Av	Mt V.	284	C2	341	B4
Wallace Pkwy	Yonk.	282	B2	340	A2
Walnut Av	Pel.	285	C4	341	B5
Walnut Av	Yonk.	283	A5	340	A3
Walnut Av (Rose Feiss Blvd)	54	259	C5	344	C1
Walnut St	N. Roch.	286	A1	342	Inset
Walnut St	Yonk.	282	B3	340	A2
Walsh Rd	Yonk.	282	A2	340	A2
Walton Av		258	A2	343	C6
1-890	51	258	A2	343	C6
891-1649	52	266	A3	343	B6
1650-2293	53	274	B2	344	A1
2294-OUT	68	274	B3	344	A1
Walton Pl	Mt V.	280	B2	341	C4
Warburton Av	Yonk.	282	A2	340	A2
Ward Av	72	269	A4	344	B2
Waring Av		275	B5	344	A2
1-899	67	275	B5	344	A2
900-OUT	69	276	B1	344	A3
Waring Pl	Yonk.	282	A2	340	A2
Warren Pl	Mt V.	280	B2	341	C4
Warren St	N. Roch.	286	A1	342	Inset
Warwick Av	Mt V.	280	A3	341	B5
Warwick Rd	Yonk.	283	A5	340	A3
Washington Av		274	C3	344	B1
1-929	51	267	C5	344	C1
931-1505 & 930-1510	56	267	A6	344	B1
1507-2289 & 1512-2288	57	274	C3	344	B1
2290-OUT	58	275	B4	344	A1
Washington Av	N. Roch.	286	A1	342	Inset
Washington Av	Pel. M.	281	B4	341	C5
Washington Blvd	Mt V.	280	B2	341	C4
Washington Pl	Mt V.	284	C1	341	B4
Washington Pl	Tuck.	284	A3	341	A5
Washington St	Mt V.	280	A2	341	B4
Water St	N. Roch.	281	B6	341	C6
Water St	Yonk.	282	B1	340	A1
Waterbury Av		270	A3	344	B3
1-2599	62	270	A3	344	B3
2600-3099	61	271	A5	345	B4
3100-OUT	65	271	A5	345	B4
Waterloo Pl	6	275	C4	344	B1
Waters Pl	61	276	C2	344	B3
Watkins Pl	N. Roch.	285	C5	341	B6
Watson Av		269	B5	344	B2
1-2199	72	269	B5	344	B2
2200-OUT	62	270	B3	344	B3
Watt Av	65	276	C3	345	B4
Waverly Av	Eastch.	284	A3	341	A5
Waverly Pl	Yonk.	282	B3	340	A2
Waverly St	Yonk.	282	B2	340	A2
Wayne Av	67	279	C4	340	C2
Webb Av	68	274	A2	344	A1
Webster Av		267	A5	344	B1
1-1505	56	267	A5	344	B1
1506-2285	57	274	C3	344	B1
2287-3025 & 2286-3010	58	275	A4	344	A1
3027-3899 & 3012-3898	67	279	C5	340	C3
3900-OUT	7	279	B5	340	C3
Webster Av	N. Roch.	286	A1	342	Inset
Webster Av	Yonk.	282	B3	340	A2
Weeks Av	57	274	C2	344	B1
Weeks Pl	N. Roch.	285	B6	341	A6
Weiher Ct	56	267	B5	344	B1
Wellesley Av	Yonk.	282	C2	340	B2
Wellington Av	N. Roch.	285	A5	341	A6
Wellington Cir	B'ville	284	A2	341	A4
Wellman Av	61	276	C2	345	B4
Wells Av	Yonk.	282	B1	340	A1
Wellyn Cl	Yonk.	284	B1	341	A4
Wellyn Rd	Yonk.	284	B1	341	A4
Wendel Pl	Yonk.	282	A3	340	A2
Wendover Rd	Yonk.	282	C3	340	B2
Wenner Pl	65	271	C4	344	C3
West 1st St	Mt V.	280	A1	341	B4
West 2nd St	Mt V.	280	A1	341	B4
West 3rd St	Mt V.	280	A1	341	B4
West 4th St	Mt V.	280	A1	341	B4
West 5th St	Mt V.	280	A1	341	B4
West 7th St	Mt V.	280	B2	341	C4
West 8th St	Mt V.	280	B2	341	C4
West 159th St	51	266	B3	343	B6
West 161st St	52	266	B1	343	B6
West 162nd St	52	266	B2	343	B6
West 163rd St	52	266	A2	343	B6
West 164th St	52	266	A2	343	B6
West 165th St	52	266	A2	343	B6
West 166th St	52	266	A2	343	B6
West 167th St	52	266	A2	343	B6
West 168th St	52	274	C1	343	B6
West 169th St	52	274	C1	343	B6
West 170th St	52	274	C1	343	B6
West 171st St	52	274	C1	343	B6
West 172nd St	52	274	C1	343	B6
West 174th St	53	274	C1	343	B6
West 175th St	53	274	C1	343	B6
West 176th St	53	274	C1	343	B6
West 177th St	53	274	B2	344	A1
West 179th St	53	274	B2	344	A1
West 180th St	53	274	B2	344	A1
West 181st St	53	274	B2	344	A1
West 182nd St	53	274	B2	344	A1
West 183rd St	53	274	B2	344	A1
West 184th St	68	274	B3	344	A1
West 188th St	68	274	A3	344	A1
West 190th St	68	274	A3	344	A1
West 192nd St	68	274	A3	344	A1
West 193rd St	63	274	A2	344	A1
West 195th St	68	274	A3	344	A1
West 197th St	68	274	A3	344	A1
West 205th St	68	278	C3	340	C2
West 225th St	68	274	A2	344	A1
West 227th St	63	278	C1	340	C1
West 229th St	63	274	A3	344	A1
West 230th St	63	278	C1	340	C1
West 231st St	63	278	C1	340	C1
West 232nd St	63	278	C1	340	C1
West 233rd St	63	278	C2	340	C1
West 234th St	63	278	C2	340	C1
West 235th St	63	278	C2	340	C1
West 236th St	63	278	C2	340	C1
West 237th St	63	278	B1	340	C1
West 238th St	63	278	B1	340	C1
West 239th St	63	278	B1	340	C1
West 240th St		278	B2	340	C1
1-499	63	278	C2	340	C1
500-OUT	71	278	B2	340	C1
West 242nd St	63	278	B2	340	C1
West 244th St	71	278	B2	340	C1
West 245th St	71	278	B2	340	C1
West 246th St	71	278	B1	340	C1
West 247th St	71	278	B1	340	C1
West 248th St	71	278	B2	340	C1
West 249th St	71	278	B2	340	C1
West 250th St	71	278	B2	340	C1
West 251st St	71	278	B3	340	C2
West 252nd St	71	278	A2	340	B1
West 253rd St	71	278	A2	340	B1
West 254th St	71	278	A2	340	B1
West 255th St	71	278	A1	340	B1
West 256th St	71	278	A2	340	B1
West 258th St	71	278	A2	340	B1
West 259th St	71	278	A2	340	B1
West 260th St	71	278	A2	340	B1
West 261st St	71	278	A2	340	B1
West 262nd St	71	278	A3	340	B2
West 263rd St	71	278	A2	340	B1
West Av	62	270	A1	344	B3
West Blvd	Pel.	281	A4	341	B5
West Castle Pl	N. Roch.	286	B2	342	Inset
West Clarke Pl	52	274	C1	343	B6
West Dr	Yonk.	283	B5	340	A3
West Farms Rd		268	B2	344	B1
1-1381	59	268	B2	344	B1
1382-OUT	6	268	A3	344	B2
West Fordham Rd	68	274	A2	344	A1
West Grand St	Mt V.	284	A2	341	A4
West Gun Hill Rd	67	279	C4	340	C2
West Kingsbridge Rd		274	A3	344	A1
1-148	68	274	A3	344	A1
149-OUT	63	274	A3	344	A1
West Lincoln Av	Mt V.	284	C1	341	B4
West Mosholu Pkwy N	67	279	C4	340	C2
West Mosholu Pkwy S	68	279	C4	340	C2
West Pondfield Rd	B'ville	284	A2	341	A4
West Sidney Av	Mt V.	284	C1	341	B4
West St	75	280	B3	341	C5
West St	Pel. M.	280	B3	341	C5
West Tremont Av	53	274	B2	343	A6
West Way	B'ville	284	B3	341	A5
Westchester Av		259	A4	343	C6
1-839	55	259	A4	343	C6
841-1399 & 840-1326	59	268	C1	344	C1
1401-1899 & 1328-1898	72	269	B4	344	B2
1900-2379	62	270	A2	344	B3
2380-OUT	61	276	C1	344	B3
Westchester Av	Mt V.	284	C2	341	B4
Westchester Pl	N. Roch.	286	A2	342	Inset
Western Av	Yonk.	282	C2	340	B2
Westervelt Av	69	276	B2	344	A3
Westery St	Yonk.	283	B5	340	B3
Westminster Ct	N. Roch.	285	C5	341	B6
Westmoreland Dr	Yonk.	279	A5	340	B3
Westview Av	Tuck.	284	A2	341	A4
Westward La	Pel. M.	281	B4	341	C5
Westwood Av	N. Roch.	285	B4	341	A5
Weyman Av	N. Roch.	286	C1	342	Inset
Whalen St	71	278	A3	340	B2
Wheeler Av		269	B4	344	B2
1-999	73	269	C4	344	C2
1000-OUT	72	269	B4	344	B2
Whelan Pl	Yonk.	282	A2	340	A2
White Oak St	N. Roch.	285	B5	341	A6
White Plains Post Rd	B'ville	284	A3	341	A5
White Plains Rd		270	C1	344	C3
1-999	73	270	C1	344	C3
1000-1299	72	270	B1	344	B3
1300-2199	62	269	A6	344	B2
2200-3899	67	275	A6	344	A2
3900-4399	66	279	B6	340	C3
4400-OUT	7	279	B6	340	C3
White Plains Rd	Eastch.	284	A3	341	A5
Whitehall Pl	66	279	B6	340	C3
Whitestone Pl	N. Roch.	285	C4	341	B5
Whitewood Av	N. Roch.	281	B5	341	C5
Whitfield Ter	N. Roch.	285	B5	341	A6
Whitlock Av	59	268	C2	344	C1
Whittier Av	Yonk.	283	C5	340	B3
Whittier St	74	260	B3	344	C2
Wicker St	Yonk.	282	A2	340	A2
Wickford Rd	N. Roch.	285	C4	341	B5
Wickham Av		276	A2	345	A4
1-3499	69	276	A2	345	A4
3500-OUT	66	279	B6	340	C3
Wilbur Pl	Yonk.	284	A1	341	A4
Wilbur St	Yonk.	283	B4	340	A3
Wilcox Av	65	272	A1	345	B4
Wilcox Av	Yonk.	282	C3	340	B2
Wild Way	Yonk.	284	B1	341	A4
Wildcliff Dr	N. Roch.	287	A4	342	Inset
Wilder Av		280	A1	341	B4
1-4799	66	280	B1	341	C4
4800-OUT	7	280	A1	341	B4
Wilgarth Rd	Yonk.	284	B1	341	A4
Wilkinson Av	61	276	B1	344	A3
Willard Av	Mt V.	284	C3	341	B5
Willett Av	67	279	C5	340	C3
William Av	64	277	C6	345	B5
William Delamater St	Yonk.	282	B2	340	A1
William Pl	61	276	C2	345	B4
William Schroeder St	Yonk.	282	B2	340	A1
William St	Mt V.	284	C1	341	B4
William St	Yonk.	282	B3	340	A2
Williamsbridge Rd		276	B1	344	A3
1-2199	61	276	B1	344	A3
2200-2899	69	275	A6	344	A3
2900-OUT	67	275	A6	344	A3
Willis Av		258	B3	343	C6
1-439	54	258	B3	343	C6
440-OUT	55	258	A3	343	C6
Willow Av	54	259	C4	343	C6
Willow Av	Pel.	285	C4	341	B5
Willow Dr	N. Roch.	286	C3	342	Inset
Willow La	61	276	C3	345	B4
Willow Pl	Mt V.	284	C2	341	B4
Willow Pl	Yonk.	282	A2	340	A2
Willow Rd	B'ville	284	A2	341	A4
Willow St	Yonk.	282	B2	340	A2
Wilson Av		276	A1	344	A3
1-2199	61	276	B1	344	A3
2200-OUT	69	276	A1	344	A3
Wilson Block	Mt V.	284	B2	341	A4
Wilson Pl	Mt V.	280	A1	341	B4
Wiltshire Pl	Yonk.	284	A1	341	A4
Wiltshire St	Yonk.	284	A1	341	A4
Wilwood Av	Mt V.	280	B2	341	C4
Winans Dr	Yonk.	283	A5	340	A3
Winchester Av	Yonk.	283	A5	340	A3
Winchester Oval	N. Roch.	287	B4	342	Inset
Windham Pl	63	274	A3	344	A1
Windsor Oval	N. Roch.	287	B4	342	Inset
Windsor Pl	Pel. M.	281	B4	341	C5
Windward La	64	277	C6	345	B6
Winfield Av	Mt V.	284	C2	341	B4
Winfred Av	Yonk.	283	C5	340	B3
Wingate Pl	Yonk.	282	B3	340	A2
Wingate Rd	Yonk.	282	C3	340	B2
Winslow Cir	Tuck.	284	A3	341	A5
Winston Pl	Yonk.	283	A4	340	A3
Winter Hill Rd	Tuck.	284	A3	341	A5
Winters St	64	277	C6	345	B5
Winthrop Av	N. Roch.	285	C5	341	B6
Winyah Ter	N. Roch.	285	C5	341	B6
Wissman Av	65	272	C3	345	C5
Witherbee Av	Pel. M.	281	A4	341	B5
Witherell St	Yonk.	284	A1	341	A4
Wolfe St	Yonk.	282	C2	340	B2
Wolfs La	Pel.	281	A4	341	B5
Wolfs La	Pel. M.	280	A3	341	B5
Wood Av		269	A6	344	B2
1-1879	6	269	A6	344	B2
1880-OUT	62	269	A6	344	B2
Wood La	N. Roch.	285	A5	341	A6
Wood Pl	N. Roch.	285	C5	341	B6
Wood Pl	Yonk.	282	A2	340	A2
Wood Rd	62	269	A6	344	B2
Woodbine Av	N. Roch.	285	C5	341	B6
Woodbine St	Yonk.	279	A6	340	B3
Woodbury St	N. Roch.	286	C1	342	Inset
Woodcut La	N. Roch.	285	A6	341	A6
Woodend La	B'ville	284	B2	341	A4
Woodhull Av	69	276	B2	344	A3
Woodland Av	B'ville	284	A2	341	A4
Woodland Av	N. Roch.	286	B2	342	Inset
Woodland Av	Yonk.	282	A3	340	A2
Woodland Ter	Mt V.	284	B3	341	A5
Woodlawn Av	N. Roch.	285	A6	341	A6
Woodlawn Av	Yonk.	279	A5	340	B3
Woodmansten Pl	61	275	B6	344	A3
Woodmansten Pl	62	275	B6	344	A3
Woodrow Wilson Sq	73	262	B1	344	C3
Woodruff Av	Yonk.	283	B5	340	A3
Woodworth Av	Yonk.	282	A2	340	A2
Woodycrest Av	52	266	A2	343	B6
Woodycrest Av	Yonk.	282	A3	340	A2
Worth St	Yonk.	282	A3	340	A2
Worthen St	74	260	A1	344	C1
Wrexham Rd	Yonk.	284	B1	341	A4
Wright Av	75	280	C2	341	C4
Wright Pl	Yonk.	283	C5	340	B3
Wyatt St	6	275	C5	344	B2
Wykagyl Ter	N. Roch.	285	A5	341	A6
Wykagyl Ter	N. Roch.	285	A4	341	A5
Wyndmere Rd	Mt V.	284	B3	341	A5
Wynnewood Rd	Pel. M.	281	B4	341	C5
Wythe Pl	52	274	C2	343	B6
Xavier Dr	Yonk.	283	B5	340	A3
Yates Av		276	B1	344	A3
1-2199	61	276	B1	344	A3
2200-OUT	69	276	A1	344	A3
Yerks Pl	Yonk.	282	C1	340	B1
Yonkers Av	Tuck.	284	A2	341	A4
Yonkers Av	Yonk.	282	B3	340	A2
Yonkers Ter	Yonk.	279	A6	340	B3
York Pl	Eastch.	284	A3	341	A5
Yorkshire Pl	Yonk.	282	A3	340	A2
Young Av	69	276	A1	344	A3
Young Av	Pel.	281	A4	341	B5
Yznaga Pl	65	263	A4	344	C3
Zerega Av		270	A3	344	B3
1-999	73	271	C4	344	C3
1000-OUT	62	270	A3	344	B3
Zulette Av	61	276	C2	345	B4

AIRPORTS

Evers S P B	65	277	C4	345	B4

BRIDGES & TUNNELS

Bronx Whitestone Br (Toll)	65	263	C6	345	C4
City Island Br	64	277	B5	345	A5
Henry Hudson	63	278	C1	340	C1
Macombs Dam Br	52	266	B1	343	B6
Madison Avenue Br	51	258	A1	343	C6
Throgs Neck Bridge (Toll)	65	265	A5	345	C5
University Heights Br	68	274	A2	343	A6
Washington Br	52	274	C1	343	B6
Willis Avenue Br	54	258	C2	343	C6
3rd Avenue Br	54	258	C1	343	C6
145th Street Br	51	266	C1	343	C6

Brooklyn

NEIGHBORHOODS

Bath Beach	14	188	A1	361	B4
Bay Ridge	9	180	A3	360	A3
Bedford-Stuyvesant	16	159	C5	354	B2
Bensonhurst	14	188	A2	361	B5
Bergen Beach	34	184	C3	362	B3
Boerum Hill	17	166	A3	354	B1
Borough Park	4	182	B3	361	A5
Brighton Beach	35	189	C4	362	C1
Broadway Junction	33	176	A2	355	B4
Brooklyn Heights	1	143	C6	354	B1
Brownsville	12	176	B1	355	C4
Bushwick	21	160	B3	355	A4
Canarsie	36	184	A3	362	A3
Carroll Gardens	31	166	B1	354	B1
City Line	8	177	B5	355	C6
Clinton Hill	5	158	C3	354	B2
Cobble Hill	1	147	C6	354	B1
Coney Island	24	194	B2	368	Inset
Crown Heights	16	168	C2	354	C2
Cypress Hills	8	177	A4	355	B5
Ditmas Park	26	183	A4	362	A1
Downtown Brooklyn	1	148	A3	354	B1
Dyker Heights	28	182	C1	361	B4
East Flatbush	34	184	B1	362	A2
East New York	7	176	B3	355	C5
East Williamsburg	11	156	C2	354	A3
Farragut	3	183	A6	362	A2
Flatbush	1	183	B5	362	A1
Flatlands	34	184	C2	362	B3
Fort Hamilton	28	187	B4	360	B3
Fulton Ferry (Dumbo)	1	144	B1	354	A1
Georgetown	34	184	B3	362	A3
Gerritsen Beach	29	190	B1	362	C2
Gowanus	15	166	C2	354	C1
Gravesend	23	188	B3	361	C5
Greenpoint	22	150	C1	348	C1
Greenwood Heights	32	171	C6	353	C6
Highland Park	8	177	A4	355	B5
Homecrest	23	189	B4	362	C1
Kensington	18	182	A3	361	A5
Manhattan Beach	35	189	C6	362	C2
Mapleton	4	182	C3	361	B5
Marine Park	34	190	A1	362	B2
Midwood	3	183	C5	362	B1
Mill Basin	34	184	C3	362	B3
Mill Island	34	190	A3	362	B3
New Lots	7	176	C3	355	C5
New Utrecht	28	182	C2	361	B5
Northside	11	153	B5	354	A2
Ocean Hill	33	176	A1	355	B4
Ocean Parkway	3	183	C4	362	B1
Paerdergat Basin	36	184	B3	362	A3
Park Slope	15	167	C4	354	C1
Parkville	18	182	B3	361	A5
Prospect Heights	38	167	B6	354	B2
Prospect Lefferts Gardens	25	174	B2	354	C2
Prospect Park South	18	183	A4	362	A1
Red Hook	31	165	B4	353	B6
Remsen Village	36	176	C1	355	C4
Rugby	3	183	A6	362	A2
Sea Gate	24	192	A1	368	Inset
Sheepshead Bay	35	189	B6	362	C2
Southside	11	154	B3	354	A2
Spring Creek	7	177	C4	355	C5
Starrett City	39	185	A5	363	A4
Stuyvesant Heights	16	169	A4	354	B3
Sunset Park	2	182	A1	361	A4
Vinegar Hill	1	144	A3	354	A1
Weeksville	13	169	C4	354	C3
Williamsburg	11	155	C5	354	A2
Windsor Terace	18	173	C4	354	C1
Wingate	25	175	A4	354	C3

NUMBERED STREETS

1st Av		179	A5	361	A4
1-5299	32	171	C4	353	C6
5300-6899	2	179	A5	361	A4
6900-OUT	9	179	B4	360	A3
1st Ct	23	189	A4	362	B1
1st Pl	31	165	A6	353	B6
1st St		166	A2	354	B1
1st St	28	187	B4	360	B3

1-105	31	166	A2	354	B1
106-OUT	15	166	C3	354	C1
2nd Av		166	C1	354	C1
1-216	15	166	C1	354	C1
217-5299	32	171	B5	353	C6
5300-6899	2	179	A5	361	A4
6900-OUT	9	179	C4	360	A3
2nd Pl	31	165	B6	353	B6
2nd St		166	B1	354	B1
1-166	31	166	B1	354	B1
167-OUT	15	166	C3	354	C1
3rd Av		166	C2	354	C1
1-250	17	166	A3	354	B1
251-617 & 252-612	15	166	C2	354	C1
619-4399 & 614-4398	32	171	B6	353	C6
4400-6899	2	179	A6	361	A4
6900-OUT	9	181	A4	360	A3
3rd Pl	31	165	B6	353	B6
3rd St		166	B1	354	B1
1-166	31	166	B1	354	B1
167-OUT	15	166	C3	354	C1
4th Av		172	A2	354	C1
1-213 & 2-222	17	167	A4	354	B1
215-617 & 224-630	15	172	A2	354	C1
619-4399 & 632-4398	32	171	B6	353	C6
4400-6899	2	179	B5	361	A4
6900-OUT	9	186	A3	360	B3
4th Pl	31	165	B6	353	B6
4th St		166	B1	354	B1
1-113	31	166	B1	354	B1
114-OUT	15	166	C3	354	C1
5th Av		167	B5	354	B1
1-206	17	167	B5	354	B1
207-723	15	172	A2	354	C1
724-4399	32	171	C6	353	C6
4400-6899	2	179	B6	361	A4
6900-OUT	9	181	A5	361	A4
5th St		166	B1	354	B1
1-76	31	166	B1	354	B1
77-OUT	15	166	C3	354	C1
6th Av		167	B4	354	B1
1-207 & 2-204	17	167	B4	354	B2
209-759 & 206-758	15	172	B2	354	C1
760-4399	32	172	B2	354	C1
4400-6899	2	179	C6	361	A4
6900-OUT	9	181	B5	361	B4
6th St	15	166	C3	354	C1
7th Av		172	B2	354	C1
1-94	17	167	B5	354	B2
95-630	15	172	B2	354	C1
631-4399	32	172	B2	354	C1
4400-6899	2	179	C6	361	A4
6900-7898 (even)	9	181	A6	361	A4
6901-OUT (odd)	28	187	B5	361	B4
7th St	15	166	C3	354	C1
8th Av		166	C3	354	C1
1-72	17	167	B5	354	B2
73-2599	15	173	A4	354	C2
2600-4399	32	182	A2	361	A5
4400-6899	2	179	C6	361	A4
6900-OUT	28	181	A6	361	A4
8th St	15	166	C3	354	C1
9th Av		182	B1	361	A4
1-330	15	167	C5	354	C2
331-4399	32	182	A2	361	A5
4400-OUT	2	182	B1	361	A4
9th St		165	B6	353	B6
1-39	31	165	B6	353	B6
40-OUT	15	172	A3	354	C1
10th Av		172	C3	354	C1
1-2000	15	172	C3	354	C1
2101-6899	19	182	A2	361	A5
6900-OUT	28	181	B6	361	B4
10th St	15	172	A3	354	C1
11th Av		173	C4	354	C1
1-1690	15	173	B4	354	C1
1691-2099	18	173	C4	354	C1
2100-6899	19	182	B1	361	A5
6900-OUT	28	181	B6	361	A4
11th St	15	172	A3	354	C1
12th Av		182	B1	361	A4
1-4099	18	182	A2	361	A5
4100-6899	19	182	B1	361	A4
6900-OUT	28	187	A6	361	B4
12th St	15	172	A3	354	C1
13th Av		182	B2	361	A5
1-4099	18	182	A3	361	A5
4100-6899	19	182	B2	361	A5
6900-OUT	28	187	A6	361	B4
13th St	15	172	A2	354	C1
14th Av		182	B2	361	A5
1-4099	18	182	A3	361	A5
4100-6899	19	182	B2	361	A5
6900-OUT	28	187	B6	361	B4
14th St	15	172	A2	354	C1
15th Av		187	C6	361	B4
1-4099	18	182	A3	361	A5
4100-6899	19	182	B2	361	A5
6900-OUT	28	187	C6	361	B4
15th St	15	172	A2	354	C1
16th Av		182	B2	361	A5
1-4099	18	182	B3	361	A5
4100-7499	4	182	B2	361	A5
7500-OUT	14	187	A6	361	B4
16th St	15	172	A2	354	C1
1-587 & 2-558	15	172	A2	354	C1
589-OUT & 560-OUT	18	173	B4	354	C1
17th Av		182	C2	361	B5
1-7499	4	182	C2	361	B5
7500-OUT	14	188	A1	361	B4
17th Ct	14	188	A1	361	B4
17th St		172	A1	354	C1
1-115 & 2-108	32	172	A1	354	C1
117-559 & 110-566	15	172	B3	354	C1
561-OUT & 568-OUT	18	173	B4	354	C1
18th Av		188	A1	361	B4
1-4399	18	182	B3	361	A5
4400-7499	4	182	C2	361	B5
7500-OUT	14	188	A1	361	B4
18th St		172	A1	354	C1
1-115 & 2-108	32	172	A1	354	C1
117-567 & 110-556	15	172	B3	354	C1
569-OUT & 558-OUT	18	173	C4	354	C1
19th Av		182	C3	361	B5
1-7499	4	182	C3	361	B5
7500-OUT	14	188	A1	361	B4
19th La	14	188	B1	361	C4
19th St		172	A1	354	C1
0-223	32	172	A1	354	C1
237-500	15	172	B3	354	C1
541-699	18	173	C4	354	C1
20th Av		182	C3	361	B5
1-7499	4	182	C3	361	B5
7500-OUT	14	188	A1	361	B4
20th Dr	14	188	B1	361	C4
20th La	14	188	B1	361	C4
20th St		172	A1	354	C1
1-236	32	172	A1	354	C1
237-540	15	172	B3	354	C1
541-OUT	18	173	C4	354	C1
21st Av		182	C3	361	B5
1-7499	4	182	C3	361	B5
7500-OUT	14	188	A2	361	B5
21st Dr	14	188	B1	361	C4
21st La	14	188	B1	361	C4
21st St		172	A1	354	C1
1-236	32	172	A1	354	C1
237-OUT	15	172	B2	354	C1
22nd St		172	A1	354	C1
1-236	32	172	A1	354	C1
237-OUT	15	172	B2	354	C1
23rd Av	4	182	C3	361	B5
1-7499	4	182	C3	361	B5
7500-OUT	14	188	B2	361	C5
23rd St		172	B1	354	C1
1-236	32	172	B1	354	C1
237-OUT	15	172	B2	354	C1
24th Av		188	A3	361	B5
1-7499	4	188	A3	361	B5
7500-OUT	14	188	B2	361	C5
24th St	32	172	B1	354	C1
25th Av	14	188	B2	361	C5
25th St	32	172	B1	354	C1
26th Av	14	188	B2	361	C5
26th St	32	171	B6	353	C6
27th Av	14	188	B2	361	C5
27th St	32	171	B6	353	C6
28th Av	14	188	B3	361	C5
28th St	32	171	B6	353	C6
29th St	32	171	B6	353	C6
30th St	32	171	B6	353	C6
31st St	32	171	B6	353	C6
32nd St	32	171	B6	353	C6
33rd St	32	171	B5	353	C6
34th St	32	171	B5	353	C6
35th St		171	B5	353	C6
1-899	32	171	B5	353	C6
900-OUT	18	182	A3	361	A5
36th St		171	B5	353	C6
1-899	32	171	B5	353	C6
900-OUT	18	182	A3	361	A5
37th St		171	C5	353	C6
1-899	32	171	C5	353	C6
900-1099	19	182	A2	361	A5
1100-OUT	18	182	A2	361	A5
38th St		171	C5	353	C6
1-899	32	171	C5	353	C6
900-1099	19	182	A2	361	A5
1100-OUT	18	182	A2	361	A5
39th St		171	C6	353	C6
1-899	32	171	C6	353	C6
900-1099	19	182	A2	361	A5
1100-OUT	18	182	A2	361	A5
40th St		171	C5	353	C6
1-899	32	171	C5	353	C6
900-1099	19	182	A2	361	A5
1100-OUT	18	182	A2	361	A5
41st St		171	C5	353	C6
1-899	32	171	C5	353	C6
900-1099	19	182	A2	361	A5
1100-OUT	18	182	A2	361	A5
42nd St		171	C5	353	C6
1-899	32	171	C5	353	C6
900-1599	19	182	A2	361	A5
1600-OUT	4	182	B3	361	A5
42nd St	2	171	C5	353	C6
43rd St		171	C4	353	C6
1-899	32	171	C4	353	C6
900-1599	19	182	A2	361	A5
1600-OUT	4	182	B3	361	A5
	2	171	C5	353	C6
44th St		171	C4	353	C6
1-299	32	171	C4	353	C6
300-899	2	171	C5	353	C6
900-1599	19	182	A2	361	A5
1600-OUT	4	182	B3	361	A5
45th St		182	A1	361	A4
1-899	2	182	A1	361	A4
900-1599	19	182	A2	361	A5
1600-OUT	4	182	B3	361	A5
45th St	32	171	C4	353	C6
46th St		182	A1	361	A4
1-899	2	182	A1	361	A4
900-1599	19	182	A2	361	A5
1600-OUT	4	182	B3	361	A5
46th St	32	171	C4	353	C6
47th St		171	C4	353	C6
1-199	32	171	C4	353	C6
200-899	2	182	A1	361	A4
900-1599	19	182	A2	361	A4
1600-OUT	4	182	B3	361	A5
48th St		171	C4	353	C6
1-199	32	171	C4	353	C6
200-899	2	179	A6	361	A4
900-1599	19	182	A2	361	A4
1600-OUT	4	182	B3	361	A5
49th St		179	A6	361	A4
1-199	32	179	A6	361	A4
200-899	2	179	A6	361	A4
900-1599	19	182	B2	361	A4
1600-OUT	4	182	B3	361	A5
50th St		179	A6	361	A4
1-199	32	179	A6	361	A4
200-899	2	179	A6	361	A4
900-1599	19	182	B2	361	A4
1600-OUT	4	182	B3	361	A5
51st St		179	A6	361	A4
1-199	32	179	A6	361	A4
200-899	2	179	A6	361	A4
900-1599	19	182	B2	361	A4
1600-OUT	4	182	B3	361	A5
52nd St		179	A6	361	A4
1-199	32	179	A6	361	A4
200-899	2	179	A6	361	A4
900-1599	19	182	B2	361	A4
1600-OUT	4	182	B3	361	A5
53rd St		179	A6	361	A4
1-199	32	179	A6	361	A4
200-899	2	179	A6	361	A4
900-1599	19	182	B2	361	A4
1600-OUT	4	182	B3	361	A5
54th St		179	A5	361	A4
1-899	2	179	A5	361	A4
900-1599	19	182	B2	361	A4
1600-OUT	4	182	B3	361	A5
55th St		179	A5	361	A4
1-899	2	179	A5	361	A4
899-1599	19	182	B2	361	A4
1600-OUT	4	182	B3	361	A5
56th Dr	34	190	A2	362	B3
56th St	2	179	A5	361	A4
56th St	19	182	B2	361	A4
56th St	4	182	B2	361	A5
57th St		179	A5	361	A4
1-899	2	179	A5	361	A4
900-1599	19	182	B1	361	A4
1600-OUT	4	182	B2	361	A5
58th St		179	A5	361	A4
1-899	2	179	A5	361	A4
900-1599	19	182	B1	361	A4
1600-OUT	4	182	B2	361	A5
59th St		179	B5	361	A4
1-899	2	179	B5	361	A4
900-1599	19	182	B1	361	A4
1600-2999	4	182	C3	361	A5
60th St		179	B5	361	A4
1-899	2	179	B5	361	A4
900-1599	19	182	B1	361	A4
1600-OUT	4	182	C3	361	B5
61st St		179	B5	361	A4
1-899	2	179	B5	361	A4
900-1599	19	182	B1	361	A4
1600-OUT	4	182	C3	361	B5
62nd St		179	B5	361	A4
1-899	2	179	B5	361	A4
900-1599	19	182	B1	361	A4
1600-OUT	4	182	C3	361	B5
63rd St		179	B5	361	A4
1-899	2	179	B5	361	A4
900-1599	19	182	B1	361	A4
1600-OUT	4	182	C3	361	B5
64th St		179	C6	361	A4
1-899	2	179	C6	361	A4
900-1599	19	182	B1	361	A4
1600-OUT	4	182	C3	361	B5
65th St		179	B4	360	A3
1-899	2	179	B4	360	A3
900-1599	19	182	B1	361	A4
1600-OUT	4	182	C3	361	B5
66th St		179	C5	361	A4
1-899	2	179	C5	361	A4
900-1599	19	182	B1	361	A4
1600-OUT	4	182	C2	361	B5
67th St		179	B4	360	A3
1-899	2	179	B4	360	A3
900-1599	19	182	B1	361	A4
1600-OUT	4	182	C2	361	B5
68th St		178	B3	360	A3
1-899	2	178	B3	360	A3
900-1599	19	182	B1	361	A4
1600-OUT	4	182	C2	361	B5
70th St		181	A6	361	A4
1-699	9	178	C3	360	A3
700-1599	28	181	A6	361	A4
1600-2999	4	182	C2	361	B5
71st St		178	C3	360	A3
1-699	9	178	C3	360	A3
700-1599	28	181	A6	361	A4
1600-2999	4	182	C2	361	B5
72nd Ct	9	178	C3	360	A3
72nd St	9	178	C3	360	A3
72nd St	28	181	A6	361	A4
72nd St	4	182	C2	361	B5
73rd St		178	C3	360	A3
1-699	9	178	C3	360	A3
700-1599	28	181	A6	361	A4
1600-2999	4	182	C2	361	A4
74th St		178	C3	360	A3
1-699	9	178	C3	360	A3
700-1599	28	181	A6	361	A4
1600-2999	4	182	C2	361	A4
76th St		178	C3	360	A3
1-699	9	178	C3	360	A3
700-1599	28	181	B6	361	B4
1600-2599	14	188	A2	361	B5
77th St		180	A3	360	A3
1-699	9	180	A3	360	A3
700-1599	28	181	B6	361	B4
1600-2999	14	188	A2	361	B5
78th St		180	A3	360	A3
1-699	9	180	A3	360	A3
700-1599	28	181	B6	361	B4
1600-2999	14	188	A2	361	B5
79th St		180	A3	360	A3
1-699	9	180	A3	360	A3
700-1599	28	181	B6	361	B4
1600-2999	14	188	A2	361	B5
80th St		180	A3	360	A3
1-699	9	180	A3	360	A3
700-1599	28	181	B6	361	B4
1600-2999	14	188	A2	361	B5
81st St		180	A3	360	A3
1-679	9	180	A3	360	A3
680-1599	28	181	B6	361	B4
1600-2999	14	188	A2	361	B5
82nd St		180	A3	360	A3
1-668	9	180	A3	360	A3
669-1599	28	181	B5	361	B4
1600-2999	14	188	A2	361	B5
83rd St		180	A3	360	A3
1-663	9	180	A3	360	A3
664-1599	28	181	B5	361	B4
1600-2999	14	188	A2	361	B5
84th St		180	A3	360	A3
1-650	9	180	A3	360	A3
651-1599	28	187	A6	361	B4
1600-2999	14	188	A2	361	B5
85th St		180	A3	360	B3
1-656	9	180	A3	360	A3
657-1599	28	187	A6	361	B4
1600-2999	14	188	A2	361	B5
86th St		180	B3	360	B3
1-673 & 2-610	9	180	B3	360	A3
675-1599 & 612-1598	28	187	A5	361	B4
1600-2599	14	188	A2	361	B5
2600-2999	23	188	B3	361	C5
87th St	9	180	B3	360	B3
88th St		180	B3	360	B3
1-623	9	180	B3	360	B3
624-2999	28	187	A5	361	B4
89th St	9	180	B3	360	B3
90th St		180	B3	360	B3
1-620	9	180	B3	360	B3
621-OUT	28	187	A5	361	B4
91st St	9	180	B3	360	B3
92nd St		180	B3	360	B3
1-599	9	180	B3	360	B3
600-OUT	28	187	A4	360	B3
93rd St	9	186	A3	360	B3
94th St	9	186	A3	360	B3
95th Av	8	177	A5	355	B6
95th St	9	186	A3	360	B3
96th St	9	186	A3	360	B3
97th St	9	186	A3	360	B3
98th St	9	186	A3	360	B3
99th St	9	186	A3	360	B3
100th St	9	186	A3	360	B3
101st St	9	186	B3	360	B3
Interstate 278	1	147	B5	354	B1
Interstate 278	5	158	B1	354	B2
Interstate 278	9	186	B2	360	B3
Interstate 278	32	179	A6	361	A4
NY 27	8	177	C5	355	C6
NY 27	26	174	C2	354	C2

NAMED STREETS

Abbey Ct	29	190	B2	362	C3
Aberdeen St	7	176	A2	355	B4
Academy Park Pl	17	167	A4	354	B1
Adams St	1	148	B2	354	B1
Adelphi St		158	B1	354	B2
1-325 & 2-336	5	158	B1	354	B2
327-OUT & 338-OUT	38	167	A5	354	B2
Adler Pl	8	177	A5	355	B6
Agate Ct	13	169	B4	354	B3
Ainslie St	11	156	B1	354	A2
Aitken Pl	1	147	B6	354	B1
Alabama Av	7	176	B3	355	C5
Albany Av		184	B1	362	A2
1-33	16	169	B4	354	B3
34-469	13	169	C4	354	C3
470-1500	3	175	B4	354	C3
1501-OUT	1	184	B1	362	A2
Albee Sq	1	149	C4	354	B1
Albemarle Rd		182	A3	361	A5
1-1299	18	182	A3	361	A5
1300-OUT	26	183	A5	362	A1
Albemarle Ter	26	183	A5	362	A1
Alben Sq	19	182	A2	361	A5
Alice Ct	13	169	B4	354	B3
Allen Av	29	190	B1	362	C2
Alton Pl	1	183	C6	362	B2
Amber St	8	177	B6	355	C6
Amboy St	12	176	B1	355	C4
Amersfort Pl	1	183	B5	362	A1
Ames La	36	184	A3	362	A3
Amherst St	35	189	C5	362	C1
Amity St	1	147	C6	354	B1
Anchorage Pl	1	144	B2	354	A1
Angela Dr	23	189	B4	362	C1
Anna Ct	7	176	C3	355	C5
Anthony St	22	157	A4	354	A3
Applegate Ct	23	188	A3	361	B5
Appollo St	22	151	C4	348	C2
Archie C. Ketchum Sq	23	188	A3	361	B5
Ardsley Lp	39	177	C4	355	C5
Argyle Rd		183	A4	362	A1
1-530	18	183	A4	362	A1
531-OUT	3	183	B4	362	A1
Arion Pl	6	160	B1	354	B3
Arkansas Dr	34	190	A3	362	B3
Arlington Av		176	A3	355	B5
1-240	7	176	A3	355	B5
241-OUT	8	177	A4	355	B5
Arlington Pl	16	168	A2	354	B2
Ash St	22	150	A2	348	C1
Ashford St	7	177	B4	355	B5
Ashland Pl		149	B5	354	B1
1-169	1	149	B5	354	B1
170-OUT	17	149	C5	354	B1
Aster Ct	29	190	B1	362	C2
Atkins Av	8	177	A4	355	B5
Atlantic Av		148	C1	354	B1
1-346	1	148	C1	354	B1
347-733 & 348-752	17	166	A3	354	B1
735-1081 & 754-1130	38	167	A5	354	B2
1083-1453 & 1132-1518	16	168	B2	354	B2
1455-1727 & 1520-1800	13	169	B5	354	B3
1729-2463 & 1802-2464	33	169	B6	354	B3
2465-2957 & 2466-2950	7	176	A3	355	B5
2959-3599 & 2952-3598	8	177	A4	355	B5
3600-OUT	24	192	B1	368	Inset
Atlantic Commons	17	167	A5	354	B2
Atwater Ct	23	189	C4	362	C1
Auburn Pl	5	149	A6	354	B1
Aurelia Ct	1	183	B6	362	A2
Autumn Av	8	177	A5	355	B6
Autumn La	8	177	C5	355	C6
Avenue A		176	C1	355	C4
1-9599	36	176	C1	355	C4
9600-OUT	12	176	C1	355	C4
Avenue B	36	184	A2	362	A3
Avenue C	18	182	A3	361	A5
Avenue D		183	A6	362	A2
1-3299	26	183	A5	362	A1
3300-5999	3	183	A6	362	A2
6000-OUT	36	184	A2	362	A3
Avenue F	18	182	B3	361	A5
Avenue H		183	B4	362	A1
1-1999	3	183	B4	362	A1
2000-4399	1	183	B6	362	A1
4400-OUT	34	184	B1	362	A2
Avenue I		183	B4	362	A1
1-1999	3	183	B4	362	A1
2000-4399	1	183	B6	362	A1
4400-OUT	34	184	B1	362	A2
Avenue J		183	C4	362	B1
1-1999	3	183	C4	362	B1
2000-4399	1	183	B6	362	A1
4400-7499	34	184	B1	362	A2
7500-OUT	36	184	B3	362	A3
Avenue K		183	C4	362	B1
1-1999	3	183	C4	362	B1
2000-4399	1	183	C6	362	B2
4400-7499	34	184	B1	362	A2
7500-OUT	36	184	B3	362	A3
Avenue L		183	C4	362	B1
1-1999	3	183	C4	362	B1
2000-3999	1	183	C6	362	B1
4000-7499	34	184	C1	362	B2
7500-OUT	36	185	A4	363	A4
Avenue M		183	C4	362	B1
1-1999	3	183	C4	362	B1
2000-3499	1	183	C6	362	B1
3500-7499	34	184	C1	362	B2
7500-OUT	36	185	A4	363	A4
Avenue N		183	C4	362	B1
1-1999	3	183	C4	362	B1
2000-3199	1	183	C6	362	B1
3200-7499	34	184	C1	362	B2
7500-OUT	36	185	B4	363	A4
Avenue O		188	A3	361	B5
1-199	4	188	A3	361	B5
200-1999	3	189	A4	362	B1
2000-2699	1	183	C5	362	B1
2700-OUT	34	184	C1	362	B2
Avenue P		189	A4	362	B1
1-391	4	188	A3	361	B5
392-1099	23	189	A4	362	B1
1100-2964	29	189	A5	362	B1
2965-OUT	34	183	C6	362	B2
Avenue R		189	A4	362	B1
1-1199	23	189	A4	362	B1
1200-3064	29	189	A5	362	B1
3065-OUT	34	184	C1	362	B2
Avenue S		188	A3	361	B5
1-1199	23	188	A3	361	B5
1200-3199	29	189	A5	362	B1
3200-OUT	34	190	A1	362	B2
Avenue T		188	B3	361	C5
1-1199	23	188	B3	361	C5
1200-3299	29	189	A6	362	B2
3300-OUT	34	184	C2	362	B2
Avenue U		188	B3	361	C5
1-1199	23	188	B3	361	C5
1200-3299	29	189	B5	362	C1
3300-OUT	34	190	A1	362	B2
Avenue V	23	188	B3	361	C5
1-1199	23	188	B3	361	C5
1200-3399	29	189	B6	362	C2
3400-OUT	34	184	C3	362	B3
Avenue W	23	188	B3	361	C5
1-1199	23	188	B3	361	C5
1200-3399	29	189	B6	362	C1
3400-OUT	34	184	C3	362	B3
Avenue X		188	B3	361	C5
1-499	23	188	B3	361	C5
500-3186	35	189	B5	362	C1
3187-3399	29	190	B1	362	C2
3400-OUT	34	184	C3	362	B3
Avenue Y		189	B4	362	C1
61-550	23	189	B4	362	C1
551-3399	35	189	B5	362	C1
3400-OUT	34	184	C3	362	B3
Avenue Z		188	C3	361	C5
1-282	23	189	C4	362	C1
283-753	35	189	B5	362	C1
754-3399	24	189	C4	362	C1
Aviation Rd	34	191	C4	363	C4
Bainbridge St	33	169	B5	354	B3
Balfour Pl	25	174	A3	354	C3
Baltic St		147	C5	354	B1
1-399	1	147	C5	354	B1
400-OUT	17	166	A2	354	B1
Bancroft Pl	33	176	A1	355	B4
Bank St	36	176	C3	355	C5
Banker St	22	150	C2	348	C1
Banner 3rd Rd	35	189	C4	362	C1
Banner Av	35	189	C4	362	C1
Barbey St	7	176	A3	355	B5
Barlow Dr N	34	190	A3	362	B3
Barlow Dr S	34	190	A3	362	B3
Bartel Prichard Cir	15	173	B4	354	C1
Bartlett Pl	29	190	B2	362	C2
Bartlett St	6	159	A5	354	A3
Barwell Ct	9	186	A3	360	B3
Bassett Av	34	190	A3	362	B3
Bassett Wk	34	190	A3	362	B3
Batchelder St		189	A6	362	B2
1-2399	29	189	A6	362	B2
2400-OUT	35	189	B6	362	C2
Bath Av		187	B6	361	B4
1-1599	28	187	B6	361	B4
1600-OUT	14	188	B2	361	B5
Battery Av		187	A4	360	B3
1-83	28	187	A4	360	B3
84-OUT	9	187	B4	360	B3
Baughman Pl	34	184	C1	362	B2
Bay 7th St	28	187	B6	361	B4
Bay 8th St	28	187	C6	361	B4
Bay 10th St	28	187	C6	361	B4
Bay 11th St	28	187	C6	361	B4
Bay 13th St	14	187	C6	361	B4
Bay 14th St	14	188	A1	361	B4
Bay 16th St	14	188	A1	361	B4
Bay 17th St	14	188	A1	361	B4
Bay 19th St	14	188	A1	361	B4
Bay 20th St	14	188	A1	361	B4
Bay 22nd St	14	188	A1	361	B4
Bay 23rd St	14	188	A1	361	B4
Bay 25th St	14	188	A1	361	B4
Bay 26th St	14	188	B1	361	C4
Bay 28th St	14	188	B2	361	C5
Bay 29th St	14	188	B2	361	C5
Bay 31st St	14	188	B2	361	C5
Bay 32nd St	14	188	B2	361	C5
Bay 34th St	14	188	B2	361	C5
Bay 35th St	14	188	B2	361	C5
Bay 37th St	14	188	B2	361	C5
Bay 38th St	14	188	B2	361	C5
Bay 40th St	14	188	B2	361	C5
Bay 41st St	14	188	B2	361	C5
Bay 43rd St	14	188	B2	361	C5
Bay 44th St	14	188	B2	361	C5
Bay 46th St	14	188	B2	361	C5
Bay 47th St	14	188	B3	361	C5
Bay 48th St	14	188	C2	361	C5
Bay 49th St	14	188	C2	361	C5
Bay 50th St	14	188	C3	361	C5
Bay 52nd St	14	188	C2	361	C5
Bay 53rd St	14	188	C2	361	C5
Bay 54th St	14	188	C2	361	C5
Bay 56th St	14	188	C2	361	C5
Bay Av		183	C5	362	B1
1-1999	3	183	C5	362	B1
2000-OUT	1	183	C5	362	B1
Bay Cliff Ter	2	179	B4	360	A3
Bay Ct	35	189	C5	362	C1
Bay Pkwy		188	A2	361	B5
1-5499	3	183	C4	362	A1
5500-7499	4	182	C3	361	B5
7500-OUT	14	188	A2	361	B5
Bay Ridge Av		178	B3	360	A3
1-899	2	178	B3	360	A3

Brooklyn

Brooklyn

21 159 C6 354 B3
Lafayette Wk 9 186 A3 360 B3
Lake Av 35 189 C6 362 C2
Lake Pl 23 188 B3 361 C5
Lake St 23 188 B3 361 C5
Lama Ct 23 188 B3 361 C5
Lamont Ct 25 174 A3 354 C3
Lancaster Av 23 189 B4 362 C1
Landis Ct 29 190 B2 362 C2
Langham St 35 189 C6 362 C2
Laurel Av 24 192 A1 368 Inset
Lawn Ct 35 189 C5 362 C1
Lawrence Av 3 182 B3 361 A5
Lawrence St 1 148 B3 354 B1
Lawton St 21 160 B2 354 B3
Lee Av 158 A3 354 A2
1-199 & 2-196 11 158 A3 354 A2
201-OUT & 198-OUT
6 159 A4 354 A2
Lefferts Av 174 B1 354 C2
1-557 & 2-554 25 174 B1 354 C2
559-883 & 556-884
3 175 A4 354 C3
885-OUT 13 175 A5 354 C3
Lefferts Pl 38 168 A1 354 B2
Legion St 12 176 B1 355 C4
Leif Ericson Dr (Shore Pkwy)
9 180 A2 360 A3
14 188 B1 361 C4
2 178 B3 360 A3
28 187 C4 360 B3
Lenox Rd 174 C2 354 C2
1-374 26 174 C2 354 C2
375-950 3 175 C4 354 C3
951-OUT 12 176 C1 355 C4
Leonard St 156 C2 354 A3
1-210 6 156 C2 354 A3
221-401 & 212-394
11 156 B2 354 A3
403-OUT & 396-OUT
22 150 C2 348 C1
Lester Ct 29 190 B2 362 C2
Lewis Av 159 B6 354 B3
1-115 & 2-120 6 159 B6 354 B3
117-331 & 122-334 21 160 C1 354 B3
333-OUT & 336-OUT 33 169 A5 354 A3
Lewis Pl 18 183 A4 362 A1
Lexington Av 168 A1 354 B2
1-125 & 2-116 38 168 A1 354 B2
127-425 & 118-410
16 168 A2 354 B2
427-OUT & 412-OUT
21 160 C1 354 B3
Liberty Av 176 A3 355 B5
1-175 12 176 B2 355 C4
176-675 7 176 A3 355 B5
676-1240 8 177 A4 355 B5
Lincoln Av 8 177 A5 355 B6
Lincoln Pl 167 B4 354 B1
1-261 & 2-266 17 167 B4 354 B1
263-571 & 268-560
38 167 C6 354 B2
573-871 & 562-872
16 174 B1 354 C2
873-1540 13 168 C3 354 C3
1541-OUT 33 176 B1 355 C4
Lincoln Rd 25 174 B1 354 C2
Lincoln Ter 13 175 A6 354 C3
Lincoln Ter 35 189 C6 362 C2
Linda Ct 36 184 A2 362 A3
Linden Blvd 174 C2 354 C2
1-335 26 174 C2 354 C2
336-966 3 175 B4 354 C3
967-1720 12 176 C1 355 C4
1721-2250 7 176 C3 355 C4
2251-OUT 8 177 B4 355 C5
Linden St 160 C3 355 B4
1-253 21 160 C3 355 B4
254-OUT 37 161 B4 355 B5
Linwood St 8 177 A4 355 B5
Little Nassau St 5 158 B3 354 B2
Little St 1 145 B5 354 A1
Livingston St 148 B1 354 B1
1-251 & 2-270 1 148 B1 354 B1
253-OUT & 272-OUT
17 149 C4 354 B1
Livonia Av 176 C1 355 C4
1-450 12 176 C1 355 C4
451-OUT 7 176 B3 355 C4
Lloyd Ct 23 188 A3 361 B5
Lloyd St 26 174 C2 354 C2
Locust Av 3 183 C4 362 B1
Locust St 6 159 B6 354 B3
Logan St 8 177 A4 355 B5
Lois Av 29 190 B2 362 C3
Lombardy St 22 157 A4 354 A3
Lorimer St 156 C2 354 A2
1-480 6 156 C2 354 A2
481-740 11 156 B2 354 A3
741-OUT 22 156 A1 354 A2
Loring Av 8 177 B5 355 C6
Lorraine St 31 165 C5 353 C6
Losee Ter 35 189 C6 362 C2
Lott Av 12 176 C2 355 C4
Lott Pl 34 184 C1 362 B2
Lott St 26 183 A5 362 A1
Lotts La 18 182 B3 361 A5
Louis Pl 33 176 A1 355 B4
Louisa St 18 182 A3 361 A5
Louise Ter 9 178 C3 360 A3
Louisiana Av 176 C3 355 C5
1-599 7 176 C3 355 C5
600-OUT 39 185 A5 363 A4
Love La 1 147 A6 354 B1
Ludlam Pl 25 174 A2 354 C2
Luquer St 31 165 B6 353 B6
Lyme Av 24 192 A1 368 Inset
Lynch St 158 A3 354 A2
1-17 11 158 A3 354 A2
18-OUT 6 158 A3 354 A2
MacDonough St 16 169 A4 354 B3
1-209 & 2-220 16 169 A4 354 B3
211-OUT & 222-OUT
33 169 A6 354 B3
MacDougal St 33 176 A1 355 B4
Mackay Pl 9 178 C3 360 A3
Mackenzie St 35 189 C6 362 C2
Macon St 168 A3 354 B3
1-339 & 2-320 16 168 A3 354 B3
341-OUT & 322-OUT
33 169 A6 354 B3
Madeline Ct 2 179 C4 360 A3
Madison Pl 29 189 A6 362 B2
Madison St 168 A1 354 B2
1-76 38 168 A1 354 B2
77-350 16 168 A2 354 B2
351-1300 21 169 A5 354 B3
1301-OUT 37 161 B5 355 B4
Madoc Av 29 190 C1 362 C2
Main St 1 144 B1 354 A1
Malbone St 25 174 A3 354 C3
Malcolm X Blvd 160 C2 354 B3
1-222 21 160 C2 354 B3
233-374 33 169 A6 354 B3
Malta St 7 176 C3 355 C5
Manhattan Av 156 C2 354 A3
1-231 & 2-240 6 156 C2 354 A3
233-409 & 242-414
11 156 B2 354 A3
411-1299 & 416-1298
22 156 A2 354 A3
Manhattan Av (Sea Gate)
24 188 A1 368 Inset
Manhattan Ct 189 B4 362 C1
1-59 23 189 B4 362 C1
60-OUT 35 189 B4 362 C1
Manor Ct 35 189 C5 362 C1
Mansfield Pl (E. 24th St) 183 B5 362 A1
1-1551 1 183 B5 362 A1
1552-2399 29 189 A6 362 B1
2400-OUT 35 189 B6 362 C2
Maple Av 24 192 A1 368 Inset
Maple St 174 B1 354 C2
1-548 25 174 B1 354 C2
549-OUT 3 175 B4 354 C3
Marconi Pl 33 176 A1 355 B4
Marcus Garvey Blvd 159 B6 354 B3
1-153 6 159 B6 354 B3
166-383 21 159 C6 354 B3
383-467 16 169 A4 354 B3
Marcy Av 155 C6 354 A2
1-331 & 2-344 11 155 C6 354 A2
333-665 & 346-664
6 159 A4 354 A2
666-OUT 16 159 C5 354 B3
Margaret Ct 35 189 B5 362 C1
Marginal St 32 171 B5 353 C6
Marginal St E 7 176 A3 355 B5
Marginal St W 7 176 A3 355 B5
Marine Av 9 186 A3 360 B3
Marine Pkwy 34 189 A6 362 B2
Marion St 13 169 B6 354 B3
Marlborough Ct 3 183 B4 362 A1
Marlborough Rd 26 183 A4 362 A1
Marshall St 1 145 A4 354 A1
Martense Ct 26 174 C1 354 C2
Martense St 26 174 C2 354 C2
Martin Luther King Jr Pl
6 159 B5 354 B3
Maspeth Av 11 156 B3 354 A3
Matthews Ct 18 183 A4 362 A1
Matthews Pl 36 185 B4 363 A4
Maujer St 6 156 C2 354 A3
Mayfair Dr N 34 190 A3 362 B3
Mayfair Dr S 34 190 A2 362 B3
McClancy Pl 7 177 B4 355 C5
McDonald Av 172 C3 354 C1
1-953 18 172 C3 354 C1
954-1799 3 182 C3 361 A5
1800-OUT 23 189 B4 362 C1
McGuinness Blvd 22 150 B2 348 C1
McKeever Pl 25 174 A1 354 C1
McKenny St 1 143 B6 354 A2
McKibbin St 6 159 A5 354 A3
McKinley Av 8 177 A5 355 B6
Meadow St 157 C4 354 A3
1-80 6 157 C4 354 A3
81-OUT 37 157 B5 354 A3
Meeker Av 156 B1 354 A2
1-390 11 156 B1 354 A2
391-OUT 22 156 A3 354 A3
Melba Ct 29 190 B2 362 C2
Melrose St 160 A2 354 B3
1-285 & 2-300 6 160 A2 354 A3
287-OUT & 302-OUT
37 160 A2 354 A3
Menahan St 160 B3 355 B4
1-170 21 160 B3 355 B4
171-OUT 37 161 A4 355 B4
Merit Ct 29 190 B2 362 C2
Mermaid Av 24 193 B4 368 Inset
Mesereau Ct 35 189 C6 362 C2
Meserole Av 22 150 C1 348 C1
Meserole St 156 C2 354 A3
1-377 & 2-392 6 156 C2 354 A3
379-OUT & 394-OUT
37 157 C5 354 A3
Metropolitan Av 153 C4 354 A2
1-1125 11 153 C4 354 A2
1126-4599 37 157 B5 354 A3
Miami Ct 25 174 B3 354 C3
Micieli Pl 18 182 A3 361 A5
Middagh St 1 143 B6 354 A1
Middleton St 6 159 A4 354 A2
Midwood St 174 B1 354 C2
1-545 25 174 B1 354 C2
546-OUT 3 175 B4 354 C3
Milford St 8 177 A4 355 B5
Mill Av 34 184 C2 362 B3
Mill La 34 184 C2 362 B3
Mill Rd 14 188 B2 361 C5
Mill St 31 165 B6 353 B6
Miller Av 7 176 A3 355 B5
Milton St 22 150 C1 348 C1
Minna St 18 182 A3 361 A5
Moffat St 161 C6 355 B4
1-283 & 2-290 7 161 C6 355 B4
285-OUT & 292-OUT
37 161 C6 355 B4
Monaco Pl 33 176 A2 355 B4
Monitor St 22 157 C4 348 C2
Monroe Pl 1 148 A1 354 B1
Monroe St 168 A1 354 B2
1-63 & 2-68 38 168 A1 354 B2
65-337 & 70-354 16 168 A2 354 B2
339-OUT & 356-OUT
21 169 A5 354 B3
Montague St 1 147 A6 354 B1
Montague Ter 1 147 A5 354 B1
Montana Pl 34 190 A3 362 B3
Montauk Av 8 177 A4 355 B5
Montauk Ct 35 189 C5 362 C1
Montgomery Pl 15 167 C5 354 C2
Montgomery St 174 A1 354 C2
1-668 25 174 A1 354 C2
669-OUT 13 175 A4 354 C3
Montieth St 6 160 A1 354 A3
Montrose Av 6 156 C2 354 A3
Moore Pl 29 189 A5 362 B1
Moore St 6 159 A5 354 A3
Morgan Av 157 C4 354 A3
1-265 & 2-272 37 157 C4 354 A3
67-423 & 274-418
11 157 B4 354 A3
425-OUT & 420-OUT
22 156 A3 354 A3
Morton St 11 155 C4 354 A2
Mother Gaston Blvd 176 A2 355 B4
1-228 33 176 A2 355 B4
231-OUT 12 176 B2 355 C4
Moultrie St 22 150 C3 348 C2
Murdock Ct 23 189 C4 362 C1
Myrtle Av 159 B4 354 B2
1-278 1 149 B5 354 B1
279-751 & 280-75
5 149 B6 354 B1
753-1173 & 756-1132
6 159 B4 354 B2
1175-1373 & 1134-1350
21 160 B2 354 B3
1375-5399 & 1352-5398
37 161 B4 355 B4
Myrtle La 34 184 C3 362 B3
Narrows Av 178 C3 360 A3
1-6899 2 178 B3 360 A3
6900-OUT 9 178 C3 360 A3
Nassau Av 22 156 A2 354 A3
Nassau Ct 35 189 C5 362 C1
Nassau St 1 145 C4 354 B1
National Dr 34 190 A2 362 B3
Nautilus Av 24 192 B1 368 Inset
Navy St 1 145 C5 354 B1
Nelson St 31 165 B6 353 B6
Neptune Av 188 C1 361 C4
1-389 & 2-396 35 189 C4 362 C1
391-OUT & 398-OUT
24 193 A4 368 Inset
Neptune Ct 35 189 C5 362 C1
Neptune St 24 195 A4 368 Inset
Nevins St 166 A3 354 B1
1-303 & 2-298 17 166 A3 354 B1
05-OUT & 300-OUT
15 166 B2 354 B1
New Dock St 1 143 A6 354 A1
New Jersey Av 7 176 A3 355 B5
New Lots Av 177 B4 355 C5
1-160 12 176 C2 355 C4
161-760 7 176 B3 355 C4
761-OUT 8 177 B4 355 C5
New Utrecht Avenue 182 C2 361 B5
1-6899 19 182 B2 361 A5
6900-7299 28 182 C2 361 B5
7300-7499 4 182 C2 361 B5
7500-OUT 14 188 A1 361 B4
New York Av 168 C3 354 C3
1-298 16 168 C3 354 B3
299-392 13 168 C3 354 C3
393-584 25 174 A3 354 C3
585-1400 3 174 B3 354 C3
1401-2199 1 183 B6 362 A2
2200-OUT 34 183 C6 362 B2
Newel St 22 150 C3 348 C2
Newkirk Av 183 B4 362 A1
1-1399 3 183 B4 362 A1
1400-3299 26 183 A5 362 A1
3300-OUT 3 183 A6 362 A2
Newport St 176 C1 355 C4
1-400 12 176 C1 355 C4
401-OUT 7 176 C3 355 C4
Newton St 22 156 A2 354 A3
Nichols Av 8 177 A5 355 B6
Nixon Ct 23 189 C4 362 C1
Noble St 22 150 C1 348 C1
Noel Av 29 190 B2 362 C3
Nolans La 36 184 A3 362 A3
Noll St 160 A1 354 A3
1-158 6 160 A1 354 A3
159-OUT 37 160 A2 354 A3
Norfolk St 35 189 C6 362 C2
Norman Av 22 150 C3 348 C2
Norman Pl 7 176 A2 355 B4
North 1st St 11 153 C4 354 A2
North 3rd St 11 153 C4 354 A2
North 4th St 11 153 C5 354 A2
North 5th St 11 153 C5 354 A2
North 6th St 11 153 C6 354 A2
North 7th St 11 153 C6 354 A2
North 8th St 11 153 C6 354 A2
North 9th St 11 153 B6 354 A2
North 10th St 11 153 B6 354 A2
North 11th St 11 153 B6 354 A2
North 12th St 11 153 A6 354 A2
North 13th St 11 153 A6 354 A2
North 14th St 11 153 A6 354 A2
North 15th St 11 153 A6 354 A2
North Conduit Av 8 177 A5 355 B6
North Elliott Pl 5 145 C6 354 B1
North Henry St 22 150 C3 348 C2
North Oxford St 5 145 C6 354 B1
North Portland Av 5 149 A6 354 B1
Norwood Av 8 177 A4 355 B5
Nostrand Av 159 B4 354 B2
1-135 (odd only) 6 159 B4 354 B2
137-259 & 2-290 5 159 B4 354 B2
261-791 & 292-832
16 168 A2 354 B2
793-1261 & 834-1268
25 174 A2 354 C2
1263-1925 & 1270-1926
26 174 C2 354 C2
1927-2799 & 1928-2802
1 183 C6 362 B2
2801-3693 & 2804-3694
29 189 A6 362 B2
3695-OUT 35 189 B6 362 C2
Nova Ct 29 190 C1 362 C2
Oak St 22 150 C1 348 C1
Oakland Pl 26 183 A5 362 A1
O'Brien Pl 8 177 A5 355 B6
Ocean Av 183 A5 362 A1
1-325 25 173 B6 354 C2
326-1060 26 183 A5 362 A1
1061-2099 3 183 B5 362 A1
2100-2812 29 189 A5 362 B1
2813-OUT 35 189 B5 362 C1
Ocean Ct 189 B4 362 C1
1-51 23 189 B4 362 C1
52-OUT 35 189 B4 362 C1
Ocean Pkwy 183 A4 362 A1
1-619 & 2-630 18 183 A4 362 A1
621-1599 & 632-1608
3 183 C4 362 A1
1601-2399 & 1610-2398
23 189 A4 362 B1
2400-OUT 35 189 C4 362 C1
Ocean View Av 189 C4 362 C1
1-3799 35 189 C4 362 C1
3800-OUT 24 188 C1 361 C4
Oceanic Av 24 192 B2 368 Inset
Ohio Wk 34 184 C3 362 B3
Old Fulton St 1 143 B6 354 A1
Old Mill Rd 8 177 C5 355 C6
Old New Utrecht Rd 182 B3 361 A5
1-4099 18 182 A3 361 A5
4100-OUT 4 182 B3 361 A5
Olean St 1 183 C5 362 B1
Olive St 11 156 B3 354 A3
Oliver St 9 180 B2 360 B3
Opal Ct 29 190 C1 362 C2
Orange St 1 143 C6 354 B1
Orient Av 11 156 B3 354 A3
Oriental Blvd 35 189 C6 362 C1
Osborn St 12 176 C2 355 C4
Otsego St 31 165 C5 353 C6
Overbaugh Pl 1 184 C1 362 B2
Ovington Av 179 C4 360 A3
1-699 9 179 C4 360 A3
700-899 2 181 A6 361 A4
900-OUT 19 182 B1 361 A4
Ovington Ct 4 182 C2 361 B5
Owls Head Ct 2 178 B3 360 A3
Oxford St 35 189 C6 362 C2
Pacific St 148 C1 354 B1
1-331 1 148 C1 354 B1
333-777 & 332-736
17 166 A3 354 B1
779-1145 & 738-1120
38 168 B1 354 B2
1147-1503 & 1122-1460
16 168 C2 354 B2
1505-1795 & 1462-1750
13 169 B5 354 B3
1797-OUT & 1752-OUT
33 169 B6 354 B3
Paerdegat Av N 36 184 B3 362 A3
Paerdegat Av S 34 184 B2 362 A3
Paerdegat 1st St 36 184 B2 362 A3
Paerdegat 2nd St 36 184 B3 362 A3
Paerdegat 3rd St 36 184 B3 362 A3
Paerdegat 4th St 36 184 B3 362 A3
Paerdegat 5th St 36 184 B3 362 A3
Paerdegat 6th St 36 184 B3 362 A3
Paerdegat 7th St 36 184 B3 362 A3
Paerdegat 8th St 36 184 B3 362 A3
Paerdegat 9th St 36 184 B3 362 A3
Paerdegat 10th St 36 184 B3 362 A3
Paerdegat 11th St 36 184 B3 362 A3
Paerdegat 12th St 36 184 B3 362 A3
Paerdegat 13th St 36 184 B3 362 A3
Paerdegat 14th St 36 184 B3 362 A3
Paerdegat 15th St 36 184 B3 362 A3
Paidge Av 22 150 B2 348 C1
Palm Ct 25 174 B3 354 C3
Palmetto St 160 C3 355 B4
1-280 21 160 C3 355 B4
281-OUT 37 161 B4 355 B4
Parade Pl 26 173 C6 354 C2
Park Av 158 B3 354 B2
1-45 1 149 A5 354 B1
47-569 & 46-560 5 158 B3 354 B2
571-OUT & 562-OUT
6 159 B4 354 B2
Park Pl 167 B4 354 B1
1-159 & 2-168 17 167 B4 354 B1
161-637 & 170-638 38 167 B6 354 B2
639-912 16 168 C2 354 C2
913-1570 13 168 C3 354 C3
1571-OUT 33 176 B1 355 C4
Park St 6 159 B6 354 B3
Parkside Av 26 174 C1 354 C2
Parkside Ct 26 174 C1 354 C2
Parkville Av 3 182 B3 361 A5
Parkway Ct 189 B4 362 C1
1-41 23 189 B4 362 C1
42-OUT 35 189 B4 362 C1
Parrott Pl 28 187 A5 361 B4
Patchen Av 160 C2 354 B3
1-179 & 2-176 21 160 C2 354 B3
181-OUT & 178-OUT
33 169 A5 354 B3
Pearl St 1 144 C2 354 B1
Pearson St 34 184 C2 362 B3
Pedestrian St 35 189 C6 362 C2
Pembroke St 35 189 C6 362 C2
Penn St 11 158 A3 354 A2
Pennsylvania Av (Granville Payne Av)
176 C3 355 C5
1-1140 7 176 C3 355 C5
1141-OUT 39 177 C4 355 C5
Percival St 31 165 C6 353 C6
Peri La 34 184 C3 362 B3
Perry Pl 16 168 B2 354 B2
Perry Ter 9 179 C4 360 A3
Pierrepont Pl 1 147 A5 353 B6
Pierrepont St 1 147 A6 354 B1
Pilling St 7 176 A2 355 B4
Pine St 8 177 A5 355 B6
Pineapple St 1 143 C6 354 B1
Pioneer St 31 165 B4 353 B6
Pitkin Av 176 B1 355 C4
1-1454 33 176 B1 355 C4
1455-1900 12 176 B1 355 C4
1901-2385 7 176 B3 355 C5
2386-2999 8 177 B4 355 C5
Plaza St East 38 167 B5 354 B2
Plaza St West 15 167 C5 354 C2
Pleasant Pl 33 176 A2 355 B4
Plumb 1st St 29 190 B1 362 C2
Plumb 2nd St 29 190 B1 362 C2
Plumb 3rd St 35 190 C1 362 C2
Plumb Beach Av 29 190 C1 362 C2
Plymouth St 1 144 A3 354 A1
Polar St 24 188 C1 361 C4
Polhemus Pl 15 167 C4 354 C1
Poly Pl 28 187 B4 360 B3
Poole La 35 189 C6 362 C1
Poplar Av 24 188 C1 361 C4
Poplar St 1 144 B1 354 A1
Portal St 33 175 A6 354 C3
Porter Av 157 C5 354 A3
1-226 37 157 C5 354 A3
227-OUT 22 157 A4 354 A3
Post Ct 29 190 C2 362 C2
Powell St 12 176 B2 355 C4
Powers St 11 156 C1 354 A2
Prescott Pl 33 176 A1 355 B4
President St 165 A6 353 B6
1-436 31 165 A6 353 B6
437-969 & 438-958
15 167 B4 354 B1
971-1261 & 960-1262
25 168 C1 354 C2
1263-OUT 13 175 A4 354 C3
Preston Ct 184 A2 362 A2
1-7999 34 184 A2 362 A2
8000-OUT 36 184 A2 362 A3
Prince St 1 149 A4 354 B1
Prospect Av 172 A2 354 C1
1-618 15 172 A2 354 C1
619-OUT 18 173 C4 354 C1
Prospect Expwy 15 172 B3 354 C1
Prospect Park Southwest 173 B4 354 C1
1-78 15 173 B4 354 C1
79-OUT 18 173 C5 354 C1
Prospect Park West 15 173 A4 354 C1
Prospect Pl 168 B1 354 B2
141-605 & 152-604
38 168 B1 354 B2
606-878 16 168 C2 354 C2
879-1546 13 168 C3 354 C3
1547-OUT 33 176 B1 355 C4
Prospect St 1 144 b2 354 B1
Provost St 22 150 B2 348 C1
Pulaski St 159 C4 354 B2
1-409 & 2-420 6 159 C4 354 B2
411-OUT & 422-OUT
21 160 B1 354 B3
Putnam Av 168 A1 354 B2
1-129 38 168 A1 354 B2
153-423 & 130-422
16 168 A2 354 B2
424-1396 21 169 A5 354 B3
1397-1599 37 161 B5 355 B4
Quay St 22 150 C1 348 C1
Quentin Rd 188 A3 361 B5
1-1099 23 188 A3 361 B5
1100-3008 29 189 A5 362 B1
3009-OUT 34 183 C6 362 B2
Quentin St 35 190 C1 362 C2
Quincy St 168 A1 354 B2
1-106 38 168 A1 354 B2
107-396 16 168 A2 354 B2
397-OUT 21 160 C1 354 B3
Rabbi Joel Teitelbaum Pl
11 158 A3 354 A2
Radde Pl 33 176 A1 355 B4
Railroad Av 22 151 B4 348 C2
Raleigh Pl 26 174 C3 354 C3
Ralph Av 160 C3 355 B4
1-127 21 160 C3 355 B4
128-625 33 176 A1 355 B4
626-757 12 176 B1 355 C4
759-1853 & 758-1864
36 184 A2 362 A3
1855-OUT & 1866-OUT
34 184 B2 362 A3
Randolph St 37 157 C5 354 A3
Rapelye St 31 165 B6 353 B6
Red Cross Pl 1 144 C2 354 B1
Red Hook La 1 148 B2 354 B1
Reed St 31 165 B4 353 B6
Reeve Pl 18 173 C4 354 C1
Regent Pl 26 183 A5 362 A1
Remsen Av 175 B6 354 C3
1-479 12 175 B6 354 C3
480-OUT 36 184 A3 362 A3
Remsen St 1 147 A5 354 B1
Revere Pl 13 168 B3 354 B3
Rewe St 11 157 B4 354 A3
Richards St 31 165 B5 353 B6
Richardson St 156 B1 354 A2
1-153 & 2-160 11 156 B1 354 A2
155-OUT & 162-OUT
22 156 A3 354 A3
Richmond St 8 177 A4 355 B5
Ridge Blvd 180 A3 360 A3
1-6899 2 181 B4 360 A3
6900-OUT 9 180 A3 360 A3
Ridge Ct 9 179 C4 360 A3
Ridgecrest Ter 9 178 C3 360 A3
Ridgewood Av 177 A4 355 B5
1-72 7 176 A3 355 B5
73-600 8 177 A4 355 B5
Ridgewood Pl 37 161 B5 355 E4
Riegelmann Boardwalk (Boardwalk W)
24 193 B5 368 Inset
River St 11 152 C3 354 A2
Riverdale Av 176 C1 355 C4
1-425 12 176 C1 355 C4
426-OUT 7 176 B3 355 C4
Rochester Av 169 C5 354 C3
1-127 33 169 B6 354 B3
128-OUT 13 169 C5 354 C3
Rock St 6 160 A1 354 A3
Rockaway Av 176 B2 355 C4
1-325 33 176 A2 355 B4
326-1021 12 176 B2 355 C4
1022-OUT 36 176 C2 355 C4
Rockaway Pkwy 176 B1 355 C4
1-601 12 176 B1 355 C4
602-OUT 36 185 A4 363 A4
Rockwell Pl 17 149 C5 354 B1
Roder Av 3 183 C4 362 B1
Rodney St 11 155 C6 354 A2
Roebling St 11 155 C5 354 A2
Rogers Av 174 A2 354 C2
1-199 & 2-176 16 168 C2 354 B2
201-633 & 178-634
25 174 A2 354 C2
635-1280 26 174 C2 354 C2
1281-OUT 1 183 A5 362 A1
Roosevelt Ct 32 172 B1 354 C1
Roosevelt Pl 33 176 A1 355 B4
Rose St 36 184 A3 362 A3
Ross St 11 158 A2 354 A2
Rost Pl 36 185 B4 363 A4
Royce Pl 34 184 C3 362 B3
Royce St 34 184 C3 362 B3
Ruby St 8 177 B6 355 C6
Rugby Rd 183 A4 362 A1
1-530 26 183 A4 362 A1
531-OUT 3 183 B4 362 A1
Russell St 22 150 C3 348 C2
Rutherford Pl 14 188 A1 361 B4
Rutland Rd 174 B1 354 C2
1-400 25 174 B1 354 C2
401-914 3 175 B4 354 C3
915-OUT 12 175 B6 354 C3
Rutledge St 11 158 A3 354 A2
Ryder Av 3 183 C4 362 B1
Ryder St 34 184 C1 362 B2
Ryerson St 5 158 B2 354 B2
Sackett St 165 A6 353 B6
1-516 31 165 A6 353 B6
517-OUT 17 166 B3 354 B1

Brooklyn

Sackman St		176	B2	355	C4
1-160	33	176	A2	355	B4
161-OUT	12	176	B2	355	C4
Saint Andrews Pl	16	169	B4	354	B3
Saint Charles Pl	16	168	C1	354	C2
Saint Edwards St		149	A5	354	B1
1-125	5	149	A5	354	B1
126-OUT	1	149	A5	354	B1
Saint Felix St	17	149	C6	354	B1
Saint Francis Pl	16	168	C1	354	C2
Saint James Pl		158	C2	354	B2
1-50	5	158	C2	354	B2
51-OUT	38	167	A6	354	B2
Saint Johns Pl		167	C6	354	C2
1-267	17	167	B4	354	B1
269-621 & 268-624	38	167	C6	354	C2
623-925 & 626-924	16	168	C2	354	C2
927-1571 & 926-1588	13	169	C4	354	C3
1573-OUT & 1590-OUT	33	176	B1	355	C4
Saint Jude Pl	36	185	B4	363	A4
Saint Marks Av		166	A3	354	B2
1-135 & 2-144	17	166	A3	354	B2
137-537 & 146-552	38	167	B5	354	B2
539-759 & 554-778	16	168	C2	354	B2
761-1315 & 780-1316	13	169	B4	354	C3
1317-OUT	33	176	B1	355	C4
Saint Marks Pl	17	167	B4	354	B1
Saint Nicholas Av	37	157	C6	355	A4
Saint Pauls Ct	26	174	C1	354	C2
Sandford Pl	5	159	B4	354	B2
Sands St	1	144	A2	354	A1
Saratoga Av		176	A1	355	B4
1-475	33	176	A1	355	B4
476-OUT	12	176	B1	355	C4
Schaefer St	7	161	C5	355	B4
Schenck Av	7	177	C4	355	C5
Schenck Ct	7	176	A3	355	B5
Schenck Pl	36	185	B4	363	A4
Schenck St	7	176	A3	355	B5
Schenck St	36	185	B4	363	A4
Schenectady Av		169	C5	354	C3
1-430	13	169	C5	354	C3
431-1529	3	175	C5	354	C3
1530-OUT	34	184	B1	362	A2
Schermerhorn St		148	B1	354	B1
1-257 & 2-250	1	148	B1	354	B1
259-OUT & 252-OUT	17	166	A3	354	B1
Scholes St		156	C2	354	A3
1-376	6	156	C2	354	A3
377-OUT	37	157	C5	354	A3
School La	36	184	A3	362	A3
Schroeders Av	39	185	A5	363	A4
Schweikerts Wk	24	194	B3	368	Inset
Scott Av		157	C6	355	A4
1-215	37	157	C6	355	A4
216-OUT	22	157	A5	354	A3
Sea Gate Av	24	192	A2	368	Inset
Sea Pl	24	193	C4	368	Inset
Seabreeze Av	24	189	C4	362	C1
Seabring St	31	165	A5	353	B6
Seacoast Ter	35	189	C5	362	C1
Seaview Av		185	B4	363	A4
1-112-44	36	185	B4	363	A4
112-45-OUT	39	185	A5	363	A4
Seaview Av	8	177	C5	355	C6
Seaview Ct	36	185	A4	363	A4
Seba Av	29	190	B2	362	C2
Sedgwick Pl	2	179	B4	360	A3
Sedgwick St	31	165	A6	353	B6
Seeley St	18	173	C4	354	C1
Seigel St	6	159	A5	354	A3
Senator St	2	179	B4	360	A3
Seton Pl	3	182	B3	361	A5
Shale St	35	190	C1	362	C2
Sharon St	11	156	B3	354	A3
Sheepshead Bay Rd		195	A5	368	Inset
1-999	24	195	A5	368	Inset
1000-1148 & 1001-1153	29	189	B5	362	C1
1150-OUT & 1155-OUT	35	189	C5	362	C1
Sheffield Av	7	176	B3	355	C5
Shell Rd		188	C3	361	C5
1-2819 & 2-2840	23	188	C3	361	C5
2821-OUT & 2842-OUT	24	188	C3	361	C5
Shepherd Av	8	177	A4	355	B5
Sheridan Av	8	177	A5	355	B6
Sherlock Pl	33	176	A2	355	B5
Sherman St		173	B4	354	C1
1-70	15	173	B4	354	C1
71-OUT	18	173	B4	354	C1
Shore Blvd	35	189	C5	362	C1
Shore Ct	9	180	B2	360	B3
Shore Pkwy	36	185	B5	363	A4
Shore Pkwy (Belt Pkwy)	23	188	C3	361	C5
	29	190	C2	362	C3
	35	189	C5	362	C1
Shore Parkway (Leif Ericson Dr)	9	180	A2	360	A3
	14	188	B1	361	C4
	2	178	B3	360	A3
	28	187	C4	360	B3
Shore Rd		180	A2	360	A3
1-6899	2	178	B3	360	A3
6900-OUT	9	180	A2	360	A3
Shore Rd Ext		187	C6	361	B4
1-1118	28	187	C6	361	B4
1119-OUT	14	188	A1	361	B4
Shore Road Dr	2	179	B4	360	A3
Sidney Pl	1	147	B6	354	B1
Sigourney St	31	165	C5	353	C6
Skidmore Av	36	185	B4	363	A4
Skidmore La	36	184	A3	362	A3
Skidmore Pl	36	185	B4	363	A4
Skillman Av	11	156	B2	354	A3
Skillman St	5	158	B3	354	B2
Sloan Pl	23	189	B4	362	C1
Slocum Pl	18	183	A4	362	A1
Smith St		148	B2	354	B1
1-223 & 2-220	1	148	B2	354	B1
225-OUT & 222-OUT	31	166	B1	354	B1
Smiths La	36	184	A3	362	A3
Snediker Av	7	176	B2	355	C4
Snyder Av		183	A5	362	A1
1-3299	26	183	A5	362	A1
3300-OUT	3	183	A6	362	A1
Somers St	33	176	A2	355	B4
South 1st St	11	155	A5	354	A2
South 2nd St	11	155	A5	354	A2
South 3rd St	11	155	B6	354	A2
South 4th St	11	155	B5	354	A2
South 5th Pl	11	155	B5	354	A2
South 5th St	11	155	B4	354	A2
South 6th St	11	155	B4	354	A2
South 8th St	11	155	C4	354	A2
South 9th St	11	155	C4	354	A2
South 10th St	11	154	C3	354	A2
South 11th St	11	154	C3	354	A2
South Conduit Av	8	177	A5	355	B6
South Elliott Pl	17	149	C6	354	B1
South Lake Dr		173	C5	354	C2
South Oxford St	17	167	A5	354	B2
South Portland Av	17	149	C6	354	B1
Southgate Ct	23	189	B4	362	C1
Spencer Ct	5	159	B4	354	B2
Spencer Pl	16	168	A2	354	B2
Spencer St	5	159	B4	354	B2
Stagg St		156	C1	354	A2
1-376	6	156	C1	354	A2
377-OUT	37	157	C5	354	A3
Stanhope St		160	B2	354	B3
1-156	21	160	B2	354	B3
157-OUT	37	160	A3	355	B4
Stanley Av		176	C3	355	C5
1-820	7	176	C3	355	C5
821-OUT	8	177	C4	355	C5
Stanton Rd	35	190	C1	362	C2
Stanwix St	6	160	A1	354	A3
Starr St		160	A2	354	A3
1-50	21	160	A2	354	A3
51-OUT	37	160	A2	354	A3
State St	1	148	C1	354	B1
1-309 & 2-334	1	148	C1	354	B1
311-OUT & 336-OUT	17	166	A3	354	B1
Stephens Ct	26	183	A5	362	A1
Sterling Pl	17	167	B4	354	B1
1-159 & 2-184	17	167	B4	354	B1
161-649 & 186-650	38	167	B6	354	B2
651-940	16	168	C2	354	C2
Sterling Pl	13	168	C3	354	C3
Sterling Pl	33	176	B1	355	C4
Sterling St	25	174	A1	354	C2
Steuben St	5	158	B2	354	B2
Stewart Av		157	C5	354	A3
1-227 & 2-234	37	157	C5	354	A3
229-399 & 236-400	11	157	B4	354	A3
401-OUT	22	157	A4	354	A3
Stewart St	7	176	A2	355	B4
Stillwell Av		188	A3	361	B5
1-1599	4	188	A3	361	B5
1600-2649	23	188	A3	361	B5
2650-OUT	24	195	B5	368	Inset
Stillwells Pl	36	184	B3	362	A3
Stockholm St		160	B2	354	B3
1-160	21	160	B2	354	B3
161-OUT	37	160	A3	355	B4
Stockton St	6	159	B5	354	B3
Stoddard Pl	25	174	A1	354	C2
Story St	18	182	A3	361	A5
Stratford Rd	18	183	A4	362	A1
Strauss St	12	176	B1	355	C4
Strickland Av	34	190	A2	362	B3
Strong Pl	31	166	A1	354	B1
Stryker Ct	23	189	B4	362	C1
Stryker St	23	189	B4	362	C1
Stuart St	29	189	A6	362	B2
Stuyvesant Av		160	C1	354	B3
1-287 & 2-300	21	160	C1	354	B3
289-OUT & 302-OUT	33	169	A5	354	B3
Sullivan Pl	25	174	A1	354	C2
Sullivan St	31	165	B4	353	B6
Summit St	31	165	A6	353	B6
Sumner Pl	6	159	A6	354	A3
Sumpter St	33	176	A1	355	B4
Sunnyside Av	7	176	A3	355	B5
Sunnyside Ct	7	176	A3	355	B5
Sunset Ct	24	188	C1	361	C4
Surf Av	24	193	C5	368	Inset
Sutter Av		176	B1	355	C4
1-470	12	176	B1	355	C4
471-950	7	176	B3	355	C5
951-1599	8	177	B4	355	C5
Sutton St	22	151	C4	348	C2
Suydam Pl	33	169	B6	354	B3
Suydam St		160	B2	354	B3
1-200	21	160	B2	354	B3
201-OUT	37	160	A3	355	A4
Taaffe Pl	5	158	B3	354	B2
Tabor Ct	19	182	B1	361	A4
Tampa Ct	25	174	B3	354	C3
Tapscott Av	12	175	A6	354	C3
Tapscott St	12	176	B1	355	C4
Taylor St	11	158	A2	354	A2
Tech Pl	1	148	A3	354	B1
Tehama St	18	182	A3	361	A5
Temple Ct	18	173	C5	354	C2
Ten Eyck St		156	C2	354	A3
1-25 & 2-28	6	156	C2	354	A3
27-OUT & 30-OUT	37	157	B5	354	A3
Tennis Ct	26	183	A5	362	A1
Terrace Pl	18	173	C4	354	C1
Thames St	6	160	A1	354	A3
Thatford Av	12	176	C2	355	C4
Thatford St	12	176	B2	355	C4
Thomas S Boyland St (Hopkinson Av)		176	A1	355	C4
1-418	33	176	A1	355	B4
444-1049	12	176	C2	355	C4
Thomas St	22	151	C5	348	C2
Thornton St	6	159	A5	354	B3
Throop Av		159	A5	354	A3
1-325 & 2-350	6	159	A5	354	A3
327-543 & 352-574	21	159	C6	354	B3
545-OUT & 576-OUT	16	169	A4	354	B3
Tiemans La	36	185	A4	363	A4
Tiffany Pl	31	165	A6	353	B6
Tilden Av		183	A5	362	A1
1-3299	25	183	A5	362	A1
3300-OUT	3	183	A6	362	A2
Tillary St	1	148	A2	354	B1
Tompkins Av		159	B6	354	B3
1-205 & 2-202	6	159	B6	354	B3
207-OUT & 204-OUT	16	159	C5	354	B3
Tompkins Pl	31	166	A1	354	B1
Townsend St	22	151	C5	348	C2
Troutman St		160	B1	354	B3
1-215	6	160	B1	354	B3
216-OUT	37	160	A2	354	A3
Troy Av		169	C5	354	C3
1-430	13	169	C5	354	C3
431-1575	3	175	C5	354	C3
1576-OUT	34	184	B1	362	A2
Troy Pl	34	184	B1	362	A2
Trucklemans La	36	185	A4	363	A4
Trust Sq	34	184	C1	362	B2
Truxton St	33	176	A2	355	B4
Turnbull Av	36	184	A3	362	A3
Turner Pl	18	183	A4	362	A1
Twin Pines Dr	39	185	A5	363	A4
Underhill Av	38	167	B6	354	C2
Union Av		156	B1	354	A2
1-185 & 2-168	6	159	A4	354	B2
187-OUT & 170-OUT	11	156	B1	354	A2
Union St		165	A6	353	B6
1-515 & 2-476	31	165	A6	353	B6
517-971 & 478-922	15	167	B4	354	B1
973-1325 & 924-1300	25	168	C1	354	C2
1327-1901 & 1302-1850	13	175	A4	354	C3
1903-1991 & 1852-1923	33	176	B1	355	C4
1993-OUT & 1930-OUT	12	176	B1	355	C4
Utica Av		175	B5	354	C3
1-50	33	169	B6	354	B3
51-440	13	175	A5	354	B3
441-1460	3	175	B5	354	C3
1461-OUT	34	184	B1	362	A2
Van Brunt St	31	165	B4	353	B6
Van Buren St	21	159	C6	354	B3
Van Dam St	22	151	C5	348	C2
Van Dyke St	31	165	B4	353	B6
Van Sicklen St	23	188	B3	361	C5
Van Siclen Av		176	A3	355	B5
1-1022	7	176	A3	355	B5
1023-OUT	39	177	C4	355	C5
Van Sinderen Av	7	176	B2	355	C4
Vandalia Av		177	C4	355	C5
1-414	39	185	A5	363	A4
415-OUT	8	177	C5	355	C6
Vanderbilt Av		158	B1	354	B2
1-331	5	158	B1	354	B2
332-OUT	38	167	B5	354	B2
Vanderbilt St	18	173	C4	354	C1
Vanderveer Pl	26	183	A5	362	A1
Vanderveer St	7	176	A2	355	B4
Vandervoort Av	22	157	A4	354	A3
Vandervoort Pl	37	160	A2	354	A3
Varet St	6	159	A5	354	A3
Varick Av		157	C5	354	A3
1-258	37	157	C5	354	A3
259-400	11	157	A4	354	A3
401-OUT	22	157	A4	354	A3
Varick St	22	151	C5	348	C2
Varkens Hook Rd	36	184	A3	362	A3
Verandah Pl	1	147	C6	354	B1
Vermont Av	7	176	A3	355	B5
Vermont Ct	7	176	A3	355	B5
Vermont St	7	176	A3	355	B5
Vernon Av		159	B4	354	B2
1-399	6	159	B4	354	B2
400-OUT	21	160	B1	354	B3
Verona Pl	16	168	B3	354	B3
Verona St	31	165	B5	353	B6
Veronica Pl	26	183	A5	362	A1
Veterans Av	34	184	C2	362	B3
Victor Rd	3	183	A6	362	A2
Village Ct	23	189	B4	362	C1
Village Rd E	23	189	B4	362	C1
Village Rd N	23	189	B4	362	C1
Village Rd S	23	188	B3	361	C5
Vine St	1	143	B6	354	A1
Virginia Pl	13	169	C4	354	C3
Visitation Pl	31	165	B5	353	B6
Vista Pl	2	179	C5	361	A4
Voorhies Av	35	189	C5	362	C1
Wakeman Pl	2	179	B4	360	A3
Waldane Ct	35	190	C1	362	C2
Waldorf Ct	3	183	B4	362	A1
Walker St	7	177	C5	355	C6
Wallabout St		158	B3	354	B2
1-97 & 2-148	11	158	B3	354	B2
99-OUT & 150-OUT	6	158	B3	354	B2
Wallaston Ct	4	182	C2	361	B5
Walsh Ct	3	183	B4	362	A1
Walton St	6	159	A4	354	A2
Walworth St	5	159	B4	354	B2
Warren Pl	1	147	C5	354	B1
Warren St		147	C4	353	B6
1-396	1	147	C4	353	B6
397-OUT	17	166	A3	354	B1
Warsoff Pl	5	159	B4	354	B2
Warwick St	7	176	A3	355	B5
Washington Av		158	C2	354	B2
1-350	5	158	C2	354	B2
351-811 & 352-860	38	167	A6	354	B2
813-OUT & 862-OUT	25	174	A1	354	C2
Washington Park	5	158	C1	354	B2
Washington St	1	144	B2	354	A1
Washington Wk (Walt Whitman Houses)	5	158	B1	354	B2
Water St	1	144	B3	354	A1
Waterbury St	6	156	C3	354	A3
Watkins St	12	176	B2	355	C4
Waverly Av		158	B2	354	B2
1-335	5	158	B2	354	B2
336-OUT	38	167	A6	354	B2
Weber's Ct	35	189	C6	362	C2
Weber's Ter	35	189	C6	362	C2
Webster Av	3	182	B3	361	A5
Webster Pl	15	172	A2	354	C1
Weirfield St		161	C4	355	B4
1-289	21	161	C4	355	B4
290-OUT	37	161	B5	355	B4
Weldon St	8	177	A5	355	B6
Wellington Ct	3	183	B4	362	A1
Wells St	8	177	A4	355	B5
West 1st St		188	A3	361	B5
1-1599	4	188	A3	361	B5
1600-2699	23	188	A3	361	B5
2700-OUT	24	189	C4	362	C1
West 2nd Pl	24	189	C4	362	C1
West 2nd St		188	A3	361	B5
1-1599	4	188	A3	361	B5
1600-2699	23	188	A3	361	B5
2700-OUT	24	189	C4	362	C1
West 3rd St		188	A3	361	B5
1-1599	4	188	A3	361	B5
1600-2699	23	188	A3	361	B5
2700-OUT	24	189	C4	362	C1
West 4th St		188	A3	361	B5
1-1599	4	188	A3	361	B5
1600-OUT	23	188	A3	361	B5
West 5th St		188	A3	361	B5
1-1600	4	188	A3	361	B5
1601-2699	23	188	A3	361	B5
2700-OUT	24	195	A6	368	Inset
West 6th St		188	A3	361	B5
1-1599	4	188	A3	361	B5
1600-2699	23	188	A3	361	B5
2700-OUT	24	195	A5	368	Inset
West 7th St		188	A3	361	B5
1-1600	4	188	A3	361	B5
1601-OUT	23	188	A3	361	B5
West 8th St		188	A3	361	B5
1-1599	4	188	A3	361	B5
1600-2699	23	188	A3	361	B5
2700-OUT	24	195	A5	368	Inset
West 9th St		165	B6	353	B6
1-213	31	165	B6	353	B6
214-1599	4	188	A3	361	B5
1600-OUT	23	188	A3	361	B5
West 10th St		188	A3	361	B5
1-1599	4	188	A3	361	B5
1600-2699	23	188	A3	361	B5
2700-OUT	24	195	B5	368	Inset
West 11th St		188	A3	361	B5
1-1599	4	188	A3	361	B5
1600-OUT	23	188	A3	361	B5
West 12th St		188	A3	361	B5
1-1599	4	188	A3	361	B5
1600-2699	23	188	A3	361	B5
2700-OUT	24	195	A4	368	Inset
West 13th St	23	188	A3	361	B5
West 15th Pl	14	188	C3	361	C5
West 15th St		188	C3	361	C5
1-2659	14	188	C3	361	C5
2660-OUT	24	194	A3	368	Inset
West 16th St		188	C3	361	C5
1-2699	14	188	C3	361	C5
2700-OUT	24	194	A3	368	Inset
West 17th St		188	C3	361	C5
1-2699	14	188	C3	361	C5
2700-OUT	24	194	A2	368	Inset
West 19th St		188	C3	361	C5
1-2699	14	188	C3	361	C5
2700-OUT	24	194	B2	368	Inset
West 20th St		188	C2	361	C5
1-2699	14	188	C2	361	C5
2700-OUT	24	194	A2	368	Inset
West 21st St		188	C2	361	C5
1-2799	14	188	C2	361	C5
2800-OUT	24	194	B1	368	Inset
West 22nd St		188	C2	361	C5
1-2699	14	188	C2	361	C5
2700-OUT	24	194	B1	368	Inset
West 23rd St	24	194	B1	368	Inset
West 24th St	24	193	B6	368	Inset
West 25th St	24	193	B6	368	Inset
West 27th St	24	193	A6	368	Inset
West 28th St	24	193	A5	368	Inset
West 29th St	24	193	A5	368	Inset
West 30th St	24	193	A5	368	Inset
West 31st St	24	193	A4	368	Inset
West 32nd St	24	193	B4	368	Inset
West 33rd St	24	192	A3	368	Inset
West 35th St	24	192	B3	368	Inset
West 36th St	24	192	B3	368	Inset
West 37th St	24	192	B3	368	Inset
West Av	24	189	C4	362	C1
West Brighton Av	24	189	C4	362	C1
West Dr		173	A4	354	C2
West End Av	35	189	C5	362	C1
West Lake Dr		173	C5	354	C2
West Shore Av	14	188	C2	361	C5
West St		150	B1	348	C1
1-399	22	150	B1	348	C1
400-OUT	23	189	B4	362	C1
Westbury Ct	25	174	B1	354	C2
Westerly La	9	180	A2	360	A3
Westminster Rd	18	183	A4	362	A1
Wharton Pl	8	236	A1	355	B5
Whipple St	6	159	A5	354	A3
White St	6	160	A1	354	A3
Whitman Dr	34	190	A3	362	B3
Whitney Av	29	190	B1	362	C2
Whitney Pl	23	189	B4	362	C1
Whitty La	3	184	A1	362	A2
Whitwell Pl	15	166	B3	354	B1
Will Pl	7	176	C3	355	C5
William Ct	35	189	C5	362	C1
William J Hennessy Sq	35	189	C4	362	C1
Williams Av	7	176	B2	355	C4
Williams Pl	7	176	A2	355	B4
Williamsburg Pl	5	158	B2	354	B2
Williamsburg Pl	11	158	B2	354	B2
Williamsburg St E	11	158	A3	354	A2
Williamsburg St W		158	A3	354	A2
1-344	11	158	A3	354	A2
345-OUT	11	158	A3	354	B2
Willmohr St	12	176	C1	355	C4
Willoughby Av		158	C1	354	B2
1-438	5	158	C1	354	B2
439-840	6	159	B4	354	B2
841-1100	21	160	B1	354	B3
1101-OUT	37	160	A3	355	A4
Willoughby St	1	148	B3	354	B1
Willow Pl	1	147	B5	354	B1
Willow St	1	143	C6	354	B1
Wilson Av		160	A2	354	A3
1-333 & 2-318	37	160	A2	354	A3
335-527 & 320-512	21	161	B4	355	B4
529-OUT & 514-OUT	7	161	C5	355	B4
Wilson St	11	158	A2	354	A2
Windsor Pl		172	B3	354	C1
1-254	15	172	B3	354	C1
255-OUT	18	173	B4	354	C1
Winthrop St		174	B1	354	C2
1-370	25	174	B1	354	C2
371-965	3	174	B3	354	C3
966-OUT	12	175	B6	354	C3
Withers St		156	B1	354	A3
1-275 & 2-272	11	156	B1	354	A3
277-OUT & 274-OUT	22	157	A4	354	A3
Wogan Ter	9	187	A4	360	B3
Wolcott St	31	165	B4	353	B6
Wolf Pl	23	188	B3	361	C5
Woodbine St		161	C4	355	B4
1-280	21	161	C4	355	B4
281-1599	37	161	B4	355	B5
Woodhull St	31	165	A6	353	B6
Woodpoint Rd	11	156	B3	354	A3
Woodrow Ct	32	171	B6	353	C6
Woodruff Av	26	173	C6	354	C2
Woods Pl	26	183	A5	362	A1
Woodside Av	23	189	A4	362	B1
Wortman Av		176	C3	355	C5
1-433	7	176	C3	355	C5
434-OUT	8	177	C5	355	C6
Wyckoff Av	37	160	A3	355	A4
Wyckoff St		166	A2	354	B1
1-129 & 2-132	1	166	A2	354	B1
131-OUT & 134-OUT	17	166	A3	354	B1
Wyona St	7	176	B3	355	C5
Wythe Av	11	154	B3	354	A2
Wythe Pl	11	158	A2	354	A2
York St	1	144	A3	354	A1

BRIDGES & TUNNELS

Brooklyn Battery Tunnel (Toll)	31	165	A6	353	B6
Brooklyn Br	1	143	A6	354	A1
Kosciuszko Br	22	151	C6	348	C2
Manhattan Br	1	144	A2	354	A1
Marine Parkway Gil Hodges Mem Br (Toll)	34	191	C5	363	C4
Verrazano-Narrows Br (Toll)	9	186	B2	360	B3
Williamsburg Br	11	154	A1	354	A2

Manhattan

Manhattan

West 165th St	32	135	A4	343	B5
West 166th St	32	135	A4	343	B5
West 167th St	32	135	A4	343	B5
West 168th St	32	135	A4	343	B5
West 169th St	32	136	C2	343	B5
West 170th St	32	136	C2	343	B5
West 171st St	32	136	C2	343	B5
West 172nd St	32	136	C2	343	B5
West 173rd St	32	136	C2	343	B5
West 174th St	33	136	C3	343	B5
West 175th St	33	136	C3	343	B5
West 176th St	33	136	C3	343	B5
West 177th St	33	136	C3	343	B5
West 178th St	33	136	C3	343	B5
West 179th St	33	136	B2	343	A5
West 180th St	33	136	B3	343	A5
West 181st St	33	136	B3	343	A5
West 182nd St	33	136	B3	343	A6
West 183rd St	33	136	B3	343	A6
West 184th St	33	136	B3	343	A6
West 185th St	33	136	B3	343	A5
West 186th St	33	137	B4	343	A6
West 187th St	33	136	A3	343	A5
West 188th St	4	137	B4	343	A6
West 189th St	4	137	A4	343	A6
West 190th St	4	137	A4	343	A6
West 191st St	4	137	A4	343	A6
West 192nd St	4	137	A4	343	A6
West 193rd St	4	137	A4	343	A6
West 196th St	4	138	C2	343	A6
West 201st St	34	139	C4	343	A6
West 202nd St	34	139	C4	343	A6
West 203rd St	34	139	C4	343	A6
West 204th St	34	139	C4	343	A6
West 205th St	34	139	C4	343	A6
West 206th St	34	139	C4	343	A6
West 207th St	34	139	C4	343	A6
West 208th St	34	139	C4	343	A6
West 211th St	34	139	B4	343	A6
West 212th St	34	139	B4	343	A6
West 213th St	34	139	B4	343	A6
West 214th St	34	139	B4	343	A6
West 215th St	34	139	B4	343	A6
West 216th St	34	139	B5	343	A6
West 217th St	34	139	B4	343	A6
West 218th St	34	139	B5	343	A6
West 219th St	34	139	B5	343	A6
West 220th St	34	139	B5	343	A6
West 225th St	63	278	C2	344	A1
West 227th St	63	278	C2	340	C1
West 228th St	63	278	C2	340	C1
West Broadway		29	C6	336	B3
1-95	7	29	C6	336	B3
97-373 & 96-368	13	38	C2	336	B3
375-OUT & 370-OUT	12	39	A4	336	B3
West Dr	28	20	C3	336	C2
West End Av		99	C4	347	B5
1-341	23	99	C4	347	B5
343-637 & 342-640	24	107	C4	347	A5
639-OUT & 642-OUT	25	124	C3	347	A5
West Houston St		39	A5	337	A4
1-177 & 2-170	12	39	A5	337	A4
179-OUT & 172-OUT	14	45	C5	336	A3
West Rd	44	69	A5	339	B5
West St		21	B4	336	C2
21-114	6	21	B4	336	C2
115-185	7	29	C4	336	B2
186-324	13	37	C5	336	B3
325-OUT	14	44	C2	336	A3
West Thames St	28	20	C3	336	C2
White St	13	30	A2	336	B3
Whitehall St	4	16	A3	336	C2
Willett St (Bialystocker Pl)	2	33	B6	337	B5
William St		17	A5	336	C3
1-9 & 2-6	4	17	A5	336	C3
11-83 & 8-78	5	21	C6	336	C3
85-OUT & 80-OUT	38	22	B1	336	C3
Wooster St		38	C3	336	B3
1-55 & 2-58	13	38	C3	336	B3
57-OUT & 60-OUT	12	38	B3	336	B3
Worth Sq	1	59	C4	338	C2
Worth St	13	30	B2	336	B3
York Av		85	B5	339	A5
1101-1509 & 1100-1512	21	85	B5	339	A5
1511-1655 & 1514-1656	28	96	B1	339	A6
1657-OUT & 1658-OUT	128	104	C3	348	A2
York St	13	38	C2	336	B3

AIRPORTS

West 30th St Heliport	1	62	A3	338	B1
Downtown Manhattan Heliport	4	17	B5	336	C3
East 34th St Heliport	16	61	C5	339	C4

BRIDGES & TUNNELS

145th St Br	39	133	A6	343	C6
3rd Avenue Br	35	133	C6	343	C6
Alexander Hamilton Br	33	137	C4	343	B6
Brooklyn Battery Tunnel (Toll)	4	21	C4	336	C2
Brooklyn Br	38	19	B5	337	C4
George Washington Br (Toll)	33	136	B1	343	A5
Henry Hudson Br (Toll)	34	138	A3	340	C1
High Br (Closed)	32	137	C4	343	B6
Holland Tunnel (Toll-Eastbound)	13	38	B2	336	B3
Lincoln Tunnel (Toll)	18	71	B5	338	B2
Macombs Dam Br	39	135	C5	343	B6
Madison Avenue Br	37	133	B6	343	C6
Manhattan Br	2	24	B2	337	C4
Queensboro Br (59th St Bridge)	22	77	C5	339	B5
Queens-Midtown Tunnel (Toll)	17	68	C1	339	C4
Roosevelt Island Br	44	86	C2	339	A6
Triborough Br (Toll)	35	131	B4	348	A2
University Heights Br	34	139	C5	343	A6
Washington Br	33	137	C4	343	B6
Williamsburg Br	2	35	C4	337	B6
Willis Avenue Br	35	130	A3	343	C6

Queens

NEIGHBORHOODS

Arverne	92	248	C2	364	C3
Astoria	3	208	A2	348	B3
Auburndale	58	219	A5	350	B3
Bay Terrace	60	204	B1	350	A3
Bayside	61	219	A6	350	B3
Bayswater	91	249	A4	365	B4
Beechhurst	57	203	B5	350	A2
Bellaire	29	232	B3	357	A4
Belle Harbor	94	250	B3	369	B6
Bellerose	26	233	A4	351	C5
Blissville	1	213	C4	348	C2
Breezy Point	97	252	B3	368	B3
Briarwood	35	230	B3	356	A2
Broad Channel	93	247	A6	364	B2
Brookville	13	239	C4	357	C4
Cambria Heights	11	239	A5	357	B5
College Point	56	202	B2	349	A6
Corona	68	217	A5	349	C5
Ditmars	5	199	B4	348	A3
Douglas Manor	63	204	C3	351	A4
Douglaston	63	220	A3	351	B4
Dutch Kills	1	207	C5	348	B2
East Elmhurst	69	210	A3	349	B4
Edgemere	91	248	B3	364	C3
Elmhurst	73	216	B2	349	C4
Far Rockaway	91	249	B5	365	B4
Floral Park	26	221	C5	351	C6
Flushing	54	218	A2	349	B6
Forest Hills	75	225	C6	355	A6
Forest Hills Gardens	75	230	B1	356	A1
Fresh Meadows	65	219	C6	350	C3
Glen Oaks	4	221	B5	351	B6
Glendale	85	228	B1	355	A5
Hammels	93	248	C1	364	C2
Hillcrest	66	231	A5	356	A2
Hollis	23	232	B1	357	A4
Hollis Hill	27	220	C2	351	C4
Holliswood	23	232	A1	357	A4
Hook Creek	59	243	B5	365	A5
Howard Beach	14	240	A3	356	C1
Hunters Pt	1	212	B1	348	C1
Jackson Hgts	72	209	C6	349	B4
Jamaica	35	231	C4	356	A2
Jamaica Ests	32	231	A6	356	A3
Jamaica Hills	32	231	B5	356	A3
Kew Gardens Hills	67	230	A2	349	C6
Kew Gardens	15	230	B2	356	A1
Laurelton	13	239	B5	357	C5
Linden Hill	54	203	C4	350	B2
Lindenwood	14	236	C2	355	C6
Little Neck	63	205	C4	351	B5
Long Island City	1	212	A3	348	C2
Malba	57	202	B3	349	A6
Maspeth	78	223	C4	355	A4
Middle Village	79	224	C1	355	A5
Murray Hill	55	218	A3	350	B2
Neponsit	94	250	C2	369	B5
Oakland Gardens	64	220	B2	351	C4
Ozone Park	19	237	A4	356	B1
Pomonok	65	219	C4	350	C2
Queens Village	28	232	A3	357	A5
Queensboro Hill	55	218	B2	349	C6
Queensbridge	1	206	C3	348	B2
Ravenswood	6	207	A4	348	B2
Rego Park	74	225	A4	349	C5
Richmond Hill	18	230	C2	356	B1
Ridgewood	85	226	B3	355	A4
Rockaway Park	94	251	B4	364	C1
Rosedale	22	239	C5	357	C5
Roxbury	95	253	A5	369	B4
Saint Albans	12	232	C2	357	B4
Seaside	94	251	A6	364	C1
Somerville	92	248	B2	364	C3
South Jamaica	36	238	B1	356	B3
South Ozone Park	20	237	B5	356	C2
Springfield Gdns	34	238	B3	357	C4
Steinway	5	200	C1	349	A4
Sunnyside	4	214	A1	348	C3
Sunnyside Gdns	77	214	A2	348	C3
West Maspeth	78	222	A1	348	C3
Whitestone	57	203	B4	350	A2
Woodhaven	21	236	A1	355	B6
Woodside	77	215	A4	348	C3

NUMBERED STREETS

1st St	14	241	A4	356	C1
1st St	2	198	C1	348	B2
1st St	22	243	B5	365	A5
2nd St		198	B1	348	A2
25-00 - 29-99	2	198	B1	348	A2
50-00 - 56-99	1	212	B1	348	C1
2nd St	22	243	B5	365	A5
3rd Av	57	203	A4	350	A2
3rd Rd	93	247	A6	364	B2
3rd St	2	198	B1	348	B2
3rd St	22	243	B5	365	A5
4th Av	57	203	A4	350	A2
4th Av	97	252	B2	368	B3
4th St	2	198	C1	348	B2
5th Av		202	B2	349	A6
115-00 - 126-99	56	202	B2	349	A6
144-00 - 149-99	57	203	A4	350	A2
5th St	1	212	B1	348	C1
6th Av		202	B2	349	A6
119-00 - 129-99	56	202	B2	349	A6
145-00 - 150-99	57	203	A4	350	A2
6th Rd	57	203	A4	350	A2
7th Av		202	B2	349	A6
119-00 - 130-99	56	202	B2	349	A6
145-00 - 161-99	57	203	B4	350	A2
8th Av	56	202	B2	349	A6
117-00 - 121-99	56	202	B2	349	A6
145-00 - 150-99	57	203	B4	350	A2
8th Rd	57	203	B4	350	A2
8th St	2	198	C1	348	B2
9th Av		202	B1	349	A5
115-00 - 129-99	56	202	B1	349	A5
138-00 - OUT	57	203	B5	350	A2
9th Rd	56	202	B2	349	A6
9th St		207	B4	348	B2
25-01 - 26-99	2	198	C2	348	B2
33-01 - 36-99	6	207	B4	348	B2
37-01 - 44-99	1	207	B4	348	B2
10th Av		202	B1	349	A5
115-00 - 126-99	56	202	B1	349	A5
138-00 - OUT	57	203	B5	350	A2
10th St		207	B4	348	B2
33-01 - 36-99	6	207	B4	348	B2
37-01 - 44-99	1	206	C3	348	B2
11th Av		202	B2	349	A6
121-00 - 130-99	56	202	B2	349	A6
138-00 - 160-99	57	203	B4	350	A2
11th Pl	1	212	B2	348	C1
11th St		207	B4	348	B2
32-00 - 36-99	6	207	B4	348	B2
37-00 - 53-99	1	207	B4	348	B2
12th Av	56	202	B2	349	A6
117-00 - 121-99	56	202	B1	349	A5
147-00 - 168-99	57	203	B5	350	A2
12th Rd	57	203	B5	350	A2
12th St		207	B4	348	B2
25-00 - 30-99	2	198	C1	348	B2
31-00 - 36-99	6	207	B4	348	B2
37-00 - 43-99	1	206	C3	348	B2
13th Av		202	B3	349	A6
122-00 - 125-99	56	202	B2	349	A6
138-00 - 162-99	57	202	B3	349	A6
13th Rd	57	202	B3	349	A6
13th St		207	C4	348	B2
33-01 - 36-99	6	207	A5	348	B2
37-01 - 43-99	1	207	C4	348	B2
14th Av		202	B3	349	A6
109-00 - 137-99	56	202	B1	349	A5
138-00 - 168-99	57	203	B4	350	A2
208-00 - 214-99	60	204	B1	350	A3
14th Pl		198	C2	348	B2
25-01 - 26-99	2	198	C2	348	B2
32-01 - 32-99	6	207	A5	348	B2
14th Rd		202	B3	349	A6
110-00 - 132-99	56	202	B3	349	A6
149-00 - 167-99	57	203	B5	350	A2
14th St		207	B4	348	B2
25-00 - 30-99	2	198	C2	348	B2
31-00 - 36-99	6	207	A5	348	B2
37-00 - 37-99	1	207	B4	348	B2
15th Av		202	B1	349	A5
109-00 - 131-99	56	202	B1	349	A5
138-00 - 167-99	57	203	B4	350	A2
208-00 - 214-99	60	204	B1	350	A3
15th Dr		203	B4	350	A2
147-00 - 166-99	57	203	B4	350	A2
208-00 - OUT	60	204	B1	350	A3
15th Rd		203	B4	350	A2
144-00 - 149-99	57	203	B4	350	A2
200-00 - 216-99	60	204	B1	350	A3
16th Av		203	B5	350	A2
157-00 - 199-99	57	203	B5	350	A2
200-00 - 214-99	60	204	B1	350	A3
16th Dr	57	203	B5	350	A2
16th Rd	57	203	B4	350	A2
17th Av		203	B5	350	A2
145-00 - 199-99	57	203	B5	350	A2
200-00 - 216-99	60	203	B6	350	A3
17th Rd	57	203	B4	350	A2
18th Av		202	B2	349	A6
119-00 - 130-99	56	202	B2	349	A6
145-00 - 168-99	57	203	B4	350	A2
209-00 - 214-99	60	204	B1	350	A3
18th St		199	A4	348	A3
20-01 - 20-99	5	199	A4	348	A3
25-01 - 27-99	2	198	C2	348	B2
19th Av		199	B6	348	A3
35-01 - 48-99	5	199	B6	348	A3
49-00 - 80-99	70	200	C2	349	B4
138-00 - 199-99	57	203	B4	350	A2
200-00 - OUT	60	203	C6	350	A3
19th Dr	70	200	C2	349	B4
19th Rd	70	200	C2	349	B4
19th St		198	B3	348	A3
20-00 - 23-99	5	199	A4	348	A3
24-00 - 24-99	2	198	B3	348	A3
20th Av		199	A4	348	A3
18-00 - 48-99	5	199	A4	348	A3
49-00 - 84-99	70	200	C1	349	B4
109-00 - 130-99	56	202	B3	349	A6
143-00 - 169-99	57	203	B4	350	A2
20th Rd		199	A4	348	A3
18-00 - 45-99	5	199	A4	348	A3
146-00 - 166-99	57	203	B5	350	A2
20th St	5	199	A4	348	A3
21st Av		199	A4	348	A3
18-00 - 48-99	5	199	A4	348	A3
49-00 - 84-99	70	200	C1	349	B4
122-00 - 123-99	56	202	C2	349	A6
143-00 - 199-99	57	203	C4	350	A2
200-00 - OUT	60	203	C6	350	A3
21st Dr	5	198	A3	348	A3
21st Rd		199	A4	348	A3
18-00 - 21-99	5	199	A4	348	A3
143-00 - 143-99	57	202	C3	349	A6
160-00 - 169-99	57	203	C5	350	A2
21st St		207	A5	348	B2
20-01 - 23-99	5	199	B4	348	A3
24-01 - 30-99	2	198	B3	348	A3
31-01 - 36-99	6	207	A5	348	B2
37-01 - 51-99	1	207	C4	348	B2
22nd Av		202	C2	349	A6
118-00 - 128-99	56	202	C2	349	A6
138-00 - 199-99	57	203	C4	350	A2
200-00 - 223-99	60	203	C6	350	A3
22nd Dr		198	B3	348	A3
19-00 - 21-99	5	198	B3	348	A3
98-00 - 98-99	69	201	C5	349	B5
22nd Rd		199	B4	348	A3
19-00 - 21-99	5	199	B4	348	A3
143-00 - 144-99	57	202	C3	349	A6
22nd St		207	C4	348	B2
25-01 - 26-99	2	198	C3	348	B3
36-01 - 36-99	6	207	B5	348	B2
37-01 - 43-99	1	207	C4	348	B2
23rd Av		199	B4	348	A3
19-01 - 46-99	5	198	B3	348	A3
85-00 - 101-99	69	210	A2	349	B4
119-00 - 130-99	56	202	B3	349	A6
138-00 - 199-99	57	203	C5	350	A2
200-00 - 223-99	60	204	C1	350	A3
23rd Dr	5	198	B3	348	A3
23rd Rd		198	B3	348	A3
19-00 - 42-99	5	198	B3	348	A3
102-00 - 102-99	69	210	A3	349	B5
207-00 - 217-99	60	204	B1	350	A3
23rd St		199	B4	348	A3
20-01 - 23-99	5	199	B4	348	A3
24-01 - 30-99	2	198	C3	348	A3
31-01 - 36-99	6	207	A6	348	B2
37-01 - 51-99	1	207	C4	348	B2
23rd Ter	5	198	B3	348	A3
24th Av		198	B3	348	A3
19-01 - 32-99	2	198	B3	348	A3
33-01 - 38-99	3	199	C4	348	B3
77-00 - 84-99	70	209	B6	349	B4
85-00 - 102-99	69	210	A2	349	B4
145-00 - 199-99	57	203	C5	350	A2
200-00 - 215-99	60	203	C6	350	A3
24th Dr	2	198	B3	348	A3
24th Rd		198	B3	348	A3
19-00 - 31-99	2	198	B3	348	A3
90-00 - 102-99	69	210	A2	349	B4
149-00 - 199-99	57	203	C5	350	A2
200-00 - OUT	60	203	C6	350	A3
24th St		198	C3	348	B3
20-01 - 23-99	5	199	B4	348	A3
24-01 - 24-99	2	198	C3	348	B3
34-01 - 36-99	6	207	B5	348	B2
37-01 - 43-99	1	207	C4	348	B2
25th Av		208	A3	348	B3
40-01 - 48-99	3	208	A3	348	B3
49-00 - only	77	209	A4	348	B3
71-00 - 84-99	70	209	B6	349	B4
85-00 - 102-99	69	210	A2	349	B4
120-00 - 129-99	56	202	C2	349	A6
141-00 - 199-99	57	203	C5	350	A2
25th Dr		203	C5	350	B2
118-00 - 157-99	54	203	C4	350	B2
158-00 - 199-99	58	203	C5	350	B2
25th Rd		198	C2	348	B2
18-01 - 26-99	2	198	C2	348	B2
118-00 - 146-99	54	202	C2	349	A6
25th St (Crescent St)		213	A4	348	C2
20-01 - 23-99	5	199	B4	348	A3
24-01 - 30-99	2	198	C3	348	B3
31-01 - 36-99	6	207	A6	348	B2
49-01 - 51-99	1	207	C4	348	B2
26th Av		198	B1	348	A2
1-00 - 18-99	2	198	C2	348	B2
118-00 - 157-99	54	202	C2	349	B6
158-00 - 199-99	58	203	C5	350	B2
200-00 - 223-99	60	204	C1	350	B3
26th Rd		198	C2	348	B2
18-00 - 21-99	2	198	C2	348	B2
97-00 - 97-99	69	210	B3	349	B5
26th St	5	198	C3	348	B3
20-01 - 23-99	5	199	B5	348	A3
24-01 - 24-99	2	198	C3	348	B3
27th Av		198	B1	348	A2
1-01 - 18-99	2	198	B1	348	A2
60-00 - 60-99	77	209	B4	348	B3
99-00 - 107-99	69	211	A4	349	B5
118-00 - 157-99	54	203	C4	350	B2
158-00 - 199-99	58	203	C5	350	B2
200-00 - 217-99	60	204	C1	350	B3
27th Rd	2	198	C2	348	B2
27th St		198	C3	348	B3
20-00 - 23-99	5	199	B4	348	A3
24-00 - 27-99	2	198	C3	348	B3
37-00 - 51-99	1	207	C4	348	B2
28th Av		198	C2	348	B2
11-01 - 32-99	2	198	C2	348	B2
33-01 - 48-99	3	208	A2	348	B3
49-00 - 69-99	77	209	B4	348	B3
118-00 - 157-99	54	202	C2	349	B6
158-00 - 199-99	58	203	C5	350	B2
200-00 - 217-99	60	204	C1	350	B3
28th Rd		208	A1	348	B3
31-01 - 31-99	2	208	A1	348	B3
138-00 - 141-99	54	202	C3	349	B6
209-00 - 216-99	60	204	C1	350	B3
28th St		199	C4	348	B3
20-01 - 23-99	5	199	B5	348	A3
24-01 - 26-99	2	198	C3	348	B3
33-01 - 36-99	6	207	B6	348	B2
37-01 - 46-99	1	207	C5	348	B2
29th Av		198	C2	348	B2
12-01 - 23-99	2	198	C2	348	B2
102-00 - 107-99	69	211	B4	349	B5
118-00 - 157-99	54	202	C2	349	B6
158-00 - 199-99	58	203	C5	350	B2
200-00 - 217-99	60	204	C1	350	B3
29th Rd	54	202	C3	349	B6
29th St		199	C4	348	B3
20-00 - 23-99	5	199	B5	348	A3
24-00 - 30-99	2	198	C3	348	B3
31-00 - 36-99	6	207	B6	348	B2
37-00 - 53-99	1	207	C5	348	B2
30th Av		198	C2	348	B2
11-01 - 32-99	2	198	C2	348	B2
33-01 - 48-99	3	208	A1	348	B3
49-00 - 69-99	77	208	B3	348	B3
70-00 - 84-99	70	209	B6	349	B4
85-00 - 95-99	69	210	B2	349	B4
119-00 - 120-99	54	202	C2	349	B6
198-00 - 198-99	58	203	C6	350	B3
208-00 - 209-99	60	204	C1	350	B3
30th Dr	2	198	C1	348	B2
30th Pl	1	213	B5	348	C2
30th Rd		198	C1	348	B2
8-00 - 25-99	2	198	C1	348	B2
44-00 - 46-99	3	208	B3	348	B3
30th St		208	A1	348	B3
26-00 - 30-99	2	208	A1	348	B3
31-00 - 36-99	6	207	B6	348	B2
37-00 - 52-99	1	207	C5	348	B2
31st Av		198	C1	348	B2
8-01 - 36-99	6	198	C1	348	B2
37-01 - 48-99	3	208	B2	348	B3
49-01 - 69-99	77	208	B3	348	B3
70-00 - 84-99	70	209	B6	349	B4
85-00 - 107-99	69	210	B3	349	B4
120-00 - 130-00	54	202	C2	349	B6
31st Dr	6	207	A5	348	B2
11-01 - 23-99	6	207	A5	348	B2
108-00 - 108-99	69	211	B5	349	B5
134-00 - OUT	54	202	C3	349	B6
31st Pl	1	213	B5	348	C2
31st Rd		207	A5	348	B2
14-01 - 23-99	6	207	A5	348	B2
118-00 - 157-99	54	202	C3	349	B6
216-00 - 217-99	60	204	C2	351	A4
31st St		199	B5	348	A3
20-00 - 23-99	5	199	B5	348	A3
24-00 - 30-99	2	208	A1	348	B3
31-00 - 36-99	6	207	B6	348	B3
37-00 - 49-99	1	207	C5	348	B2
32nd Av		208	C3	348	B3
51-00 - 69-99	77	208	C3	348	B3
70-00 - 84-99	70	209	B6	349	B4
85-00 - 109-99	69	210	B3	349	B4
130-00 - 157-99	54	218	A2	349	B6
158-00 - 199-99	58	203	C5	350	B2
200-00 - 217-99	61	204	C1	350	B3
32nd Dr	61	204	C1	350	B3
32nd Pl	1	213	B5	348	C2
32nd Rd		219	A5	350	B3
198-00 - 199-99	58	219	A5	350	B3
214-00 - 214-99	61	204	C1	351	B4
32nd St		199	B5	348	A3
20-00 - 23-99	5	199	B5	348	A3
24-00 - 30-99	2	208	A1	348	B3
31-00 - 36-99	6	207	B6	348	B3
37-00 - 39-99	1	207	C6	348	B2
33rd Av		207	A5	348	B2
11-01 - 28-99	6	207	A5	348	B2
130-00 - 157-99	54	218	A2	349	B5
158-00 - 199-99	58	219	A4	350	B2
200-00 - 215-99	61	204	C1	350	B3
33rd Rd		207	A4	348	B2
9-01 - 23-99	6	207	A4	348	B2
131-00 - 157-99	54	218	A3	350	B2
200-00 - 223-99	61	204	C1	350	B3
33rd St		208	A1	348	B3
20-00 - 23-99	5	199	B5	348	A3
24-00 - 30-99	2	208	A1	348	B3
31-00 - 36-99	6	207	C6	348	B3
37-00 - 48-99	1	207	C6	348	B2
34th Av		207	A4	348	B2
8-01 - 36-99	6	207	A4	348	B2
37-01 - 46-99	1	208	C1	348	B3
58-00 - 69-99	77	209	C4	348	B3
70-00 - 95-99	72	210	C1	349	B4
96-00 - 127-99	68	211	C4	349	B5
131-00 - 157-99	54	218	A2	349	B6
158-00 - 199-99	58	219	A5	350	B3
200-00 - 223-99	61	219	A6	350	B3
250-00 - 254-99	63	205	C4	351	A5
34th Rd		210	C3	349	B5
70-00 - 95-99	72	210	C3	349	C5
131-00 - 157-99	54	218	A2	349	B6
200-00 - 223-99	61	204	C1	350	B3
34th St		208	B1	348	B3
25-00 - 30-99	3	208	A1	348	B3
31-00 - 36-99	6	207	C6	348	B3
37-00 - OUT	1	207	C6	348	B2
35th Av		207	A4	348	B2
7-01 - 36-99	6	207	B5	348	B2
37-01 - 43-99	1	208	C1	348	B3
54-00 - 69-99	77	215	A5	349	C4
70-00 - 92-99	72	210	C1	349	B4
96-00 - 127-99	68	211	C4	349	B5
131-00 - 157-99	54	218	A2	349	B6
159-00 - 199-99	58	219	A4	350	B2
200-00 - 223-99	61	219	A6	350	B3
35th Rd	72	215	A5	349	C4
35th St		208	B1	348	B3
20-00 - 23-99	5	199	B5	348	A3
24-00 - 30-99	3	208	A1	348	B3
31-00 - 36-99	6	207	C6	348	B3
37-00 - OUT	1	207	C6	348	B2
36th Av		207	B4	348	B2
7-01 - 36-99	6	207	B5	348	B2
37-01 - 41-99	1	208	C1	348	B2
108-00 - 127-99	68	211	C5	349	B5
200-00 - 223-99	61	219	A6	350	B3
36th Rd	54	218	A2	349	B6
36th St		208	B1	348	B3
19-00 - 23-99	5	199	B5	348	A3
24-00 - 30-99	3	208	A2	348	B3
31-00 - 36-99	6	207	C6	348	B3
37-00 - 48-99	1	207	C6	348	B2
37th Av		208	C3	348	B3
8-01 - 52-99	1	207	B4	348	B2

53-00 - 69-99	77	208	C3	348	B3
70-00 - 95-99	72	216	A1	349	C4
96-00 - 127-99	68	211	C5	349	B5
131-00 - 157-99	54	218	A3	350	B2
158-00 - 199-99	58	219	A5	350	B3
200-00 - 223-99	61	204	C1	351	B4
224-00 - OUT					
EX 1-399	63	205	C4	351	A5
37th Dr	68	211	C5	349	B5
37th Rd		208	C3	348	B3
53-00 - 69-99	77	208	C3	348	B3
70-00 - 95-99	72	215	A6	349	C4
96-00 - 127-99	68	211	C4	349	B5
37th St		208	B1	348	B3
19-00 - 23-99	5	199	C5	348	B3
24-00 - 32-99	3	208	B1	348	B3
34-00 - OUT	1	207	C6	348	B2
38th Av		207	B4	348	B2
8-01 - 52-99	1	207	B4	348	B2
54-00 - 69-99	77	214	A3	348	C3
96-00 - 127-99	68	211	C5	349	B5
131-00 - 157-99	54	218	A2	349	B6
200-00 - 223-99	61	219	A6	350	B3
224-00 - OUT					
E 1-399	63	205	C4	351	B5
38th Dr (Little Neck Rd)	63	204	C3	351	B4
38th St		208	B1	348	B3
18-00 - 23-99	5	199	C5	348	B3
24-00 - 32-99	3	208	B1	348	B3
34-00 - OUT	1	208	C1	348	B3
39th Av		207	C4	348	B2
21-01 - 32-99	1	207	C4	348	B2
44-02 - 48-98 (even)	4	214	A2	348	C3
44-01 - 52-99 (odd)	4	214	A2	348	C3
49-00 - 52-98 (even)	77	214	A3	348	C3
53-00 - 69-99	77	214	A3	348	C3
96-00 - 127-99	68	211	C5	349	B5
131-00 - 157-99	54	218	A2	349	B6
158-00 - 199-99	58	219	A5	350	B3
200-00 - 223-99	61	219	A6	350	B3
224-00 - OUT	63	204	C3	351	B4
39th Dr	77	214	A3	348	C3
39th Pl	4	213	B6	348	C2
39th Rd		214	A3	348	C3
52-00 - 52-99	77	214	A3	348	C3
223-00 - 233-99	63	205	C4	351	B5
39th St		213	B6	348	C2
36-00 - 40-99	1	213	A6	348	C2
41-00 - OUT	4	213	B6	348	C2
40th Av		206	C3	348	B2
8-00 - 30-99	1	207	C4	348	B2
213-00 - 220-99	61	220	A1	351	B4
233-00 - OUT	63	205	C4	351	B5
40th Dr	73	216	A3	349	C5
40th Rd		207	C5	348	B2
29-00 - 29-99	1	207	C5	348	B2
94-00 - 95-99	73	216	A3	349	C5
96-00 - 127-99	68	217	A4	349	C5
131-00 - 135-99	54	218	A2	349	B6
40th St	4	213	B6	348	C2
41st Av		206	C3	348	B2
10-01 - 30-99	1	206	C3	348	B2
52-00 - 73-99	77	214	A3	348	C3
74-00 - 95-99	73	215	A6	349	C4
96-00 - 127-99	68	217	A5	349	C5
131-00 - 149-99	55	218	A2	349	B6
150-00 - 157-99	54	218	A2	349	B6
158-00 - 199-99	58	219	A5	350	B3
200-00 - 223-99	61	219	A6	350	B3
224-00 - OUT	63	205	C4	351	B5
41st Dr		214	B3	348	C3
58-00 - 58-99	77	214	B3	348	C3
250-00 - 260-99	63	205	C4	351	B5
41st Rd		206	C3	348	B2
10-00 - 11-99	1	206	C3	348	B2
94-00 - 95-99	73	216	A3	349	C5
131-00 - 157-99	55	218	B2	349	B6
222-00 - 222-99	61	220	A2	351	B4
250-00 - 260-99	63	205	C4	351	B5
41st St		208	B2	348	B3
19-00 - 23-99	5	200	B1	349	A4
24-00 - 32-99	3	208	B2	348	B3
34-00 - 36-99	1	208	C1	348	B3
41-00 - OUT	4	214	B1	348	C3
42nd Av (Sanford Av)		217	A5	349	C5
94-00 - 95-99	73	216	A3	349	C5
96-00 - 127-99	68	217	A5	349	C5
131-00 - 157-99	55	218	B2	349	B6
158-00 - 199-99	58	219	A5	350	B3
200-00 - 223-99	61	219	A6	350	B3
234-00 - 260-99	63	205	C4	351	B5
42nd Pl	1	208	C1	348	B3
42nd Rd		213	A4	348	B2
23-00 - 28-99	1	213	A4	348	B2
196-00 - 196-99	58	219	A6	350	B3
42nd St		208	B2	348	B3
18-00 - 23-99	5	200	B1	349	A4
24-00 - 32-99	3	208	B2	348	B3
34-00 - 35-99	1	208	C1	348	B3
41-00 - 50-99	4	214	B1	348	C3
43rd Av		206	C2	348	B1
7-01 - 38-99	1	206	C2	348	B1
39-01 - 48-99	4	213	A6	348	C2
49-00 - 73-99	77	214	B3	348	C3
74-00 - 95-99	73	216	B2	349	C4
96-00 - 127-99	68	217	A5	349	C5
131-00 - 157-99	55	219	A4	350	B2
158-00 - 199-99	58	219	A4	350	B2
200-00 - 223-99	61	219	A6	350	B3
224-00 - 260-99	63	205	C4	351	B5
43rd Rd		206	C3	348	B2
8-00 - 11-99	1	206	C3	348	B2
158-00 - 199-99	58	219	A5	350	B3
43rd St		208	B2	348	B3
18-01 - 23-99	5	200	B1	349	A4
24-00 - 32-99	3	208	B2	348	B3
34-00 - 38-99	1	208	C1	348	B3
39-01 - 47-24	4	214	A1	348	C3
47-25 - 50-99	77	214	C1	348	C3
52-00 - 55-99	78	213	C6	348	C2
44th Av		212	A3	348	C1
8-01 - 22-99	1	212	A3	348	C1
58-00 - 73-99	77	214	C3	348	C3
74-00 - 95-99	73	216	B1	349	C4
96-00 - 127-99	68	217	A5	349	C5
158-00 - 199-99	58	219	B5	350	B3
200-00 - 223-99	61	219	A6	350	B3
224-00 - 260-99	63	220	A3	351	B5
44th Dr	1	212	A3	348	C1
44th Rd	1	212	A2	348	C1
44th St		208	B2	348	B3
24-01 - 32-99	3	208	B2	348	B3
34-01 - 34-99	1	208	C2	348	B3
39-01 - 45-99	4	214	A1	348	C3
47-00 - 51-09	77	214	C1	348	C3

51-10 - 54-99	78	222	A1	348	C3
45th Av		212	A2	348	C1
5-00 - 23-99	1	212	A2	348	C1
69-00 - 73-99	77	215	B5	349	C4
74-00 - 95-99	73	216	B2	349	C4
96-00 - 127-99	68	217	A5	349	C5
131-00 - 157-99	55	218	B3	350	B2
158-00 - 199-99	58	219	B4	350	B2
200-00 - 223-99	61	219	A6	350	B3
45th Dr		219	B6	350	B3
158-00 - 199-99	58	219	B5	350	B3
200-00 - 223-99	61	219	B6	350	B3
45th Rd	1	212	A2	348	C1
10-01 - 23-99	1	212	A2	348	C1
158-00 - 199-99	58	219	B5	350	B3
200-00 - 223-99	61	219	A6	350	B3
45th St		208	B2	348	B3
18-00 - 23-99	5	200	B1	349	A4
24-00 - 32-99	3	208	B2	348	B3
34-00 - 34-99	1	208	C2	348	B3
39-01 - 45-50	4	214	A1	348	C3
45-51 - 51-99	77	214	C1	348	C3
46th Av		212	A2	348	C1
5-00 - 21-99	1	212	A2	348	C1
74-00 - 95-99	73	215	B6	349	C4
96-00 - 127-99	68	217	A5	349	C5
131-00 - 157-99	55	219	B4	350	B2
158-00 - 199-99	58	219	B4	350	B2
200-00 - 223-99	61	219	B6	350	B3
46th Rd		212	A2	348	C1
4-01 - 21-99	1	212	A2	348	C1
189-00 - 199-99	58	219	B5	350	B3
200-00 - 223-99	61	219	B6	350	B3
46th St		208	B3	348	B3
18-00 - 23-99	5	200	C1	349	A4
24-00 - 32-99	3	208	B3	348	B3
34-00 - 34-99	1	208	C2	348	B3
39-01 - 45-32	4	214	A2	348	C3
45-35 - 51-99	77	214	C1	348	C3
52-00 - 56-99	78	222	A1	348	C3
47th Av		212	A2	348	C1
4-00 - 38-99	1	212	A2	348	C1
39-00 - 43-99	4	213	B6	348	C2
44-00 - 73-99	77	214	B3	348	C3
74-00 - 95-99	73	216	B1	349	C4
96-00 - 127-99	68	217	A5	349	C5
131-00 - 157-99	68	217	A5	349	C5
158-00 - 199-99	58	219	B5	350	B3
200-00 - 223-99	61	219	B6	350	B3
47th Rd		212	A2	348	C1
4-00 - 11-99	1	212	A2	348	C1
217-00 - 218-99	61	219	B6	350	B3
47th St		208	B3	348	B3
18-01 - 23-99	5	200	C1	349	B4
24-01 - 32-99	3	208	B3	348	B3
39-01 - 45-16	4	214	A2	348	C3
45-17 - 51-99	77	214	C1	348	C3
55-00 - 58-99	78	214	C1	348	C3
48th Av		212	A1	348	C1
4-00 - 38-99	1	212	A1	348	C1
39-00 - 41-99	4	213	B5	348	C2
42-00 - 73-99	77	214	B3	348	C3
74-00 - 95-99	73	216	B3	349	C5
96-00 - 127-99	68	217	A5	349	C5
158-00 - 199-99	65	219	B6	350	C3
200-00 - 233-99	64	220	B1	351	B4
48th St		208	B3	348	B3
18-01 - 22-99	5	200	C1	349	B4
23-01 - 32-99	3	208	B3	348	B3
34-01 - 36-99	1	208	C2	348	B3
37-01 - 43-99	4	214	A2	348	C3
45-00 - 51-99	77	214	B2	348	C3
52-00 - 57-99	78	222	A1	348	C3
49th Av		212	B3	348	C2
10-01 - 27-99	1	212	B1	348	C1
66-00 - 73-99	77	215	C5	349	C4
74-00 - 95-99	73	216	B3	349	C5
96-00 - 127-99	68	217	A5	349	C5
158-00 - 199-99	65	219	B6	350	B3
200-00 - 233-99	64	220	B1	351	B4
49th Rd	64	220	A2	351	B4
49th St		208	B3	348	B3
18-01 - 22-99	5	200	C1	349	B4
23-01 - 30-99 (odd)	3	208	B3	348	B3
23-02 - 32-98 (even)	3	208	B3	348	B3
31-01 - 31-99 (odd)	77	214	B2	348	C3
32-01 - 32-99 (odd)	3	208	C2	348	B3
39-01 - 43-99	4	214	A2	348	C3
45-00 - 50-99	77	214	B2	348	C3
57-00 - 58-99	78	222	B1	355	A4
50th Av		212	B1	348	C1
2-00 - 27-99	1	212	B1	348	C1
39-00 - 41-99	4	213	B6	348	C2
42-00 - 73-99	77	215	C4	348	C3
74-00 - 95-99	73	216	B3	349	C5
96-00 - 127-99	68	217	A6	349	C5
158-00 - 199-99	65	219	B5	350	C3
200-00 - 23-99	64	220	B1	351	B4
50th St		208	B3	348	B3
24-00 - 37-99	77	208	B3	348	B3
38-01 - 38-99	4	214	A2	348	C3
39-00 - 45-99	77	214	B2	348	C3
53-00 - 54-99	78	222	A2	348	C3
51st Av		212	B1	348	C1
2-01 - 27-99	1	212	B1	348	C1
43-00 - 73-99	77	215	C5	349	C4
74-00 - 95-99	73	216	B2	349	C4
96-00 - 109-99	68	217	B5	349	C5
196-00 - 198-99	65	219	B6	350	C3
200-00 - 23-99	64	220	B1	351	B4
240-00 - 251-99	62	221	A4	351	B5
51st Dr	77	215	C6	349	C4
51st Rd	77	215	C5	349	C4
51st St	77	214	B2	348	C3
52nd Av		215	C6	349	C4
42-00 - 44-99	78	215	C6	349	C4
58-00 - 59-99	77	214	C3	348	C3
60-99 - 73-99	78	215	C5	349	C4
74-00 - 95-99	73	216	B3	349	C4
96-00 - 127-99	68	217	B6	349	C5
240-00 - 254-99	62	221	A4	351	B5
52nd Ct	78	215	C6	349	C4
52nd Dr	78	215	C5	349	C4
52nd Rd		215	C5	349	C4
66-00 - 73-99	78	215	C5	349	C4
254-00 - 254-99	62	221	A4	351	B5
52nd St		214	A3	348	C3
38-01 - 38-99	4	214	A3	348	C3
39-00 - 43-99	77	214	A3	348	C3
53rd Av		212	B2	348	C1
10-01 - 11-99	1	212	B2	348	C1
42-00 - 73-99	78	215	C4	348	C3
74-00 - 95-99	73	216	B3	349	C4
96-00 - 127-99	68	217	B6	349	C5
158-00 - 199-99	65	219	B6	350	C3

200-00 - 233-99	64	220	B1	351	B4
240-00 - 254-99	62	221	A4	351	B5
53rd Dr	78	223	A4	348	C3
53rd Pl	77	208	C3	348	B3
53rd Rd		223	A5	349	C4
66-00 - 73-99	78	223	A5	349	C4
254-00 - 254-99	62	221	A4	351	B5
53rd St	77	214	A3	348	C3
54th Av		212	B1	348	C1
1-01 - 5-99	1	212	B1	348	C1
42-00 - 73-99	78	214	C1	348	C3
74-00 - 95-99	73	216	C2	349	C4
96-00 - 127-94	68	217	B6	349	C5
200-00 - 233-99	64	220	B2	351	B4
242-00 - 260-99	62	221	A4	351	B5
54th Dr	78	222	A1	348	C2
54th Pl	78	222	C3	355	A4
54th Rd	78	222	A1	348	C3
54th St		208	C3	348	B3
30-00 - 43-99	77	208	C3	348	B3
58-00 - 60-99	78	222	C3	355	A4
55th Av		222	A1	348	C2
42-00 - 73-99	78	222	A1	348	C2
74-00 - 95-99	73	216	C3	349	C4
96-00 - 127-99	68	217	B4	349	C5
55th Dr	78	222	A2	348	C3
55th Rd		222	A3	348	C3
43-00 - 73-99	78	222	A3	348	C3
74-00 - 95-99	73	216	C2	349	C4
55th St		222	C3	355	A4
31-00 - 43-99	77	208	C3	348	B3
58-00 - 61-99	78	222	C3	355	A4
56th Av		222	B3	355	A4
1-01 - 1-99	1	222	B3	355	A4
43-00 - 73-99	78	222	B3	355	A4
74-00 - 95-99	73	216	C3	349	C4
96-00 - 127-99	68	217	B6	349	C5
131-00 - 157-99	55	218	B2	349	C6
158-00 - 199-99	65	219	B6	350	C3
200-00 - 231-99	64	220	B1	351	C4
56th Dr	78	222	B3	355	A4
56th Pl	77	209	B4	348	B3
56th Rd		222	B3	355	A4
42-00 - 73-99	78	222	B3	355	A4
131-00 - 157-00	55	218	B3	350	C2
223-00 - 226-99	64	220	B2	351	B4
56th St		209	C4	348	B3
31-00 - 43-99	77	209	C4	348	B3
58-00 - 62-99	78	222	B2	355	A4
56th Ter	78	222	B2	355	A4
57th Av		223	A6	349	C4
56-00 - 73-99	78	223	A6	349	C4
74-00 - 95-99	73	216	C2	349	C4
96-00 - 127-99	68	217	C4	349	C5
132-00 - 134-00	55	218	B2	349	C6
223-00 - 231-99	64	220	B2	351	B4
243-00 - 263-99	62	221	A4	351	B5
57th Dr		222	B3	355	A4
57-00 - 73-99	78	222	B3	355	A4
244-00 - 246-99	62	221	A4	351	B5
57th Pl	78	222	B2	355	A4
57th Rd		222	B3	355	A4
56-00 - 73-99	78	222	B3	355	A4
74-00 - 95-99	73	224	A1	349	C4
130-00 - 138-00	55	218	B2	349	C6
223-00 - 230-99	64	220	B2	351	B4
57th St		214	A3	348	C3
32-00 - 43-99	77	209	C4	348	B3
58-00 - 61-99	78	222	B2	355	A4
58th Av		222	B3	355	A4
46-00 - 73-99	78	222	B3	355	A4
74-00 - 95-99	73	224	A1	349	C4
96-00 - 127-99	68	217	B5	349	C5
132-00 - 134-00	55	218	B2	349	C6
158-00 - 199-99	65	219	C5	350	C3
200-00 - 233-99	64	220	B1	351	C4
58th Dr	78	222	B3	355	A4
58th La	77	214	C3	348	C3
58th Pl		214	C3	348	C3
48-00 - 53-99	77	214	C3	348	C3
54-00 - 58-99	78	222	B3	355	A4
58th Rd		222	B3	355	A4
58-00 - 73-99	78	222	B3	355	A4
74-00 - 95-99	73	224	B1	355	A5
130-00 - 157-99	55	218	B2	349	C6
230-00 - 230-99	64	220	B3	351	B5
58th St		209	C4	348	B3
30-00 - 53-99	77	209	C4	348	B3
54-00 - 58-99	78	222	C3	355	A4
59th Av		222	C3	355	A4
48-00 - 73-99	78	222	C3	355	A4
74-00 - 95-99	73	216	C3	349	C5
96-00 - 127-99	68	217	C5	349	C5
130-00 - 157-00	55	218	B2	349	C6
158-00 - 199-99	65	219	C4	350	C2
221-00 - 228-99	64	220	B2	351	B4
262-00 - 262-98	62	221	A5	351	B6
59th Dr	78	222	C3	355	A5
59th Pl		215	B4	348	C3
47-00 - 53-99	77	215	B4	348	C3
54-00 - 60-99	78	222	B3	355	A4
59th Rd	78	222	C3	355	A5
59th St		215	A4	348	C3
33-00 - 53-99	77	209	C4	348	B3
56-00 - 60-99	78	222	B3	355	A4
60th Av		223	C4	355	A4
59-00 - 73-99	78	223	C4	355	A4
74-00 - 95-99	73	224	A3	349	C4
96-00 - 127-99	68	217	C5	349	C5
130-00 - 153-00	55	218	C2	349	C6
243-00 - 264-99	62	221	A4	351	B5
60th Ct	78	223	C4	355	A4
60th Dr		223	C4	355	A4
60-00 - 73-99	78	223	C4	355	A4
83-00 - 86-99	73	224	A3	349	C4
60th La		223	C4	355	A4
58-00 - 62-99	78	223	C4	355	A4
63-00 - 79-99	85	227	B5	355	A4
60th Pl		209	C4	348	B3
33-00 - 33-99	77	209	C4	348	B3
53-00 - 62-08	78	223	B4	355	A4
62-47 - 76-99	85	227	A4	355	A4
60th Rd		223	C4	355	A4
59-00 - 73-99	78	223	C4	355	A4
74-00 - 95-99	73	224	A2	349	C4
262-00 - 264-99	62	221	A5	351	B6
60th St		209	C4	348	B3
30-00 - 50-99	77	209	C4	348	B3
52-00 - 62-20	78	222	B3	355	A4
62-30 - 79-99	85	227	B5	355	A4
61st Av	62	221	A4	351	B5
61st Dr	79	224	B2	355	A5
61st Rd		223	C6	355	A5
61-00 - 84-99	79	223	C6	355	A5
85-00 - 85-99	74	224	A3	349	C5

131-00 - 157-99	67	218	C2	349	C6
61st St		209	C4	348	B3
31-00 - 51-99	77	209	C4	348	B3
52-00 - 60-99	78	223	A4	348	C3
62-00 - 79-99	85	227	C5	355	B5
62nd Av		222	C3	355	A4
56-00 - 60-99	78	222	C3	355	A4
61-00 - 84-99	79	223	C5	355	A4
85-00 - 99-99	74	224	A3	349	C5
100-00 - 112-99	75	217	C6	349	C5
131-00 - 157-99	67	218	C2	349	C6
245-00 - 259-99	62	221	B4	351	B5
62nd Dr		223	C6	355	A5
69-00 - 84-99	79	223	C6	355	A5
85-00 - 99-99	74	217	C5	349	C5
100-00 - 112-99	75	217	C6	349	C5
62nd Rd		223	C5	355	A4
61-00 - 84-99	79	223	C5	355	A4
85-00 - 99-99	74	224	A3	349	C5
100-00 - 112-99	75	217	C6	349	C5
131-00 - 157-99	67	218	C2	349	C6
62nd St		209	C4	348	B3
32-00 - 51-99	77	209	C4	348	B3
52-00 - 60-99	78	223	A4	348	C3
61-00 - 61-99	79	223	C5	355	A5
67-00 - 80-99	85	227	B5	355	A5
63rd Av		224	B3	355	A6
69-00 - 84-99	79	224	B3	355	A6
85-00 - 99-99	74	225	A4	349	C5
102-00 - 112-99	75	217	C6	349	C5
131-00 - 157-99	67	218	C2	349	C6
245-00 - 255-99	62	221	B4	351	B5
63rd Dr		225	A5	349	C5
85-00 - 99-99	74	225	A5	349	C5
102-00 - 112-99	75	217	C6	349	C5
63rd Pl	78	223	A4	348	C3
63rd Rd		224	B3	355	A6
61-00 - 84-99	79	224	B3	355	A6
85-00 - 99-99	74	225	A5	349	C5
102-00 - 112-99	75	217	C6	349	C5
131-00 - 157-99	67	218	C2	349	C6
63rd St		215	B4	348	C3
35-00 - 51-99	77	215	B4	348	C3
52-00 - 60-99	78	223	A4	348	C3
61-00 - 61-99	79	223	C5	355	A5
64th Av		225	A5	349	C5
97-00 - 99-99	74	225	A5	349	C5
102-00 - 112-99	75	217	C6	349	C5
131-00 - 157-99 330					
	67	218	C2	349	C6
158-00 - 199-99	65	219	C5	350	C3
200-00 - 233-99	64	220	B2	351	C4
249-00 - 249-99	62	221	B4	351	B5
64th Cir	65	219	C6	350	C3
64th La	85	227	C6	355	B5
64th Pl	85	227	B6	355	A5
64th Rd		224	B3	355	A6
61-00 - 84-99	79	224	B3	355	A6
85-00 - 99-99	74	225	A5	349	C5
102-00 - 112-99	75	217	C6	349	C5
136-00 - 137-99	67	218	C2	349	C6
64th St		209	C5	349	B4
34-00 - 51-99	77	209	C5	349	B4
52-00 - 59-99	78	223	A4	348	C3
61-00 - 62-99	79	223	C5	355	A5
66-00 - 80-99	85	227	B5	355	A5
65th Av		225	A5	349	C5
85-00 - 99-99	74	225	A5	349	C5
102-00 - 112-99	75	225	A6	349	C5
131-00 - 157-99	67	230	A3	350	C2
158-00 - 199-99	65	219	C4	350	C2
200-00 - 233-99	64	220	B2	351	C4
234-00 - OUT	62	220	B3	351	B5
65th Cres	65	219	C6	350	C3
65th Dr		224	C1	355	A5
69-00 - 84-99	79	224	C1	355	A5
85-00 - 99-99	74	225	B5	355	A6
65th La	79	227	A5	355	A5
65th Pl		215	C4	348	C3
39-00 - 51-99	77	215	B5	349	C4
52-00 - 59-99	78	223	A4	348	C3
64-00 - 64-99	79	227	A5	355	A5
67-00 - 72-99	85	227	B6	355	A5
65th Rd		225	B4	355	A6
35-00 - 99-99	74	225	B4	355	A6
61-00 - 84-99	75	225	A6	349	C5
65th St		215	C4	348	C3
34-00 - 51-99	77	215	A5	349	C4
52-00 - 59-99	78	223	B4	355	A4
61-00 - 64-99	79	223	C5	355	A5
67-00 - 80-99	85	227	B6	355	A5
66th Av		225	C4	355	A6
85-00 - 99-99	74	225	C4	355	A6
102-00 - 112-99	75	225	A6	349	C5
234 - OUT	62	220	B3	351	B5
66th Dr	79	224	C1	355	A5
66th Pl	85	227	B6	355	A5
66th Rd		224	C1	355	A5
61-00 - 84-99	79	224	C1	355	A5
85-00 - 99-99	74	225	C5	355	A6
102-00 - 112-99	75	225	A6	349	C5
66th St		215	C5	349	C4
41-00 - 51-99	77	215	B5	349	C4
52-00 - 60-99	78	223	A5	349	C4
69-00 - 72-99	85	227	B6	355	A5
67th Av		227	B4	355	A4
59-00 - 60-99	85	227	B4	355	A4
85-00 - 101-99	74	225	C5	355	A6
102-00 - 112-99	75	225	A6	349	C5
158-00 - 199-99	65	219	C4	350	C2
200-00 - 233-99	64	220	B2	351	C4
234-00 - 240-99	62	220	B3	351	B5
67th Dr		228	A2	355	A5
69-00 - 84-99	79	228	A2	355	A5
85-00 - 85-99	74	225	C5	355	A6
100-00 - 112-99	75	225	A6	349	C5
67th Pl	85	228	B1	355	A5
67th Rd		228	A2	355	A5
73-00 - 84-99	79	228	A2	355	A5
85-00 - 85-99	74	225	C5	355	A6
99-00 - 112-99	75	225	A6	349	C5
67th St		215	C5	349	C4
40-00 - 51-99	77	215	C5	349	C4
52-00 - 60-99	78	223	A5	349	C4
61-00 - 61-99	79	223	C6	355	A5
69-00 - 72-99	85	227	B6	355	A5
68th Av		227	B4	355	A4
59-00 - 72-99	85	227	B4	355	A4
73-00 - 84-99	79	228	A2	355	A5
85-00 - 85-99	74	225	C5	355	A6
89-00 - 112-99	75	225	C6	355	A6
131-00 - 157-99	67	218	C3	350	C2
158-00 - 199-99	65	219	C5	350	C3
216-00 - 220-99	64	220	C2	351	C4
240-01 - 240-83	62	220	B3	351	B5

68th Dr		230	A1	356	A1
103-00 - 112-99	75	230	A1	356	A1
135-00 - 157-99	67	218	C3	350	C2
68th Pl	85	228	B1	355	A5
68th Rd		227	B4	355	A4
59-00 - 72-99	85	227	B4	355	A4
73-00 - 84-99	79	228	A3	355	A5
85-00 - 85-99	74	225	C5	355	A6
131-00 - 157-99	67	218	C3	350	C2
68th St		209	C5	349	B4
30-00 - 51-99	77	209	C5	349	B4
52-00 - 60-99	78	223	A5	349	C4
61-00 - 61-99	79	223	C6	355	A5
69-00 - 72-99	85	228	B1	355	A5
69th Av		227	B4	355	A4
58-00 - 72-99	85	227	B4	355	A4
73-00 - 79-00	79	228	A3	355	A5
87-00 - 112-99	75	230	A1	356	A1
131-00 - 157-99	67	230	A3	350	C2
158-00 - 199-99	65	219	C4	350	C2
200-00 - 233-99	64	220	C2	351	C4
234-00 - 259-99	62	220	B3	351	B5
260-00 - OUT (Floral Park)					
	4	221	B5	351	B6
69th Dr	79	228	A3	355	A5
69th La		223	B6	355	A5
54-00 - 60-99	78	223	B6	355	A5
61-00 - 62-99	79	224	C1	355	A5
69th Pl		215	C5	349	C4
50-00 - 51-99	77	215	C5	349	C4
52-00 - 60-99	78	223	A5	349	C4
61-00 - 64-99	79	224	C1	355	A5
69-00 - 76-99	85	228	B1	355	A5
69th Rd		228	A2	355	A5
73-00 - 79-99	79	228	A2	355	A5
86-00 - 112-99	75	229	A6	355	A6
131-00 - 157-99	67	230	A3	350	C2
69th St		209	B5	349	B4
30-00 - 51-99	77	209	B5	349	B4
52-00 - 60-99	78	223	A5	349	C4
61-00 - 66-99	79	223	C6	355	A5
69-00 - 73-99	85	228	B1	355	A5
70th Av		227	B4	355	A5
58-00 - 73-49	85	227	B4	355	A4
73-50 - 84-99	79	228	A2	355	A5
89-00 - 112-99	75	225	C6	355	A6
131-00 - 157-99	67	230	A2	349	C6
234-00 - 252-99	62	220	B3	351	C5
70th Dr	75	229	A6	355	A6
70th Rd		230	A1	356	A1
88-00 - 112-99	75	230	A1	356	A1
131-00 - 157-99	67	230	A2	349	C6
70th St		209	B5	349	B4
22-00 - 32-99	70	209	B5	349	B4
33-00 - 35-99	72	209	C5	349	B4
40-00 - 51-99	77	215	C5	349	C4
52-00 - 60-99	78	215	C5	349	C4
61-00 - 66-99	79	224	C1	355	A5
69-00 - 76-99	85	228	B1	355	A5
71st Av		227	B5	355	A5
58-00 - 89-99	85	227	B5	355	A5
74-00 - 74-99	79	228	A2	355	A5
90-00 - 112-99	75	230	A1	356	A1
131-00 - 157-99	67	230	A2	349	C6
158-00 - 199-99	65	231	A4	350	C2
251-00 - 252-99	26	221	B5	351	B6
71st Cres	65	219	C6	350	C3
71st Dr	75	230	B1	356	A1
71st Pl	85	228	B2	355	A5
71st Rd		229	A6	355	A6
91-00 - 112-99	75	229	A6	355	A6
131-00 - 157-99	67	230	A2	349	C6
251-00 - 252-99	26	221	B5	351	B6
71st St		209	B5	349	B4
21-00 - 32-99	70	209	B5	349	B4
33-00 - 35-99	72	209	C5	349	B4
40-00 - 51-99	77	215	C6	349	C4
52-00 - 60-99	78	215	C6	349	C4
61-00 - 66-99	79	224	C1	355	A5
61-00 - 77-99	85	228	B2	355	A5
72nd Av		230	B1	356	A1
83-00 - 89-99	85	228	B2	355	A5
131-00 - 157-99	67	230	A2	356	A1
158-00 - 199-99	65	231	A4	350	C2
243-00 - 244-99	62	221	B4	351	C5
251-00 - 252-99	26	221	B5	351	B6
72nd Cres	67	230	A3	356	A2
72nd Dr		230	A1	356	A1
97-00 - 112-99	75	230	A1	356	A1
131-00 - 157-99	67	230	A3	350	C2
72nd Pl		215	C6	349	C4
50-00 - 51-99	77	215	C6	349	C4
52-00 - 53-99	78	215	C6	349	C4
70-00 - 77-99	85	228	B2	355	A5
72nd Rd		230	A1	356	A1
96-00 - 113-99	75	230	A1	356	A1
131-00 - 157-99	67	230	A3	356	A1
266-00 - OUT (Floral Park)					
	4	221	B5	351	B6
72nd St		209	B5	349	B4
21-00 - 32-99	70	209	B5	349	B4
33-00 - 37-99	72	209	C5	349	B4
40-00 - 51-99	77	215	B6	349	C4
52-00 - 60-99	78	215	C6	349	C4
61-00 - 64-99	79	224	C1	355	A5
70-00 - 77-99	85	228	B2	355	A5
73rd Av		229	A4	355	A6
84-00 - 89-99	85	229	A4	355	A6
100-00 - 112-99	75	230	A1	356	A1
131-00 - 157-99	67	230	A3	356	A2
158-00 - 199-99	66	231	A4	350	C2
200-00 - 233-99	64	220	C1	351	C4
243-00 - 244-99	62	221	B4	351	C5
253-00 - OUT (Floral Park)					
	4	221	B5	351	B6
73rd Pl		215	C6	349	C4
50-00 - 50-99	77	215	C6	349	C4
54-00 - 60-99	78	215	C6	349	C4
61-00 - 69-99	79	228	A2	355	A5
70-00 - 78-99	85	228	B2	355	A5
73rd Rd		230	B1	356	A1
110-00 - 110-99	75	230	B1	356	A1
214-00 - 216-99	64	220	C2	351	C4
253-00 - OUT	4	221	B5	351	C6
73rd St		209	B5	349	B4
21-00 - 32-99	70	209	B5	349	B4
33-00 - 37-99	72	209	C6	349	B4
40-00 - 51-99	77	215	A6	349	C4
52-00 - 60-99	78	215	C6	349	C4
70-00 - 78-99	85	228	B2	355	A5
73rd Ter	67	230	A2	356	A1
74th Av		227	C6	355	A6
62-00 - 89-99	85	227	C6	355	B5
93-00 - 112-99	75	230	B1	356	A1
158-00 - 199-99	66	231	A5	350	C3

Queens

108th Av		236	B2	355	B6
84-00 - 95-99	17	236	B2	355	B6
150-00 - 175-99	33	231	C5	356	B3
220-00 - 228-99	29	233	B4	357	A5
108th Dr	33	231	C5	356	B3
108th Pl	35	237	A6	356	B2
108th Rd	33	231	C5	356	B3
108th St		211	B5	349	B5
19-00 - 32-99	69	211	B5	349	B5
33-00 - 60-99	68	211	C5	349	B5
61-00 - 71-99	75	217	C6	349	B5
84-00 - 91-99	18	230	C1	356	B1
94-00 - 107-99	19	237	A4	356	B1
109-00 - 110-99	20	237	B4	356	B1
109th Av		236	B2	355	B6
84-00 - 107-99	17	236	B2	355	B6
108-00 - 135-99	20	237	B4	356	B1
137-00 - 149-99	35	237	A6	356	B2
150-00 - 176-99	33	238	A1	356	B3
188-00 - 205-99	12	232	C1	357	A4
206-00 - OUT	29	233	B4	357	A5
109th Dr	33	238	A1	356	B3
109th Rd		237	A6	356	B2
139-00 - 139-99	35	237	A6	356	B2
150-00 - 169-99	33	231	C6	356	B3
190-00 - 194-99	12	232	C1	357	A4
109th St		211	C5	349	B5
33-00 - 36-99	68	211	C5	349	B5
84-00 - 91-99	18	230	C1	356	A1
94-00 - 107-99	19	237	A4	356	B1
109-00 - OUT	20	237	B4	356	B1
110th Av		236	B1	356	B2
77-00 - 92-99	17	236	B1	356	B2
143-00 - 149-99	35	237	A6	356	B3
150-00 - 180-99	33	238	A1	356	B3
194-00 - 205-99	12	232	C1	357	A4
208-00 - 223-99	29	232	B3	357	A5
110th Rd		238	A1	356	B3
147-00 - 147-99	35	238	A1	356	B3
150-00 - 169-99	33	238	A1	356	B3
190-00 - 194-99	12	232	C1	357	A4
216-00 - 217-99	29	232	B3	357	A5
110th St		202	B1	349	A5
1-00 - 14-99	56	202	B1	349	A5
32-00 - 32-99	69	211	B5	349	B5
33-00 - 34-99	68	211	C5	349	B5
61-00 - 72-99	75	218	C1	349	C6
84-00 - 91-99	18	230	C1	356	A1
94-00 - 107-99	19	237	A4	356	B1
109-00 - OUT	20	237	B4	356	B1
111th Av		237	B4	356	B1
109-01 - 135-99	20	237	B4	356	B1
137-00 - 149-99	35	237	A6	356	B2
150-00 - 176-99	33	238	A1	356	B3
190-00 - 205-99	12	232	C2	357	A4
206-00 - OUT	29	233	C4	357	A4
111th Rd		238	A1	356	B3
150-00 - 153-99	33	238	A1	356	B3
190-00 - 205-99	12	232	C1	357	A4
206-00 - 215-99	29	232	C3	357	A5
111th St		202	B1	349	A5
1-00 - 14-99	56	202	B1	349	A5
31-00 - 32-99	69	211	B5	349	B5
33-00 - 60-99	68	211	C5	349	B5
61-00 - 66-99	75	230	A1	349	C6
85-00 - 91-99	18	230	C1	356	A1
94-00 - 107-99	19	237	A4	356	B1
109-00 - OUT	20	237	B4	356	B1
112th Av		238	A1	356	B3
148-00 - 148-99	35	238	A1	356	B3
150-00 - 179-99	33	238	A1	356	B3
190-00 - 205-99	12	232	C2	357	A4
206-00 - OUT	29	232	C3	357	A5
112th Pl	69	211	B5	349	B5
112th Rd		238	A1	356	B3
162-00 - 162-99	33	238	A1	356	B3
191-00 - 205-99	12	232	C1	357	B4
206-00 - 227-99	29	232	C3	357	A5
112th St		202	B1	349	A5
1-00 - 14-99	56	202	B1	349	A5
32-00 - 32-99	69	211	B5	349	B5
33-00 - 60-99	68	211	C5	349	B5
61-00 - 72-99	75	218	C1	349	C6
84-00 - 93-99	18	230	C1	356	A1
94-00 - 107-99	19	237	A4	356	B1
109-00 - OUT	20	237	B4	356	B1
113th Av		238	A2	356	B3
150-00 - 173-99	33	238	A2	356	B3
181-00 - 205-99	12	232	C2	357	B4
206-00 - OUT	29	232	C3	357	A5
113th Dr	29	233	C4	357	A5
113th Pl	75	230	B2	356	A1
113th Rd	12	232	C2	357	B4
113th St		202	B1	349	A5
1-00 - 14-99	56	202	B1	349	A5
34-00 - 34-98	68	211	C6	349	B5
61-00 - 78-99	75	230	A2	356	A1
84-00 - 91-99	18	230	C2	356	A1
94-00 - 107-99	19	237	A4	356	B1
109-00 - OUT	20	237	B4	356	B1
114th Av	11	232	C3	357	A5
114th Dr		232	C1	357	B4
188-00 - 205-99	12	232	C1	357	B4
227-00 - 228-99	11	233	C4	357	B5
114th Pl	20	237	B4	356	C1
114th Rd		238	A1	356	B3
150-00 - 180-99	34	238	A1	356	B3
181-00 - 205-99	12	232	C2	357	B4
216-00 - 229-99	11	232	C3	357	A5
114th St		202	B1	349	A5
1-00 - 14-99	56	202	B1	349	A5
37-00 - 43-99	68	211	C6	349	B5
84-00 - 93-99	18	230	C2	356	A1
94-00 - 107-99	19	237	A4	356	B1
109-00 - 150-99	20	237	B4	356	B1
114th Ter	11	233	C4	357	B5
115th Av		232	C2	357	B5
117-01 - 135-99	20	237	B5	356	B2
137-00 - 149-99	36	237	A6	356	B2
150-00 - 180-99	34	238	A1	356	B3
181-00 - 205-99	12	232	C2	357	B4
206-00 - 231-99	11	232	C3	357	B5
115th Ct	11	232	C3	357	A5
115th Dr		238	A1	356	B3
150-00 - 155-99	34	238	A1	356	B3
190-00 - 205-99	12	232	C2	357	B4
115th Rd		238	A1	356	B3
150-00 - 159-99	34	238	A1	356	B3
187-00 - 205-99	12	232	C2	357	B4
215-00 - 232-99	11	232	C3	357	B5
115th St		202	B1	349	A5
1-00 - 14-99	56	202	B1	349	A5
83-00 - 91-99	18	230	C2	356	A1
94-00 - 107-99	19	237	A4	356	B1
109-00 - 150-99	20	237	B5	356	B1
115th Ter	11	232	C3	357	B5
116th Av		237	B5	356	B2
122-01 - 135-99	20	237	B5	356	B2
137-00 - 149-99	36	237	B6	356	B2
150-00 - 180-99	34	238	A1	356	B3
181-00 - 205-99	12	232	C2	357	B4
206-00 - 233-99	11	232	C3	357	B5
116th Dr	34	238	A1	356	B3
116th Rd		237	B6	356	B2
142-00 - 142-99	36	237	B6	356	B2
150-00 - 155-99	34	238	A1	356	B3
189-00 - 205-99	12	239	A4	357	B4
206-00 - 209-99	11	232	C3	357	B5
116th St		202	B1	349	A5
1-00 - 14-99	56	202	B1	349	A5
82-00 - 91-99	18	230	C2	356	A1
94-00 - 107-99	19	237	A4	356	B1
109-00 - 150-99	20	237	B5	356	B1
117th Rd		237	B6	356	C2
132-00 - 132-99	20	237	B6	356	C2
189-00 - 194-99	12	239	A4	357	B4
216-00 - 216-99	11	232	C3	357	B5
117th St		202	B1	349	A5
1-00 - 14-99	56	202	B1	349	A5
83-00 - 91-99	18	230	C2	356	B1
94-00 - 107-99	19	237	A4	356	B1
109-00 - 154-99	20	237	B5	356	B2
118th Av		238	A2	356	B3
150-00 - 170-99	34	238	A2	356	B3
188-00 - 205-99	12	239	A4	357	B4
216-00 - 235-99	11	239	A5	357	B5
118th Rd		238	A2	356	B3
160-00 - 170-99	34	238	A2	356	B3
186-00 - 191-99	12	239	A4	357	B4
118th St		202	B1	349	A5
1-00 - 14-99	56	202	B1	349	A5
83-00 - 85-99	15	230	C2	356	A1
86-00 - 91-99	18	230	C2	356	B1
94-00 - 107-99	19	237	A4	356	B1
109-00 - 150-99	20	237	B5	356	B2
119th Av		238	B1	356	B3
143-00 - 149-99	36	238	B1	356	B3
150-00 - 172-99	34	238	A2	356	B3
188-00 - 205-99	12	239	A4	357	B4
216-00 - 236-99	11	239	A5	357	B5
119th Dr		238	A3	357	B4
160-00 - 161-99	34	238	A3	357	B4
187-00 - OUT	12	238	A3	357	B4
119th Rd		238	B1	356	B3
142-00 - 142-99	36	238	B1	356	B3
150-00 - 180-99	34	238	B1	356	B3
181-00 - 188-99	12	239	A4	357	B4
119th St		202	B2	349	A6
5-00 - 22-00	56	202	B2	349	A6
25-00 - 31-99	54	202	C2	349	B6
120th Av		237	B6	356	C2
132-00 - 135-99	20	237	B6	356	C2
137-00 - 148-99	36	237	B6	356	C2
150-00 - 180-99	34	238	A2	356	B3
181-00 - 203-99	12	239	A4	357	B4
216-00 - 237-99	11	239	A5	357	B5
120th Rd	12	239	A4	357	B4
120th St		202	C2	349	A6
9-00 - 23-00	56	202	C2	349	A6
25-00 - 31-99	54	202	C2	349	B6
84-00 - 85-99	15	230	C2	356	A1
86-00 - 91-99	18	230	C2	356	A1
94-00 - 107-99	19	237	A4	356	B1
109-00 - OUT	20	237	B5	356	B2
121st Av		238	A2	356	B3
150-00 - 161-99	34	238	A2	356	B3
186-00 - 201-99	12	239	A4	357	B4
216-00 - 238-99	11	232	C3	357	B5
121st St		202	C2	349	A6
9-00 - 23-00	56	202	C2	349	A6
25-00 - 32-99	54	202	C2	349	B6
84-00 - 85-99	15	230	C2	356	A1
86-00 - 91-99	18	230	C2	356	A1
94-00 - 107-99	19	237	A4	356	B1
109-00 - OUT	20	237	B5	356	B2
122nd Av		238	B1	356	C3
142-00 - 142-99	36	238	B1	356	C3
150-00 - 64-99	34	238	A2	356	B3
186-00 - 201-99	13	239	A4	357	B4
122nd Pl	20	237	B5	356	C2
122nd St		202	C3	349	B6
28-01 - 29-99	54	202	C3	349	B6
84-00 - 85-99	15	230	C2	356	A1
86-00 - 86-99	18	230	C2	356	A1
104-00 - 107-99	19	237	A5	356	B2
109-00 - OUT	20	237	B5	356	B2
123rd Av		237	B6	356	C2
140-00 - 147-99	36	237	B6	356	C2
150-00 - 154-99	34	238	B1	356	B3
123rd St		202	B2	349	A6
5-00 - 23-00	56	202	B2	349	A6
25-00 - 32-99	54	202	C2	349	A6
84-00 - 85-99	15	230	C2	356	A1
86-00 - 87-99	18	230	C2	356	A1
93-00 - 107-99	19	237	A5	356	B2
109-00 - OUT	20	237	B5	356	B2
124th Av	34	238	B1	356	B3
124th Pl	15	230	C2	356	A1
124th St		202	B2	349	A6
5-00 - 23-00	56	202	B2	349	A6
25-00 - 32-99	54	202	C2	349	A6
84-00 - 85-99	15	230	C2	356	A1
86-00 - 87-99	18	230	C2	356	A1
93-00 - 107-99	19	237	A5	356	B2
109-00 - OUT	20	237	B5	356	B2
125th Av		238	A3	357	B4
150-00 - 177-99	34	238	A3	357	B4
181-00 - 232-99	13	239	A6	357	B5
125th St		202	B2	349	A6
3-00 - 23-00	56	202	B2	349	A6
25-00 - 32-99	54	202	C2	349	A6
83-00 - 85-99	15	230	B2	356	A1
86-00 - 87-99	18	230	C2	356	A1
94-00 - 107-00	19	237	A5	356	B2
109-00 - 152-99	20	237	B5	356	B2
126th Av		238	B3	357	B4
168-00 - 176-99	34	238	B3	357	B4
231-00 - 232-99	13	239	A6	357	B5
126th Pl	68	218	A1	349	B6
126th St		202	B2	349	A6
3-00 - 23-00	56	202	B2	349	A6
25-00 - 32-99	54	202	C2	349	A6
33-00 - 40-90	68	218	A1	349	B6
84-00 - 85-99	15	230	C2	356	A1
86-00 - 89-99	18	230	C2	356	A1
94-00 - 107-99	19	237	A5	356	B2
109-00 - OUT	20	237	B5	356	B2
127th Av	34	238	B3	357	B4
127th Pl	68	218	A1	349	B6
127th St		202	B2	349	A6
3-00 - 23-00	56	202	B2	349	A6
25-00 - 32-99	54	202	C2	349	A6
33-00 - 35-99	68	218	A1	349	B6
84-00 - 85-99	15	230	C2	356	A1
86-00 - 89-99	18	230	C3	356	A2
94-00 - 107-99	19	237	A5	356	B2
109-00 - OUT	20	237	A5	356	B2
128th Av		238	B2	356	C3
157-00 - 174-99	34	238	B2	356	C3
231-00 - 232-99	13	239	A6	357	B5
233-00 - 240-99	22	239	A6	357	B5
128th Dr		239	A6	357	B5
231-00 - 232-99	13	239	A6	357	B5
240-00 - OUT	22	239	B6	357	B5
128th Rd		239	A6	357	B5
231-00 - 232-99	13	239	A6	357	B5
240-00 - OUT	22	239	B6	357	B5
128th St		202	B2	349	A6
5-00 - 23-00	56	202	B2	349	A6
104-00 - 107-99	19	237	A5	356	B2
109-00 - 152-99	20	237	A5	356	B2
129th Av		238	B1	356	C3
142-00 - 146-99	36	238	B1	356	C3
156-00 - 180-99	34	238	B2	356	C3
181-00 - 232-99	13	239	A5	357	B5
233-00 - OUT	22	239	B6	357	B5
129th Rd	22	239	B6	357	B5
129th St		202	B2	349	A6
5-00 - 23-00	56	202	B2	349	A6
84-00 - 85-99	15	230	C3	356	A2
86-00 - 89-99	18	230	C3	356	A2
94-00 - 107-99	19	237	A5	356	B2
118-00 - OUT	20	237	C5	356	C2
130th Av		237	B6	356	C2
114-00 - 135-99	20	237	B6	356	C2
137-00 - 149-99	36	237	B6	356	C2
150-00 - 180-99	34	238	B2	356	C3
181-00 - 232-99	13	239	A5	357	B4
233-00 - 245-99	22	239	B6	357	B5
130th Dr	13	239	A5	357	B5
130th Pl		237	C6	356	C2
133-01 - 135-99	20	237	C6	356	C2
133-01 - 135-99	30	237	C6	356	C2
130th Rd		238	B3	357	B4
178-00 - 180-99	34	238	B3	357	B4
219-00 - 219-99	13	239	A5	357	B5
242-00 - 243-99	22	239	B6	357	B5
130th St		202	C2	349	A6
7-00 - 23-00	56	202	C2	349	A6
84-00 - 85-99	15	230	C3	356	A2
86-00 - 91-99	18	230	C3	356	A2
94-00 - 107-99	19	237	A5	356	B2
109-00 - OUT	20	237	B6	356	B2
131st Av		237	B6	356	C2
130-00 - 135-99	20	237	B6	356	C2
137-00 - 142-99	36	237	B6	356	C2
159-00 - 178-99	34	238	B2	356	C3
216-00 - 232-99	13	239	A5	357	B4
233-00 - OUT	22	239	B6	357	B4
131st Rd	22	239	B6	357	B5
131st St		202	B2	349	A6
11-00 - 18-00	56	202	B2	349	A6
85-00 - 85-99	15	230	C3	356	A2
86-00 - 87-99	18	230	C3	356	A2
94-00 - 107-99	19	237	A5	356	B2
109-00 - 135-99	20	237	B6	356	B2
140-00 - OUT	30	237	C6	356	C2
132nd Av		238	B2	356	C3
73-00 - 180-99	34	238	B2	356	C3
181-00 - 219-99	13	239	A4	357	B4
241-00 - 243-99	22	239	B6	357	B5
132nd Rd		239	A4	357	B4
216-00 - 219-99	13	239	A4	357	B4
241-00 - 243-99	22	239	B6	357	B5
132nd St		202	B3	349	A6
1-00 - 24-99	56	202	B3	349	A6
86-00 - 89-99	18	230	C3	356	B2
94-00 - 107-99	19	237	A5	356	B2
109-00 - 135-99	20	237	B6	356	B2
140-00 - OUT	30	237	C6	356	C2
133rd Av		236	B2	355	C6
75-00 - 78-99	14	236	B2	355	C6
79-00 - 107-99	17	236	B2	355	C6
108-00 - 135-99	20	237	B6	356	C2
137-00 - 149-99	36	237	C6	356	C2
151-00 - 180-99	34	238	B2	356	C3
181-00 - 232-99	13	239	B5	357	B5
233-00 - OUT	22	239	B6	357	C5
133rd Dr	22	239	B6	357	C5
133rd Pl	56	202	B3	349	A6
133rd Rd		238	B3	357	B4
176-00 - 180-99	34	238	B3	357	B4
181-00 - 218-99	13	239	B4	357	B4
245-00 - OUT	22	239	B6	357	C5
133rd St		218	B2	349	C6
55-01 - 55-99	55	218	B2	349	C6
87-00 - 89-99	18	230	C3	356	A2
94-00 - 107-99	19	237	A5	356	B2
109-00 - 135-99	20	237	B6	356	B2
140-00 - 140-99	13	239	B4	357	B4
134th Av		236	B3	356	C1
94-00 - 97-99	17	236	B3	356	C1
132-00 - 135-99	20	237	C6	356	C2
137-00 - 137-99	36	237	C6	356	C2
151-00 - 179-99	34	238	C2	356	C3
242-00 - 246-99	22	239	B6	357	C5
134th Pl	20	237	C6	356	C2
134th Rd		236	B3	356	C1
96-00 - 97-99	17	236	B3	356	C1
165-00 - 165-99	34	238	B3	357	C4
217-00 - 223-99	13	239	B4	357	B4
234-00 - OUT	22	239	B6	357	C5
134th St		218	B2	349	C6
41-00 - 60-99	55	218	B2	349	C6
61-00 - 61-99	67	218	C2	349	C6
80-00 - 82-99	35	230	B3	356	A2
86-00 - 89-99	18	230	C3	356	A2
94-00 - 107-99	19	237	A5	356	B2
109-01 - 135-99	20	237	B6	356	B2
148-00 - OUT	30	237	C6	356	C2
135th Av		237	B5	356	C1
75-00 - 135-99	20	237	B5	356	C2
137-00 - 149-99	36	238	C1	356	C3
150-00 - 180-99	34	238	C2	356	C3
181-00 - 228-99	13	239	B4	357	B4
234-00 - 247-99	22	239	B6	357	C5
135th Dr	17	236	B3	356	C1
135th Pl	20	237	B6	356	C2
135th Rd		236	B3	356	C1
97-00 - 97-99	17	236	B3	356	C1
246-00 - 247-99	22	239	B6	357	C5
135th St		202	B3	349	A6
11-00 - 18-00	56	202	B3	349	A6
41-00 - 60-99	55	218	B2	349	C6
61-00 - 79-99	67	218	C2	349	C6
80-00 - 82-99	35	230	B3	356	A2
86-00 - 89-99	18	230	C3	356	A2
102-00 - 107-99	19	237	A5	356	B2
109-00 - 135-99	20	237	B6	356	B2
136th Av		238	B3	357	B4
93-00 - 180-99	34	238	B3	357	B4
181-00 - 221-99	13	239	B4	357	B4
234-00 - 247-99	22	239	B6	357	C5
136th Rd		239	B4	357	B4
216-00 - 217-99	13	239	B4	357	B4
244-00 - 247-99	22	239	C6	357	C5
136th St		202	B3	349	A6
11-00 - 18-00	56	202	B3	349	A6
41-00 - 60-99	55	218	B2	349	C6
61-00 - 79-99	67	218	C2	349	C6
86-00 - 88-99	18	230	C3	356	A2
137th Av		238	C2	356	C3
181-00 - 232-99	13	239	B4	357	C4
233-00 - 247-99	22	239	C6	357	C5
137th Pl	55	218	B3	350	C2
137th Rd		239	B4	357	B4
217-00 - 220-99	13	239	B4	357	B4
235-00 - 247-99	22	239	C6	357	C5
137th St		202	B3	349	A6
11-00 - 18-00	56	202	B3	349	A6
25-00 - 40-99	54	202	C3	349	B6
41-00 - 60-99	55	218	B2	349	C6
61-00 - 88-99	67	218	C2	349	C6
138th Av		239	B4	357	C5
152-00 - 180-99	34	238	B3	357	C4
181-00 - 232-99	13	239	B4	357	C4
233-00 - 244-99	22	239	C6	357	C5
138th Pl	35	230	C3	356	B2
138th Rd	13	239	B4	357	C4
138th St		202	B3	349	A6
11-00 - 18-00	56	202	B3	349	A6
25-00 - 40-99	54	202	C3	349	B6
41-00 - 60-99	55	218	B2	349	C6
61-00 - 79-99	67	218	C2	349	C6
80-00 - 111-99	35	230	B3	356	A2
114-00 - 115-99	36	237	B6	356	C2
139th Av		239	B4	357	C4
186-00 - 232-99	13	239	B4	357	C4
233-00 - 253-99	22	239	C6	357	C5
139th Rd	34	238	B3	357	C4
139th St		202	B3	349	A6
13-00 - 14-00	57	202	B3	349	A6
25-00 - 40-99	54	202	C3	349	B6
61-00 - 79-99	67	230	A2	349	C6
81-00 - 111-99	35	230	B3	356	A2
114-00 - 119-99	36	237	B6	356	B2
140th Av		238	C2	356	C3
153-00 - 180-99	34	238	C2	356	C3
181-00 - 219-99	13	239	B4	357	C4
241-00 - OUT	22	239	C6	357	C5
140th St		202	B3	349	A6
13-00 - 14-00	57	202	B3	349	A6
25-00 - 40-99	54	202	C3	349	B6
61-00 - 79-99	67	230	A2	349	C6
111-00 - 111-99	35	237	A6	356	B2
114-00 - 135-99	36	237	B6	356	B2
141st Av		238	B3	357	C4
180-00 - 180-99	34	238	B3	357	C4
181-00 - 232-99	13	239	B4	357	C4
233-00 - 241-99	22	239	C5	357	C5
141st Pl	67	230	A3	356	A2
141st Rd	13	239	B4	357	C4
141st St		202	B3	349	A6
13-00 - 14-99	57	202	B3	349	A6
25-00 - 40-99	54	202	C3	349	B6
56-00 - 56-99	55	218	B3	350	C2
61-00 - 79-99	67	218	C2	349	C6
82-00 - 111-99	35	230	B3	356	A2
114-00 - 120-99	36	237	A6	356	B2
142nd Av		238	B3	357	C4
167-00 - 179-99	34	238	B3	357	C4
240-00 - 241-99	22	239	C5	357	C5
142nd Pl	36	238	B1	356	B3
142nd Rd	13	239	C4	357	C4
142nd St		202	B3	349	A6
13-00 - 14-99	57	202	B3	349	A6
56-00 - 60-99	55	218	B3	350	C2
103-00 - 111-99	35	237	A6	356	B2
114-00 - 135-99	36	238	B1	356	B2
143rd Av		238	B3	357	C4
179-00 - 180-99	34	238	B3	357	C4
181-00 - 232-99	13	239	C4	357	C4
233-00 - 247-99	22	239	C5	357	C5
143rd Pl	57	202	B3	349	A6
143rd Rd		238	B3	357	C4
170-00 - 180-99	34	238	B3	357	C4
181-00 - 225-99	13	239	C4	357	C4
143rd St		202	B3	349	A6
13-00 - 23-99	57	202	B3	349	A6
29-00 - 33-99	54	202	C3	349	B6
84-00 - 111-99	35	230	B3	356	A2
114-00 - 135-99	36	238	B1	356	B2
144th Av		238	C3	357	C4
162-00 - 180-99	34	238	C3	357	C4
181-00 - 230-99	13	239	C4	357	C4
240-00 - 243-99	22	239	C5	357	C5
144th Dr	34	238	C2	356	C3
144th Pl		203	B4	350	A2
13-00 - 14-99	57	203	B4	350	A2
90-00 - 91-99	35	231	C4	356	A2
144th Rd	13	239	C4	357	C4
	34	238	C2	356	C3
144th St		203	B4	350	A2
15-01 - 23-99	57	203	B4	350	A2
85-00 - 111-99	35	230	B3	356	A2
114-00 - 135-99	36	238	B1	356	B2
144th Ter	34	238	C2	356	C3
145th Av		238	C2	356	C3
155-00 - 180-99	34	238	C2	356	C3
181-00 - 231-99	13	239	C4	357	C4
240-00 - 259-99	22	239	C5	357	C5
145th Dr		238	C2	356	C3
154-00 - 180-99	34	238	C2	356	C3
181-00 - 183-99	13	238	C3	357	C4
145th Pl		203	B4	350	A2
1300 - 1500	57	203	B4	350	A2
29-00 - 33-99	54	218	A3	350	B2
145th Rd		238	C2	356	C3
157-00 - 180-99	34	238	C2	356	C3
181-00 - 227-99	13	239	C4	357	C4
145th St		218	A3	350	B2
1-00 - 24-99	57	203	C4	350	B2
25-00 - 40-99	54	218	A3	350	B2
88-00 - 111-99	35	231	C4	356	A2
114-00 - 133-99	36	238	B1	356	B3
146th Av		238	C2	356	C3
156-00 - 180-99	34	238	C2	356	C3
181-00 - 231-99	13	239	C4	357	C4
240-00 - 241-99	22	239	C5	357	C5
146th Dr	13	238	C3	357	C4
146th Pl		203	B4	350	A2
1300 - 1500	57	203	B4	350	A2
61-00 - 61-99	67	218	C3	350	C2
146th Rd		238	C3	357	C4
167-00 - 180-99	34	238	C3	357	C4
181-00 - 183-99	13	238	C3	357	C4
146th St		203	B4	350	A2
1-00 - 24-99	57	203	B4	350	A2
25-00 - 40-99	54	203	C4	350	A2
41-00 - 60-99	55	218	B3	350	C2
61-00 - 79-99	67	218	C3	350	C2
87-00 - 111-99	35	231	C4	356	A2
114-00 - 133-99	36	238	B1	356	B3
146th Ter		238	C3	357	C4
178-00 - 180-99	34	238	C3	357	C4
181-00 - 183-99	13	238	C3	357	C4
147th Av		238	C3	357	C4
150-00 - 180-99	34	238	C3	357	C4
181-00 - 232-99	13	239	C4	357	C4
233-00 - 245-99	22	239	C5	357	C5
147th Dr	22	243	A5	357	C5
147th Pl		203	A4	350	A2
200 - 300	57	203	A4	350	A2
25-00 - 40-99	54	203	C4	350	B2
92-00 - 97-99	35	231	C4	356	A2
147th Rd	22	243	A5	357	C5
147th St		203	B4	350	A2
1-00 - 24-99	57	203	B4	350	A2
25-00 - 40-99	54	203	C4	350	B2
41-00 - 60-99	55	218	A3	350	B2
61-00 - 79-99	67	230	A3	350	C2
110-00 - 111-99	35	238	A1	356	B3
114-00 - 133-99	36	238	B1	356	C3
148th Av		238	C3	357	C4
167-00 - 176-99	34	238	C3	357	C4
225-00 - 231-99	13	239	C4	357	C4
253-00 - 257-99	22	243	A5	357	C5
148th Dr	13	238	C3	357	C4
	22	243	A5	357	C5
148th Pl		218	C3	350	C2
61-00 - 61-99	67	218	C3	350	C2
91-00 - 91-99	35	231	C4	356	A2
148th Rd		238	C3	357	C4
167-00 - 175-99	34	238	C3	357	C4
235-00 - 259-99	22	243	A5	357	C5
148th St		203	A4	350	A2
1-00 - 24-99	57	203	A4	350	A2
25-00 - 40-99	54	203	C4	350	A2
41-00 - 60-99	55	218	C3	350	C2
61-00 - 79-99	67	218	C3	350	C2
110-00 - 111-99	35	238	A1	356	B3
114-00 - 133-99	36	238	A1	356	B3
149th Av		236	C2	355	C6
78-00 - 87-99	14	236	C2	355	C6
94-00 - 107-99	17	236	B3	356	C1
108-00 - 135-99	20	237	C5	356	C2
175-00 - 179-99	34	238	C3	357	C4
182-00 - 232-99	13	238	C3	357	C4
233-00 - OUT	22	243	A5	357	C5
149th Dr	22	243	A6	357	C5
149th Pl		203	A4	350	A2
200 - 300	57	203	A4	350	A2
25-00 - 40-99	54	218	A3	350	B2
41-00 - 60-99	55	218	A3	350	B2
149th Rd		238	C3	357	C4
169-00 - 180-99	34	238	C3	357	C4
181-00 - 182-99	13	238	C3	357	C4
236-00 - OUT	22	243	A6	357	C5
149th St		203	B4	350	A2
1-00 - 24-99	57	203	B4	350	A2
25-00 - 40-99	54	203	C4	350	A2
41-00 - 60-99	55	218	A3	350	B2
61-00 - 79-99	67	218	C3	350	C2
85-00 - 95-99	35	231	C4	356	A2
114-00 - 133-99	36	238	A1	356	B3
150th Av		237	C5	356	C1
114-00 - 129-99	20	237	C5	356	C1
130-00 - 130-99	30	237	C6	356	C2
175-01 - 179-01	34	238	C3	357	C4
182-00 - 183-99	13	238	C3	357	C4
150th Dr	13	242	A3	357	C4
150th Pl		203	B5	350	A2
600 - 16-00	57	203	B5	350	A2
25-00 - 40-99	54	218	A3	350	B2
150th Rd		236	C3	356	C1
95-00 - 95-99	17	236	C3	356	C1
179-00 - 179-99	34	242	A3	357	C4
182-00 - 183-99	13	242	A3	357	C4
150th St		203	B4	350	A2
200 - 24-00	57	203	B4	350	A2
24-00 - 40-99	54	203	C4	350	B2
41-00 - 60-99	55	218	A3	350	B2
61-00 - 79-99	67	230	A3	350	C2
80-00 - 107-99	35	231	C4	356	A2
130-00 - 174-99	36	238	C1	356	C3
151st Av	14	236	C3	356	C1
151st Dr	13	242	A3	357	C4
151st Pl	34	238	C2	356	C3
151st St		203	A4	350	A2
600 - 799	57	203	A4	350	A2
54-00 - 54-99	55	218	B3	350	C2
84-00 - 88-99	32	231	B4	356	A2
92-00 - 92-99	33	231	C4	356	A2
152nd Av	20	237	C5	356	C2
152nd St		203	A5	350	A2
600 - 14-00	57	203	A5	350	A2
25-00 - 40-99	54	203	C5	350	B2
41-00 - 60-99	55	218	B3	350	C2
61-00 - 79-99	67	218	C3	350	C2
84-00 - 88-99	32	231	B4	356	A2
118-00 - 123-99	34	238	B1	356	B3
153rd Av	14	236	C2	355	C6
153rd Ct	34	238	C2	356	C3
153rd La	34	238	C2	356	C3
153rd Pl		203	B5	350	A2
15-00 - 15-99	57	203	B5	350	A2
144-00 - OUT	34	238	C2	356	C3
153rd Rd	67	230	A3	350	C2
153rd St		219	A4	350	B2
25-00 - 40-99	54	219	A4	350	B2
41-00 - 60-99	55	218	C3	350	C2
61-00 - 79-99	67	230	A3	350	C2
87-00 - 90-99	32	231	C4	356	A2
92-00 - 113-99	33	238	A1	356	B3
114-00 - 129-99	34	238	B1	356	B3
153rd Wy	34	238	C2	356	C3
154th Pl		203	A5	350	A2
600 - 8-59	57	203	A5	350	A2
59-00 - 59-99	55	218	C3	350	C2
154th St		203	B5	350	A2
700 - 24-00	57	203	B5	350	A2
25-00 - 40-99	54	203	C5	350	B2
41-00 - 60-99	55	203	C5	350	B2
61-00 - 73-99	67	231	A4	356	A2
106-00 - 113-99	33	231	C4	356	B2

Queens

114-00 - 140-99	34	238	B2	356	C3
155th Av	14	236	C3	356	C1
155th St		203	B5	350	A2
14-00 - 16-00	57	203	B5	350	A2
25-00 - 40-99	54	219	A4	350	B2
41-00 - 60-99	55	219	A4	350	B2
61-00 - 79-99	67	218	C3	350	C2
106-00 - 113-99	33	231	C5	356	B3
114-00 - 147-99	34	238	B2	356	C3
156th Av	14	236	C2	355	C6
156th Ct	54	203	C5	350	B2
156th Pl	33	231	C4	356	B2
156th St		203	B5	350	A2
14-00 - 16-00	57	203	B5	350	A2
25-00 - 40-99	54	219	A4	350	B2
41-00 - 60-99	55	219	B4	350	B2
61-00 - 79-99	67	218	C3	350	C2
105-00 - 113-99	33	231	C5	356	B3
114-00 - 146-99	34	238	B2	356	C3
157th Av	14	236	C2	355	C6
157th St		203	B5	350	A2
7-00 - 24-99	57	203	B5	350	A2
24-00 - 40-99	54	219	A4	350	B2
41-00 - 60-99	55	219	B4	350	B2
61-00 - 79-99	67	219	C4	350	C2
95-00 - 113-99	33	231	C5	356	B3
114-00 -146-99	34	238	A1	356	B3
158th Av	14	236	C2	355	C6
158th St		203	B5	350	A2
600 - 14-00	57	203	B5	350	A2
25-00 - 47-99	58	219	A4	350	B2
48-00 - 72-99	65	219	C4	350	C2
94-00 - 113-99	33	231	C4	356	A2
114-00 - 145-99	34	238	B2	356	C3
159th Av	14	236	C3	356	C1
159th Rd	14	237	C4	356	C1
159th St		203	B5	350	A2
600 - 15-00	57	203	B5	350	A2
25-00 - 47-99	58	219	A4	350	B2
48-00 - 72-99	65	219	C4	350	C2
73-00 - 79-99	66	231	A4	356	B3
80-00 - 90-99	32	231	B4	356	A2
92-00 - 113-99	33	231	C5	356	B3
114-00 - 145-99	34	238	B2	356	C3
160th Av	14	240	A2	355	C6
160th St		203	B5	350	A2
6-00 - 24-00	57	203	B5	350	A2
25-00 - 47-99	58	219	A4	350	B2
48-00 - 72-99	65	219	C4	350	C2
73-00 - 79-99	66	231	A4	350	C2
80-00 - 90-99	32	231	B4	356	A2
92-00 - 113-99	33	231	C5	356	B3
114-00 - 140-99	34	238	B2	356	B3
161st Av	14	240	A2	355	C6
161st Pl	34	238	B1	356	B3
161st St		203	B5	350	A2
6-00 - 14-00	57	203	B5	350	A2
25-00 - 47-99	58	219	A4	350	B2
48-00 - 72-99	65	219	C4	350	C2
73-00 - 79-99	66	231	A4	356	A2
80-00 - 90-99	32	231	B4	356	A2
92-00 - 113-99	33	231	C5	356	A3
114-00 - 144-99	34	238	B2	356	B3
162nd Av	14	240	A3	356	C1
162nd St		203	B5	350	A2
7-00 - 14-00	57	203	B5	350	A2
25-00 - 47-99	58	219	A4	350	B2
48-00 - 72-99	65	219	C4	350	C2
73-00 - 79-99	66	231	A4	350	C2
80-00 - 89-99	32	231	B4	356	A2
92-00 - 113-99	33	231	C5	356	A3
114-00 - 144-99	33	231	C5	356	A3
163rd Av	14	240	A3	356	C1
163rd Dr	14	241	A4	356	C1
163rd Pl	58	219	B4	350	B2
163rd St		203	C5	350	A2
14-00 - 24-99	57	203	C5	350	A3
25-00 - 47-99	58	219	A4	350	B2
48-00 - 78-99	65	219	C4	350	C2
88-00 - OUT	32	231	B5	356	A3
164th Av	14	240	A3	364	A1
164th Dr	14	241	A4	356	C1
164th Pl		231	B4	356	A2
80-00 - 83-99	32	231	B4	356	A2
103-00 - 113-99	33	231	C5	356	B3
164th Rd	14	241	A4	356	C1
164th St		203	B6	350	A3
14-00 - 24-99	57	203	B6	350	A3
25-00 - 47-99	58	219	A4	350	B2
48-00 - 72-99	65	219	C4	350	C2
73-00 - 78-99	66	231	A4	356	A2
79-00 - 89-99	32	231	B5	356	A2
103-00 - 110-99	33	231	C5	356	A3
116-00 - 120-99	34	238	A2	356	B3
165th Av	14	240	A3	364	A1
165th St		203	B6	350	A3
14-00 - 24-99	57	203	B6	350	A3
25-00 - 47-99	58	219	A4	350	B2
48-00 - 72-99	65	219	C4	350	C2
73-00 - 78-99	66	231	A4	356	A2
80-00 - 89-99	32	231	B4	356	A2
92-00 - 113-99	33	231	C5	356	A3
114-00 - 120-99	34	238	A2	356	B3
166th Pl	34	238	B3	357	C4
166th St		203	B6	350	A3
7-00 - 24-00	57	203	B6	350	A3
25-00 - 47-99	58	219	A4	350	B2
48-00 - 72-99	65	219	C4	350	C2
73-00 - 78-99	66	231	A4	350	C2
80-00 - 91-99	32	231	A4	356	A2
92-00 - 113-99	33	238	A2	356	B3
114-00 - 146-99	34	238	A2	356	B3
167th St		219	A5	350	B3
25-00 - 47-99	58	219	A5	350	B3
48-00 - 72-99	65	219	C4	350	C2
73-00 - 78-99	66	231	A4	350	C2
80-00 - 87-99	32	231	B5	356	A2
114-00 - 145-99	34	238	A2	356	B3
168th Pl		231	B5	356	A3
83-00 - 89-99	32	231	B5	356	A3
92-00 - 103-99	33	231	C5	356	A3
137-00 - OUT	34	238	A2	356	B3
168th St		219	A5	350	B3
25-00 - 47-99	58	219	A5	350	B3
48-00 - 72-99	65	219	C4	350	C2
73-00 - 79-99	66	231	A4	350	C2
80-00 - 91-99	32	231	B5	356	A2
92-00 - 113-99	33	231	C5	356	A3
114-00 - 142-99	34	238	A2	356	B3
169th Pl	33	231	C6	356	B3
169th St		203	C6	350	A3
18-00 - 24-00	57	203	C6	350	A3
25-00 - 47-99	58	219	A5	350	B3
48-00 - 72-99	65	219	C4	350	C3
73-00 - 78-99	66	231	A4	350	C2
80-00 - 91-99	32	231	B5	356	A3
170th Pl	65	219	B5	350	C3
170th St		219	A5	350	B3
25-00 - 47-99	58	219	A5	350	B3
48-00 - 72-99	65	219	C5	350	C3
73-00 - 77-99	66	231	A5	350	C3
80-00 - 91-99	32	231	B5	356	A3
92-00 - 113-99	33	231	C5	356	A3
114-00 - 151-99	34	238	A2	356	B3
171st Pl		219	B5	350	B3
25-00 - 47-99	58	219	B5	350	B3
105-00 - 110-99	33	231	C6	356	A3
171st St		219	A5	350	B3
25-00 - 47-99	58	219	A5	350	B3
48-00 - 72-99	65	219	C5	350	C3
73-00 - 77-99	66	231	A5	350	C3
84-00 - 91-99	32	231	B5	356	A3
103-00 - 113-99	33	231	C6	356	A3
114-00 - 140-99	34	238	A2	356	B3
172nd St		219	A5	350	B3
25-00 - 47-99	58	219	A5	350	B3
48-00 - 72-99	65	219	C5	350	C3
73-00 - 77-99	66	231	A5	350	C3
82-00 - 91-99	32	231	B5	356	A3
92-00 - 113-99	33	231	C6	356	A3
114-00 - 140-99	34	238	A2	356	B3
173rd St		219	C5	350	C3
48-00 - 72-99	65	219	C5	350	C3
73-00 - 77-99	66	231	A5	350	C3
87-00 - 91-99	32	231	B5	356	A3
92-00 - 113-99	33	231	C6	356	A3
114-00 - 140-99	34	238	A2	356	B3
174th Pl	34	238	B3	357	B4
174th St		219	C5	350	C3
48-00 - 72-99	65	219	C5	350	C3
73-00 - 77-99	66	231	A5	350	C3
108-00 - 111-99	33	231	C6	356	B3
114-00 - 142-99	34	238	A2	356	B3
175th Pl		219	C5	350	C3
49-00 - 56-99	65	219	C5	350	C3
112-00 - 113-99	33	231	C6	356	B3
114-00 - 115-99	34	238	A3	357	B4
175th St		219	C5	350	C3
48-00 - 72-99	65	219	C5	350	C3
73-00 - 77-99	66	231	A5	350	C3
87-00 - 91-99	32	231	B6	356	A3
92-00 - 113-99	33	231	C6	356	A3
114-00 - 148-99	34	238	A2	356	A3
176th Pl	34	238	B3	357	B4
176th St		231	A5	350	C3
73-00 - 77-99	66	231	A5	350	C3
90-00 - 90-99	32	231	B6	356	A3
92-00 - 113-99	33	231	C6	356	A3
114-00 - 146-99	34	238	B3	357	B4
177th Pl	33	231	B6	356	A3
177th St		231	A5	350	C3
73-00 - 72-99	66	231	A5	350	C3
92-00 - 113-99	33	231	C6	356	A3
114-00 - 151-99	34	238	B3	357	B4
178th Pl		231	B6	356	A3
92-00 - 113-99	33	231	B6	356	A3
114-00 - 145-99	34	238	A3	357	B4
178th St		219	C5	350	C3
48-00 - 72-99	65	219	C5	350	C3
73-00 - 75-99	66	231	A5	350	C3
83-00 - 91-99	32	231	B6	356	A3
92-00 - 113-99	33	231	C6	356	A3
114-00 - 131-99	34	238	A3	357	B4
179th Pl		231	B6	356	A3
88-00 - 90-99	32	231	B6	356	A3
92-00 - OUT	33	231	B6	356	A3
179th St		219	C5	350	C3
48-00 - 72-99	65	219	C5	350	C3
73-00 - 75-99	66	231	A5	350	C3
88-00 - 90-99	32	231	B6	356	A3
111-00 - 113-99	33	231	C6	356	B3
114-00 - 145-99	34	238	A3	357	B4
180th Pl	33	231	B6	356	A3
180th St		219	C5	350	C3
48-00 - 72-99	65	219	C5	350	C3
73-00 - 75-99	66	231	A5	350	C3
88-00 - 91-99	32	231	B6	356	A3
92-00 - 113-99	33	231	C6	356	A3
114-00 - 145-99	34	238	A3	357	B4
181st Pl		231	B6	356	A3
92-00 - 92-99	33	231	B6	356	A3
143-00 - 144-99	13	238	C3	357	C4
181st St		219	C5	350	C3
48-00 - 72-99	65	219	C5	350	C3
73-00 - 75-99	66	231	A5	350	C3
88-00 - 92-99	23	231	B6	356	A3
140-00 - 147-99	13	239	C4	357	C4
182nd Pl		231	B6	356	A3
88-00 - 92-99	23	231	B6	356	A3
143-00 - OUT	13	238	C3	357	C4
182nd St		219	C5	350	C3
48-00 - 72-99	65	219	C5	350	C3
73-00 - 75-99	66	231	A5	350	C3
88-00 - 93-99	23	231	B6	356	A3
139-00 - 150-99	13	238	C3	357	C4
183rd Pl	12	232	C1	357	A4
183rd St		219	C5	350	C3
48-00 - 72-99	65	219	C5	350	C3
73-00 - 75-99	66	231	A6	350	C3
88-00 - 93-99	23	231	B6	356	A3
137-00 - 147-99	13	238	C3	357	C4
184th Pl	23	231	B6	356	A3
184th St		219	C5	350	C3
48-00 - 72-99	65	219	C5	350	C3
73-00 - 75-99	66	231	A6	350	C3
88-00 - 102-99	23	231	B6	356	A3
104-00 - 104-99	12	232	C1	357	A4
141-00 - 147-99	13	238	C3	357	C4
185th St		219	C5	350	C3
48-00 - 72-99	65	219	C5	350	C3
73-00 - 75-99	66	231	A6	350	C3
88-00 - 102-99	23	231	B6	356	A3
104-00 - 104-99	12	232	C1	357	A4
141-00 - 146-99	13	239	B4	357	C4
186th La	65	219	C6	350	C3
186th St		219	C5	350	C3
48-00 - 72-99	65	219	C5	350	C3
73-00 - 75-99	66	231	A6	350	C3
88-00 - 103-99	23	231	B6	356	A3
104-00 - OUT	12	232	C1	357	A4
187th Pl	23	232	B1	357	A4
187th St		219	C5	350	C3
25-00 - 47-99	58	219	B5	350	B3
48-00 - 72-99	65	219	C5	350	C3
73-00 - 75-99	66	231	A6	350	C3
88-00 - 103-99	23	232	B1	357	A4
104-00 - 105-99	12	232	C1	357	A4
188th St		219	B5	350	B3
25-00 - 47-99	58	219	B5	350	B3
48-00 - 72-99	65	219	C6	350	C3
73-00 - 75-99	66	231	A6	350	C3
80-00 - 103-99	23	231	A6	350	C3
104-00 - 105-99	12	232	C1	357	A4
189th St		219	A5	350	B3
25-00 - 47-99	58	219	A5	350	B3
48-00 - 72-99	65	219	B5	350	C3
73-00 - 75-99	66	231	A6	350	C3
80-00 - 103-99	23	231	A6	350	C3
104-00 - 120-99	12	232	C1	357	A4
190th La	65	219	C6	350	C3
190th Pl	12	232	C1	357	A4
190th St		219	A5	350	B3
25-00 - 47-99	58	219	A5	350	B3
48-00 - 72-99	65	219	B5	350	C3
73-00 - 75-99	66	219	C6	350	C3
80-00 - 97-99	23	231	A6	350	C3
116-00 - 120-99	12	239	A4	357	B4
121-00 - 122-99 (Lucas St)	13	239	A4	357	B4
191st St		219	A5	350	B3
25-00 - 47-99	58	219	A5	350	B3
85-00 - 103-99	23	232	B1	357	A4
104-00 - 120-99	12	232	C1	357	A4
121-00 - 122-99	13	239	A4	357	B4
192nd St		219	A5	350	B3
25-00 - 47-99	58	219	A5	350	B3
48-00 - 72-99	65	219	C6	350	C3
73-00 - 75-99	66	219	C6	350	C3
80-00 - 103-99	23	232	B1	357	A4
104-00 - 120-99	12	232	C1	357	A4
121-00 - 122-99	13	239	A4	357	B4
193rd La	65	219	C6	350	C3
193rd St		219	A5	350	B3
25-00 - 47-99	58	219	A5	350	B3
48-00 - 72-99	65	219	B6	350	C3
73-00 - 75-99	66	219	C6	350	C3
80-00 - 103-99	23	232	B1	357	A4
104-00 - 120-99	12	232	C1	357	A4
121-00 - 124-99	13	239	A4	357	B4
194th La	65	219	C6	350	C3
194th St		219	A5	350	B3
25-00 - 47-99	58	219	A5	350	B3
48-00 - 72-99	65	219	B6	350	B3
73-00 - 75-99	66	219	C6	350	C3
99-00 - 103-99	23	232	B1	357	A4
104-00 - 120-99	12	232	C2	357	A4
121-00 - 122-99	13	239	A4	357	B4
195th La	65	219	C6	350	C3
195th Pl	23	232	B1	357	A4
195th St		219	A6	350	B3
25-00 - 47-99	58	219	A6	350	B3
48-00 - 72-99	65	219	B6	350	B3
73-00 - 75-99	66	219	C6	350	C3
88-00 - 103-99	23	232	B1	357	A4
104-00 - 120-99	12	232	C2	357	A4
121-00 - 122-99	13	239	A4	357	B4
196th Pl		219	B6	350	B3
25-00 - 47-99	58	219	B6	350	B3
48-00 - 72-99	65	219	B6	350	B3
73-00 - 75-99	66	219	C6	350	C3
196th St		219	A6	350	B3
25-00 - 47-99	58	219	A6	350	B3
48-00 - 72-99	65	219	B6	350	B3
73-00 - 75-99	66	219	C6	350	C3
88-00 - 103-99	23	232	B1	357	A4
104-00 - 120-99	12	232	C2	357	A4
121-00 - 122-99	13	239	A4	357	B4
197th St		219	B6	350	B3
25-00 - 47-99	58	219	B6	350	B3
48-00 - 72-99	65	219	C6	350	B3
73-00 - 75-99	66	220	C1	351	C4
87-00 - 103-99	23	232	B1	357	A4
104-00 - 120-99	12	232	C2	357	A4
121-00 - 123-99	13	239	A4	357	B4
198th St		219	B6	350	B3
25-00 - 47-99	58	219	B6	350	B3
48-00 - 72-99	65	219	C6	350	B3
73-00 - 75-99	66	220	C1	351	C4
88-00 - 103-99	23	232	B1	357	A4
104-99 - 120-99	12	232	C2	357	A4
121-00 - OUT	13	239	A4	357	B4
199th St		219	B6	350	B3
25-00 - 47-99	58	219	B6	350	B3
48-00 - 72-99	65	219	B6	350	C3
73-00 - 75-99	66	220	C1	351	C4
88-00 - 103-99	23	232	B2	357	A4
104-00 - 120-99	12	232	C2	357	A4
121-00 - OUT	13	239	A4	357	B4
200th St		219	A5	350	B3
13-00 - 31-99	60	203	B6	350	A3
32-00 - 47-99	61	219	A5	350	B3
99-00 - 103-99	23	232	B2	357	A4
104-00 - 120-99	12	232	C2	357	A4
121-00 - OUT	13	239	A4	357	B4
201st Pl	12	239	A4	357	B4
201st St		203	B6	350	A3
13-00 - 31-99	60	203	B6	350	A3
32-00 - 47-99	61	219	A6	350	B3
48-00 - 79-99	64	219	B6	350	B3
88-00 - 103-99	23	232	B2	357	A4
104-00 - 120-99	12	232	C2	357	A4
121-00 - OUT	13	239	A4	357	B4
202nd St		203	B6	350	A3
13-00 - 31-99	60	203	B6	350	A3
32-00 - 47-99	61	219	A6	350	B3
48-00 - 79-99	64	219	B6	350	B3
87-00 - 103-99	23	232	B2	357	A4
104-00 - 120-99	12	232	C2	357	A4
203rd Pl	60	203	C6	350	B3
203rd St		203	C6	350	A3
13-00 - 3199	60	203	C6	350	A3
32-00 - 47-99	61	219	A6	350	B3
48-00 - 79-99	64	219	B6	350	B3
90-00 - 103-99	23	232	B2	357	A4
104-00 - 119-99	12	232	C2	357	A4
204th St		203	C6	350	A3
13-00 - 31-99	60	203	C6	350	A3
32-00 - 47-99	61	219	A6	350	B3
48-00 - 79-99	64	219	B6	350	B3
87-00 - 103-99	23	232	B2	357	A4
104-00 - 119-99	12	232	C2	357	A4
205th Pl		232	B2	357	A4
100-00 - 103-99	23	232	B2	357	A4
104-00 - 109-99	12	232	B2	357	A4
205th St		203	C6	350	A3
13-00 - 31-99	60	203	C6	350	A3
32-00 - 47-99	61	219	A6	350	B3
48-00 - 79-99 (Clearview Expwy)	64	219	B6	350	B3
88-00 - 103-99	23	232	B2	357	A4
104-00 - 118-99	12	232	C2	357	A4
206th St		203	C6	350	A3
13-00 - 31-99	60	203	C6	350	A3
32-00 - 47-99	61	219	A6	350	B3
48-00 - 79-99	64	220	B1	351	B4
80-00 - 89-99	27	232	A2	357	A4
90-00 - 94-99	28	232	B2	357	A4
95-00 - 113-99	29	232	B2	357	A4
114-00 - 118-99	11	232	C3	357	A5
207th St		204	C1	350	A3
13-00 - 31-99	60	204	C1	350	A3
32-00 - 47-99	61	219	A6	350	B3
48-00 - 79-99	64	220	B1	351	B4
80-00 - 89-99	27	232	A2	357	A4
90-00 - 94-99	28	232	B2	357	A4
95-00 - 113-99	29	232	B2	357	A4
114-00 - 116-99	11	232	C3	357	A5
208th Pl	60	204	B1	350	A3
208th St		204	B1	350	A3
13-00 - 31-99	60	204	B1	350	A3
32-00 - 47-99	61	219	A6	350	B3
48-00 - 79-99	64	220	B1	351	B4
80-00 - 89-99	27	232	A2	357	A4
90-00 - 94-99	28	232	B2	357	A4
95-00 - 113-99	29	232	B2	357	A4
114-00 - 116-99	11	232	C3	357	A5
209th Pl		204	C1	350	B3
12-00 - 29-99	60	204	C1	350	B3
109-00 - 111-99	29	232	B3	357	A5
209th St		204	B1	350	A3
13-00 - 31-99	60	204	B1	350	A3
32-00 - 47-99	61	219	A6	350	B3
48-00 - 79-99	64	220	C2	351	C4
80-00 - 89-99	27	220	C2	351	C4
90-00 - 94-99	28	232	B2	357	A4
95-00 - 113-99	29	232	B3	357	A4
114-00 - 116-99	11	232	C3	357	A5
210th Pl		204	C1	350	A3
12-00 - 29-99	60	204	C1	350	A3
89-00 - 89-99	27	232	A2	357	A4
90-00 - 94-99	28	232	B2	357	A4
210th St		204	C1	350	A3
13-00 - 31-99	60	204	C1	350	A3
32-00 - 47-99	61	219	A6	350	B3
48-00 - 79-99	64	220	B1	351	B4
80-00 - 89-99	27	220	C2	351	C4
90-00 - 94-99	28	232	B2	357	A4
95-00 - 113-99	29	232	B3	357	A5
114-00 - 116-99	11	232	C3	357	A5
211th Pl		232	A2	357	A4
90-00 - 94-99	28	232	A2	357	A4
95-00 - 104-99	29	232	B3	357	A5
211th St		204	C1	350	A3
13-00 - 31-99	60	204	C1	350	A3
32-00 - 47-99	61	219	A6	350	B3
48-00 - 79-99	64	220	B1	351	B4
80-00 - 89-99	27	220	C2	351	C4
90-00 - 94-99	28	232	B2	357	A5
95-00 - 113-99	29	232	B3	357	A5
114-00 - OUT	11	232	C3	357	A5
212th Pl		232	A2	357	A4
88-00 - 89-99	27	232	A2	357	A4
90-00 - 94-99	28	232	A3	357	A5
95-00 - 109-99	29	232	B3	357	A5
212th St		204	B1	350	A3
13-00 - 31-99	60	204	B1	350	A3
32-00 - 47-99	61	204	C1	350	B3
48-00 - 79-99	64	220	B1	351	B4
80-00 - 89-99	27	220	C2	351	C4
90-00 - 94-99	28	232	A3	357	A5
95-00 - 113-99	29	232	B3	357	A5
114-00 - OUT	11	232	C3	357	A5
213th St		204	C1	350	A3
13-00 - 31-99	60	204	C1	350	A3
32-00 - 47-99	61	204	C1	350	B3
48-00 - 79-99	64	220	B1	351	B4
80-00 - 89-99	27	220	C2	351	C4
90-00 - 94-99	28	232	A3	357	A5
95-00 - 113-99	29	232	B3	357	A5
214th La	61	220	A1	351	B4
214th Pl		232	A3	357	A5
92-00 - 94-99	28	232	A3	357	A5
28-00 - 29-99	60	204	C2	351	A4
32-01 - 43-99	61	220	A1	351	B4
214th St		204	C2	351	A4
14-00 - 31-99	60	204	C2	351	A4
32-00 - 47-99	61	204	C1	351	B4
48-00 - 79-99	64	220	B1	351	B4
80-00 - 89-99	27	220	C2	351	C4
90-00 - 94-99	28	232	A3	357	A5
95-00 - 113-99	29	232	B3	357	A5
215th Pl		204	C2	351	A4
14-00 - 31-99	60	204	C2	351	A4
32-00 - 47-99	61	220	A1	351	B4
80-00 - 89-99	27	232	A3	351	C4
90-00 - OUT	28	232	A3	357	A5
215th St		204	B1	350	A3
14-00 - 31-99	60	204	B1	350	A3
32-00 - 47-99	61	220	A1	351	B4
48-00 - 79-99	64	220	B1	351	B4
80-00 - 89-99	27	220	C2	351	C4
90-00 - 94-99	28	232	A3	357	A5
95-00 - 113-99	29	232	B3	357	A5
216th St		204	B1	350	A3
14-00 - 31-99	60	204	B1	350	A3
32-00 - 47-99	61	220	A1	351	B4
48-00 - 79-99	64	220	B1	351	B4
80-00 - 89-99	27	232	A3	351	C5
90-00 - 94-99	28	232	A3	357	A5
95-00 - 113-99	29	232	B3	357	A5
217th La	29	232	B3	357	A5
217th Pl	29	232	B3	357	A5
217th St		204	B1	350	A3
14-00 - 31-99	60	204	B1	350	A3
32-00 - 47-99	61	220	A1	351	B4
48-00 - 79-99	64	220	B2	351	B4
80-00 - 89-99	27	232	A3	351	C4
90-00 - 94-99	28	232	A3	357	A5
95-00 - 113-99	29	232	B3	357	A5
115-00 - 120-99	11	232	C3	357	B5
130-00 - 135-99	13	239	B4	357	B4
218th Pl		232	A3	351	C5
80-00 - 89-99	27	232	A3	351	C5
90-00 - 94-99	28	232	A3	357	A5
102-00 - OUT	29	233	B4	357	A5
218th St		204	C2	351	A4
14-00 - 31-99	60	204	C2	351	A4
32-00 - 47-99	61	220	A1	351	B4
48-00 - 79-99	64	220	B2	351	B4
81-00 - 89-99	27	232	A3	351	C4
90-00 - 94-99	28	232	A3	357	A5
95-00 - 104-99	29	232	B3	357	A5
115-00 - 120-99	11	232	C3	357	B5
130-00 - OUT	13	239	B4	357	B4
219th St		220	A1	351	B4
32-00 - 47-99	61	220	A1	351	B4
48-00 - 79-99	64	220	B2	351	B4
80-00 - 89-99	27	232	A3	351	C4
90-00 - 94-99	28	232	A3	351	C5
95-00 - 113-99	29	233	B4	357	A5
114-00 - 120-99	11	232	C3	357	A5
130-00 - 141-99	13	239	B4	357	B4
220th Pl		220	A2	351	B4
32-00 - 47-99	61	220	A2	351	B4
48-00 - 79-99	64	220	C2	351	C4
135-00 - 137-99	13	239	B4	357	B4
220th St		220	A1	351	B4
32-00 - 47-99	61	220	A1	351	B4
48-00 - 79-99	64	220	B2	351	B4
80-00 - 89-99	27	232	A3	351	C5
90-00 - 94-99	28	233	A4	357	A5
95-00 - 108-99	29	233	B4	357	A5
114-00 - 120-99	11	239	A5	357	B5
130-00 - 146-99	13	239	B5	357	B5
221st Pl		232	A3	351	C5
80-00 - 89-99	27	232	A3	351	C5
90-00 - 94-99	28	232	A3	351	C5
221st St		220	A2	351	B4
32-00 - 47-99	61	220	A2	351	B4
48-00 - 79-99	64	220	C2	351	C4
80-00 - 89-99	27	220	C3	351	C5
90-00 - 94-99	28	232	A3	351	C5
95-00 - 113-99	29	233	B4	357	A5
114-00 - 120-99	11	239	A5	357	B5
130-00 - 145-99	13	239	B5	357	B5
222nd St		220	A2	351	B4
32-00 - 47-99	61	220	A2	351	B4
48-00 - 79-99	64	220	C3	351	C4
80-00 - 89-99	27	220	C3	351	C5
90-00 - 94-99	28	233	A4	351	C5
95-00 - 113-99	29	233	B4	357	A5
114-00 - 120-99	11	239	A5	357	B5
130-00 - 146-99	13	239	B5	357	B5
223rd Pl	64	220	B2	351	C4
223rd Rd	61	220	A2	351	B4
223rd St		220	A2	351	B4
32-00 - 47-99	61	220	A2	351	B4
48-00 - 79-99	64	220	B2	351	B4
80-00 - 89-99	27	220	C3	351	C5
95-00 - 113-99	29	233	B4	357	A5
114-00 - 120-99	11	239	A5	357	B5
130-00 - 147-99	13	239	B5	357	B5
224th St		220	B2	351	B4
57-00 - 69-99	64	220	B2	351	B4
91-00 - 94-99	28	233	A4	351	C5
95-00 - 113-99	29	233	B4	357	A5
114-00 - 120-99	11	239	A5	357	B5
130-00 - 147-99	13	239	B5	357	B5
225th St		220	B2	351	B4
48-00 - 79-99	64	220	B2	351	B4
92-00 - 92-99	26	233	A4	357	A5
94-00 - 94-99	28	233	A4	357	A5
95-00 - 112-99	29	233	C4	357	A5
114-00 - 120-99	11	239	A5	357	B5
130-00 - 148-99	13	239	B5	357	B5
226th St		220	B2	351	B4
56-01 - 78-99	64	220	B2	351	B4
114-00 - 120-99	11	239	A6	357	B5
128-00 - 148-99	13	239	B5	357	B5
227th St		233	C4	357	A5
101-00 - 113-99	29	233	C4	357	A5
114-00 - 120-99	11	239	A6	357	B5
130-00 - OUT	13	239	B5	357	B5
228th St		220	B2	351	C5
48-00 - 79-99	64	220	B2	351	B4
114-00 - 120-99	11	239	A6	357	B5
130-00 - 148-99	13	239	B5	357	B5
229th St		220	B2	351	B4
48-00 - 79-99	64	220	B2	351	B4
81-00 - 83-99	27	220	C3	351	C5
114-00 - 120-99	11	239	A6	357	B5
130-00 - 148-99	13	239	B5	357	B5
230th Pl	13	239	C5	357	C4
230th St		220	B2	351	B4
48-00 - 79-99	64	220	B2	351	B4
80-00 - 80-99	27	220	C3	351	C5
114-00 - 120-99	11	239	A6	357	B5
130-00 - 148-99	13	239	B5	357	B5
231st St		220	A2	351	B4
50-00 - 64-99	63	220	A3	351	B5
80-00 - 86-99	27	220	C3	351	C5
114-00 - 120-99	11	239	A6	357	B5
130-00 - 148-99	13	239	B5	357	B5
232nd St		220	A2	351	B4
48-00 - 79-99	64	220	A2	351	B4
80-00 - 88-99	27	220	C3	351	C5
115-00 - 120-99	11	239	A6	357	B5
129-00 - 148-99	13	239	B5	357	B5
233rd Pl	63	204	C3	351	B4
233rd St		204	C3	351	B4
38-00 - 38-99	63	204	C3	351	B4
48-00 - 79-99	64	220	B3	351	B5
80-00 - 86-99	27	220	C3	351	C5
114-00 - 120-99	11	239	A6	357	B5
121-00 - OUT	22	239	B6	357	B5
234th Pl	22	239	C5	357	C5
234th St		204	C3	351	E4
25-00 - 44-99	63	204	C3	351	E4
80-00 - 89-99	27	221	C4	351	C5
116-00 - 120-99	11	239	A6	357	B5
121-00 - OUT	22	239	B6	357	B5
235th Ct	27	233	A4	351	C5
235th St		205	C4	351	B5
25-00 - 44-99	63	205	C4	351	B5
80-00 - 89-99	27	221	C4	351	C5
117-00 - 120-99	11	239	A6	357	B5
121-00 - OUT	22	239	B6	357	B5
236th St		221	C4	351	C5
80-00 - 82-99	27	221	C4	351	C5
88-00 - 89-99	26	233	A4	357	A5
118-00 - 120-99	11	239	A6	357	B5
121-00 - OUT	22	239	B6	357	B5
237th St		221	C4	351	C5
80-00 - 80-99	27	221	C4	351	C5
81-00 - 89-99	26	233	A4	351	C5
119-00 - 120-99	11	239	A6	357	B5
121-00 - OUT	22	239	B6	357	B5
238th St		233	A4	351	C5
88-00 - 95-99	26	233	A4	351	C5
119-00 - 120-99	11	239	A6	357	B5
121-00 - 128-99	22	239	A6	357	B5
239th St		233	A4	351	C5
85-00 - 95-99	26	233	A4	351	C5
120-00 - OUT	11	239	A6	357	B5
240th Pl	62	220	A3	351	B5
240th St		205	C4	351	B5
25-00 - 44-99	63	205	C4	351	B5
45-00 - 71-99	62	220	A3	351	B5
83-00 - 95-99	26	233	A4	351	C5
147-00 - OUT	22	239	C5	357	C5
241st St		220	A3	351	B5
45-00 - 53-99	62	220	A3	351	B5
82-00 - 94-99	26	233	A4	351	C5
134-00 - 146-99	22	239	C5	357	C5
242nd St		220	A3	351	B5

25-00 - 44-99	63	220	A3	351	B5
45-00 - 72-99	62	221	B4	351	B5
80-00 - 95-99	26	221	C4	351	C5
131-00 - 138-99	22	239	B6	357	B5
243rd St		205	C4	351	B5
25-00 - 44-99	63	205	C4	351	B5
45-00 - 72-99	62	220	A3	351	B5
80-00 - 95-99	26	221	C4	351	C5
130-00 - 146-99	22	239	B6	357	B5
244th St		220	A3	351	B5
25-00 - 44-99	63	220	A3	351	B5
45-00 - 73-99	62	220	A3	351	B5
80-00 - 93-99	26	221	C4	351	C5
130-00 - 138-99	22	239	B6	357	B5
245th La	62	221	B4	351	B5
245th Pl	62	221	B4	351	B5
245th St		220	A3	351	B5
45-00 - 71-99	62	220	A3	351	B5
91-00 - 93-99	26	233	A5	351	C6
133-00 - 146-99	22	239	B6	357	C5
246th Cres	62	221	A4	351	B5
246th Pl	62	221	A4	351	B5
246th St		221	C5	351	C6
80-00 - 93-99	26	221	C5	351	C6
134-00 - 140-99	22	239	B6	357	C5
247th St		205	C4	351	B5
40-00 - 43-99	63	205	C4	351	B5
45-00 - 66-99	62	220	A3	351	B5
77-00 - 92-99	26	221	C5	351	C6
138-00 - 155-99	22	239	C6	357	C5
248th St		205	C4	351	B5
25-00 - 44-99	63	205	C4	351	B5
45-00 - 66-99	62	220	A3	351	B5
80-00 - 89-99	26	221	C5	351	C6
138-00 - 155-99	22	239	C6	357	C5
249th St		205	C4	351	B5
25-00 - 44-99	63	205	C4	351	B5
75-00 - 89-99	26	221	C5	351	C6
137-00 - 146-99	22	239	C6	357	C5
250th St		205	C4	351	B5
25-00 - 44-99	63	205	C4	351	B5
45-00 - 66-99	62	221	A4	351	B5
75-00 - 89-99	26	221	C5	351	C6
137-00 - 142-99	22	239	C6	357	C5
251st Pl	62	221	A4	351	B5
251st St		221	C5	351	C6
45-00 - 66-99	62	221	A4	351	B5
75-00 - 87-99	26	221	C5	351	C6
137-00 - OUT (Caney Lane)	22	239	C6	357	C5
252nd St		221	B4	351	B5
45-00 - 66-99	62	221	B4	351	B5
70-00 - 87-99	26	221	C5	351	C6
253rd Pl	22	239	C6	357	C5
253rd St		221	A4	351	B5
45-00 - 66-99	62	221	A4	351	B5
83-00 - 87-99	26	221	C5	351	C6
137-00 - OUT	22	239	C6	357	C5
254th St		205	C4	351	A5
25-00 - 44-99	63	205	C4	351	A5
45-00 - 66-99	62	221	A4	351	B5
79-00 - 85-99	4	221	C5	351	C6
86-00 - 87-99	26	233	A5	351	A5
139-00 - 144-99	22	239	C6	357	C5
255th St		205	C4	351	A5
33-00 - 38-99	63	205	C4	351	A5
45-00 - 66-99	62	221	A4	351	B5
75-00 - 83-99 (Floral Park)	4	221	C5	351	C6
140-00 - 149-99	22	239	C6	357	C5
256th St		221	A4	351	B5
57-00 - 68-99	62	221	A4	351	B5
79-00 - 83-99	4	221	C5	351	C6
84-00 - 87-101	1	221	C6	351	C6
137-00 - OUT	22	239	C6	357	C5
257th St		221	C5	351	C6
79-00 - 83-99	4	221	C5	351	C6
84-00 - 87-86 (Floral Park)	1	221	C6	351	C6
137-00 - 149-99	22	243	A6	357	C5
258th St		221	C6	351	C6
79-00 - 83-99 (Floral Park)	4	221	C6	351	C6
84-00 - 87-69 (Floral Park)	1	221	C6	351	C6
149-00 - OUT	22	243	A6	357	C5
259th St		221	C6	351	C6
79-00 - 83-99	4	221	C6	351	C6
84-00 - 87-69 (Floral Park)	1	221	C6	351	C6
147-00 - OUT	22	243	A6	357	C5
260th Pl	4	221	B5	351	B6
260th St		221	A5	351	B6
55-00 - 59-99	62	221	A5	351	B6
69-00 - 83-99	4	221	B5	351	C6
84-00 - 87-32 (Floral Park)	1	221	C6	351	C6
261st St		221	B6	351	C6
69-00 - 83-99 (Floral Park)	4	221	B6	351	C6
84-00 - 86-59 (Floral Park)	1	221	C6	351	C6
262nd St		221	A5	351	B6
57-00 - 60-99	62	221	A5	351	B6
77-00 - 83-99 (Floral Park)	4	221	B6	351	C6
84-00 - OUT (Floral Park)	1	221	C6	351	C6
149-00 - 149-98	22	243	A6	357	C5
263rd St		221	A5	351	B6
57-00 - 58-99	62	221	A5	351	B6
73-00 - 83-99 (Floral Park)	4	221	B6	351	B6
84-00 - OUT (Floral Park)	1	221	C6	351	C6
264th St		221	A5	351	B6
58-00 - 60-99	62	221	A5	351	B6
76-00 - 83-99 (Floral Park)	4	221	B6	351	C6
84-00 - OUT (Floral Park)	1	221	C6	351	C6
265th St		221	B6	351	B6
76-01 - 77-99 (New Hyde Park)	40	221	B6	351	B6
78-00 - 83-99 (Floral Park)	4	221	B6	351	C6
84-00 - OUT (Floral Park)	1	221	C6	351	C6
266th St		221	B6	351	B6
76-01 - 77-99 (New Hyde Park)	40	221	B6	351	B6
78-00 - 83-99 (Floral Park)	4	221	B6	351	C6
84-00 - OUT (Floral Park)	1	221	C6	351	C6
267th St		221	B6	351	B6
76-01 - 77-99 (New Hyde Park)	40	221	B6	351	B6
78-00 - 83-99 (Floral Park)	4	221	B6	351	C6
84-00 - OUT (Floral Park)	1	221	C6	351	C6
268th St		221	B6	351	B6
76-01 - 77-99 (New Hyde Park)	40	221	B6	351	B6
78-00 - 83-99 (Floral Park)	4	221	B6	351	C6
84-00 - OUT	1	221	C6	351	C6
269th St	40	221	B6	351	B6
270th St	40	221	B6	351	B6
271st St	40	221	B6	351	B6
Interstate 278	77	209	C5	349	B4
Interstate 278	78	212	Inset	348	C2
Interstate 295	60	204	B1	350	A3
Interstate 295	64	220	C1	351	C4
Interstate 495	1	213	C5	348	C2
Interstate 495	55	218	C1	349	C6
Interstate 495	64	220	B2	351	B4
Interstate 495	78	222	A2	348	C3
Interstate 678	19	237	A6	356	B2
Interstate 678	30	241	A6	364	A2
Interstate 678	35	237	A6	356	B2
Interstate 678	54	218	B1	349	B6
NY 25	1	213	A6	348	C2
NY 25	23	232	B1	357	A4
NY 25	35	231	C4	356	A2
NY 25	74	225	A4	349	C5
NY 25A	54	218	A3	350	B2
NY 25A	63	220	A2	351	B4
NY 25A	72	209	C5	349	B4
NY 27	13	239	C4	357	C4
NY 27	14	237	C4	356	C1
NY 878	20	237	C6	356	C2

NAMED STREETS

Abbott Rd	59	204	A1	350	A3
Aberdeen Rd		231	A6	356	A3
180-00 - 187-99	32	231	A6	356	A3
188-00 - OUT	23	231	A6	350	C3
Abigail Adams Av	32	231	B4	356	A2
Abingdon Rd	15	230	B2	356	A1
Acme Ter	93	247	A6	364	B2
Adair St	13	239	A4	357	B4
Adelaide Rd	33	238	A2	356	B3
Admiral Av	79	227	A5	355	A5
Aguilar Av	67	230	A3	350	C2
Alameda Av	62	220	A3	351	B5
Albert Rd	17	236	B3	356	C1
Albion Av	73	216	B1	349	C4
Alderton St	74	225	A4	349	C5
Alecia Av	13	239	B4	357	C4
Alison St	62	221	A4	351	B5
Allendale St	35	231	C4	356	B2
Almeda Av		248	B1	364	C3
51-00 - 53-99	91	248	B3	364	C2
54-00 - OUT	92	248	B1	364	C2
Almont Rd	91	249	B6	365	B5
Alonzo Rd	91	249	A6	365	B5
Alston Pl	63	204	C3	351	B4
Alstyne Av		216	B3	349	C5
94-00 - 95-99	73	216	B3	349	C5
96-00 - OUT	68	217	B4	349	C5
Alwick Rd	20	237	B6	356	C2
Amboy La	29	233	B4	357	A5
Amelia Rd	34	238	A3	357	B4
Amory Ct	85	226	A3	355	A4
Amstel Blvd	92	248	C1	364	C2
Anapolis St	91	249	B6	365	B5
Anchor Dr	91	249	A4	365	B4
Anderson Rd	34	238	A3	357	B4
Andrews Av	78	222	C3	355	A4
Ankener Av	73	216	C1	349	C4
Annandale La	62	221	A4	351	B5
Apex Pl	75	217	C6	349	C5
Arcade Av	12	232	C1	357	A4
Arcadia Wk	97	252	B3	368	B3
Arch St	1	212	A3	348	C2
Archer Av		231	C4	356	B2
139-00 - 149-99	35	231	C4	356	B2
150-00 - OUT	33	231	C5	356	A2
Archway Pl	75	230	B1	356	A1
Ardsley Rd	63	204	C3	351	B4
Arion Rd	17	236	B3	356	C1
Arleigh Rd	63	204	C3	351	A4
Arlington Ter		237	A6	356	B2
145-00 - 147-99	35	237	A6	356	B2
150-00 - 155-99	33	238	A1	356	B3
Arnold Av	78	222	C3	355	A4
Arthur St	13	239	C4	357	C4
Arverne Blvd	92	248	C2	364	C3
Ascan Av	75	230	B1	356	A1
Ash Av	55	218	B3	350	B2
Ashby Av	58	219	B5	350	B3
Ashford St	27	232	A3	351	C5
Aske Pl	73	216	A3	349	C5
Aske St	73	216	A3	349	C5
Aspen Pl	32	231	B5	356	A3
Asquith Cres	74	225	B5	355	A6
Astoria Blvd		199	C4	348	B3
1-01 - 32-99	2	199	C4	348	B3
Astoria Blvd N 33-01 - 38-99 (odd)	3	199	C4	348	B3
Astoria Blvd S 33-02 - 48-98 (even)	3	208	A2	348	B3
40-01 - 47-99	5	199	C4	348	B3
49-00 - 85-99	70	209	A5	349	B4
86-00 - 112-98	69	209	A6	349	B4
Astoria Park S	2	198	B2	348	A2
Astoria Sq	2	198	C2	348	B2
Atlantic Av		236	A1	355	B6
74-00 - 107-98 (even)	16	236	A1	355	B6
74-01 - 99-99 (odd)	21	236	A1	355	B6
100-01 - 135-99 (odd)	18	236	A3	356	B1
108-00 - 135-98 (even)	19	237	A4	356	B1
Atlantic Wk	97	252	B3	368	B3
Aubrey Av	85	229	A4	355	A6
Auburndale La	58	219	B5	350	C3
Audley St		230	B2	356	A1
1-00 - 121-99	15	230	B2	356	A1
120-99 - 116-99	18	230	B2	356	A1
Augusta Ct	34	238	A1	356	B3
Augustina Av	91	249	A5	365	B4
Austell Pl	1	213	B4	348	C2
Austin St		225	A4	349	C5
61-00 - 66-99	74	225	A4	349	C5
67-00 - 79-99	75	225	B6	355	A6
80-00 - 85-99	15	230	B2	356	A1
Ava Pl	32	231	B5	356	A3
Avery Av	55	218	B2	349	B6
Avon Rd		231	A6	356	A3
182-00 - 186-99	32	231	A6	356	A3
188-00 - OUT	23	231	A6	356	A3
Avon St	32	231	B6	356	A3
Aztec Pl	91	249	B5	365	C4
Babbage St	18	230	C2	356	A1
Babylon Av	12	232	C1	357	A4
Bagley Av	58	219	B5	350	B3
Bailey Ct	91	249	A4	365	B4
Baisley Blvd		238	A3	357	B4
131-00 - 180-99	34	238	C2	356	C3
181-00 - 188-99	12	238	A3	357	B4
Balsam Ct	91	249	B6	365	B5
Barbadoes Dr	92	248	B1	364	C2
	93	251	A6	364	C2
Barclay Av	55	218	A3	350	B2
Bardwell Av	29	232	B3	357	A5
Barrington St	32	231	B6	356	A3
Barnett Av	4	214	A2	348	C3
Barnwell Av	73	216	B1	349	C4
Barron St	34	238	A1	356	B3
Barrows Ct	62	220	A3	351	B5
Barton Av	54	218	A3	350	B2
Bascom Av	36	237	B6	356	C2
Bates Rd	62	205	C5	351	B5
Bath Wk	97	252	B3	368	B3
Battery Rd	91	249	A5	365	B4
Baxter Av	73	216	A1	349	C4
Bay 24th St	91	249	B4	365	B4
Bay 25th St	91	249	B4	365	B4
Bay 27th St	91	249	B4	365	B4
Bay 28th St	91	249	A4	365	B4
Bay 30th St	91	249	B4	365	B4
Bay 31st St	91	249	B4	365	B4
Bay 32nd Pl	91	249	B4	365	B4
Bay 32nd St	91	249	B4	365	B4
Bay Ct	91	249	A4	365	B4
Bay Park Dr	56	202	B1	349	A5
Bay Park Pl	91	249	B4	365	B4
Bay St	63	204	C3	351	B4
Bay Ter	97	252	B3	368	B3
Bay Club Dr	60	204	C1	350	A3
Bayfield Av	92	248	B1	364	C2
Bayport Pl	91	249	B5	365	B4
Bayside Av		203	C4	350	B2
118-00 - 157-99	54	203	C4	350	B2
158-00 - 199-99	58	203	C5	350	B2
Bayside Dr	97	252	B3	368	B3
Bayside La	58	203	C5	350	B2
Bayside St	59	204	B1	350	A3
Bayside Wk	97	252	B3	368	B3
Bayswater Av	91	249	A4	365	B4
Bayview Av	14	241	C4	356	C1
Bayview Wk	97	252	B3	368	B3
Baywater Ct	91	249	A4	365	B4
Bayway Wk	97	252	B3	368	B3
Beach 3rd St	91	249	B6	365	C5
Beach 4th St	91	249	B6	365	C5
Beach 5th St	91	249	B6	365	C5
Beach 6th St	91	249	B6	365	C5
Beach 7th St	91	249	B6	365	C5
Beach 8th St	91	249	B6	365	C5
Beach 9th St	91	249	B6	365	B5
Beach 11th St	91	249	B6	365	C5
Beach 12th St	91	249	B6	365	B5
Beach 13th St	91	249	B6	365	C5
Beach 14th St	91	249	B6	365	C5
Beach 15th St	91	249	B6	365	C4
Beach 16th St	91	249	B5	365	C4
Beach 17th St	91	249	B5	365	C4
Beach 18th St	91	249	B5	365	B4
Beach 19th St	91	249	B5	365	C4
Beach 20th St	91	249	B5	365	C4
Beach 21st St	91	249	B5	365	B4
Beach 22nd St	91	249	B5	365	C4
Beach 24th St	91	249	B5	365	C4
Beach 25th St	91	249	B5	365	C4
Beach 26th St	91	249	B5	365	C4
Beach 27th St	91	249	B5	365	C4
Beach 28th St	91	249	B5	365	C4
Beach 29th St	91	249	B4	365	C4
Beach 30th St	91	249	B4	365	B4
Beach 31st St	91	249	B4	365	B4
Beach 32nd St	91	249	B4	365	C4
Beach 33rd St	91	249	B4	365	C4
Beach 34th St	91	249	B4	365	C4
Beach 35th St	91	249	B4	365	C4
Beach 36th St	91	249	B4	365	C4
Beach 37th St	91	249	B4	365	C4
Beach 38th St	91	249	B4	365	C4
Beach 39th St	91	249	B4	365	C4
Beach 40th St	91	249	B4	365	C4
Beach 41st St	91	249	B4	365	C4
Beach 42nd St	91	249	C4	365	C4
Beach 43rd St	91	248	B3	364	C3
Beach 44th St	91	248	B3	364	C3
Beach 45th St	91	248	B3	364	C3
Beach 46th Pl	91	248	C3	364	C3
Beach 46th St	91	248	B3	364	C3
Beach 46th Wy	91	248	C3	364	C3
Beach 47th St	91	248	B3	364	C3
Beach 47th Wy	91	248	C3	364	C3
Beach 48th St	91	248	B3	364	C3
Beach 48th Wy	91	248	C3	364	C3
Beach 49th St	91	248	B3	364	C3
Beach 50th St	91	248	B3	364	C3
Beach 51st St	91	248	B3	364	C3
Beach 52nd St	91	248	C3	364	C3
Beach 53rd St	91	248	C3	364	C3
Beach 54th St	92	248	B3	364	C3
Beach 55th St	92	248	C3	364	C3
Beach 56th Pl	92	248	C3	364	C3
Beach 56th St	92	248	C3	364	C3
Beach 57th St	92	248	C2	364	C3
Beach 58th St	92	248	B2	364	C3
Beach 59th St	92	248	C2	364	C3
Beach 60th St	92	248	C2	364	C3
Beach 61st St	92	248	C2	364	C3
Beach 62nd St	92	248	C2	364	C3
Beach 63rd St	92	248	B2	364	C3
Beach 64th St	92	248	B2	364	C3
Beach 65th St	92	248	B2	364	C3
Beach 66th St	92	248	B2	364	C3
Beach 67th St	92	248	B2	364	C3
Beach 68th St	92	248	B2	364	C3
Beach 69th St	92	248	B2	364	C3
Beach 70th St	92	248	C2	364	C3
Beach 71st St	92	248	C1	364	C3
Beach 72nd St	92	248	B2	364	C2
Beach 73rd St	92	248	C1	364	C2
Beach 74th St	92	248	C1	364	C2
Beach 75th St	92	248	C1	364	C2
Beach 76th St	92	248	C1	364	C2
Beach 77th St	92	248	C1	364	C2
Beach 79th St	93	248	C1	364	C2
Beach 80th St	93	248	C1	364	C2
Beach 81st St	93	248	C1	364	C2
Beach 82nd St	93	248	C1	364	C2
Beach 83rd St	93	248	C1	364	C2
Beach 84th St	93	248	C1	364	C2
Beach 85th St	93	248	C1	364	C2
Beach 86th St	93	248	C1	364	C2
Beach 87th St	93	251	A6	364	C2
Beach 88th St	93	251	A6	364	C2
Beach 89th St	93	251	A6	364	C2
Beach 90th St	93	251	A6	364	C2
Beach 91st St	93	251	A6	364	C2
Beach 92nd St	93	251	A6	364	C2
Beach 93rd St	93	251	A6	364	C2
Beach 94th St	93	251	A6	364	C2
Beach 95th St	93	251	A6	364	C2
Beach 96th St	93	251	A6	364	C2
Beach 97th St	93	251	A6	364	C2
Beach 98th St	93	251	A6	364	C2
Beach 99th St	94	251	A6	364	C2
Beach 100th St	94	251	A6	364	C2
Beach 101st St	94	251	A6	364	C2
Beach 102nd La	94	251	A6	364	C2
Beach 102nd St	94	251	A6	364	C2
Beach 104th St	94	251	A5	364	C1
Beach 105th St	94	251	A5	364	C1
Beach 106th La	94	251	B5	364	C1
Beach 106th St	94	251	A5	364	C1
Beach 108th St	94	251	A5	364	C1
Beach 109th St	94	251	B5	364	C1
Beach 110th St	94	251	B5	364	C1
Beach 111th St	94	251	B5	364	C1
Beach 112th St	94	251	B5	364	C1
Beach 113th St	94	251	B5	364	C1
Beach 114th St	94	251	B5	364	C1
Beach 115th St	94	251	B5	364	C1
Beach 116th St	94	251	B4	364	C1
Beach 117th St	94	251	B4	364	C1
Beach 118th St	94	251	B4	364	C1
Beach 119th St	94	251	B4	364	C1
Beach 120th St	94	251	B4	364	C1
Beach 121st St	94	251	B4	364	C1
Beach 122nd St	94	251	B4	364	C1
Beach 123rd St	94	251	B4	364	C1
Beach 124th St	94	251	B4	364	C1
Beach 125th St	94	251	B4	364	C1
Beach 126th St	94	251	B4	364	C1
Beach 127th St	94	251	B4	364	C1
Beach 128th St	94	251	B4	364	C1
Beach 129th St	94	250	B3	363	C5
Beach 130th St	94	250	B3	363	C5
Beach 131st St	94	250	B3	363	C5
Beach 132nd St	94	250	B3	363	C5
Beach 133rd St	94	250	B3	363	C5
Beach 134th St	94	250	B3	363	C5
Beach 135th St	94	250	B3	363	C5
Beach 136th St	94	250	B3	363	C5
Beach 137th St	94	250	B3	363	C5
Beach 138th St	94	250	B3	363	C5
Beach 139th St	94	250	B3	363	C5
Beach 140th St	94	250	B3	363	C5
Beach 141st St	94	250	B3	363	C5
Beach 142nd St	94	250	B3	363	C5
Beach 143rd St	94	250	B3	369	B6
Beach 144th St	94	250	B3	369	B6
Beach 145th St	94	250	A3	369	B5
Beach 146th St	94	250	A3	369	B5
Beach 147th St	94	250	A3	369	B5
Beach 148th St	94	250	A3	369	B5
Beach 149th St	94	250	A3	369	B5
Beach 169th St	94	253	A6	369	B5
Beach 193rd St	95	253	B4	369	B4
Beach 201st St	97	253	B4	369	B4
Beach 204th St	97	252	B3	368	B3
Beach 207th St	97	252	B3	368	B3
Beach 208th St	97	252	B3	368	B3
Beach 209th St	97	252	B3	368	B3
Beach 210th St	97	252	B3	368	B3
Beach 213th St	97	252	B3	368	B3
Beach 214th St	97	252	B3	368	B3
Beach 215th St	97	252	B3	368	B3
Beach 216th St	97	252	B3	368	B3
Beach 217th St	97	252	B2	368	B3
Beach 219th St	97	252	B2	368	B3
Beach 220th St	97	252	B2	368	B3
Beach 221st St	97	252	B2	368	B3
Beach 222nd St	97	252	B2	368	B3
Beach Channel Dr		249	B4	365	C4
1 - 53-99	91	249	B4	365	B4
54-00 - 77-99	92	248	C2	364	C3
78-00 - 97-99	93	251	A6	364	C2
98-00 - OUT	94	251	A5	364	C2
Beacon Pl	91	249	A4	365	B4
Beatrice Ct	91	249	B5	365	B4
Beaver Rd	33	231	C4	356	B2
Beck Rd	91	249	B6	365	B5
Bedell St		238	A1	356	B3
112-00 - 113-99	33	238	A1	356	B3
114-00 - 136-99	34	238	A2	356	B3
137-00 - OUT	13	238	B3	357	C4
Bedford Av	97	252	B3	368	B3
Beech Av	55	218	B3	350	B2
Beech Cir	56	202	B2	349	A6
Beech Ct	56	202	B2	349	A6
Beechknoll Av	62	221	A4	351	B5
Beechknoll Pl	75	230	B1	356	A1
Belknap St	13	239	B4	357	B4
	34	239	B4	357	B4
Bell Blvd		204	B1	350	A3
12-00 - 31-99	60	204	B1	350	A3
32-00 - 47-99	61	220	A1	351	B4
48-00 - 79-99	64	220	B1	351	B4
80-00 - 85-99	27	232	A2	351	C4
Bellaire Pl	29	232	B2	357	A4
Belmont Av	17	236	B2	355	C6
Belt Pkwy	13	239	C4	357	C4
Belt Pkwy	14	240	A2	355	C6
Benham St	73	216	A3	349	C5
Bennett Ct	34	239	B4	357	B4
Bennett St		239	B4	357	C4
132-00 - 136-99	34	239	B4	357	C4
137-00 - OUT	13	239	B4	357	C4
Bentley Rd	22	243	A5	357	C5
Benton St	12	239	A4	357	B4
	13	239	A4	357	B4
Bergen Rd	30	237	C5	356	C2
Berrian Blvd	5	200	B1	349	A4
Bert Rd W	93	247	A6	364	B2
Bessemer St	18	230	C2	356	A1
Bessemund Av	91	249	B4	365	B4
Beverly Rd	15	230	B2	356	A1
Beverly Rd	63	204	C3	351	A4
Billings St	27	232	A3	351	C5
Birds Al	54	218	A2	349	B6
Birdsall Av	91	249	A5	365	B4
Birmington Pkwy	64	220	A2	351	B4
Bleecker St	85	227	A4	355	A4
Blossom Av	55	218	B2	349	B6
Boardwalk		248	C2	364	C3
1-00 - 53-99	91	249	B4	365	C4
54-00 - 77-99	92	248	C2	364	C3
78-00 - 97-99	93	248	C1	364	C2
98-00 - OUT	94	251	B5	364	C2
Boelsen Cres	74	225	B5	355	A6
Boker Ct	56	202	B2	349	A6
Bolton Rd	91	249	A6	365	B5
Bonnie La	60	204	B1	350	A3
Boody St	70	209	B5	349	B4
Booth Memorial Av		218	B2	349	C6
132-00 - 157-99	55	218	B2	349	C6
158-00 - OUT	65	219	C4	350	C2
Booth St		224	A3	349	C5
60-00 - 60-99	73	224	A3	349	C5
61-00 - 66-99	74	225	A4	349	C5
67-00 - 68-99	75	225	B6	355	A6
Borage Pl	75	230	B1	356	A1
Borden Av		212	B2	348	C1
2-01 - 38-99	1	212	B2	348	C1
44-00 - 68-99	78	222	A3	348	C3
Borkel Pl	28	232	A3	351	C5
Borough Pl	77	209	B4	348	B3
Boss St	17	237	B4	356	B1
Boundary Rd	59	204	B1	350	A3
Boundary Rd N	30	238	C2	356	C3
Bourton St	74	225	A4	349	C5
Bow St	75	230	B1	356	A1
Bowden Av	61	219	A6	350	B3
Bowne St		218	A2	349	B6
36-00 - 40-99	54	218	A2	349	B6
41-00 - 52-99	55	218	B3	350	B2
Boyce Av	61	219	A6	350	B3
Braddock Av		232	A3	351	C5
220-00 - 221-99	27	232	A3	351	C5
221-00 - 235-99	28	233	A4	351	C5
236-00 - OUT	26	233	A4	351	C5
Bradley Av	1	213	C5	348	C2
Brant Wk	97	252	B3	368	B3
Brattle Av	62	221	A4	351	B5
Breezy Point Blvd	97	252	B2	368	B3
Brevoort St	15	230	C2	356	A1
Brian Cres	60	203	B6	350	A3
Briar Pl	91	249	B5	365	C4
Bridge St	14	237	C4	356	C1
Bridgeton St	14	237	C4	356	C1
Bridgewater Av	4	221	B5	351	B6
Brinkerhoff Av	12	232	C1	357	A4
Brisbin St	35	231	C4	356	B2
Bristol Av	17	236	B3	356	C1
Britton Av	73	216	B1	349	C4
Broadway		208	B1	348	B3
8-01 - 36-99	6	207	A5	348	B2
37-01 - 48-99	3	208	B2	348	B3
49-00 - 69-99	77	209	C4	348	B3
70-00 - 73-99	72	215	A5	349	C4
74-00 - OUT	73	216	B1	349	C4
Brocher Rd	34	238	A3	357	B4
Brookhaven Av	91	249	B5	365	C4
Brooklyn Queens Expwy	77	214	B2	348	C3
Brooklyn Queens Expwy E	77	209	B5	349	B4
Brooklyn Queens Expwy W	77	209	A4	348	B3
Brookside St	63	205	C4	351	A5
Brookville Blvd	22	239	C5	357	C5
Brown Pl	78	223	B5	355	A5
Browns Blvd	97	253	A5	369	B4
Browvale La	62	221	A4	351	B5
Brunswick Av	91	249	A5	365	B4
Budd Pl	54	218	A2	349	B6
Buell St	69	211	B5	349	B5
Bulova St	77	209	B4	348	B3
Bunnecke Ct	85	227	A4	355	A4
Burchell Av	92	248	B1	364	C2
Burchell Rd	92	248	B2	364	C3
Burden Cres	35	230	B3	356	A2
Burdette Pl	32	231	C4	356	A2
Burling St	55	218	B3	350	B2
Burns St		225	B6	355	A6
6 - 68-04	75	225	B6	355	A6
66-00 - 66-99	74	225	B5	355	A6
Burrough Pl	77	215	B5	349	C4
Burton St	57	203	B6	350	A3
Butler Av	85	226	A3	355	A4
Butler St	69	211	A4	349	B5
Bye St	75	230	B1	356	A1
Byrd St	55	218	B2	349	B6
Byron St	34	238	C2	356	C3
Cabot Rd	85	234	A3	355	B5
Caffrey Av	91	249	B6	365	C5
Calamus Av		215	C5	349	C4
69-00 - 73-99	77	215	C5	349	C4
74 - OUT	73	216	C1	349	C4
Calamus Cir	73	216	C1	349	C4
Caldwell Av		223	B6	355	A5
68-00 - 73-99	78	223	B6	355	A5
74-00 - 81-99	73	224	B1	355	A5
82-00 - 82-99	79	224	B2	355	A5
Calloway St	68	217	C5	349	C5
Cambria Av	62	220	A3	351	B5
Cambridge Rd	32	231	B6	356	A3
Camden Av	12	232	C1	357	A4
Camp Rd	91	249	B5	365	C4
Caney La	22	239	C6	357	C5
Caney Rd	22	239	C5	357	C5
Capstan Ct	56	202	A2	349	A6
Cargo Plz	30	238	C1	356	C3
Cargo Service Rd	30	237	C6	356	C2
Carlton Pl	54	218	A2	349	B6
Carlton St	74	225	B4	355	A6
Carolina Rd	62	220	A3	351	B5
Carpenter Av	23	232	B1	357	A4
Carson St	13	239	B4	357	B4
Cary Pl	63	220	A3	351	B5
Case St	72	216	A2	349	C4
Castlewood St	4	221	B6	351	C6
Catalpa Av	85	227	B4	355	A4
Cedar Hill Rd	91	249	B6	365	B5
Cedar La	63	204	C3	351	B4
Cedarcroft Rd	32	231	B5	356	A3
Cedarlawn Av	91	249	B6	365	B5
Cedric Rd	20	237	B6	356	C2
Celtic Av	77	214	C1	348	C3
Center Blvd	1	212	A1	348	C1
Center Cargo Rd	30	238	C1	356	C3

Queens

Center Dr 57 202 B3 349 A6
Center Dr 63 204 C3 351 A4
Center St 97 253 A5 369 B4
Centerville St 17 236 B3 356 C1
Central Av 85 227 B5 355 B5
Central Av 91 249 B5 365 B4
Centre St 85 227 C4 355 B4
Champlain Rd 93 247 A6 364 B2
Chandler St 91 249 A5 365 B4
Channel Rd 93 247 B6 364 C2
Channing Rd 91 249 A6 365 B5
Chapel Wk 97 252 B3 368 B3
Chapin Ct 32 231 B4 356 A2
Chapin Pkwy 32 231 B4 356 A2
Charlecote Ridge 32 231 B5 356 A3
Charlotte St 85 226 A1 355 A4
Charter Rd 35 230 B3 356 A2
Chelsea St 32 231 B6 356 A3
Cheney St 34 239 B4 357 B4
Cherry Av 55 218 B3 350 B2
Cherry St 63 205 C4 351 B5
Chester Wk 97 252 B3 368 B3
Chevy Chase St 32 231 A6 350 C3
Chicot Rd 17 236 B3 356 B1
Christie Av 68 217 B4 349 C5
Church Av 97 253 A5 369 B4
Church Rd 93 247 A6 364 C2
Church St 14 237 C4 356 C1
Circle Dr 59 204 A1 350 A3
Circle Rd 63 205 C4 351 B5
Claran Ct 78 223 A4 348 C3
Claremont Ter 73 216 B2 349 C4
Claude Av 33 238 A1 356 B3
Clearview Expwy 204 C1 350 A3
14-00 - 31-99 60 204 C1 350 A3
32-00 - 47-99 61 219 A6 350 B3
48-00 - OUT 64 220 B1 351 B4
Clinton Av 78 223 B4 355 A4
Clinton Pl 32 231 B5 356 A3
Clinton Ter 32 231 B5 356 A3
Clinton Wk 97 252 B3 368 B3
Clintonville St 57 203 B5 350 A2
Clio St 23 232 A1 357 A4
Clover Hill Dr 23 232 B1 357 A4
Clover Pl 23 232 B1 357 A4
Clover Pl 85 234 A3 355 B5
Cloverdale Blvd 64 220 B2 351 B4
Clyce St 225 B6 355 A6
66-00 - 66-99 74 225 B5 355 A6
67-00 - 68-99 75 225 B6 355 A6
Codwise Pl 73 216 C1 349 C4
Cody Av 85 227 A4 355 B4
Cohancy St 237 C4 356 C1
150-00 - 150-99 17 237 C4 356 C1
155-00 - 155-99 14 237 C4 356 C1
Colden St 55 218 B3 350 C2
Coldspring Rd 91 249 B4 365 B4
Coleman Sq 14 237 C4 356 C1
Colfax St 232 C3 357 A5
109-00 - 113-99 29 232 C3 357 A5
114-00 - OUT 11 232 C3 357 A5
College Pl 56 202 B2 349 A6
College Point Blvd 202 C2 349 A6
1 - 24-99 56 202 C2 349 A6
25-00 - 40-99 54 202 C2 349 B6
41-00 - 60-00 55 218 B2 349 B6
Collier Av 91 249 C4 365 C4
Collins Pl 54 218 A2 349 B6
Colonial Av 75 218 C1 349 C6
Columbus Sq 2 199 C4 348 B3
Commissary Rd 30 237 C5 356 C2
Commonwealth Blvd 221 B4 351 B5
63-00 - 73-99 62 221 B4 351 B5
74-01 - 90-98 26 221 C5 351 C5
Como Av 23 232 A1 357 A4
Compass Rd 30 238 C1 356 C3
Conch Rd 91 248 B3 364 C3
Concord St 62 205 C5 351 B5
Congressman Rosenthal Av
54 218 A2 349 B6
Continental Av (71st Av)
75 229 A6 355 A6
Cook Av 79 228 A2 355 A5
Coolidge Av 230 B3 356 A2
135-00 - 149-99 35 230 B3 356 A2
150-00 - OUT 32 231 B4 356 A2
Coombs St 13 239 B4 357 C4
Cooper Av 228 B2 355 A5
75-00 - 89-31 85 227 C5 355 B5
89-34 - 89-98 74 229 A5 355 A6
Cooper Ter 85 227 C6 355 B5
Corbett Rd 61 204 C2 351 B4
Cornaga Av 91 249 B4 365 B4
Cornaga Ct 91 249 B6 365 B5
Cornelia St 85 226 C3 355 B4
Cornell La 63 205 C4 351 B5
Cornish Av 73 216 B1 349 C4
Corona Av 216 B2 349 C4
84-00 - 95-99 73 216 B2 349 C4
96-00 - 112-99 68 217 B4 349 C5
Corporal Kennedy St 204 C1 350 A3
1-00 - 31-99 60 204 C1 350 A3
32-00 - 47-99 61 219 A6 350 B3
Corporal Stone St 61 220 A1 351 B4
Couch Pl 69 211 B4 349 B5
Court Sq 1 213 A4 348 C2
Courtney Av 58 219 B5 350 B3
Courtney La 97 253 B4 369 B4
Cove Ct 56 202 B2 349 A6
Covert St 85 227 C4 355 B4
Cowles Ct 79 224 C3 355 A6
Cpl Larry Muss Mem Sq
57 203 C5 350 A2
Craft Av 22 243 A6 365 A5
Crandall Av 34 239 B4 357 B4
Crane St 1 212 A3 348 C2
Cranford Rd 75 230 B1 356 A1
Cranston St 34 238 B2 356 C3
Creekside Av 97 253 A5 369 B4
Crescent St 198 C3 348 B3
20-01 - 23-99 5 199 B4 348 C3
24-01 - 30-99 2 198 C3 348 B3
31-01 - 36-99 6 207 A6 348 B2
37-01 - 44-99 1 207 C4 348 B2
Cresskill Pl 35 231 C4 356 B2
Crest Rd 91 249 B5 365 C4
Crocheron Av 58 219 A4 350 B2
Crommeling St 55 218 B2 349 B6
Cromwell Cres 74 225 B4 355 A6
Cronston Av 94 250 B2 369 B5
Cross Bay Blvd 236 B3 356 B1
105-00 - 149-99 17 236 B3 356 B1
152-00 - 165-99 14 240 A3 356 C1
93 247 B6 364 A1
Cross Island Pkwy 203 B5 350 A2
10-01 - 12-99 57 203 B5 350 A2
80-00 - 88-19 26 221 C5 351 C5
99-00 - 112-98 29 233 B4 357 A5
114-00 - OUT 11 233 C4 357 A5
Croydon Rd 32 231 B5 356 A3
Crugers Rd 92 248 C1 364 C2
Cryder's La 57 203 B5 350 A2
Cullman Av 62 221 B4 351 B5
Culloden Pl 16 236 A2 355 C6
Curtis St 69 211 A4 349 B5
Curzon Rd 18 230 C2 356 A1
Cuthbert Rd 15 230 B2 356 A1
Cypress Av 85 226 A1 355 A4
Cypress Hills St 85 227 B5 355 A5
Dahlia Av 55 218 B2 349 B6
Daisy Pl 26 221 B4 351 B5
Dalny Rd 32 231 B6 356 A3
Dana Ct 79 224 B3 355 A6
Dane Pl 75 225 B5 355 A6
Daniels St 35 230 B3 356 A2
Darren Dr 60 204 B1 350 A3
Dartmouth St 75 225 B6 355 A6
Davenport Av 233 A4 357 A5
220-00 - 235-99 28 233 A4 357 A5
236-00 - 237-99 26 233 A4 351 C5
Davenport St 14 241 A4 356 C1
Davies Rd 91 249 B6 365 C5
Davis Ct 1 213 B4 348 C2
Davis St 1 212 A3 348 C2
De Costa Av 92 248 B1 364 C2
Deauville Wk 97 252 B3 368 B3
Decatur St 85 227 A4 355 B4
Deepdale Av 62 220 A3 351 B5
Deepdale Pl 62 221 A4 351 B5
Deepdene Pl 75 230 B1 356 A1
Deerfield Rd 91 249 B4 365 C4
Defoe St 13 239 B4 357 B4
Dekalb Av 85 226 A2 355 A4
Delaware Av 55 218 A3 350 B2
Delevan St 29 232 C3 357 A5
Delong St 218 B2 349 B6
40-00 - 40-99 54 218 B2 349 B6
41-00 - 41-99 55 218 B2 349 B6
Demerest Rd 93 247 B6 364 C2
Denman St 73 216 A2 349 C4
Dennis St 34 239 B4 357 B4
Depew Av 63 205 C4 351 B5
Depot Rd 219 A4 350 B2
156-00 - 157-99 54 219 A4 350 B2
158-00 - OUT 58 219 A4 350 B2
Desarc Rd 17 236 B3 356 C1
Desota Rd 93 251 A6 364 C2
Devon Wk 97 252 B3 368 B3
Devonshire Rd 32 231 B5 356 A3
Dexter Ct 21 236 A1 355 B6
Diane Pl 60 204 B1 350 A3
Dickens St 91 249 B5 365 B4
Dieterle Cres 74 225 B4 355 A6
Digby Pl 16 236 A2 355 B6
Dillion St 33 238 A1 356 B3
Dinsmore Av 91 249 B6 365 B5
Ditmars Blvd 199 B4 348 A3
18-01 - 48-99 5 199 B4 348 A3
49-00 - 84-99 70 209 A5 349 B4
85-00 - 112-99 69 210 A1 349 B4
Dix Av 91 249 B5 365 B4
Donald Ct 91 249 B6 365 C5
Doncaster Pl 32 231 A5 356 A3
Dongan Av 73 216 B1 349 C4
Doran Av 85 229 A4 355 B4
Dorian Ct 91 249 B6 365 B5
Doris La 97 253 B4 369 B4
Dormans Rd 12 232 C1 357 B4
Dorothy Pl 2 199 C4 348 B3
Douglas Av 33 231 C5 356 A3
Douglas Rd 63 205 C4 351 A5
Douglaston Pkwy 220 A3 351 B5
38-00 - 44-99 63 220 A3 351 B5
45-00 - 72-99 62 220 A3 351 B5
Downing St 54 218 A2 349 B6
Doxey Pl 17 236 B3 356 C1
Drew St 16 236 A2 355 B6
Dry Harbor Rd 79 224 B3 355 A6
Duane Rd 59 204 B1 350 A3
Dumfries Pl 32 231 A5 356 A3
Dumont Av 236 B2 355 C6
75-00 - 78-99 14 236 B2 355 C6
83-01 - 87-99 17 236 B2 355 C6
Dunbar St 91 249 A4 365 B4
Dunkirk St 232 C1 357 A4
Dunlop Av 12 232 C1 357 A4
Dunton Av 23 232 A1 357 A4
Dunton St 23 232 A1 357 A4
Dutch Kills St 1 213 A4 348 C2
Dwight Av 91 249 B4 365 B4
Eagle Nest La 55 218 B2 349 B6
East 1st Rd 93 247 A6 364 B2
East 4th Rd 93 247 A6 364 B2
East 5th Rd 93 247 A6 364 B2
East 6th Rd 93 247 A6 364 B2
East 7th Rd 93 247 A6 364 B2
East 8th Rd 93 247 A6 364 B2
East 9th Rd 93 247 B6 364 B2
East 10th Rd 93 247 B6 364 B2
East 12th Rd 93 247 B6 364 B2
East 14th Rd 93 247 B6 364 B2
East 16th Rd 93 247 B6 364 B2
East 18th Rd 93 247 B6 364 C2
East 20th Rd 93 247 B6 364 C2
East Dr 63 204 C3 351 A4
East Gate Plz 13 239 B4 357 B4
East Hampton Blvd 64 220 A2 351 B4
East Hangar Rd 30 241 A6 356 C2
East Lp 59 204 B2 351 A4
East Williston Av 1 221 C6 351 C6
Eckford Av 17 236 B3 356 C1
Edgemere Av 91 248 C3 364 C3
Edgemere Rd 91 249 C4 365 C4
Edgerton Blvd 32 231 B5 356 A3
Edgerton Rd 32 231 A5 356 A3
Edgewood Av 13 239 B4 357 C4
Edgewood St 22 243 A5 357 C5
Edmore Av 233 A4 357 A5
221-00 - 235-99 28 233 A4 357 A5
236-00 - OUT 26 233 A4 351 C5
Edsall Av 85 228 B2 355 A5
Effington Av 58 219 B5 350 C3
Eggert Pl 91 249 A5 365 B4
Egmont Pl 91 249 A4 365 B4
Elbertson St 73 216 A2 349 C4
Elder Av 55 218 B2 349 C6
Eliot Av 223 C4 355 A4
60-00 - 61-07 78 223 C4 355 A4
61-08 - 84-99 79 223 C5 355 A4
85-00 - 89-00 74 224 A3 349 C5
Elizabeth Av 248 B1 364 C2
200 - 299 91 248 B3 364 C2
6800 - 7299 92 248 B1 364 C2
Elizabeth Rd 92 248 B2 364 C3
Elk Dr 91 249 B5 365 C4
Elkmont Av 26 221 C5 351 C6
Elks Rd 73 216 C1 349 C4
Ellwell Cres 74 225 B4 355 A6
Elm Av 55 218 B3 350 B2
Elmhurst Av 216 B2 349 C4
84-00 - 89-99 73 216 B2 349 C4
90-00 - 91-99 72 216 A2 349 C4
Elmira Av 12 232 C1 357 A4
Elvira Av 91 249 B6 365 B5
Emily Rd 60 203 B6 350 A3
Empire Av 91 249 B6 365 B5
Enfield Pl 64 220 A2 351 B4
Enright Rd 91 249 A5 365 B4
Epsom Course 232 A1 357 A4
198-00 - 200-99 23 232 A1 357 A4
201 - OUT 27 232 A1 357 A4
Ericsson St 69 211 A4 349 B5
Essex Ct 93 247 B6 364 B2
Essex Wk 97 252 B3 368 B3
Estates Dr 60 204 B1 350 A3
Estates La 60 204 B1 350 A3
Eton St 32 231 B6 356 A3
Evelith Rd 34 238 B3 357 B4
Everdell Av 91 249 B5 365 B4
Everitt Pl 12 238 A3 357 B4
Everton St 74 225 B4 355 A6
Exeter St 75 225 B6 355 A6
Faber Ter 91 249 A4 365 B4
Fairbury Av 233 A4 357 A5
221-00 - 235-99 28 233 A4 357 A5
236-00 - OUT 26 233 A4 357 A5
Fairchild Av 58 219 B5 350 C3
Fairview Av 85 226 A3 355 A4
Fairway Close 75 230 B1 356 A1
Falcon Av 91 249 B4 365 C4
Far Rockaway Blvd 91 249 B4 365 C4
Farmers Blvd 232 C1 357 A4
99-00 - 103-99 23 232 B1 357 A4
104-00 - 120-99 12 232 C1 357 A4
121-00 - 122-26 13 239 A4 357 B4
122-44 - 147-99 34 238 B3 357 B4
Farrington St 54 218 A2 349 B6
Federal Cir 30 237 C6 356 C2
Fern Pl 33 231 C6 356 A3
Ferndale Av 35 237 A6 356 B2
Fernside Pl 91 249 B5 365 C4
Finnard Av 93 248 C1 364 C2
Firwood Pl 12 232 C1 357 A4
Fitchett St 74 225 B4 355 A6
Fleet Ct 79 225 B4 355 A6
Fleet St 225 B6 355 A6
65-00 - 70-99 75 225 B6 355 A6
85-00 - 86-99 74 225 B6 355 A6
Flushing Av 226 A1 355 A4
17-00 - 19-99 85 226 A1 355 A4
51-00 - 64-99 78 222 C3 355 A4
Foam Pl 91 249 B5 365 B4
Foch Blvd 237 B6 356 B2
126-00 - 135-99 20 237 B6 356 B2
137-00 - 149-99 36 237 B6 356 B2
150-00 - 171-99 34 238 A2 356 B3
186-00 - OUT 12 238 A3 357 B4
Fonda Av 12 232 C1 357 B4
Foothill Av 23 232 B1 357 A4
Forest Av 85 227 A4 355 B4
Forest Park Dr 18 230 C1 356 A1
21 229 C4 355 B6
Forest Pkwy 21 229 C4 355 B6
Forest Rd 63 205 C4 351 B5
Forley St 73 216 A2 349 C4
Fowler Av 55 218 B2 349 B6
Frame Pl 55 218 B2 349 B6
Francis Lewis Blvd 203 B5 350 A2
16-00 - 24-99 57 203 B5 350 A2
25-00 - 36-99 58 203 C6 350 B3
37-00 - 47-99 61 219 A6 350 B3
48-00 - 58-99 64 219 B6 350 B3
86-00 - 89-99 27 232 A1 351 C4
90-00 - 94-99 28 232 B2 357 A5
95-00 - 113-99 29 232 B2 357 A5
114-00 - 226-99 11 232 C3 357 A5
121-00 - 137-99 13 239 B5 357 B5
138-01 - 262-99 22 239 C6 357 C5
Franklin Av 55 218 B2 349 B6
Frankton St 22 239 C6 357 C5
Freedom Dr 18 230 C1 356 A1
Fremont St 85 227 A5 355 B5
Fresh Meadow La 219 C5 350 C3
46-00 - 47-99 58 219 B5 350 B3
48-00 - 69-98 65 219 C5 350 C3
Fresh Pond Rd 223 C4 355 A4
55-00 - 60-99 78 223 C4 355 A4
61-00 - 62-29 79 223 C4 355 A4
62-30 - OUT 85 227 A5 355 A4
Frisco Av 91 249 B6 365 B5
Fuller Pl 55 218 B2 349 B6
Fulton Wk 97 252 B3 368 B3
Furmanville Av 79 224 C2 355 A5
Galasso Pl 78 222 B2 355 A4
Gale Av 1 213 B5 348 C2
Galway Av 12 232 C1 357 B4
Garfield Av 77 215 C5 349 C4
Garland Dr 64 220 A2 351 B4
Garrett St 34 238 B3 357 B4
Gaskell Rd 62 221 A4 351 B5
Gates Av 85 227 A4 355 B4
Gateway Blvd 91 249 B5 365 C4
General R W Berry Rd
59 204 B2 351 A4
George St 85 227 C4 355 B4
Georgia Rd 55 218 B3 350 B2
Geranium Av 55 218 B3 350 C2
Gerard Pl 75 230 A1 356 A1
Gettysburg St 26 233 A4 351 C5
Gillmore St 69 211 A4 349 B5
Gipson St 91 249 B5 365 B4
Gladwin Av 58 219 B5 350 C3
Glassboro Av 35 237 A6 356 B2
Gleane St 73 216 A2 349 C4
Glenmore Av 17 236 B2 355 B6
Glenn Av 32 231 B4 356 A2
Glenwood St 205 C4 351 B5
25-00 - 44-99 63 205 C4 351 B5
45-00 - 48-99 62 205 C4 351 B5
Goethals Av 32 231 B4 356 A2
Gold Rd 17 236 B3 356 C1
Goldington Ct 79 225 B4 355 A6
Goldsmith St 73 216 C2 349 C4
Goodwood Rd 75 230 B1 356 A1
Gorsline St 73 216 C1 349 C4
Gotham Rd 20 237 B6 356 C2
Gotham Wk 97 252 B3 368 B3
Gothic Dr 32 231 B5 356 A3
Gouverneur Av 92 248 C1 364 C2
Grace Ct 32 231 C4 356 A2
Graham Ct 54 202 C2 349 B6
Graham Pl 97 253 B4 369 B4
Granada Pl 91 249 A4 365 B4
Grand Av 222 C1 355 A4
45-00 - 73-99 78 222 C1 355 A4
74-00 - OUT 73 216 C1 349 C4
Grand Central Pkwy 218 C1 349 C6
61-00 - 78-99 (St) 75 218 C1 349 C6
80-00 - 80-99 (St) 70 209 A5 349 B4
90-00 - 90-98 69 211 A4 349 B4
80-05 - 81-10 (Ave)
35 230 B3 356 A2
135-00 - 149-99 35 230 B3 356 A2
150-00 - 187-99 32 231 B4 356 A2
200-00 - 229-99 27 220 C3 351 C4
229-00 - 231-99 (odd)
64 220 C3 351 C5
244-00 - 252-98 (even)
26 221 C4 351 C5
244-01 - 265-95 (odd)
62 221 B4 351 C5
Grandview Av 85 226 A3 355 A4
Grandview Ter 91 249 B6 365 B5
Granger St 68 217 B5 349 C5
Grannatt Pl 34 238 B2 356 C3
Grassmere Ter 91 249 B5 365 C4
Gravett Rd 67 218 C3 350 C2
Gray St 79 224 C2 355 A5
Grayson St 12 239 A4 357 B4
13 239 A4 357 B4
Greene Av 85 226 A3 355 A4
Greenpoint Av 213 B6 348 C2
30-01 - 38-99 1 213 C5 348 C2
39-01 - 47-99 4 213 B6 348 C2
Greenway Cir 75 230 B1 356 A1
Greenway North 75 230 B1 356 A1
Greenway South 75 230 B1 356 A1
Greenway Ter 75 230 B1 356 A1
Greenwood Ct 91 249 B6 365 B5
Grenfell St 15 230 B2 356 A1
Grosvenor La 18 230 C2 356 A1
Grosvenor Rd 18 230 C1 356 A1
Grosvenor St 63 204 C3 351 A4
Groton St 75 225 C6 355 A6
Grove St 85 227 A4 355 A4
Guinzburg Rd 33 231 C4 356 B2
Gull Ct 93 247 A6 364 C2
Guy R Brewer Blvd 231 C5 356 A3
92-00 - 113-99 33 231 C5 356 A3
114-00 - OUT 34 238 B2 356 B3
Haddon St 32 231 A6 350 C3
Hague Pl 34 238 B2 356 C3
Haight St 55 218 B2 349 B6
Hamilton Pl 78 223 A4 348 C3
Hampton St 73 216 A2 349 C4
Hancock St 85 226 C3 355 B4
Hand Rd 62 205 C5 351 B5
Hanford St 62 220 A3 351 B5
Hangar Rd N 30 238 C2 356 C3
Hannibal St 12 232 C1 357 A4
Hanson Ct 91 249 B5 365 C4
Hantz Rd 91 248 B3 364 C3
Harbour Ct 91 249 A4 365 B4
Haring St 74 225 A4 349 C5
Harman St 85 226 A3 355 A4
Harmony Rd 97 253 A5 369 B4
Harper St 68 218 A1 349 B6
Harris St 91 249 A6 365 B5
Harrow St 75 225 C6 355 A6
Harry Van Arsdale Jr Av (Jewel Av)
65 231 A4 350 C2
Hart St 85 226 A2 355 A4
Hartland Av 27 220 C2 351 C4
64 220 C2 351 C4
Hartman La 91 249 B4 365 B4
Haspel St 73 216 C2 349 C4
Hassock St 91 249 A5 365 B4
Hawthorne Av 55 218 B3 350 B2
Hawtree Creek Rd 20 237 B5 356 C2
Hawtree St 17 236 B3 356 B1
Haywood Rd 23 232 B1 357 A4
Hazen St 70 200 C1 349 B4
Healy Av 91 249 B5 365 B4
Hempstead Av 29 232 B3 357 A5
Henderson Av 23 232 B1 357 A4
Hendrickson Pl 33 231 C5 356 B3
Henley Rd 32 231 B6 356 A3
Henry Av 77 215 C5 349 C4
Henry Rd 91 249 B6 365 B5
Hessler Av 92 248 C1 364 C2
Hewlett Av 92 221 B6 351 B6
Hewlett St 221 A5 351 B6
56-00 - 60-99 62 221 A5 351 B6
271-00 - OUT (New Hyde Park)
40 221 B6 351 B6
Heyson Rd 91 249 B6 365 C5
Hiawatha Av 23 232 B1 357 A4
Hicks Dr 77 215 B4 348 C3
Hicksville Rd 91 249 B6 365 C5
Higgins St 54 202 C2 349 B6
Highland Av 32 231 B4 356 A2
Highland Ct 91 249 B5 365 C4
Highland Pl 97 253 B4 369 B4
Hilburn Av 12 232 C1 357 B4
Hillcrest Av 63 205 C4 351 B5
Hillcrest Wk 97 252 B3 368 B3
Hillmeyer Av 92 248 B1 364 C2
Hillside Av 230 C2 356 A1
117-00 - 136-99 18 230 C2 356 A1
137-00 - 149-99 35 230 C3 356 A2
150-00 - 187-99 32 231 B4 356 A2
188-00 - 205-99 23 232 B1 357 A4
206-00 - 235-99 27 232 A2 357 A4
236-00 - 253-99 26 221 C5 351 C5
254-00 - 267-99 (Floral Park)
4 221 C6 351 C6
268-00 - OUT (even) (Floral Park)
1 221 C6 351 C6
268-01 - OUT (odd) (New Hyde Park)
40 221 C6 351 C6
97 253 A5 369 B4
Hillyer St 73 216 C1 349 C4
Himrod St 85 226 A3 355 A4
Hobart St 77 208 B3 348 B3
Hoffman Dr 73 216 C3 349 C4
Holder Pl 75 230 B1 356 A1
Holland Av 93 247 A6 364 C2
Hollis Av 232 C2 357 A4
99-00 - 192-99 23 232 B1 357 A4
193-00 - 205-99 12 232 C2 357 A4
206-00 - 218-99 29 232 B3 357 A4
Hollis Court Blvd 219 B6 350 B3
46-00 - 47-99 58 219 B5 350 B3
48-01 - 58-99 65 219 B6 350 B3
87-01 - 89-99 27 232 A2 357 A4
90-00 - 94-99 28 232 B3 357 A4
188-00 - 192-99 58 219 B6 350 C3
Hollis Hills Ter 27 232 A2 351 C4
64 220 C1 351 C4
Holly Av 55 218 B3 350 B2
Hollywood Av 204 C3 351 A4
1 - 148-00 63 204 C3 351 A4
149-00 - 149-99 55 219 B4 350 B2
Hollywood Ct 91 249 B5 365 B4
Homelawn St 32 231 B5 356 A3
Honeywell St 1 213 A6 348 C2
Hook Creek Blvd 22 239 B6 357 C5
Hoover Av 230 B3 356 A2
135-00 - 149-99 35 230 B3 356 A2
150-00 - OUT 32 231 B4 356 A2
Horace Harding Expwy
65 219 C6 350 C3
Horace Harding Expwy
74 217 C5 349 C5
Horatio Pkwy 64 220 A2 351 B4
Horton Av 91 249 A5 365 B4
Hough Pl 91 248 B3 364 C3
Hovendon Rd 32 231 B6 356 A3
Hoxie Dr 64 220 A2 351 B4
Hoyt Av N 2 198 B3 348 A3
Hoyt Av S 2 198 C3 348 B3
Hudson Wk 97 252 B3 368 B3
Hull Av 78 223 A5 349 C4
Humphreys St 69 210 A3 349 B5
Hungry Harbor Rd 22 243 A6 357 C5
Hunter St 1 213 A4 348 C2
Hunters Point Av 213 B5 348 C2
29-01 - 38-99 1 213 B5 348 C2
39-01 - 39-99 4 213 B5 348 C2
Hurley Ct 91 249 B6 365 B5
Huron St 14 236 C3 356 C1
Huxley St 22 243 A5 357 C5
Ide Ct 91 249 B5 365 B4
Ilion Av 12 232 C1 357 B4
Indiana Av 85 228 B2 355 B5
Ingram St 75 225 C6 355 A6
Inwood St 237 A6 356 B2
104-00 - 113-99 35 237 A6 356 B2
114-00 - 133-99 36 238 B1 356 B3
Iowa Rd 62 205 C5 351 B5
Ireland St 73 216 C1 349 C4
Irving Wk 97 252 B3 368 B3
Irwin Pl 34 238 A3 357 B4
Ithaca St 73 216 A1 349 C4
Ivy Close 75 230 B1 356 A1
J.F.K. Expwy 30 238 C1 356 C3
Jackie Robinson Pkwy 18 229 B6 355 A6
Jackson Av 1 212 B2 348 C1
Jackson Mill Rd 69 210 B3 349 B4
Jacobus St 73 215 C6 349 C4
Jaegers La 17 236 B3 356 C1
Jamaica Av 236 A2 355 B6
74-00 - 98-99 21 236 A2 355 B6
100-00 - 135-99 18 230 C2 356 B1
137-00 - 149-99 35 230 C3 356 A2
150-00 - 180-99 32 231 C5 356 A2
181-00 - 205-99 23 231 B6 356 A3
206-00 - 235-99 28 232 B3 357 A4
237-01 - OUT 26 233 A4 357 A5
Jamaica Wk 97 252 B3 368 B3
James Ct 34 238 A1 356 B3
Janet La 97 253 B4 369 B4
Janet Pl 54 218 A2 349 B6
Jarman Rd 59 204 B1 350 A3
Jarvis Ct 91 249 B6 365 C5
Jasmine Av 55 218 B3 350 B2
Java Pl 93 248 C1 364 C2
Jay Av 78 223 A5 349 C4
Jefferson Av 85 226 C3 355 B4
Jessie Ct 63 205 C4 351 B5
Jewel Av (Harry Van Arsdale Jr Av)
230 A1 356 A1
67-00 - 113-99 75 230 A1 356 A1
128-00 - 157-99 67 230 A2 349 C6
158-00 - OUT 65 231 A4 350 C2
John F Kennedy Cir 64 220 C2 351 C4
Jordan Av 12 232 C1 357 B4
Jordan Ct 60 204 B1 350 A3
Jordan Dr 60 204 B1 350 A3
Jordan St 58 203 C6 350 B3
Judge St 73 216 A1 349 C4
Jullius Rd 56 202 B2 349 A6
Junction Blvd 210 C3 349 B5
33-00 - 34-99 72 210 C3 349 B5
35-00 - 48-99 68 210 C3 349 B5
49-00 - 60-99 73 217 B4 349 C5
Juniper Av 55 218 B3 350 C2
Juniper Blvd N 79 224 B1 355 A5
Juniper Blvd S 79 224 C1 355 A5
Juniper Valley Rd 79 224 C1 355 A5
Juno St 75 225 C6 355 A6
Justice Av 73 216 C2 349 C4
Kalmia Av 55 218 B3 350 B2
Kearney St 69 210 B3 349 B5
Keel Ct 56 202 B2 349 A6
Keeseville Av 12 232 C1 357 B4
Kendrick Pl 32 231 B5 356 A3
Kenilworth Dr 64 220 A2 351 B4
Kenmore Rd 63 204 C3 351 A4
Keno Av 23 232 A1 357 A4
Kent St 32 231 A6 350 C3
Kessel St 75 225 C6 355 A6
Ketch Ct 56 202 B2 349 A6
Ketcham St 73 216 A1 349 C4
Kew Forest La 75 230 B2 356 A1
Kew Gardens Rd 230 B2 356 A1
9-00 - 130-99 15 230 B2 356 A1
131-00 - 136-99 18 230 C3 356 A2
Kildare Rd 32 231 A5 356 A3
Kildare Wk 97 252 B3 368 B3
Killarney St 14 236 C3 356 C1
King Rd 54 218 A2 349 B6
Kingsbury Av 64 220 C2 351 C4
Kingston Pl 32 231 B5 356 A3
Kissena Blvd 218 A2 349 B6
41-00 - 60-99 55 218 A2 349 B6
61-00 - OUT 67 218 C3 350 C2
Kneeland Av 73 216 C1 349 C4
Kneeland St 73 215 C6 349 C4
Knollwood Av 63 204 C3 351 A4
Kruger Rd 32 231 B6 356 A3
Laburnum Av 218 B3 350 C2
137-00 - 157-99 55 218 B3 350 C2
158-00 - OUT 58 219 A4 350 B2
Lafayette St 17 236 B3 356 C1

Lahn St	14	236	C3	356	C1
Lakeview Blvd	34	238	A2	356	B3
Lakeview La	34	238	B2	356	B3
Lakeview St	13	239	B4	357	C4
Lakewood Av	35	237	A6	356	B2
Lamont Av	73	216	A3	349	C5
Lanark Rd	93	247	A6	364	B2
Land Rd	62	221	A4	351	B5
Landers St	35	230	B3	356	A2
Lanett Av	91	249	B6	365	C5
Langdale St	40	221	B6	351	B6
Langston Av	4	221	B5	351	B6
Lansing Av	13	239	C5	357	C5
Larkin Av	92	248	C2	364	C3
Latham La	34	238	B3	357	C4
Latimer Pl	54	218	A2	349	B6
Laurel Av	68	217	B5	349	C5
Laurel Hill Blvd		212	Inset	348	C2
34-00 - 35-00	78	212	Inset	348	C2
44-60 - 69-99	77	215	B4	348	C3
Laurelton Pkwy		239	B6	357	B5
120-00 - 120-99	11	239	A6	357	B5
121-00 - OUT	22	239	B6	357	B5
Lawrence St	55	218	B2	349	C6
57-00 - 60-99	55	218	B2	349	C6
61-00 - OUT	67	218	C1	349	C6
Lax Av	56	202	B2	349	A6
Layton St	73	216	B1	349	C4
Leavitt St	54	218	A2	349	B6
Lee Rd	59	204	A1	350	A3
Lee St	57	203	C4	350	A2
Leeds Rd	62	221	A4	351	B5
Lefferts Blvd		230	C2	356	A1
80-00 - 85-99	15	230	C2	356	A1
86-00 - 91-99	18	230	C2	356	A1
94-00 - 107-99	19	237	A4	356	B1
109-00 - 150-99	20	237	B5	356	B2
155-00 - OUT	14	237	C5	356	C2
Leggett Pl	57	203	A4	350	A2
Leith Pl	62	221	A4	351	B5
Leith Rd	62	221	A4	351	B5
Leslie Rd	34	238	A3	357	B4
Leverich St	72	215	A5	349	C4
Lewis Av	68	217	B5	349	C5
Lewiston Av	12	232	C1	357	B4
Lewmay Rd	91	249	C4	365	C4
Liberty Av		236	B2	355	B6
74-00 - 107-99	17	236	B2	355	B6
108-00 - 135-99	19	237	A4	356	B1
137-00 - 149-99	35	231	C4	356	B2
150-00 - 180-99	33	231	C5	356	B2
181-00 - OUT	12	232	C1	357	A4
Liberty La	97	252	A3	368	B3
Lincoln St	20	237	B6	356	B2
Lincoln Wk	97	252	B3	368	B3
Linden Av	36	238	B1	356	B3
Linden Blvd		236	B2	355	C6
75-00 - 79-89	14	236	B2	355	C6
79-00 - 107-99	17	236	B3	356	C1
108-00 - 135-99	20	237	B5	356	B2
137-00 - 149-99	36	237	A6	356	B2
150-00 - 180-99	34	238	A1	356	B3
181-00 - 205-99	12	239	A4	357	B4
206-00 - 235-99	11	232	C3	357	B5
Linden Pl	54	218	A2	349	B6
Linden St	85	227	A4	355	A4
Lineaus Pl	54	218	A2	349	B6
Lithonia Av	65	219	B4	350	C2
Little Bay Rd	59	204	B1	350	A3
Little Neck Blvd	60	204	C2	351	A4
Little Neck Pkwy		205	C4	351	A5
24-00 - 44-99	63	205	C4	351	A5
45-00 - 63-99	62	221	A4	351	B5
69-00 - 83-99 (Floral Park)	4	221	B5	351	C6
84-00 - 88-99 (Floral Park)	1	233	A6	351	C6
Liverpool St	35	237	A6	356	B2
Lloyd Rd	35	237	A6	356	B2
Locke Av	57	203	B5	350	A2
Long Island Expwy (Queens Midtown Expwy)		212	B3	348	C3
1-00 - 41-99	1	212	B3	348	C2
58-00 - 73-99	78	214	C1	348	C3
74-00 - 82-99	73	224	A2	349	C4
92-00 - 101-99	74	217	C5	349	C5
102-00 - 113-99	75	217	C6	349	C5
130-00 - 157-99	67	218	C1	349	C6
158-00 - 199-99	65	219	C4	350	C2
200-00 - 239-99	64	220	B1	351	C4
248-00 - 260-99	62	221	A4	351	B5
Long St	34	238	B2	356	B3
Look St	63	221	A4	351	B5
Loretta Rd	91	249	B5	365	B4
Lori Dr	60	203	B6	350	A3
Loubet St	75	225	C6	355	A6
Louise Ct	94	251	A6	364	C2
Lovingham Pl	12	238	A3	357	B4
Lowe Ct	35	231	C4	356	A2
Lucas St		239	A4	357	B4
120-00 - 120-99	12	239	A4	357	B4
121-00 - 125-99	13	239	A4	357	B4
Ludlum Av	12	232	C1	357	A4
Luke Pl	64	220	B1	351	B4
Luther Rd	85	228	C1	355	B5
Lutheran Av	79	224	B1	355	A5
Lux Rd	35	237	A6	356	B2
Lyman St	27	233	A4	351	C5
Macintosh St	77	215	B4	348	C3
MacNish St	73	216	B2	349	C4
Madison St	73	224	A2	349	C4
Madison St	85	227	B4	355	A4
Mador Ct	91	249	B6	365	B5
Magnolia Pl	55	218	A3	350	B2
Main Av	2	198	C1	348	B2
Main St		218	A2	349	B6
36-00 - 40-99	54	218	A2	349	B6
41-00 - 60-99	55	218	B2	349	B6
61-00 - 79-99	67	218	C2	349	C6
80-00 - OUT	35	230	B3	356	A2
Malba Dr (144th St)	57	202	B3	349	A6
Mangin Av	12	232	C1	357	B4
Manilla St	73	216	C1	349	C4
Manor Rd	27	220	C3	351	C5
	63	204	C3	351	A4
Manse St	75	225	C6	355	A6
Manton St	35	230	B3	356	A2
Manville La	97	253	B4	369	B4
Maple Av	55	218	B2	349	B6
Marathon Pkwy		220	A3	351	B5
34-00 - 44-99	63	220	A3	351	B5
45-00 - 66-99	62	221	A4	351	B5
Marengo St	23	232	A1	357	A4
Margaret Pl	85	229	B5	355	A6
Marine Terminal Rd	71	209	A6	349	B4
Marinette St	63	204	C3	351	A4
Marion Wk	97	252	B3	368	B3
Marissa St	13	239	B4	357	C4
Market St	97	253	B4	369	B4
Markwood Pl	75	230	B1	356	A1
Marne Pl	33	238	A2	356	B3
Mars Pl	34	239	A4	357	B4
Marsden St	34	238	A2	356	B3
Marshall Av	97	252	B3	368	B3
Martense Av	68	217	B5	349	C5
Maryland Rd	62	220	A3	351	B5
Maspeth Av	78	222	B3	355	A4
Mathewson Ct	34	239	B4	357	B4
Mathias Av	33	238	A1	356	B3
Maurice Av		222	B3	355	A4
52-00 - 64-99	78	222	B3	355	A4
65-00 - OUT	77	215	C4	348	C3
Mayda Rd	22	239	C5	357	C5
Mayfair Rd	18	230	C1	356	A1
Mayfield Rd	32	231	B5	356	A3
Mayville St	12	232	C1	357	A4
Mazeau St	78	223	A6	349	C4
McBride St	91	249	B5	365	B4
McIntosh St	69	210	A3	349	B5
McLaughlin Av	23	231	A6	356	A3
Meadow Dr	34	238	C3	357	C4
Meehan Av	91	249	B6	365	C5
Melbourne Av	67	218	C3	350	C2
Melissa Ct	60	204	B1	350	A3
Melrose La	63	204	C3	351	B4
Melvina Pl	78	222	B3	355	A4
Memorial Cir	94	251	B4	364	C1
Memorial Dr	18	230	C1	356	A1
Memphis Av	22	239	C6	357	C5
Menahan St	85	227	A4	355	A4
Mentone St		239	C5	357	C5
225-00 - 232-99	13	239	C5	357	C4
233-00 - 236-99	22	239	C5	357	C5
Meridian Rd	55	218	B1	349	C6
Merrick Blvd	32	231	B5	356	A3
87-00 - 91-99	32	231	B5	356	A3
92-00 - 113-99	33	231	C5	356	A3
114-00 - 134-99	34	238	A2	356	B3
135-00 - 232-99	13	239	B4	357	B4
233-00 - 245-99	22	239	B6	357	C5
Merrill St	34	238	A3	357	B4
Metcalf Av	65	219	B4	350	C2
Metropolitan Av		222	C1	355	A4
46-00 - 61-48	85	222	C1	355	A4
61-49 - 80-99	79	228	A1	355	A5
89-00 - 91-99	74	229	A5	355	A6
92-00 - 108-99	75	229	A6	355	A6
115-00 - 132-99	18	230	B1	356	A1
118-00 - 129-99	15	230	C2	356	A1
Mexico St	12	238	A3	357	B4
Meyer Av		243	B5	365	A5
1-99	22	243	B5	365	A5
157-00 - 158-99	34	238	A1	356	B3
159-00 - 159-99	33	238	A1	356	B3
Michael Ct	60	204	B1	350	A3
Michael Pl	60	204	B1	350	A3
Middlemay Pl	75	230	B1	356	A1
Midland Pkwy	32	231	B6	356	A3
Milburn St	12	239	A4	357	B4
	13	239	A4	357	B4
Miller St	54	218	A2	349	B6
Minton St	91	249	A6	365	B5
Mobile Rd	91	249	B6	365	B5
Moline St	27	233	A4	351	C5
Montauk St		238	A3	357	B4
118-00 - 120-99	12	238	A3	357	B4
121-00 - OUT	13	239	A4	357	B4
Monterey St	29	232	B3	357	A5
Morenci La	62	221	A4	351	B5
Morgan St	63	205	C4	351	B5
Morse Ct	91	249	B5	365	B4
Moss Pl	91	249	A6	365	B5
Mott Av	91	249	B5	365	B4
Mount Olivet Cres		223	C4	355	A4
60-00 - 60-99	78	223	C4	355	A4
61-00 - 62-99	79	223	C5	355	A5
Mowbray Dr (82nd Dr)	15	230	B2	356	A1
Mulbach Ct	91	249	B5	365	C4
Mulberry Av	55	218	B3	350	C2
Murdock Av		238	A2	356	B3
173-00 - 180-99	34	238	A2	356	B3
181-00 - 205-99	12	232	C2	357	B4
206-00 - 211-99	11	232	C3	357	A5
212-00 - OUT	29	232	C3	357	A5
Muriel Ct	17	237	B4	356	B1
Murray Av	59	204	B1	350	A3
Murray La	54	203	C4	350	B2
Murray St		203	C4	350	A2
1-00 - 24-99	57	203	C4	350	A2
25-00 - 40-99	54	203	C4	350	B2
41-00 - 45-99	55	219	A4	350	B2
Musket St	27	233	A4	351	C5
Myrtle Av		227	B4	355	B4
54-00 - 95-99	85	227	B4	355	B4
108-00 - 117-99	18	229	B6	355	A6
Nadel Pl	33	238	A2	356	B3
Nameoke St	91	249	A5	365	B4
Nansen St	75	225	C5	355	A6
Nasby Pl	91	249	B5	365	B4
Nashville Blvd		232	C3	357	B5
116-00 - 212-99	11	232	C3	357	A5
119-00 - 120-99	12	239	A5	357	B5
121-00 - 197-99	13	239	A4	357	B4
213-00 - OUT	29	232	C3	357	A5
Nassau Blvd	62	221	A4	351	B5
Nassau Expwy	14	237	C5	356	C2
National St	68	217	A4	349	C5
Negundo Av	55	218	B3	350	C2
Neilson St	91	249	B6	365	B5
Nellis St	13	239	A4	357	B4
Neponsit Av	94	250	B2	369	B5
Nepton St	13	239	A4	357	B4
Neptune Wk	97	253	B4	369	B4
Nero Av	23	232	A1	357	A4
New Haven Av	91	249	B5	365	B4
Newburg St	12	238	A3	357	B4
Newhall Av	22	239	C5	357	C5
Newport Av	94	250	B3	369	B6
Newport Wk	97	252	B3	368	B3
Newtown Av	2	198	C3	348	B3
Newtown Rd		208	B2	348	B3
40-01 - 49-99	3	208	B2	348	B3
50-00 - 50-99	77	208	C3	348	B3
Nicolls Av	68	217	A5	349	C5
Noel Rd	93	247	A6	364	B2
Normal Rd	32	231	B4	356	A2
Norman St	85	227	A4	355	B4
North Conduit Av		236	B2	355	C6
76-00 - 170-99	17	236	B2	355	C6
108-00 - 135-99	20	237	C4	356	C1
137-00 - 149-99	36	238	C1	356	C2
150-00 - 180-99	34	238	C2	356	C3
181-00 - 232-99	13	239	C4	357	C4
233-00 - OUT	22	239	C6	357	C5
North Dr	57	202	B3	349	A6
North Lp	59	204	A1	350	A3
North Service Ct	30	242	A1	356	C3
North Service Rd	30	241	A6	356	C2
Northern Blvd		207	C5	348	B2
30-01 - 50-99	1	207	C5	348	B2
51-00 - 69-99	77	208	C3	348	B3
70-00 - 95-99	72	209	C6	349	B4
96-00 - 130-99	68	211	B4	349	B5
132-00 - 157-99	54	218	A2	349	B6
158-00 - 199-99	58	219	A4	350	B2
200-00 - 223-99	61	219	A6	350	B3
224-00 - 255-13	63	220	A2	351	B4
Norton Av	91	249	B4	365	C4
Norton Dr	91	249	B4	365	B4
Nurge Av	78	222	C3	355	A4
Oak Av		218	B3	350	C2
137-00 - 157-99	55	218	B3	350	C2
158-00 - OUT	58	219	B4	350	C2
Oak Dr	91	249	B6	365	B5
Oak La	63	205	C4	351	B5
Oak Park Dr	62	221	B4	351	C5
Ocean (Boardwalk) Promenade	94	251	B4	369	B6
Ocean Av	97	252	B3	368	B3
Ocean Crest Blvd	91	249	B4	365	C4
Oceania St		220	A1	351	B4
33-00 - 47-99	61	220	A1	351	B4
48-00 - 79-99	64	220	B1	351	B4
Oceanside Av	97	252	B3	368	B3
Oceanside Dr	97	252	B3	368	B3
Oceanview Av	95	253	A5	369	B4
O' Connell Ct	73	216	B2	349	C4
O' Donnell Rd	33	238	A2	356	B3
Officer's Dr	59	204	B1	350	A3
Olcott St	75	229	A6	355	A6
Old Beach 88th St	93	251	A6	364	C2
Old Rockaway Blvd	30	238	C3	357	C4
Old South Rd		236	B2	355	B6
76-00 - 99-99	17	236	B2	355	B6
124-00 - OUT	20	237	C5	356	C2
Olive Pl	75	230	B1	356	A1
Olive Wk	97	252	B3	368	B3
Onderdonk Av	85	226	A2	355	A4
Onslow Pl	15	230	B2	356	A1
Orchard St	1	213	A4	348	C2
Ordnance Rd	59	204	A1	350	A3
Ostend St	91	249	B5	365	C4
Otis Av	68	217	B6	349	C5
Otto Rd	85	227	B6	355	A5
Overbrook Pl	62	220	A3	351	B5
Overhill Rd	75	230	B1	356	A1
Overlook Rd	62	221	A4	351	B5
Ovid Pl	12	232	C1	357	B4
Page Pl	78	222	B2	355	A4
Palermo St	23	232	A1	357	A4
Palmer Dr	97	252	B2	368	B3
Palmetto St	85	227	A4	355	A4
Palo Alto Av	23	232	B1	357	A4
Palo Alto St	23	232	A1	357	A4
Park Cres	32	231	B4	356	A2
Park Dr E	67	230	A2	349	C6
Park End Pl	75	230	B1	356	A1
Park La	15	230	B2	356	A1
	63	204	C3	351	A4
Park La S		229	C4	355	B6
74-00 - 96-99	21	229	C4	355	B6
101-00 - 117-99	18	230	C1	356	B1
119-00 - OUT	15	230	B2	356	A1
Parsons Blvd		202	A3	349	A6
1-00 - 24-99	57	203	C4	350	A2
25-00 - 40-99	54	218	A3	350	B2
41-00 - 52-99	55	218	A3	350	B2
57-00 - 72-99	65	219	C4	350	C2
73-00 - 79-99	66	231	A4	356	A2
80-00 - OUT	32	231	B4	356	A2
Parvine Av	92	248	B2	364	C3
Pearl Rd	56	202	B2	349	A6
Pearl St	91	249	A5	365	B4
Pearson Pl	1	213	B4	348	C2
Pearson St	1	212	A3	348	C2
Peartree Av	75	230	A1	349	C6
Peck Av		218	B3	350	C2
137-00 - 153-98	55	218	B3	350	C2
175-01 - 197-98	65	219	B5	350	C3
214-01 - 215-98	64	220	C2	351	C4
217-00 - OUT	27	220	C2	351	C4
Peconic St	17	236	B3	356	C1
Pelham Wk	97	252	B3	368	B3
Pell Av	68	211	C6	349	B5
Pembroke Av	62	205	C5	351	B5
Penelope Av	79	224	C1	355	A5
Penrod St	68	217	B6	349	C5
Perry Av	78	223	B4	355	A4
Pershing Cres	35	230	B3	356	A2
Perth Rd	32	231	A6	350	C3
Petracca Pl	57	202	B3	349	A6
Pettit Av	73	216	B1	349	C4
Phlox Pl	55	218	B3	350	B2
Phroane Av	33	238	A2	356	B3
Pidgeon Meadow Rd		219	B4	350	B2
162-00 - 169-99	58	219	A4	350	B2
170-00 - 175-00	65	219	B5	350	C3
Pilot Rd	30	238	C1	356	C3
Pinegrove St	35	237	A6	356	B2
Pineville La	13	239	B4	357	B4
Pinson St	91	249	A5	365	B4
Pinto St	23	232	A1	357	A4
Pitkin Av	17	236	B2	355	B6
Plainview Av	91	249	B6	365	C5
Plattwood Av	17	236	B3	356	B1
Pleasantview St	79	224	C1	355	A5
Plunkett Av	91	249	A4	365	B4
Point Breeze Pl	91	249	A4	365	B4
Point Breezy Av	97	252	B3	368	B3
Point Cres	57	202	B3	349	A6
Polhemus Av	33	231	C6	356	A3
Polo Pl	74	229	A5	355	A6
Pompeii Av	23	232	A1	357	A4
Pompeii Rd	23	232	A1	357	A4
Pontiac St	27	233	A4	351	C5
Poplar Av	55	218	B3	350	C2
Pople Av	55	218	B2	349	B6
Poppenhusen Av	56	202	B1	349	A5
Porter Rd	34	238	C3	357	C4
Powell's Cove Blvd		202	B2	349	A6
126-00 - 129-99	56	202	B2	349	A6
147-00 - OUT	57	203	A5	350	A2
Power Rd W	93	247	B6	364	B2
Poyer St	73	216	B1	349	C4
Pratt Av	59	204	B1	350	A3
President St	91	249	B5	365	B4
Prince St	54	218	A2	349	B6
Princeton St	35	237	A6	356	B2
Prospect Av	63	205	C4	351	B5
Prospect Ct	13	239	C4	357	C4
Purves St	1	213	A4	348	C2
Putnam Av	85	227	B4	355	A4
Queens Blvd		213	A6	348	C2
29-00 - 38-99	1	213	A5	348	C2
39-00 - 48-99	4	213	A6	348	C2
48-00 - 73-99	77	214	B3	348	C3
74-00 - 91-99	73	216	C2	349	C4
92-00 - 99-99	74	225	A5	349	C5
100-00 - 118-99	75	225	A6	349	C5
120-00 - 126-99	15	230	B2	356	A1
120-55 only (Borough Hall)	24	230	A2	356	A1
137-00 - OUT	35	230	B3	356	A2
Queens Plz E	1	213	A5	348	C2
Queens Plz N (Bridge Plz N)	1	207	C4	348	B2
Queens Plz S (Bridge Plz S)	1	206	C3	348	B2
Queens St	1	213	A4	348	C2
Queens Wk	97	252	B3	368	B3
Quencer Rd	12	232	C1	357	B4
Quince Av	55	218	B3	350	C2
Race Track Rd	14	237	C4	356	C1
Radar Rd	30	238	C1	356	C3
Radcliff Av	68	217	B5	349	C5
Radnor Rd		231	A6	356	A3
84-00 - 187-99	32	231	A6	356	A3
188-00 - OUT	23	231	A6	356	A3
Radnor St	32	231	B6	356	A3
Railroad Av	1	213	C4	348	C2
Railroad Pl	78	222	B2	355	A4
Raleigh St	17	236	C3	356	C1
Range St	27	233	A4	351	C5
Ransom St	27	233	A4	351	C5
Rau Ct	14	241	A4	356	C1
Reads La	91	249	B6	365	B5
Red Cross La	59	204	B1	350	A3
Redding St	17	236	B3	356	C1
Redfern Av	91	249	B5	365	C4
Redfield St	62	220	A3	351	B5
Reeder St	73	216	C2	349	C4
Reeves Av	67	218	C3	350	C2
Regatta Pl	63	204	C3	351	B4
Regina Av	91	249	B5	365	B4
Reid Av	97	253	B4	369	B4
Reinhart Rd	91	248	B3	364	C3
Remington St	35	237	A6	356	B2
Remsen Pl	78	223	B4	355	A4
Rene Ct	85	226	A3	355	A4
Review Av	1	213	C4	348	C2
Rex Pl	33	231	C6	356	A3
Ricard St	85	226	A3	355	A4
Richardson Pl	33	231	C6	356	A3
Richland Av	64	220	C1	351	C4
Richmond Rd	63	204	C3	351	A5
Rico Pl	17	236	B3	356	C1
Ridge Rd	63	204	C3	351	A4
Ridgedale St	13	239	B4	357	B4
Riis Av	94	250	B2	369	B5
Ring Pl	34	238	A2	356	B3
Rio Dr	23	231	B6	356	A3
Riverside Dr	57	203	A5	350	A2
Riverton St	12	238	A3	357	B4
Riviera Ct	56	202	A2	349	A6
Robard La	29	232	B3	357	A5
Robert Rd	60	204	B1	350	A3
Robin La	60	203	B6	350	A3
Robinson St	55	218	B3	350	B2
Rockaway Beach Blvd		248	C1	364	C2
1-00 - 53-99	91	248	C3	364	C3
54-00 - 77-99	92	248	C2	364	C3
78-00 - 97-99	93	248	C1	364	C2
98-00 - OUT	94	250	B3	369	B6
Rockaway Blvd		236	A1	355	B6
74-00 - 79-99	21	236	A1	355	B6
80-00 - 91-99	16	236	A2	355	B6
92-00 - 107-99	17	236	B3	356	B1
108-00 - 135-99	20	237	B4	356	B1
137-00 - 149-99	36	238	B1	356	C3
150-00 - 179-99	34	238	B2	356	C3
229-00 - 232-99	13	243	A4	357	C4
233-00 - OUT	22	243	A4	365	A4
Rockaway Frwy	91	248	C3	364	C3
Rockaway Point Blvd	97	252	B2	368	B3
Rocky Hill Rd	61	219	B6	350	B3
Roe Pl	60	203	B6	350	A3
Roe Rd	34	238	A3	357	B4
Rome Dr	12	232	C1	357	B4
Romeo Ct	23	232	A1	357	A4
Roosevelt Av		214	B2	348	C3
49-00 - 69-99	77	214	A3	348	C3
70-00 - 95-99	72	216	A1	349	C4
96-00 - 127-99	68	217	A4	349	C5
131-00 - OUT	54	218	A2	349	B6
Roosevelt St	91	249	B6	365	B5
Roosevelt Wk	97	252	B3	368	B3
Rose Av	55	218	B3	350	C2
Rose Ct	91	249	B6	365	B5
Rosewood	64	219	B6	350	B3
Rosita Rd	17	237	B4	356	B1
Roxbury Av	97	253	A5	369	B4
Roxbury Blvd	97	253	A5	369	B4
Rufus King Av	32	231	C4	356	A2
Ruscoe St	33	231	C6	356	A3
Rushmore Av	62	220	A3	351	B5
Rushmore Ter	62	221	A4	351	B5
Russell Pl	75	230	B1	356	A1
Russell St	14	241	A4	356	C1
Rust St	78	222	B2	355	A4
Rutledge Av	85	229	A4	355	A6
Ryan Ct	57	203	C4	350	A2
Ryan Rd	13	239	B4	357	C4
Rye Pl	12	238	A3	357	A4
Sabre St	27	233	A4	351	C5
Sagamore Av	23	232	B1	357	A4
Sagamore Rd	23	232	B1	357	A4
Sage St	91	249	A6	365	B5
Saint Cloud Rd	92	248	B1	364	C2
Saint Felix Av	85	227	A5	355	B4
Saint James Av	73	216	B2	349	C4
Saint Johns Rd	85	226	A3	355	A4
Saint Nicholas Av	85	226	B3	355	A4
Salerno Av	23	232	A1	357	A4
Sancho St	23	232	A1	357	A4
Sanders Pl	35	231	C4	356	B2
Sandhill Rd	63	205	C4	351	B5
Sandy Rd	91	249	C5	365	C4
Sanford Av		218	B2	349	B6
131-00 - 157-99	55	218	B2	349	B6
158-00 - OUT	58	219	A4	350	B2
Santiago St	23	231	A6	356	A3
Saull St	55	218	B2	349	B6
Saultell Av	68	217	B6	349	C5
Saunders St	74	225	A4	349	C5
Sawyer Av	27	232	A3	351	C5
Sayres Av	33	238	A2	356	B3
Schaefer St	85	227	C4	355	B4
Scheer St	92	248	B1	364	C2
Schorr Dr	56	202	B2	349	A6
Scotta Gadell Pl	91	249	B5	365	B4
Seabreeze Av	97	253	A5	369	B4
Seabreeze Wk	97	252	B3	368	B3
Seabury St	73	216	C2	349	C4
Seafoam Ct	92	248	C2	364	C3
Seagirt Av	91	249	B6	365	C5
Seagirt Blvd	91	249	B5	365	C4
Seaside Av	94	251	A6	364	C1
Seasongood Rd	75	230	B1	356	A1
Selfridge St	75	225	C5	355	A6
Selover Rd	34	238	A3	357	B4
Seneca Av	85	226	A1	355	A4
Sergeant Beers Av	59	204	B1	350	A3
Sergeant Beers La	59	204	B2	351	A4
Seward Av	27	220	C3	351	C5
Shad Creek Rd	93	247	B6	364	B2
Shaler Av	85	227	B6	355	A5
Shiloh Av	26	221	C5	351	C6
Shore Av		237	A6	356	B2
143-00 - 149-99	35	237	A6	356	B2
150-00 - OUT	33	237	A6	356	B2
Shore Blvd	2	198	B2	348	A2
20-00 - 23-99	5	199	A4	348	A3
24-00 - 25-99	2	198	B3	348	A3
Shore Front Pkwy		251	B6	364	C2
73-00 - 77-99	92	248	C1	364	C2
78-00 - 97-99	93	248	C1	364	C2
98-00 - OUT	94	251	B5	364	C2
Shore Pkwy	14	236	C3	356	C1
Shore Rd	59	204	A1	350	A3
	63	204	C3	351	A4
Shorthill Pl	75	230	B1	356	A1
Shorthill Rd	75	230	B1	356	A1
Sidway Pl	34	238	A3	357	B4
Sign Test Rd	30	238	C1	356	C3
Sigourney Av	29	232	B3	357	A5
Silver Rd	17	236	B3	356	C1
Simonson St	73	216	C1	349	C4
Sitka St	17	236	B3	356	C1
Skillman Av		212	B3	348	C2
24-01 - 38-99	1	212	B3	348	C2
39-01 - 48-99	4	214	A1	348	C3
49-00 - 54-99	77	214	A3	348	C3
Sloan St	13	239	B4	357	C4
Slocum Cres	75	230	B1	356	A1
Smart St	55	218	B3	350	B2
Smedley St	35	230	B3	356	A2
Smith Ct	91	249	B5	365	B4
Smith St	34	238	A2	356	B3
Soho Dr	23	231	B6	356	A3
Somerset Rd	32	231	B6	356	A3
Sound St	5	199	C5	348	B3
South Cargo Rd	30	242	A1	356	C3
South Conduit Av		236	B2	355	C6
75-00 - 91-98	14	236	B2	355	C6
124-00 - 128-98	20	237	C5	356	C2
130-00 - 132-98	30	237	C6	356	C2
153-00 - 178-98	34	238	C2	356	C3
181-00 - 232-98	13	239	C4	357	C4
241-00 - 248-98	22	239	C6	357	C5
South Dr	57	202	B3	349	A6
South Rd		237	A6	356	B2
140-00 - 149-99	35	237	A6	356	B2
150-00 - 170-99	33	231	C4	356	B2
South Service Ct	30	242	A1	356	C3
South Service Rd	30	241	A6	356	C2
Southgate Plz	13	239	B4	357	C4
Southgate St	13	239	B4	357	C4
Spa Pl	35	237	A6	356	B2
Spencer Av	27	232	A2	351	C4
Spencito Rd	93	247	B6	364	C2
Spiller Rd	59	204	B1	350	A3
Springfield Blvd		220	B2	351	B4
41-00 - 47-99	61	220	A1	351	B4
48-00 - 79-99	64	220	B2	351	B4
80-00 - 89-99	27	232	A3	351	C5
90-00 - 94-99	28	232	A3	351	C5
95-00 - 113-99	29	233	B4	357	A5
114-00 - 120-99	11	232	C3	357	A5
121-00 - 152-99	13	239	B4	357	B4
Springfield La	13	239	C4	357	C4
Spritz Rd	17	236	B3	356	C1
Spruce St	68	217	A4	349	C5
Standish Pl	75	230	B1	356	A1
Stanhope St	85	226	B2	355	A4
Starr Av	1	213	C4	348	C2
Starr St	85	226	A2	355	A4
State Rd	97	253	A5	369	B4
Station Rd		219	A4	350	B2
157-00 - 158-99	55	219	A4	350	B2
159-01 - 196-99	58	219	A4	350	B2
Station Sq	75	230	A1	356	A1
Steinway Pl	5	199	B6	348	A3
Steinway St		208	B1	348	B3
18-00 - 23-99	5	200	B1	349	A4
24-00 - 32-99	3	208	B1	348	B3
34-00 - 36-99	1	208	C1	348	B3
Stephen St	85	227	A4	355	B4
Stewart Rd		220	C2	351	C4
217-01 - 217-99	64	220	C2	351	C4
218-01 - OUT	27	220	C2	351	C4
Stier St	85	227	B5	355	A5
Stockholm St	85	226	B2	355	A4
Story Av	59	204	B1	350	A3
Story Rd	92	248	C2	364	C3
Stratton St	54	218	A2	349	B6
Stripoll Sq	77	208	B3	348	B3
Strong Av	68	217	B5	349	C5
Stronghurst Av	27	220	C3	351	C5
Suffolk Dr	12	238	A3	357	B4
Suffolk Wk	97	252	B3	368	B3
Sullivan Rd	12	232	C1	357	B4
Summer St	75	230	B1	356	A1
Summerfield St	85	227	A4	355	B4
Summit Ct	55	218	B2	349	B6
Summit Pl	57	202	B3	349	A6
Sunbury Rd	34	238	A3	357	B4
Sunnyside St	91	249	A4	365	B4
Sunrise Hwy	22	239	C5	357	C5
Surf Rd	91	249	C4	365	C4
Surrey Pl	32	231	A5	350	C3
Sutphin Blvd		231	C4	356	A2
87-00 - 113-99	35	231	C4	356	A2
114-00 - 125-99	36	238	B1	356	B3
Sutro St	23	232	A1	357	A4

Queens

Sutter Av		236	B2	355	C6
77-00 - 107-99	17	236	B2	355	C6
108-00 - 135-99	20	237	B5	356	C2
137-00 - 149-99	36	237	B6	356	C2
Sutton Pl (161st St)	65	231	A4	350	C2
Suydam St	85	226	A2	355	A4
Swan Rd	92	248	C2	364	C3
Sybilla St (69th Av)	75	229	A6	355	A6
Sylvester La	59	204	B1	350	A3
Syringa Pl	55	218	B3	350	B2
Tahoe St	17	236	C3	356	C1
Talbot St	15	230	B2	356	A1
Tennis Pl (70th Rd)	75	230	B1	356	A1
Theater Rd	59	204	B1	350	A3
Thebes Av	62	220	A3	351	B5
Thetford La	97	253	B4	369	B4
Thomson Av	1	213	A4	348	C2
Thornhill Av	62	221	A4	351	B5
Thornton Pl		225	B5	355	A6
66-00 - 66-99	74	225	B5	355	A6
67-00 - 67-99	75	225	B5	355	A6
Thursby Av	92	248	B1	364	C2
Thurston St		239	B4	357	C4
136-00 - 136-99	34	239	B4	357	B4
137-00 - OUT	13	239	B4	357	C4
Tioga Dr	12	238	A3	357	B4
Tioga Wk	97	252	B2	368	B3
Tonsor St	85	226	A3	355	A4
Totten Av	59	204	B1	350	A3
Totten St	57	203	B6	350	A3
Traffic Av	85	227	A5	355	A5
Trappe Pl	33	231	C5	356	A3
Triboro Plz	2	198	B3	348	A2
Trimble Rd	77	215	A4	348	C3
Trist Pl	91	249	A4	365	B4
Troon Rd	32	231	A6	350	C3
Trotting Course La		229	A5	355	A6
69-00 - 70-99	74	229	A5	355	A6
73-01 - OUT	85	229	B6	355	A6
Troutman St	85	226	A1	355	A4
Troutville Rd	34	238	A3	357	B4
Tryon Pl	32	231	A5	356	A3
Tuckerton St	33	231	C4	356	B2
Tudor Rd	32	231	A5	356	A3
Turin Dr	12	238	A3	357	B4
Tyler Av	77	215	C4	348	C3
Ulmer St	54	202	C2	349	A6
Underhill Av		219	B5	350	A6
164-00 - 194-99	65	219	B5	350	C2
200-00 - OUT	64	204	B1	351	C4
Underhill Rd	59	204	B1	350	A3
Underwood Rd	75	230	B1	356	A1
Union Hall St	33	231	C5	356	A3
Union St		218	A2	349	B6
25-00 - 40-99	54	202	C3	349	A6
41-00 - 47-99	55	218	A2	349	B6
Union Tpke		229	B5	355	A6
1-00 - 96-00	85	229	B5	355	A6
103-01 - 119-99 (odd)	75	229	B5	355	A6
117-00 - 119-98 (even)	15	230	B2	356	A1
135-01 - 138-99 (odd)	67	230	B3	356	A2
135-02 - 135-98 (even)	35	230	B3	356	A2
141-00 - 157-99	67	230	B3	356	A2
158-00 - 199-99	66	231	A4	356	A2
200-00 - 230-99	64	220	C2	351	C4
231-00 - 237-99	27	221	C4	351	C5
242-00 - 252-99	26	221	C5	351	C5
253-00 - 268-98 (even) (Floral Park)	4	221	B5	351	C6
265-01 - OUT (odd) (New Hyde Park)	40	221	B6	351	C6
Upshaw Rd	75	230	B2	356	A1
Ursina Rd	34	238	A3	357	B4
Ursula Pl	75	229	A6	355	A6
Utica Wk	97	252	B2	368	B3
Utopia Pkwy		203	B6	350	A3
1-00 - 24-99	57	203	B6	350	A3
25-00 - 47-99	58	219	A5	350	B3
48-00 - 72-99	65	219	C5	350	C3
73-00 - 79-99	66	231	A5	350	C3
80-00 - 82-99	32	231	A5	356	A3
Valentine Pl	85	228	A3	355	A6
Van Brunt Rd	93	247	B6	364	C2
Van Cleef St	68	217	B6	349	C5
Van Dam St	1	213	B5	348	C2
Van Doren St	68	217	B6	349	C5
Van Horn St	73	216	C2	349	C4
Van Kleeck St	73	216	C1	349	C4
Van Loon St	73	216	C2	349	C4
Van Nostrand Ct	63	205	C4	351	A4
Van Nostrand Pl	63	204	C3	351	B4
Van Sicklen St	19	237	A5	356	B2
Van Wyck Expwy		230	B3	356	A2
84-01 - 113-99 (odd)	35	230	B3	356	A2
85-02 - 93-98 (even)	18	230	C3	356	A2
94-02 - 107-98 (even)	19	230	C3	356	B2
109-02 - 135-98 (even)	20	237	A6	356	B2
114-01 - 135-99 (odd)	36	237	B6	356	B2
140-01 - 140-99	30	241	A6	356	C2
Van Zandt Av	62	220	A3	351	B5
Vanderveer St		232	A2	351	C4
88-00 - 89-99	27	232	A2	351	C4
90-00 - 94-99	28	232	A3	357	A5
Vaux Rd	77	215	A4	348	C3
Vermont Pl	7	235	A4	355	B5
Vernon Blvd		206	B3	348	B2
29-00 - 30-99	2	198	C1	348	B2
31-00 - 36-99	6	207	B4	348	B2
37-00 - OUT	1	206	B3	348	B2
Victoria Dr	34	238	A3	357	B4
Victoria Rd	34	238	A3	357	B4
Vietor Av	73	216	B1	349	C4
Village Rd (Pvt)		230	B3	356	A2
144-00 - 149-99	35	230	B3	356	A2
150-00 - OUT	32	231	B4	356	A2
Virginia St	91	249	A6	365	B5
Vleigh Pl	67	230	A3	350	C2
Walden Av	62	205	C5	351	B5
Waldron St	68	217	B6	349	C5
Walnut St	75	229	A6	355	A6
Walter Reed Rd	59	204	A1	350	A3
Waltham St	35	231	C4	356	B2
Walton Rd	93	247	A6	364	B2
Wareham Pl	32	231	B6	356	A3
Warren St		210	C3	349	B5
37-00 - 37-99	72	216	A3	349	C5
40-00 - 41-99	73	216	A3	349	C5
Warwick Av	63	204	C3	351	A4
Warwick Cres	32	231	B5	356	A3
Water Edge Dr	60	204	B2	351	A4
Waterloo Pl	91	249	A4	365	B4
Waterview St	91	249	B4	365	B4
Watjean Ct	91	249	B5	365	C4
Watson Pl	33	231	C6	356	A3
Weaver Av	59	204	B1	350	A3
Webe Pl	57	203	B5	350	A2
Weeks La		219	B6	350	C3
47-00 - 47-99	61	219	B6	350	B3
48-00 - OUT	65	219	B6	350	B3
Weirfield St	85	227	C4	355	B4
Weller Av	22	239	C5	357	C5
Weller La	22	243	A6	357	C5
Welling Ct	2	198	C1	348	B2
Wendover Rd	75	230	B1	356	A1
West 1st Rd	93	247	A6	364	B2
West 2nd Rd	93	247	A6	364	B2
West 4th Rd	93	247	A6	364	B2
West 5th Rd	93	247	A6	364	B2
West 6th Rd	93	247	A6	364	B2
West 8th Rd	93	247	A6	364	B2
West 9th Rd	93	247	A6	364	B2
West 10th Rd	93	247	B6	364	B2
West 11th Rd	93	247	B6	364	B2
West 12th Rd	93	247	B6	364	B2
West 13th Rd	93	247	B6	364	B2
West 14th Rd	93	247	B6	364	B2
West 15th Rd	93	247	B6	364	B2
West 16th Rd	93	247	B6	364	B2
West 17th Rd	93	247	B6	364	B2
West 18th Rd	93	247	B6	364	B2
West 19th Rd	93	247	B6	364	C2
West 20th Rd	93	247	B6	364	C2
West 22nd Rd	93	247	B6	364	C2
West Dr	63	204	C3	351	A4
West Hangar Rd	30	241	A5	356	C2
West Market St	97	252	B3	368	B3
West Rd	93	247	A6	364	B2
West St	1	213	A4	348	C2
Westaway Rd	59	204	B1	350	A3
Westbourne Av	91	249	A4	365	B4
Westend Dr	62	205	C5	351	B5
Westgate St	34	238	B3	357	C4
Westmoreland Pl	63	204	C3	351	A4
Westmoreland St	63	205	C4	351	A4
Westside Av	68	217	B6	349	C5
Wetherole St		225	A4	349	C5
60-00 - 60-99	73	224	A3	349	C5
61-00 - 66-99	74	225	A4	349	C5
Wexford Ter		231	B6	356	A3
175-00 - 187-99	32	231	B6	356	A3
188-00 - OUT	23	231	B6	356	A3
Wheatley St	91	249	A5	365	B4
Whistler Av	59	204	A1	350	A3
White Oak Ct	70	209	A6	349	B4
Whitehall Ter	27	232	A2	357	A4
Whitelaw St	17	236	B3	356	C1
Whitestone Expwy		202	A3	349	A6
6-00 - 23-99	57	203	B4	350	A2
26-00 - 31-99	54	202	A3	349	A6
133-00 - 133-98	57	202	A3	349	A6
Whitney Av	73	216	B2	349	C4
Whitson St	75	230	B1	356	A1
Wicklow Pl	32	231	A6	356	A3
Willets Point Blvd		218	A1	349	B6
126-00 - 128-99	68	218	A1	349	B6
143-00 - 199-99	57	203	C4	350	A2
200-00 - OUT	60	203	B6	350	A3
Willets St	59	204	B1	350	A3
William Ct	91	249	B6	365	C5
Williamson Av	13	239	A4	357	B4
Willoughby Av	85	226	A2	355	A4
Willow St	63	205	C4	351	B5
Winchester Blvd		233	A4	351	C5
80-00 - 88-99	27	221	C4	351	C5
90-00 - 92-99	28	233	A4	351	C5
Winter St	75	230	B1	356	A1
Witthoff Av	29	232	C3	357	A5
Wood St	12	232	C1	357	B4
Woodbine St	85	227	B4	355	A4
Woodhaven Blvd		224	A3	349	C5
60-00 - 60-99	73	224	A3	349	C5
61-00 - 70-99	74	224	A3	349	C5
71-00 - 83-51	85	229	A5	355	A6
83-52 - 93-99	21	229	C6	355	B6
94-00 - 102-99	16	236	A3	356	B1
103-00 - OUT	17	236	B3	356	B1
Woodhaven Ct	16	236	A3	356	B1
Woodhull Av	23	232	B1	357	A4
Woodside Av		208	C3	348	B3
33-02 - 37-98 (even)	1	208	C3	348	B3
37-01 - 38-99 (odd)	77	208	C3	348	B3
38-02 - 38-98 (even)	4	214	A3	348	C3
39-00 - 73-99	77	214	A3	348	C3
74-00 - OUT	73	215	B6	349	C4
Woodward Av	85	226	A2	355	A4
Wren Pl	33	231	C6	356	A3
Xenia St	68	217	B5	349	C5
Yates Rd	33	237	A6	356	B2
Yellowstone Blvd		225	C5	355	A6
61-00 - 73-99	75	225	C5	355	A6
74-00 - 75-99	74	225	C5	355	A6
Zion St	62	220	A3	351	B5
Zoller Rd	34	238	B3	357	B4

AIRPORTS

John F Kennedy Intl	30	244	B3	356	C2
La Guardia Airport	71	201	C4	349	A4

BRIDGES & TUNNELS

Bronx-Whitestone Br (Toll)	57	202	A3	349	A6
Congressman Joseph Addabbo Cross Br	93	241	B4	364	A1
Cross Bay Veterans Mem Br (Toll)	93	251	A6	364	C2
Kosciuszko Br	78	212	Inset	348	C2
Roosevelt Isl Br	44	206	A3	348	B2
J J Byrne Mem Br	1	213	C4	348	C2
Marine Parkway-Gil Hodges Mem Br		250	B1	369	A5
Queensboro Br (59th St Br)	1	206	B1	348	B1
Queens-Midtown Tunnel (Toll)	1	212	A2	348	C1
Pulaski Br	1	212	B2	348	C1
Rikers Island Br	70	200	B2	349	A4
Throgs Neck Br (Toll)	57	203	A6	350	A3
Triborough Br (Toll)	2	198	A2	348	A2

Staten Island

and Bayonne, Jersey City, Hoboken, Union City, Weehawken, West New York (New Jersey)

NEIGHBORHOODS

Annadale	12	308	A1	367	B4
Arden Heights	12	307	A5	366	B3
Arlington	3	312	B2	358	A3
Arrochar	5	298	C1	360	C2
Bay Terrace	6	309	A4	367	A6
Bergen Point	B.C.	314	C1	352	C1
Bloomfield	14	300	A2	358	B2
Bull's Head	14	300	B3	358	B3
Butler Manor	9	310	C3	366	C2
Charleston	9	306	B1	366	B1
Chelsea	14	300	C2	358	C2
Clifton	4	297	B5	360	B2
Concord	4	295	C5	359	B6
Dongan Hills	5	305	A4	359	C6
Egbertville	6	304	B1	359	C4
Elm Park	2	301	A5	359	B4
Eltingville	12	308	A2	367	B4
Emerson Hill	1	295	B4	359	B6
Fox Hills	4	297	C4	359	B6
Fresh Kills	14	302	B2	366	A3
Graniteville	14	301	B4	358	B3
Grant City	6	304	B3	367	Inset
Grasmere	5	295	C6	359	C6
Great Kills	8	308	A3	367	A5
Greenridge	12	302	C2	366	A3
Grymes Hill	1	296	B2	359	B6
Harmon Cove	S.T.	324	A1	346	A1
Heartland Village	14	303	A5	358	C3
Howland Hook	3	309	Inset	358	A2
Huguenot	12	307	B5	366	B3
Huguenot Beach	12	307	C5	367	C4
Laurel Hill	S.T.	320	A1	346	B1
Lighthouse Hill	6	303	B6	367	A5
Livingston	10	293	B5	359	A5
Mariners Harbor	3	301	A4	358	A3
Midland Beach	6	305	B4	367	Inset
Mount Loretto	9	311	B4	366	C2
New Brighton	1	290	B3	359	A6
New Dorp	6	304	C2	367	A6
New Dorp Beach	6	304	C3	367	Inset
New Springville	14	300	C3	358	C3
Oakwood	6	304	C2	367	A6
Oakwood Beach	6	309	A6	367	Inset
Old Place	3	300	A2	358	A2
Old Town	5	305	A5	359	C6
Park Hill	4	295	B5	359	B6
Pleasant Plains	9	306	C3	366	B2
Port Ivory	3	312	B2	358	A3
Port Mobil	9	306	A1	366	B2
Port Richmond	2	292	C2	359	A4
Prince's Bay	9	307	C4	366	B3
Randall Manor	1	290	B2	359	A6
Richmond Town	6	303	B6	367	A5
Richmond Valley	9	310	B3	366	C2
Rosebank	5	297	C5	360	B2
Rossville	9	306	A3	366	A2
Saint George	1	291	A4	359	A6
Sandy Ground	9	306	A2	366	B2
Shore Acres	5	298	A2	360	B2
South Beach	5	305	A6	360	C2
Stapleton	4	297	A4	359	A6
Sunnyside	1	295	A4	359	B5
Todt Hill	4	294	C3	359	C5
Tompkinsville	1	291	C5	359	A6
Tottenville	7	310	C1	366	C1
Tottenville Beach	7	310	C1	366	C1
Travis	14	302	A2	358	C2
Ward Hill	4	291	C4	359	A6
West Brighton	10	294	A3	359	A5
Westerleigh	14	301	B5	359	B4
Willowbrook	14	301	C5	359	C4
Woodrow	9	306	B3	366	B3

NUMBERED STREETS

1st Av	14	301	C4	358	C3
1st Av	N.B.T.	332	B3	342	C3
1st Ct	12	308	C2	367	B4
1st St	6	304	B2	367	A6
1st St	H.C.	323	B4	346	C3
1st St	J.C.	318	B2	353	A4
2nd Av	14	301	C5	359	C4
2nd Av	N.B.T.	332	A3	342	C3
2nd Ct	12	308	C2	367	B4
2nd St	6	304	B2	367	A6
2nd St	H.C.	323	B4	346	C3
2nd St	J.C.	318	B2	353	A4
2nd St	U.C.	326	C2	346	B2
3rd Av	14	301	C5	359	B4
3rd Av	N.B.T.	332	A3	342	C3
3rd Ct	12	308	C2	367	B4
3rd St	6	304	B2	367	A6
3rd St	H.C.	323	B4	346	C3
3rd St	J.C.	318	B2	353	A4
3rd St	U.C.	326	C2	346	B2
4th Av	14	301	C5	359	B4
4th Av	N.B.T.	332	A3	342	C3
4th Ct	12	308	C2	367	B4
4th St	6	304	B2	367	A6
4th St	H.C.	323	B4	346	C3
4th St	J.C.	318	B2	353	A4
4th St	U.C.	326	C2	346	B2
5th Av	N.B.T.	332	A3	342	C3
5th St	H.C.	323	B4	346	C3
5th St	J.C.	321	A4	346	B2
5th St	J.C.	318	B2	353	A4
5th St	U.C.	326	C2	346	B2
5th St S	12	308	C1	367	B4
6th St	6	304	B2	367	A6
6th St	H.C.	323	A4	346	C3
6th St	N.B.T.	326	B1	346	B3
6th St	U.C.	326	C2	346	B2
7th St	6	304	B2	367	A6
7th St	H.C.	323	A4	346	C3
7th St	J.C.	318	A2	346	C2
7th St	N.B.T.	326	B1	346	B3
7th St	U.C.	326	B2	346	B2
8th St	6	304	C2	367	A6
8th St	H.C.	323	A4	346	C3
8th St	J.C.	318	A2	346	C2
8th St	N.B.T.	326	B1	346	B2
8th St	U.C.	326	B2	346	B2
9th St	6	304	B2	367	A6
9th St	H.C.	323	A4	346	C3
9th St	J.C.	318	A2	346	C2
9th St	N.B.T.	326	B1	346	B2
9th St	U.C.	326	B2	346	B2
10th St	6	304	C2	367	A6
10th St	H.C.	323	A5	346	C3
10th St	J.C.	318	A3	346	C2
10th St	N.B.T.	326	B1	346	B3
10th St	U.C.	326	B2	346	B2
11th St	H.C.	326	C3	346	B3
11th St	J.C.	318	A3	346	C2
11th St	N.B.T.	326	B1	346	B2
11th St	U.C.	326	B2	346	B2
12th St	H.C.	326	C3	346	B3
12th St	J.C.	318	A3	346	C2
12th St	N.B.T.	326	B1	346	B2
12th St	U.C.	326	B2	346	B2
13th St	H.C.	326	C3	346	B3
13th St	J.C.	319	A4	346	C2
13th St	N.B.T.	326	A1	346	B2
13th St	U.C.	326	B2	346	B2
14th St	H.C.	327	C4	346	B3
14th St	J.C.	322	C2	346	C2
14th St	N.B.T.	326	A1	346	B2
14th St	U.C.	326	B2	346	B2
15th St	H.C.	326	C3	346	B3
15th St	J.C.	322	C2	346	C2
15th St	U.C.	326	A2	346	B2
16th St	H.C.	326	B3	346	B3
16th St	J.C.	322	C2	346	C2
16th St	N.B.T.	326	A1	346	B2
16th St	U.C.	326	A2	346	B2
17th St	H.C.	326	B3	346	B3
17th St	J.C.	322	C2	346	C2
17th St	U.C.	326	A2	346	B2
18th St	J.C.	322	C3	346	C2
18th St	U.C.	326	A2	346	B2
18th St	W.T.	327	B4	346	B3
19th St	U.C.	326	A2	346	B2
19th St	W.T.	327	B4	346	B3
20th St	U.C.	326	A2	346	B2
21st St	N.B.T.	326	A2	346	B2
21st St	U.C.	326	A2	346	B2
22nd St	N.B.T.	325	B4	346	B2
22nd St	U.C.	326	A2	346	B2
23rd St	N.B.T.	325	B4	346	B2
23rd St	U.C.	326	A3	346	B3
24th St	N.B.T.	325	B4	346	B2
24th St	U.C.	326	A3	346	B3
25th St	U.C.	328	C1	346	B3
26th St	N.B.T.	325	B4	346	B2
26th St	U.C.	328	C1	346	B3
27th St	N.B.T.	328	C1	346	B2
27th St	U.C.	328	C1	346	B2
28th St	N.B.T.	328	C1	346	B2
28th St	U.C.	328	C1	346	B3
29th St	N.B.T.	325	A4	346	A2
29th St	U.C.	328	C1	346	B3
30th St	U.C.	328	C1	346	B3
31st St	U.C.	328	C1	346	B3
32nd St	N.B.T.	325	A4	346	A2
32nd St	U.C.	328	C2	346	B3
33rd St	U.C.	328	C2	346	B3
34th St	N.B.T.	325	A4	346	A2
34th St	U.C.	328	C2	346	B3
35th St	U.C.	328	C2	346	A3
36th St	U.C.	328	C2	346	A3
37th St	U.C.	328	C2	346	A3
38th St	N.B.T.	328	B1	346	A3
38th St	U.C.	328	B2	346	A3
39th St	N.B.T.	328	B1	346	A3
39th St	U.C.	328	B2	346	A3
40th St	N.B.T.	328	A1	346	A3
40th St	U.C.	328	B2	346	A3
41st St	N.B.T.	328	A1	346	A3
41st St	U.C.	328	B2	346	A3
42nd St	N.B.T.	328	A1	346	A3
42nd St	U.C.	328	B2	346	A3
43rd St	N.B.T.	328	A1	346	A3
43rd St	U.C.	328	B2	346	A3
44th St	N.B.T.	328	A1	346	A3
44th St	U.C.	328	B2	346	A3
45th St	U.C.	328	B3	347	A4
46th St	N.B.T.	328	A1	346	A3
46th St	U.C.	328	B3	347	A4
46th St	W.T.	329	B4	346	A3
47th St	N.B.T.	328	A1	346	A3
47th St	U.C.	328	B3	347	A4
47th St	W.T.	329	B4	346	A3
48th St	N.B.T.	328	A1	346	A3
48th St	U.C.	328	B3	347	A4
48th St	W.T.	329	B4	346	A3
49th St	N.B.T.	328	A1	346	A3
49th St	U.C.	328	A3	347	A4
49th St	W.T.	329	B4	346	A3
49th St	W.N.Y.T.	328	A3	346	A3
50th St	N.B.T.	328	A2	346	A3
50th St	W.T.	329	B4	346	A3
50th St	W.N.Y.T.	328	A3	346	A3
51st St	N.B.T.	328	A2	346	A3
51st St	W.N.Y.T.	328	A3	346	A3
52nd St	N.B.T.	328	A2	346	A3
52nd St	W.N.Y.T.	328	A3	346	A3
53rd St	N.B.T.	330	C2	346	A3
53rd St	W.N.Y.T.	328	A3	346	A3
54th St	N.B.T.	330	C2	346	A3
54th St	W.N.Y.T.	328	A3	346	A3
55th St	W.N.Y.T.	328	A3	346	A3
56th St	W.N.Y.T.	332	C1	346	A3
57th St	W.N.Y.T.	332	C1	346	A3
58th St	N.B.T.	332	C1	346	A3
58th St	W.N.Y.T.	329	A4	346	A3
59th St	W.N.Y.T.	332	C1	346	A3
60th St	N.B.T.	330	C2	346	A3
60th St	W.N.Y.T.	332	C1	346	A3
61st St	N.B.T.	332	C1	346	A3
61st St	W.N.Y.T.	332	C1	346	A3
62nd St	N.B.T.	332	B1	346	A3
62nd St	W.N.Y.T.	332	C2	346	A3
63rd St	N.B.T.	332	B1	346	A3
63rd St	W.N.Y.T.	332	C2	346	A3
64th St	N.B.T.	332	B1	346	A3
64th St	W.N.Y.T.	332	C3	347	A4
65th St	W.N.Y.T.	332	C3	347	A4
66th St	W.N.Y.T.	332	C3	347	A4
67th La	N.B.T.	332	B1	346	A3
67th St	W.N.Y.T.	332	C3	347	A4
68th St	G.T.	332	B3	347	A4
68th St	N.B.T.	332	B1	346	A3
69th St	N.B.T.	332	A1	342	C2
69th St (Franklin Av)	G.T.	332	B3	347	A4
70th St	G.T.	332	B3	347	A4
70th St	N.B.T.	332	B1	342	C2

Staten Island

Cebra Av	0	291	C4	359	A6
30-1	1	291	C4	359	A6
31-OUT	4	291	C4	359	A6
Cecil Ct	3	313	C5	358	A4
Cedar Av	5	295	C6	360	B2
Cedar Grove Av	6	309	A6	367	B6
Cedar Grove Ct	6	304	C3	367	Inset
Cedar La	S.T.	324	A3	346	A2
Cedar Pl	N.B.T.	328	A2	346	A3
Cedar St	4	296	A3	359	A6
Cedar St	J.C.	316	B1	352	A2
Cedar Ter	1	296	C2	359	B6
Cedarcliff Rd	1	296	C2	359	B6
Cedarview Av	6	304	C1	367	A6
Cedarview Av W	6	303	C5	367	A6
Cedarwood Ct	3	300	A3	358	A3
Celina La	7	310	B2	366	C2
Celtic Pl	6	304	C3	367	Inset
Center Av	S.T.	324	A3	346	A2
Center Pl	6	304	C3	367	Inset
Center St	6	303	B6	367	A5
Center St	J.C.	318	C2	353	A4
Central Av	1	291	B5	359	A6
Central Av	J.C.	322	B1	346	C2
Central Av	U.C.	326	B2	346	B2
Centre Av	4	296	C2	359	B6
Centre La	B.C.	314	B2	352	C2
Centre St	B.C.	314	A3	352	B2
Champ Ct	9	306	C2	366	C2
Champlain Av	6	304	C1	367	A6
Chandler Av	14	301	B6	359	B4
Channel View Ct	6	304	B1	359	C4
Chapel Av	J.C.	316	C2	352	B3
Chapin Av	4	295	C4	359	B5
Chappell St	10	293	C4	359	A5
Charles Av	2	292	C1	359	A4
Charles Ct	6	304	B1	359	C4
Charles Ct	N.B.T.	328	B1	346	A3
Charles Pl	3	301	A4	358	A3
Charles St	J.C.	322	A1	346	C2
Charles St	S.T.	324	B2	346	B1
Charleston Av	9	306	A3	366	B2
Charlotte Av	J.C.	320	B2	346	C1
Charter Oaks Rd	4	304	A3	359	C5
Chase Ct	B.C.	314	C2	352	C2
Chelsea Rd	14	300	C1	358	B2
Chelsea St	7	310	C1	366	C1
Chemical La	9	306	A2	366	B2
Cherokee St	5	305	B5	359	C6
Cherry Pl	14	301	C6	359	C4
Cherry St	J.C.	316	B1	352	A2
Cherrywood Ct	8	303	C6	367	A5
Cheryl Av	12	302	C3	367	A4
Chesebrough St	12	308	A2	367	B4
Cheshire Pl	1	295	A4	359	B5
Chester Av	12	307	C5	366	C3
Chester Pl	4	291	C4	359	A6
Chesterton Av	6	304	C1	367	A6
Chestnut Av	5	297	C5	360	B2
Chestnut Av	J.C.	318	A1	346	C2
Chestnut Cir	12	302	C2	366	A3
Chestnut Pl	S.T.	324	A2	346	A2
Chestnut St	4	296	B3	359	B6
Chestnut St	W.T.	326	B3	346	B3
Cheves Av	14	301	B5	359	B4
Chiang Pl	J.C.	322	C3	346	C2
Chicago Al	5	295	C6	360	B2
Chicago Av	5	295	C6	360	B2
Chisholm St	9	307	C4	366	B3
Chopin Ct	J.C.	318	B1	353	A4
Chrissy Ct	10	294	B2	359	A5
Christ St	5	295	C5	359	B6
Christine Ct	12	307	C5	367	B4
Christopher Columbus Dr	J.C.	318	B2	353	A4
Christopher La	14	301	B4	358	B3
Christopher St	3	312	C3	358	A3
Church Av	14	302	A3	358	C2
Church Ct	14	302	A3	358	C2
Church Hill Rd	N.B.T.	333	A5	342	C3
Church La	5	297	C6	360	B2
Church La	B.C.	314	B2	352	C2
Church St	2	292	B2	359	A4
Churchill Av	9	306	C2	366	B2
Cicero Av	6	303	C4	367	A4
Circle Lp	4	297	C4	359	B6
Circle Rd	4	294	C3	359	C5
City Blvd	1	295	A4	359	A5
Claire Ct	1	296	B2	359	B6
Claradon La	5	295	C6	360	B2
Claremont Av	J.C.	316	A2	352	A3
Clarence Pl	6	304	C2	367	A6
Clarion Ct	10	293	C6	359	A5
Clark La	4	291	C4	359	A6
Clark Pl	2	301	A6	359	B4
Clarke Av	6	303	C5	367	A5
Clarke Av	J.C.	316	A2	352	A3
Claudia Ct	3	301	A4	358	B3
Clawson St	6	304	B3	367	Inset
Clay Pit Rd	9	306	B1	366	B2
Clayboard St	6	304	C3	367	Inset
Claytor St	5	298	A1	360	B2
Clearmont Av	9	306	C3	366	B3
Clement St	N.B.T.	333	A5	342	C3
Clendenny Av	J.C.	316	A2	352	A3
Clendinny Av	J.C.	316	A3	352	A3
Clerk St	J.C.	317	B4	353	A4
Clermont Av	7	310	C1	366	C1
Clermont Av	9	310	C3	366	C2
Clermont Pl	14	301	B6	359	B4
Cletus St	5	305	A4	359	C6
Cleveland Al	5	295	C6	360	B2
Cleveland Av	8	308	A3	367	B5
Cleveland Pl	5	295	C6	360	B2
Cleveland St	1	291	A4	359	A6
Cliff St	5	298	A1	360	B2
Cliff St	J.C.	320	B3	346	C2
Cliff St	U.C.	326	B3	346	B2
Cliffside Av	4	296	C3	359	B6
Cliffwood Av	4	294	C3	359	C5
Clifton Av	5	297	C5	360	B2
Clifton Pl	J.C.	317	A4	353	A4
Clifton St	14	300	B3	358	B3
Clifton Ter	W.T.	328	B2	346	B3
Clinton Av	1	290	A2	359	A6
Clinton Av	J.C.	316	A3	352	A3
Clinton B Fiske Av	14	301	B6	359	B4
Clinton Ct	1	290	B2	359	A6
Clinton Pl	2	292	C1	359	A4
Clinton Rd	8	308	A3	367	B5
Clinton St	4	291	C5	359	A6
Clinton St	H.C.	323	A4	346	C3
Cloister Pl	6	304	B2	359	C5
Clove Lake Pl	10	294	B2	359	A5
Clove Rd	0	295	B4	359	B5
1-853	10	292	C3	359	A4
854-1600	1	295	B4	359	B5
1601-2075	4	295	C5	359	B6
2076-OUT	5	295	C5	359	B6
Clove Wy	14	294	A3	359	B5
Cloverdale Av	8	308	A3	367	B5
Clovis Rd	8	308	A3	367	B5
Clyde Pl	1	290	B3	359	A6
Coale Av	14	301	B6	359	B4
Coast Guard Dr	5	298	B1	360	B2
Cobblers La	4	295	C5	359	B6
Coddington Av	6	304	B2	367	A6
Cody Pl	12	307	A4	366	A3
Coke St	9	306	C2	366	B2
Cold Spring Ct	4	295	C4	359	C5
Colden St	J.C.	318	C2	353	A4
Cole St	9	306	C2	366	C2
Coles St	J.C.	318	B3	353	A5
Colfax Av	6	304	B3	359	C5
Colgate Pl	6	304	C2	367	A6
Colgate St	J.C.	318	B2	353	A4
Collard St	J.C.	320	B3	346	C2
College Av	0	301	A5	359	B4
1-529 (odd)	14	294	A2	359	B5
2-520 (even)	14	294	A2	359	B5
522-OUT (even)	2	301	A5	359	B4
531-OUT (odd)	2	301	A5	359	B4
523-529 (odd)	14	301	A6	359	B4
530-OUT	2	301	A5	359	B4
College Ct	2	301	A5	359	B4
College Dr	J.C.	316	B2	352	A3
College Pl	4	304	A3	359	C5
College St	J.C.	316	B2	352	A3
Collfield Av	0	301	B5	359	B4
1-200	2	301	A5	359	B4
201-OUT	14	301	B5	359	B4
Collyer Av	12	307	B5	366	B3
Colon Av	6	303	C5	367	A5
Colon Av	8	303	C5	367	A5
Colon St	12	307	C5	366	B3
Colonial Av	14	303	A6	359	C4
Colonial Ct	10	294	A3	359	A5
Colonial Dr	B.C.	316	C1	352	B2
Colony Rd	J.C.	315	A5	352	B3
Colony St	0	305	B4	367	Inset
1-109	5	305	B4	359	C6
110-OUT	6	305	B4	367	Inset
Colorado St	14	301	A6	359	B4
Colton St	5	295	B6	359	B6
Columbia Av	5	295	C6	360	B2
Columbia Av	J.C.	321	A4	346	B2
Columbia Av	N.B.T.	332	B1	346	A3
Columbia Ter	W.T.	329	B4	346	B3
Columbus Av	4	295	C5	359	B6
Columbus Pl	14	301	B5	359	B4
Combs Av	6	304	C1	367	A6
Comely St	12	307	C5	366	B3
Comfort Ct	12	307	B5	366	B3
Commerce Ct	14	300	B3	358	B3
Commerce St	B.C.	315	C4	352	C3
Commercial St	J.C.	317	B4	353	A4
Commodore Dr	9	311	B5	366	C3
Communipaw Av	J.C.	316	A2	352	A3
Community La	12	307	B5	367	B4
Comstock Av	14	300	B3	358	B3
Concord La	4	295	C4	359	C5
Concord Pl	4	295	B5	359	B6
Concord St	J.C.	322	C1	346	C2
Condict St	J.C.	320	C2	346	C1
Confederation Pl	3	301	A4	358	A3
Conference Ct	7	310	B1	366	C1
Conger St	5	298	C1	360	C2
Congress St	4	297	A4	359	A6
Congress St	J.C.	326	C1	346	B2
Conklin Av	3	301	A4	358	A3
Connecticut St	7	310	C1	366	C1
Connector	B.C.	314	C2	352	C2
Connor Av	6	304	B1	367	A6
Conrad Av	14	303	A6	359	B4
Constant Av	14	301	A6	359	B4
Continental Pl	3	300	A3	358	A3
Convent Av	9	306	B3	366	B2
Conyingham Av	1	290	C1	359	A5
Cook St	J.C.	320	C3	346	C2
Cooke St	14	301	B4	358	B3
Coonley Ct	3	313	C4	358	A3
Cooper Av	4	305	A4	359	C6
Cooper Pl	9	311	B5	366	C3
Cooper Pl	W.T.	329	B4	346	A3
Cooper St	B.C.	314	C2	352	C2
Cooper Ter	14	301	C4	358	C3
Copley St	14	303	A5	358	C3
Copperflag La	4	304	A3	359	C5
Copperleaf Ter	4	304	A3	359	C5
Corbin Av	8	303	C5	367	A5
Corbin Av	J.C.	320	C2	346	C1
Corcoran St	J.C.	316	B3	352	A3
Cordelia Av	9	306	C3	366	C2
Cornelia Av	12	307	C5	366	C3
Cornelia St	4	295	C5	359	C6
Cornelison Av	J.C.	317	A4	353	A4
Cornell Av	10	301	A6	359	A4
Cornell Pl	4	296	C2	359	B6
Cornell St	2	301	A5	359	A4
Cornish St	8	309	B4	367	B5
Cornwall Av	4	294	C3	359	C5
Corona Av	6	303	C6	367	A5
Correll Av	0	307	A5	366	A3
1-199	12	307	A5	366	A3
200-OUT	9	306	A3	366	B3
Corson Av	1	291	C4	359	A6
Cortelyou Av	8	308	A2	367	A6
Cortelyou Pl	1	290	B2	359	A6
Cortlandt St	2	301	A6	359	A4
Cottage Av	8	308	A3	367	B5
Cottage Av	N.B.T.	332	A2	342	C2
Cottage La	N.B.T.	324	B4	346	B2
Cottage Pl	2	292	C3	359	A4
Cottage Pl	U.C.	328	B3	346	A3
Cottage St	B.C.	314	C1	352	C1
Cottage St	J.C.	320	C3	346	C1
Cotter Av	6	303	C6	367	A5
Cottontail Ct	12	308	B1	367	B4
Cottonwood Ct	6	303	C6	367	A5
Cottonwood St	J.C.	316	B1	352	A2
Coughlan Av	10	294	A3	359	B5
Country Dr	14	303	A4	358	C3
Country Dr E	14	303	A4	358	C3
Country Dr N	14	303	A4	358	C3
Country Dr S	14	303	A4	358	C3
Country Dr W	14	303	A4	358	C3
Country La	12	307	A4	366	A3
Country Village Ct	B.C.	314	B1	352	C1
Country Village Rd	J.C.	316	C1	352	B2
Country Woods La	8	303	C6	367	A5
County Av	S.T.	324	B2	346	B1
County Rd	J.C.	320	A3	346	B2
County Rd Ext	S.T.	324	B1	346	B1
Coursen Ct	4	296	B3	359	B6
Coursen Pl	4	296	B2	359	B6
Court House Pl	J.C.	322	C1	346	C2
Court Pl	6	303	B6	367	A6
Court Pl	B.C.	314	C2	352	C2
Court St	4	296	A3	359	A6
Court St	H.C.	323	B4	346	C3
Courtney Lp	5	298	A1	360	B2
Cove N La	N.B.T.	333	B5	347	A5
Coventry Lp	12	307	A4	366	B3
Coventry Rd	4	304	A3	359	C5
Coverly Av	1	295	C4	359	B5
Coverly St	6	304	B1	367	A6
Covert Av	J.C.	320	B2	346	C1
Covington Cir	9	307	A4	366	B3
Cowen Pl	3	312	C3	358	A3
Crabapple Ct	J.C.	316	B1	352	A2
Crabbs La	14	302	A2	358	C2
Crabtree Av	9	306	B2	366	B2
Crabtree La	9	306	B2	366	B2
Crafton Av	14	301	B5	359	B4
Craig Av	7	310	C1	366	C1
Cranford Av	6	304	B1	367	A6
Cranford Ct	6	304	B1	367	A6
Cranford St	8	309	C4	367	A5
Crawford St	J.C.	317	A4	353	A4
Crescent Av	1	291	B4	359	A6
Crescent Av	J.C.	317	A4	353	A4
Crest Lp	12	308	B2	367	B5
Creston Pl	4	291	C4	359	A6
Creston St	9	306	C3	366	C3
Crittenden Pl	2	292	C1	359	A4
Croak Av	14	294	C2	359	B5
Crocheron Av	14	301	B4	358	B3
Crocker Ct	12	302	C1	366	A3
Croft Ct	6	303	C6	367	A5
Croft Pl	14	301	C4	358	B3
Cromer St	8	303	C5	367	A5
Cromwell Av	0	305	A4	359	C6
1-187	4	305	A4	359	C6
188-OUT	5	305	A4	359	C6
Cromwell Cir	4	304	A3	359	C5
Cross St	4	297	A4	359	B6
Crossfield Av	12	302	C3	367	A4
Crossgate Rd	J.C.	316	C1	352	B2
Crosshill St	1	295	A4	359	A5
Croton Av	1	295	A4	359	A5
Crowell Av	14	301	B6	359	B4
Crown Av	12	307	A5	366	B3
Crown Ct	12	307	A5	367	A4
Crown Pl	12	307	A5	366	B3
Crystal Av	0	301	B5	359	B4
1-300	2	301	A5	359	B4
301-OUT	14	301	B5	359	B4
Crystal La	1	290	B3	359	A6
Cuba Av	6	304	C3	367	Inset
Cubberly Pl	6	304	B2	367	A6
Cubberly Pl	J.C.	320	C3	346	C1
Culotta La	7	310	C2	366	C2
Culver Av	J.C.	316	A2	352	A3
Cunard Av	4	296	C2	359	B6
Cunard Pl	4	295	B5	359	B6
Cuneo Pl	J.C.	322	B2	346	C2
Cunningham Rd	9	310	B3	366	C2
Currie Av	6	304	C1	367	A6
Curtis Av	10	294	A2	359	B5
Curtis Ct	10	293	B6	359	A5
Curtis Pl	1	291	A4	359	A6
Custer Av	J.C.	316	C1	352	B2
Cypress Av	1	294	B3	359	B5
Cypress Lp	9	306	A3	366	B2
Cypress St	J.C.	316	B1	352	A2
D St	14	301	C4	358	C3
Daffodil Ct	12	307	A4	366	A3
Daffodil La	14	303	A4	358	C3
Dahlia St	12	307	A4	366	B3
Dakota Av	J.C.	317	B4	353	A4
Dakota Pl	14	301	B6	359	B4
Dale Av	6	304	B2	367	A6
Daleham St	8	303	C5	367	A5
Dalemere Rd	4	295	C4	359	C5
Dales Av	J.C.	320	C2	346	C1
Dallas St	10	294	A3	359	B5
Dalton Av	6	304	B1	367	A6
Damon St	9	310	B3	366	C2
Dana St	1	295	A4	359	A5
Danforth Av	J.C.	316	B2	352	A3
Daniel Low Ter	1	291	A4	359	A6
Darcey Av	14	301	B4	358	B3
Darien St	4	295	C5	359	B6
Darlington Av	0	307	B4	366	B3
1-402	12	307	B4	366	B3
403-OUT	9	307	B4	366	B3
Darnell La	9	306	B2	366	B2
David Pl	3	301	A5	359	A4
David St	8	308	B3	367	B5
Davidson Ct	3	312	C3	358	A3
Davidson St	3	312	C3	358	A3
Davis Av	10	293	B6	359	A5
Davis Ct	10	293	B6	359	A5
Dawson Cir	14	300	C3	358	B3
Dawson Ct	14	300	C3	358	B3
Dawson Pl	5	295	C5	359	C6
Dawson St	14	301	C5	359	B4
Dayna Dr	5	295	B6	360	B2
De Hart Av	3	313	C4	358	A3
De Kalb Av	J.C.	320	C2	346	C1
De Ruyter Pl	3	301	A4	358	A3
De Saxe La	N.B.T.	333	A5	342	C3
De Soto St	1	290	C3	359	A6
Deal Ct	5	298	A1	360	B2
Debbie St	14	301	B4	358	B3
Deborah Lp	12	307	A5	367	A4
Decatur Av	14	301	B5	359	B4
Decker Av	2	301	A5	359	A4
Deems Av	14	301	B6	359	B4
Deere Park Pl	1	295	B4	359	B5
Degroot Pl	10	292	C3	359	A4
Deisius St	12	307	C5	366	B3
Dekalb St	4	295	B5	359	B6
Dekay St	10	293	C6	359	A5
Del Monte Dr	B.C.	314	B2	352	C2
Del Ray Ct	4	297	B5	360	B2
Delafield Av	0	293	C6	359	A5
1-240	1	290	C1	359	A6
241-OUT	10	293	C6	359	A5
Delafield Pl	10	293	A6	359	A5
Delaware Av	0	305	A4	359	C6
1-199	4	305	A4	359	C6
200-OUT	5	305	A4	359	C6
Delaware Av	J.C.	320	C2	346	C1
Delaware Pl	14	294	A2	359	B5
Delaware St	4	295	C4	359	C5
Delford St	4	296	C3	359	B6
Dell Av	N.B.T.	328	A1	346	A3
Dellwood Rd	4	295	C4	359	C6
Delmar Av	12	307	B5	366	B3
Delmar Rd	J.C.	316	C1	352	B2
Delmore St	14	301	B5	359	B4
Delphine Ter	5	295	C6	359	B6
Demopolis Av	8	308	A2	367	A5
Demorest Av	14	301	B5	359	B4
Denise Ct	12	307	C5	367	B4
Denker Pl	14	303	A5	358	C3
Denning Pl	W.T.	328	C3	346	B3
Dennis Toricelli St	5	298	B1	360	B2
Denoble La	1	294	C3	359	B5
Dent Rd	8	308	A3	367	B5
Denton Pl	14	301	B5	359	B4
Depew Pl	9	306	C3	366	B3
Deppe Pl	14	301	B4	358	B3
Derby Ct	2	301	A6	359	A4
Deserre Av	12	307	B4	366	B3
Detroit Av	12	307	B5	367	B4
Devens St	2	301	A5	359	A4
Devon Lp	14	303	B5	358	C3
Devon Pl	1	290	B1	359	A5
Dewey Av	8	308	A3	367	A5
Dewey Av	W.N.Y.T.	332	C3	347	A4
Dewey Ct	8	308	A3	367	A5
Dewey Pl	8	308	A3	367	A5
Dewhurst St	14	301	C5	359	B4
Dey St	J.C.	320	B2	346	C1
Dianas Tr	4	295	B4	359	B5
Diaz Pl	6	304	C3	367	Inset
Diaz St	5	295	C6	360	C2
Dick St	J.C.	320	C3	346	C1
Dickie Av	14	301	B5	359	B4
Dierauf St	12	302	C3	367	A4
Dietz Pl	N.B.T.	325	B4	346	B2
Dimarco Pl	6	304	B1	359	C4
Dina Ct	6	303	C6	367	A5
Dinsmore St	14	300	C3	358	B3
Direnzo Ct	9	307	C4	366	C3
Dissosway Pl	10	301	A6	359	A4
Ditson St	5	297	C5	360	B2
Divine St	4	295	C5	359	C6
Division Pl	J.C.	318	A2	346	C3
Dix Pl	4	297	B4	359	B6
Dixon Av	0	301	A4	358	A3
1-100	2	301	A5	359	A4
101-OUT	3	301	A4	358	A3
Doane Av	6	303	C5	367	A5
Doane Av	8	303	C5	367	A5
Dobbs Pl	1	294	B3	359	B5
Dock St	4	297	A4	359	A6
Dodd St	W.T.	327	A4	346	B3
Dodge St	B.C.	314	C1	352	C1
Doe Ct	14	300	C3	358	C3
Doe Pl	10	293	C5	359	A5
Dogwood Dr	12	307	A4	366	B3
Dogwood La	5	295	C6	360	B2
Dogwood St	J.C.	316	B1	352	A2
Dole St	12	308	C1	367	B4
Dolson Pl	3	300	A3	358	A3
Domain St	14	301	B4	358	B3
Donald Pl	10	293	B6	359	A5
Dongan Av	14	294	B2	359	B5
Dongan Hills Av	0	304	A3	359	C5
1-99	6	304	A3	359	C5
100-OUT	5	305	A4	359	C6
Dongan St	10	292	C3	359	A4
Donley Av	5	295	B6	359	B6
Donna Ct	14	303	B4	358	C3
Dora St	14	301	B5	359	B4
Dore Ct	10	301	A6	359	A4
Doreen Dr	3	301	A4	358	B3
Dorigo La	S.T.	324	A3	346	A2
Dorothea Pl	6	304	B1	359	C4
Dorothy St	14	301	C5	359	C4
Dorval Av	12	302	C3	367	A4
Dorval Pl	12	302	C3	367	A4
Doty Av	5	305	A6	360	C2
Douglas Av	10	294	A3	359	B5
Douglas Ct	4	295	B5	359	B6
Douglas Rd	4	295	B4	359	B6
Dover Green	12	302	C2	366	A3
Downes Av	12	307	B5	367	B4
Downey Pl	3	300	A3	358	A3
Dr. Martin Luther King Expwy	2	313	C6	359	A4
Drake Av	14	294	A2	359	B5
Draper Pl	14	303	A4	358	C3
Dresden Pl	1	294	C3	359	B5
Dreyer Av	14	301	B4	358	B3
Driggs St	8	308	B3	367	B5
Driprock St	10	292	C3	359	A4
Droyers Point Blvd	J.C.	316	B1	352	A2
Droyers St	J.C.	316	B1	352	A2
Drum Av	5	298	B2	360	B2
Drumgoole Rd E	0	308	A1	367	A4
1-1276	12	308	A1	367	A4
1277-OUT	9	306	C3	366	B3
Drumgoole Rd W	0	308	A1	367	A4
1-1630	12	308	A1	367	A4
1631-OUT	9	306	C3	366	B3
Drury Av	5	305	A6	360	C2
Dryden Ct	2	301	A6	359	A4
Drysdale St	14	301	C5	359	C4
Duane Pl	1	290	B2	359	A6
Dublin Pl	3	301	A4	358	A3
Dubois Av	10	292	C3	359	A4
Dudley Av	1	295	B4	359	B5
Dudley St	J.C.	319	C4	353	A5
Duer Av	5	298	C1	360	B2
Duer La	1	290	C3	359	A6
Duer Pl	W.T.	329	C4	346	B3
Duffield Av	J.C.	320	B2	346	C1
Dugdale St	6	309	A6	367	A6
Duke Pl	14	301	C6	359	C4
Dumont Av	5	295	C5	359	C6
Dunbar St	8	303	C6	367	A5
Duncan Av	J.C.	320	C2	346	C1
Duncan Ct	J.C.	320	C2	346	C1
Duncan Rd	1	296	B2	359	B6
Duncan St	4	295	C4	359	C5
Dunham St	9	306	C3	366	B2
Dunlin Plz	S.T.	324	A1	346	A1
Duram Av	N.B.T.	328	A2	346	A3
Durant Av	0	309	A4	367	A6
1-310	6	309	A4	367	A6
311-OUT	8	309	C4	367	A5
Durgess St	4	295	C5	359	C6
Durham Av	N.B.T.	332	B1	346	A3
Dustan St	6	304	C3	367	Inset
Dutchess Av	4	295	C4	359	C5
Dwarf St	3	300	A3	358	A3
Dwight St	J.C.	316	B3	352	A3
Dyson St	4	291	C4	359	A6
Eadie Pl	1	290	A3	359	A6
Eagan Av	12	308	B1	367	B4
Eagle Rd	14	301	A4	358	B3
Earle Av	14	301	B5	359	B4
Earley Pl	7	310	B1	366	C1
East 1st St	B.C.	292	A3	359	A4
East 2nd St	B.C.	292	A3	359	A5
East 3rd St	B.C.	292	A3	359	A4
East 4th St	B.C.	292	A3	359	A4
East 5th St	B.C.	314	C1	352	C1
East 10th St	B.C.	314	C2	352	C2
East 11th St	B.C.	314	C2	352	C2
East 12th St	B.C.	314	C2	352	C2
East 14th St	B.C.	314	C2	352	C2
East 15th St	B.C.	314	C2	352	C2
East 16th St	B.C.	314	C2	352	C2
East 17th St	B.C.	314	C2	352	C2
East 18th St	B.C.	314	C2	352	C2
East 19th St	B.C.	314	C2	352	C2
East 21st St	B.C.	314	C2	352	C2
East 22nd St	B.C.	314	C2	352	C2
East 23rd St	B.C.	314	B2	352	C2
East 24th St	B.C.	314	B2	352	C2
East 25th St	B.C.	314	B2	352	C2
East 26th St	B.C.	314	B2	352	C2
East 27th St	B.C.	314	B2	352	C2
East 28th St	B.C.	314	B2	352	C2
East 29th St	B.C.	314	B2	352	C2
East 30th St	B.C.	314	B2	352	C2
East 31st St	B.C.	314	B3	352	C2
East 32nd St	B.C.	314	B3	352	C2
East 33rd St	B.C.	314	B3	352	C2
East 34th St	B.C.	314	B3	352	C2
East 35th St	B.C.	314	B3	352	C2
East 36th St	B.C.	314	B3	352	C2
East 37th St	B.C.	314	B3	352	C2
East 38th St	B.C.	314	A3	352	B2
East 39th St	B.C.	314	A3	352	B2
East 40th St	B.C.	314	A3	352	B2
East 41st St	B.C.	314	A3	352	B2
East 42nd St	B.C.	314	A3	352	B2
East 43rd St	B.C.	314	A3	352	B2
East 44th St	B.C.	314	A3	352	B2
East 45th St	B.C.	314	A3	352	B2
East 46th St	B.C.	314	A3	352	B2
East 47th St	B.C.	314	A3	352	B2
East 48th St	B.C.	314	A3	352	B2
East 49th St	B.C.	314	A3	352	B2
East 50th St	B.C.	314	A3	352	B2
East 51st St	B.C.	314	A3	352	B2
East 52nd St	B.C.	314	A3	352	B2
East 53rd St	B.C.	314	A3	352	B2
East Augusta Av	8	308	A2	367	A5
East Bidwell Av	J.C.	316	B3	352	A3
East Brandis Av	8	303	C4	367	A4
East Broadway	6	304	B1	367	A6
East Buchanan St	1	290	B3	359	A6
East Ct	B.C.	314	B2	352	C2
East Figurea Av	8	308	A2	367	A4
East Grand St	B.C.	314	A3	352	B2
East Loop Rd	4	304	A3	359	C5
East Macon Av	8	303	C4	367	A4
East Perkiomen Av	8	303	C5	367	A5
East Pulaski La	B.C.	315	A4	352	B3
East Raleigh Av	10	294	A3	359	A5
East Reading Av	8	303	C5	367	A5
East Scranton Av	8	308	A2	367	A5
East Shearwater Ct	J.C.	315	A6	353	B4
East St	J.C.	318	A1	346	C2
East Stroud Av	8	308	A2	367	A5
East View Ct	J.C.	316	B3	352	A3
Eastentry Rd	4	304	A3	359	C5
Eastern Pkwy	J.C.	316	C3	352	B3
Eastman St	12	308	B2	367	B4
Easy St	N.B.T.	331	B4	342	C2
Eaton Pl	4	313	C6	359	A4
Ebbitts St	6	304	C3	367	A6
Ebey La	12	307	A4	366	B3
Ebony St	6	304	B1	367	A6
Echo Pl	14	301	B4	358	B3
Eddy St	1	296	A2	359	A6
Eden Ct	7	310	B1	366	C1
Edgar Pl	4	295	C4	359	B6
Edgar St	W.T.	328	C3	346	B3
Edgar Ter	1	291	C4	359	A6
Edgegrove Av	0	307	B4	366	B3
1-846	12	307	B5	367	B4
847-OUT	9	307	B4	366	B3
Edgewater St	5	297	B5	360	B2
Edgewood Rd	8	308	A3	367	B5
Edinboro Rd	6	303	B6	359	C4
Edison St	6	304	C3	367	Inset
Edith Av	12	307	C5	366	C3
Edo Ct N	9	306	A3	366	B2
Edo Ct S	9	306	A3	366	B2
Edstone Dr	1	295	A4	359	A5
Edward Ct	14	303	A5	358	C3
Edward Curry Av	14	300	B1	358	B2
Edward G Baker Sq	1	291	B5	359	A6
Edward Hart Dr	J.C.	317	C4	353	B4
Edward St	N.B.T.	328	A1	346	A3
Edwards Ct	B.C.	314	C1	352	C1
Edwin St	12	308	B1	367	B4
Egan Ct	B.C.	292	A3	359	A4
Egbert Av	10	301	A6	359	A4
Egbert Pl	5	298	A1	360	B2
Ege Av	J.C.	316	A2	352	A3
Egmont Pl	1	291	A4	359	A6
Egret La	S.T.	324	A1	346	A1
Elaine Ct	4	295	C4	359	C5
Elbe Av	4	295	B5	359	B6
Elder Av	9	306	C3	366	C3
Eldorado Pl	W.T.	329	C4	346	B3
Eldridge Av	2	301	A6	359	A4
Eleanor La	8	308	A3	367	B5
Eleanor Pl	3	301	A4	358	B3
Eleanor St	6	304	B1	359	C4
Elias Pl	14	301	A6	359	B4
Elie Ct	14	303	A4	358	C3
Elise Ct	6	303	C6	367	A5
Elizabeth Av	10	293	B5	359	A5
Elizabeth Ct	7	310	B2	366	C2
Elizabeth Grove Rd	3	300	A2	358	B2
Elizabeth Pl	9	307	C4	366	C3
Elizabeth St	10	293	C4	359	A5
Elizabeth St	J.C.	318	A1	346	C2
Elk Ct	6	303	C6	367	A5
Elkhart St	8	303	C5	367	A5
Elks Pl	9	306	B3	366	B2
Ella Pl	6	304	C2	367	A6
Ellicott Pl	1	290	B2	359	A6
Ellington St	4	296	C3	359	B6
Ellis Rd	9	306	B1	366	B1
Ellis St	7	310	B1	366	C1

Ellsworth Av	12	307	B4	366	B3
Ellsworth Pl	14	294	B3	359	B5
Elm Pl	1	295	B4	359	B5
Elm St	10	293	B5	359	A5
Elm St	J.C.	320	B3	346	C1
Elmbank St	12	308	C2	367	B4
Elmhurst Av	1	294	C3	359	B5
Elmira Av	14	301	A6	359	B4
Elmira St	6	304	C2	367	A6
Elmtree Av	6	304	B3	367	Inset
Elmwood Av	8	308	A2	367	B5
Elmwood Park Dr	14	303	B5	358	C3
Elson Ct	14	301	A4	358	B3
Elson St	14	300	B3	358	B3
Eltinge St	4	295	C4	359	B6
Eltingville Blvd	12	308	A2	367	B4
Elverton Av	8	303	C5	367	A5
Elvin St	14	294	C2	359	B5
Elwood Av	14	303	A5	358	C3
Elwood Pl	1	290	C1	359	A5
Ely Av	12	307	B5	367	B4
Ely St	1	290	C3	359	A6
Emerald Ct	9	306	C2	366	C2
Emeric Ct	3	313	C5	358	A3
Emerson Av	1	295	C4	359	B5
Emerson Av	J.C.	320	C2	346	C1
Emerson Ct	4	295	C4	359	B5
Emerson Dr	4	295	B4	359	B6
Emerson La	S.T.	324	A2	346	A1
Emily Ct	7	310	B2	366	C1
Emily La	12	302	C2	366	A3
Emmet Av	6	304	C1	367	A6
Emory St	J.C.	317	A4	353	A4
End Pl	12	302	C3	367	A4
Endor Av	1	295	B4	359	B5
Enfield Pl	6	304	B1	359	C4
Engert St	9	306	A3	366	A2
Englewood Av	9	306	B1	366	B2
Enos Pl	J.C.	320	C3	346	C1
Enterprise Av	S.T.	324	A1	346	A1
Enterprise South Av	S.T.	324	B1	346	B1
Entrance Plz	J.C.	319	A4	346	C2
Erastina Pl	3	313	C4	358	A3
Eric La	8	303	C5	367	A5
Erie St	9	306	C3	366	C2
Erie St	J.C.	318	A3	346	C2
Erika Lp	12	302	C3	367	A4
Ernest La	12	308	B1	367	B4
Errington Pl	4	297	B5	360	B2
Escanaba Av	8	308	A2	367	A5
Esmac Ct N	4	295	C4	359	C5
Esmac Ct W	4	295	C4	359	C5
Essex Dr	14	303	A5	358	C3
Essex St	J.C.	319	C4	353	A5
Esther Depew St	6	304	B1	359	C4
Eton Pl	14	301	C4	358	B3
Eugene Pl	12	307	B5	366	B3
Eugene St	9	310	B2	366	C2
Eunice Pl	3	301	A4	358	B3
Eva Av	6	304	C3	367	Inset
Evan Pl	12	307	A5	367	A4
Evans St	14	303	A5	358	C3
Evelyn Pl	5	298	A1	360	B2
Everett Av	9	306	C3	366	C3
Everett Pl	9	306	C3	366	C2
Everett St	J.C.	316	A2	352	A3
Evergreen Av	0	305	A4	359	C6
1-89	4	305	A4	359	C6
90-OUT	5	305	A4	359	C6
Evergreen St	8	303	C6	367	A5
Evergreen St	B.C.	314	C1	352	C1
Everton Av	12	307	A4	366	B3
Everton Pl	12	307	A4	366	B3
Excelsior Av	9	306	C3	366	C3
Exchange Pl	J.C.	319	C5	353	A5
Exeter Rd	J.C.	316	C1	352	B2
Exeter St	8	303	C6	367	A5
Eylandt St	12	307	C5	366	B3
Faber St	2	292	C2	359	A4
Fabian St	12	308	B1	367	B4
Fahy Av	14	300	A3	358	B3
Fairbanks Av	6	304	C1	367	A6
Fairfield St	8	303	C5	367	A5
Fairlawn Av	8	309	A4	367	B5
Fairlawn Pl	8	304	A4	367	B5
Fairmount Av	J.C.	317	A4	353	A4
Fairmount Ter	J.C.	320	C2	346	C1
Fairview Av	14	294	B2	359	B5
Fairview Av	J.C.	320	C2	346	C1
Fairview Pl	4	304	A3	359	C5
Fairview Ter	W.N.Y.T.	329	B4	347	A4
Fairway Av	4	297	C4	359	B6
Fairway La	14	294	A3	359	B5
Falcon Av	6	304	C2	367	A6
Fancher Pl	3	312	B2	358	A3
Fanelli La	14	303	A6	359	C4
Fanning St	14	294	C2	359	B5
Farraday St	14	301	B4	358	B3
Farragut Av	3	300	A3	358	B3
Farragut Pl	W.N.Y.T.	333	C4	347	A4
Farrell Ct	6	304	C1	367	A6
Father Capodanno Blvd	0	305	B4	367	Inset
1-924	5	305	B5	359	C6
925-OUT	6	305	B4	367	Inset
Fawn La	6	309	C4	367	A5
Fayann La	7	310	C2	366	C1
Fayette Av	5	295	C5	359	C6
Fayette Pl	J.C.	320	C2	346	C1
Federal Pl	3	312	B2	358	A3
Feldmeyers La	14	302	A2	358	C2
Felton St	14	300	B3	358	B3
Fenway Cir	8	303	C4	367	A4
Ferguson Ct	7	310	B2	366	C2
Fern Av	8	308	A2	367	A5
Ferncliff Rd	J.C.	316	C1	352	B2
Ferndale Av	14	303	A5	358	C3
Ferndale Ct	14	303	A5	358	C3
Ferry Rd	G.T.	333	C4	347	A4
Ferry St	2	292	B2	359	A4
Ferry St	J.C.	322	B1	346	C2
Ficarelle Dr	9	306	C3	366	C3
Fiedler Av	1	291	C4	359	A6
Field Av	J.C.	320	C2	346	C1
Field St	14	301	C5	359	C4
Fields Av	14	301	C5	359	C4
Fieldstone Rd	14	300	B3	358	B3
Fieldway Av	8	309	C4	367	A5
Figurea Av	12	308	A1	367	A4
Filer St	12	308	A1	367	B4
Filipe La	8	308	B3	367	B5
Fillat St	14	301	B5	359	B4
Fillmore Av	14	301	C6	359	B4
Fillmore Pl	5	298	B1	360	B2
Fillmore Pl	W.N.Y.T.	329	A5	347	A4
Fillmore St	1	290	B1	359	A5

Fine Blvd	14	294	B3	359	B5
Fingal St	12	308	B1	367	B4
Fingerboard Rd W	0	295	A6	360	B2
500-900	5	298	A1	360	C2
901-957 (odd)	4	295	C5	359	B6
902-958 (even)	5	295	C6	359	B6
959-OUT	4	295	C5	359	B6
Finlay Av	9	306	C3	366	C3
Finlay St	7	310	C1	366	C1
Finley Av	6	304	C3	367	Inset
Fir St	J.C.	316	B1	352	A2
Firth Rd	14	300	B3	358	B3
Fish House Rd	K.T.	320	B1	346	C1
Fisher Av	7	310	B2	366	C1
Fisk St	J.C.	316	A2	352	A3
Fitzgerald Av	8	308	B3	367	B5
Flagg Ct	4	304	A3	359	C5
Flagg Pl	4	304	A3	359	C5
Flagship Cir	9	311	B5	366	C3
Fleet St	J.C.	322	C1	346	C2
Fletcher St	5	295	B6	359	B6
Flint St	6	304	C2	367	A6
Florence Pl	9	307	C4	366	C3
Florence St	8	308	A3	367	B5
Florence St	J.C.	318	B1	353	A4
Florida Av	5	298	C1	360	C2
Florida Ter	6	304	B1	359	C4
Flower Av	9	310	B3	366	C2
Floyd St	10	301	A6	359	A4
Floyd St	J.C.	320	B3	346	C1
Foch Av	5	305	A5	359	C6
Fonda Pl	9	306	C3	366	B3
Foote Av	1	296	C1	359	B5
Ford Pl	10	294	A3	359	A5
Forest Av	0	313	C4	358	A2
1-479	1	290	C2	359	A6
480-1238	10	294	A2	359	A5
1239-1700	2	301	A5	359	A4
1701-OUT	3	301	A4	359	B4
Forest Ct	3	313	C4	358	A3
Forest Green	12	307	A4	366	A3
Forest Hill Rd	14	303	A5	358	C3
Forest Rd	4	295	C4	359	C5
Forest St	14	300	C3	358	B3
Fornes Pl	12	308	B1	367	B4
Forrest St	J.C.	316	A3	352	A3
Forrest St	J.C.	317	B4	353	A4
Forrestal Av	12	302	C3	367	A4
Forrestal Ct	12	308	A1	367	A4
Fort Hill Cir	1	291	B4	359	A6
Fort Hill Pk	1	291	B4	359	A6
Fort Pl	1	291	B4	359	A6
Foster Av	14	294	C2	359	B5
Foster Rd	9	307	B4	366	B3
Four Corners Rd	4	304	A3	359	C5
Fowler Av	J.C.	316	B2	352	A3
Fox Hill Ter	5	295	B6	360	B2
Fox Hunt Ct	1	295	A4	359	B5
Fox La	6	309	A6	367	A6
Fox Pl	J.C.	320	C2	346	C1
Foxbeach Av	6	309	A6	367	A6
Foxholm St	6	304	B2	359	C5
Foye Pl	J.C.	317	A4	353	A4
Francesca La	3	301	A4	358	B3
Francine Ct	6	304	B2	367	A6
Francine La	14	301	B5	359	B4
Francis Pl	4	295	C4	359	B5
Franklin Av	1	290	A3	359	A6
Franklin D Roosevelt Boardwalk					
	5	305	A6	360	C2
Franklin La	6	303	B5	367	A5
Franklin Pl	14	294	C2	359	B5
Franklin St	J.C.	322	B1	346	C2
Fraser St	14	303	A5	358	C3
Frean St	4	296	A3	359	A6
Frede St	14	300	B3	358	B3
Frederick St	14	301	B6	359	B4
Freeborn St	0	305	B4	367	Inset
1-99	5	305	B4	359	C6
100-OUT	6	305	B4	367	Inset
Freedom Av	14	300	C3	358	C3
Freedom Pl	J.C.	316	C3	352	B3
Freedom Wy	J.C.	317	C5	353	B4
Freeman Av	J.C.	320	C1	346	C1
Freeman Pl	10	294	A3	359	A5
Fremont Av	6	304	B3	359	C5
Fremont St	1	291	B4	359	A6
Fremont St	J.C.	318	B1	353	A4
Front St	4	297	A4	359	A6
Front St	J.C.	318	A1	346	C2
Fuller Ct	6	303	C6	367	A5
Fulton Av	J.C.	316	B2	352	A3
Fulton Av	N.B.T.	331	B5	342	C3
Fulton Ct	W.N.Y.T.	329	A6	347	A4
Fulton St	4	296	B3	359	B6
Fulton St	W.T.	329	B4	346	A3
Furman St	12	308	B1	367	B4
Furness Pl	14	303	A5	358	C3
Futurity Pl	12	302	C3	367	A4
Gadsen Pl	14	303	A5	358	C3
Gail Ct	6	304	B2	367	A6
Gales La	2	292	B2	359	A4
Galesville Ct	5	298	C1	360	C2
Galloway Av	2	301	A5	359	B4
Galvaston Lp	14	303	B5	358	C3
Gannon Av	14	301	B4	358	B3
Gansevoort Blvd	14	301	B6	359	B4
Garabrant St	J.C.	317	B5	353	A4
Garden Ct	4	304	A3	359	C5
Garden St	14	294	B2	359	B5
Garden St	H.C.	323	B4	346	C3
Gardenia La	14	303	A4	358	C3
Gardner Av	J.C.	317	A4	353	A4
Garfield Av	5	298	B1	360	B2
Garfield Av	J.C.	316	C2	352	B3
Garibaldi Av	6	304	C3	367	Inset
Garretson Av	0	305	A4	359	C6
1-170	4	305	A4	359	C6
171-OUT	5	305	A4	359	C6
Garretson Av	B.C.	292	A2	359	A4
Garretson La	4	295	C5	359	B6
Garrison Av	14	301	A5	359	B4
Garrison Av	J.C.	320	C2	346	C1
Garth Ct	6	303	C6	367	A5
Gary Ct	14	301	B4	358	B3
Gary Pl	14	300	C3	358	C3
Gary St	12	302	C3	367	A4
Gates Av	J.C.	316	C1	352	B2
Gateway Dr	4	295	C5	359	B6
Gauldy Av	14	300	B3	358	B3
Gautier Av	J.C.	320	C2	346	C1
Gaw Pl	W.N.Y.T.	329	A4	346	A3
Gaynor St	9	306	C2	366	B2
Gehrs Pl	N.B.T.	328	B1	346	A3
Geldner Av	6	304	B2	359	C5

Genesee Av	0	308	A1	367	A4
1-209	8	308	A2	367	A5
210-OUT	12	308	A1	367	A4
Genesee St	1	295	B4	359	B5
Gentile Ct	12	307	C5	367	B4
George Rd	4	294	C3	359	C5
George St	7	310	B2	366	C1
George St	B.C.	314	C1	352	C1
Georges La	9	306	C3	366	C3
Georgia Ct	9	306	C2	366	C2
Gertrude St	B.C.	292	A1	359	A4
Gervil St	9	306	A3	366	B2
Getz Av	12	308	A2	367	A4
Geyser Dr	12	307	A4	366	B3
Gianna Ct	6	303	C6	367	A5
Gibson Av	8	308	A3	367	A5
Giegerich Pl	7	310	B2	366	C2
Gifford Av	J.C.	316	A3	352	A3
Giffords Glen	8	308	A3	367	B5
Giffords La	6	303	C5	367	A5
Giffords La	8	303	C5	367	A5
Gigi St	3	313	C5	358	A3
Gil Ct	12	308	A2	367	B4
Gilbert Pl	9	306	C3	366	C2
Gilbert St	6	303	B6	367	A5
Gilchrist St	J.C.	318	C2	353	A4
Giles Av	J.C.	320	C2	346	C1
Giles Pl	4	295	C5	359	B6
Gillard Av	12	308	B1	367	B4
Gilroy St	9	307	B4	366	B3
Gina Ct	14	303	A6	359	C4
Giordan Ct	3	313	C5	358	A3
Girard St	7	310	B1	366	C1
Givernaud Ter	N.B.T.	328	B1	346	A3
Gladwin St	9	306	B2	366	B2
Glascoe Av	14	301	A5	359	B4
Glen Av	1	290	C3	359	A6
Glen Rd	14	301	C4	358	C3
Glen St	14	302	A2	358	C2
Glencoe St	6	303	C4	367	A4
Glendale Av	4	295	C5	359	B6
Glenn La	J.C.	316	B2	352	A3
Glenwood Av	1	295	B4	359	B5
Glenwood Av	J.C.	320	C2	346	C1
Glenwood Pl	10	294	A3	359	B5
Globe Av	14	301	B4	358	B3
Glover St	8	308	B3	367	B5
Goethals Rd N	0	300	A3	358	B3
1-899	14	300	A3	358	B3
900-OUT	3	300	A3	358	B3
Goff Av	9	306	C3	366	B2
Gold Av	12	302	C3	367	A4
Gold St	U.C.	326	A2	346	B3
Golden Av	S.T.	324	A2	346	A2
Golden La	U.C.	328	B3	346	A3
Golfview Ct	14	303	B5	358	C3
Goll Ct	4	295	C4	359	C6
Goller Pl	14	301	C4	358	B3
Goodall St	8	308	B3	367	B5
Goodwin Av	14	301	B6	359	B4
Gordon Pl	1	290	B1	359	A5
Gordon St	4	296	B3	359	B6
Gould St	B.C.	314	A3	352	B2
Governor Rd	14	294	B2	359	B5
Gower St	14	294	C2	359	B5
Grace Ct	1	290	B2	359	A6
Grace Rd	6	304	B2	367	A6
Grace St	J.C.	326	C1	346	B2
Grafe St	9	306	A3	366	A3
Graham Av	14	300	B3	358	B3
Graham Blvd	5	305	B4	359	C6
Graham St	J.C.	326	C1	346	B2
Grand Av	1	296	C1	359	B5
Grand Av	N.B.T.	332	B1	346	C3
Grand St	H.C.	323	A4	346	C3
Grand St	J.C.	318	C1	353	A4
Grand St	W.T.	327	B4	346	B3
Grandview Av	3	312	C3	358	A3
Grandview Ter	8	308	A3	367	B5
Granite Av	3	301	A4	358	A3
Grant Av	J.C.	316	A2	352	A3
Grant Pl	6	304	B3	359	C5
Grant Pl	W.N.Y.T.	329	A4	346	A3
Grant St	1	291	C5	359	A6
Granton Av	N.B.T.	332	B1	346	A3
Granton Av Ext	N.B.T.	332	B1	346	A3
Grantwood Av	12	307	A5	367	A4
Grasmere Av	4	295	C5	359	B6
Grasmere Ct	5	295	C5	359	B6
Grasmere Dr	5	295	C6	360	B2
Grauert Pl	W.T.	328	C3	346	B3
Graves St	14	301	C6	359	B4
Gray St	4	296	A3	359	A6
Gray St	J.C.	318	B1	353	A4
Grayson St	6	304	C2	367	A6
Great Kills Rd	8	308	A3	367	A5
Greaves Av	8	303	C5	367	A5
Greaves Ct	8	303	C6	367	A5
Greaves La	8	308	A3	367	A5
Greeley Av	6	304	B3	367	Inset
Green Ct	10	301	A6	359	A4
Green St	10	294	A3	359	A5
Green Valley Rd	12	307	A4	366	A3
Greencroft Av	8	309	A4	367	B5
Greencroft La	8	309	A4	367	B5
Greene St	J.C.	319	C5	353	A5
Greenfield Av	4	297	C4	359	B6
Greenfield Ct	4	297	B5	360	B2
Greenleaf Av	10	301	A6	359	A4
Greenleaf Av S	14	301	A6	359	B4
Greenport St	4	295	C4	359	C5
Greentree La	14	301	B4	358	B3
Greenville Av	J.C.	316	B2	352	A3
Greenway Av	14	303	A6	359	C4
Greenway Dr	1	294	A3	359	B5
Greenwood Av	1	296	A1	359	A6
Gregg La	B.C.	314	B2	352	C2
Gregg Pl	1	290	C1	359	A5
Gregory Av	W.T.	327	A4	346	B3
Gregory La	14	303	B5	358	C3
Greta Pl	1	296	B2	359	B6
Gridley Av	3	301	A4	358	A3
Grieco Dr	J.C.	316	B2	352	A3
Griffith St	J.C.	322	A1	346	C2
Grille Ct	9	306	A2	366	B2
Grimsby St	6	305	B4	367	Inset
Grissom Av	14	301	C4	358	C3
Griswold Ct	1	295	A4	359	B5
Groton St	12	308	B3	367	B5
Grove Av	2	292	B2	359	A4
Grove Pl	2	292	C1	359	A4
Grove Pl	B.C.	314	B2	352	C2
Grove St	4	296	A3	359	A6
Grove St	J.C.	318	C3	353	A5
Grymes Hill Rd	1	296	B2	359	B6

Guilford St	5	298	C1	360	C2
Gulf Av	3	300	A2	358	A2
Gunton Pl	9	306	A3	366	A3
Gurdon St	14	301	B5	359	B4
Gurley Av	0	303	C5	367	A5
1-399	8	303	C5	367	A5
400-OUT	12	303	C4	367	A4
Guyon Av	6	304	C1	367	A6
Hackensack Av	J.C.	320	B1	346	C1
Hackensack Plank Rd	U.C.	328	C2	346	B3
Hackensack Plank Rd	W.T.	327	B4	346	B3
Hafstrom St	6	304	C1	367	A6
Hagaman Pl	2	301	A5	359	A4
Hague St	J.C.	326	B1	346	B2
Hale St	7	310	B2	366	C1
Hales Av	12	308	B2	367	B5
Half Moon Ct	W.N.Y.T.	333	C4	347	A4
Half-Moon Isle	J.C.	315	A6	353	B4
Hall Av	14	301	B5	359	B4
Halladay St	J.C.	318	C1	353	A4
Halleck Av	J.C.	320	B2	346	C1
Hallister St	9	306	C2	366	B2
Halpin Av	12	307	A5	366	A3
Halstead St	J.C.	316	A2	352	A3
Hamden Av	6	304	B3	359	C5
Hamilton Av	1	291	A4	359	A6
Hamilton Av	W.T.	329	C4	346	B3
Hamilton Plz	W.T.	329	C4	346	B3
Hamilton St	4	296	C2	359	B6
Hamlin Pl	2	301	A6	359	A4
Hammock La	12	307	A4	366	B3
Hampton Ct	J.C.	318	B3	353	A5
Hampton Green	12	307	A4	366	A3
Hampton Pl	9	306	A3	366	B2
Hancock Av	J.C.	322	A2	346	C2
Hancock St	5	305	A4	359	C6
Hank Pl	9	311	B5	366	C3
Hannah St	1	291	C5	359	A6
Hanover Av	4	295	B5	359	B6
Hanover Av	9	307	C4	366	C3
Harbor Blvd	W.T.	327	B5	346	B3
Harbor Dr	J.C.	315	A4	352	B3
Harbor La	3	313	C5	358	A3
Harbor Lp	3	313	C4	358	A3
Harbor Rd	3	313	C4	358	A3
Harbor View Ct	1	290	C3	359	A6
Harbor View Place E	5	298	A2	360	B2
Harbor View Place N	5	298	A2	360	B2
Harbor View Place S	5	298	A2	360	B2
Harbour Ct	8	309	B4	367	B5
Hardin Av	10	294	A3	359	A5
Hardy Pl	8	308	A3	367	A5
Hardy St	4	296	C3	359	B6
Harison Pl	10	293	B5	359	A5
Harlan Av	6	304	B1	359	C4
Harmon Blvd	S.T.	324	A1	346	A1
Harmon Meadow Blvd	S.T.	324	A3	346	A2
Harmon St	J.C.	317	A4	353	A4
Harold Av	12	308	B2	367	B4
Harold St	14	301	C6	359	B4
Harriet Av	12	311	B6	366	C3
Harris Av	14	301	C6	359	B4
Harris La	9	306	B2	366	B2
Harrison Av	2	292	C1	359	A4
Harrison Av	J.C.	316	A3	352	A3
Harrison Pl	U.C.	328	B3	346	A3
Harrison Pl	W.N.Y.T.	332	C2	346	A3
Harrison St	4	297	B4	359	B6
Harrison St	H.C.	322	B3	346	C2
Hart Av	10	294	A3	359	A5
Hart Blvd	1	290	C1	359	A5
Hart Lp	6	303	C6	367	A5
Hart Pl	7	310	B2	366	C1
Hart St	J.C.	316	B3	352	A3
Hartford Av	10	294	A3	359	A5
Hartford St	8	308	B3	367	B5
Hartley Pl	B.C.	314	C1	352	C1
Hartz Wy	S.T.	324	A1	346	A1
Harvard Av	1	290	B3	359	A6
Harvest Av	10	294	A3	359	A5
Harvey Av	14	301	B5	359	B4
Harvey St	5	298	B1	360	B2
Hasbrouck Hill Rd	4	295	C4	359	C6
Hastings Ct	9	306	C3	366	C3
Hastings St	5	298	C1	360	C2
Hatfield Pl	2	292	C1	359	A4
Haughwout Av	2	301	A6	359	A4
Hauxhurst Av	W.T.	328	C3	346	B3
Haven Av	6	305	B4	359	C6
Haven Esplanade	1	290	C3	359	A6
Havenwood Rd	1	290	C2	359	A6
Hawley Av	12	307	C4	366	B3
Hawthorne Av	14	301	B4	358	B3
Hawthorne Av	J.C.	320	C2	346	C1
Hawthorne Av S	14	301	B5	359	B4
Hay St	4	295	C5	359	B6
Haynes St	9	307	C4	366	B3
Haywood St	7	310	B2	366	C2
Heaney Av	3	301	A4	358	A3
Heather Ct	3	301	A4	358	B3
Heberton Av	2	292	C2	359	A4
Hecker St	7	310	B2	366	C1
Heckman Dr	J.C.	316	C1	352	B2
Heenan Av	12	307	B5	366	B3
Heffernan St	12	302	C3	367	A4
Heindel Av	N.B.T.	331	B4	342	C3
Heinz Av	8	308	B3	367	B5
Helen St	S.T.	324	B2	346	B1
Helena Rd	4	294	C3	359	C5
Helene Ct	9	306	B3	366	B2
Helios Pl	9	306	B3	366	B3
Hemlock Ct	9	306	A3	366	B2
Hemlock La	9	306	B2	366	B2
Hemlock St	9	306	A3	366	B3
Hemlock St	J.C.	316	B1	352	A2
Hempstead Av	6	305	B4	367	Inset
Henderson Av	0	293	C5	359	A5
1-370	1	290	B2	359	A6
371-OUT	10	293	C5	359	A5
Hendricks Av	1	291	B4	359	A6
Henning St	14	294	B3	359	B5
Henry Pl	5	305	A4	359	C6
Henry St	J.C.	318	A1	346	C2
Henry St	S.T.	324	B2	346	B2
Henry St	U.C.	328	C1	346	B3
Herbert Pl	J.C.	320	C3	346	C1
Herbert St	9	307	C4	366	C3
Hereford St	8	303	C5	367	A5
Herkimer St	1	295	A4	359	B5
Herrick Av	9	306	C2	366	B2
Herrick Ct	B.C.	314	C2	352	C2
Hervey St	9	306	A3	366	A2
Hett Av	6	304	C3	367	Inset
Heusden St	3	313	C5	358	A3
Hewitt Av	1	295	B4	359	B5

Hickory Av	5	295	C6	360	C2
Hickory Cir	12	307	A5	366	A3
Hickory Ct	9	306	A3	366	B2
High St	5	298	A1	360	B2
High St	J.C.	318	A1	346	C2
Highland Av	1	296	B1	359	B6
Highland Av	J.C.	320	C2	346	C1
Highland La	8	308	B3	367	B5
Highland Pl	W.N.Y.T.	329	A5	347	A4
Highland Rd	8	308	A3	367	A5
Highmount Rd	8	308	A3	367	B5
Highpoint Av	W.T.	327	A4	346	B3
Highpoint Rd	4	294	C3	359	B5
Highview Av	1	290	A3	359	A6
Highview Rd	J.C.	316	B2	352	A3
Highwood Av	W.T.	328	C3	346	B3
Highwood Ter	W.T.	328	C3	346	B3
Hill St	4	296	B3	359	B6
Hill St	J.C.	322	C2	346	C2
Hillbrook Ct	5	295	B6	360	B2
Hillbrook Dr	5	295	C6	360	B2
Hillcrest Av	8	308	A3	367	B5
Hillcrest Ct	4	295	C5	359	B6
Hillcrest Pl	N.B.T.	331	B5	342	C3
Hillcrest Rd	1	296	B2	359	B6
Hillcrest St	0	308	B2	367	B5
1-243	8	308	B3	367	B5
244-OUT	12	308	B2	367	B5
Hillcrest Ter	5	295	C5	359	B6
Hilldale Ct	5	295	B6	360	B2
Hillis St	12	308	B1	367	B4
Hillman Av	14	300	B3	358	B3
Hillridge Ct	5	295	B6	360	B2
Hillside Av	4	296	C2	359	B6
Hillside Pl	N.B.T.	328	B2	346	A3
Hillside Rd	W.N.Y.T.	329	A6	347	A4
Hillside Ter	8	308	A3	367	A5
Hilltop Pl	8	308	A3	367	B5
Hilltop Rd	12	308	B2	367	B5
Hilltop Ter	4	304	A3	359	C5
Hillview La	4	295	C4	359	C5
Hillview Pl	4	295	C4	359	C5
Hillwood Ct	5	295	B6	360	B2
Hinton St	12	302	C3	367	A4
Hitchcock Av	6	304	B1	359	C4
Hobart Av	B.C.	293	A4	359	A5
Hoboken Av	J.C.	322	C1	346	C2
Hobson St	J.C.	322	A3	346	C2
Hoda Pl	12	307	B5	367	B4
Hodges Pl	14	294	B2	359	B5
Holbernt Ct	2	301	A6	359	A4
Holcomb Av	12	307	A5	366	B3
Holden Blvd	14	301	C6	359	B4
Holdridge Av	12	308	B2	367	B4
Holgate St	14	301	B5	359	B4
Holiday Dr	3	301	A4	358	B3
Holiday Wy	14	301	A4	358	B3
Holland Av	3	312	C2	358	A3
Holland St	J.C.	322	A3	346	C2
Holly Av	8	308	A3	367	B5
Holly Pl	6	304	B2	367	A6
Holly St	4	295	C4	359	C6
Holly St	J.C.	316	B1	352	A2
Holmes Av	J.C.	320	C2	346	C1
Holsman Rd	1	295	B5	359	B6
Holton Av	9	311	B5	366	C3
Home Av	5	298	A1	360	B2
Home Pl	0	301	B5	359	B4
1-69	2	301	B5	359	B4
70-OUT	14	301	B5	359	B4
Homer St	4	291	C5	359	A6
Homestead Av	2	292	C1	359	A4
Homestead Pl	J.C.	320	C3	346	C2
Hook Rd	B.C.	315	C4	352	C3
Hook Rd	B.C.	314	C2	352	C2
Hooker Pl	0	313	C6	359	A4
1-199	2	313	C6	359	A4
200-OUT	3	313	C6	359	A4
Hooper Av	6	309	A4	367	A6
Hope Av	5	298	A1	360	B2
Hope La	5	298	A1	360	B2
Hopkins Av	6	304	C1	367	A6
Hopkins Av	J.C.	322	C1	346	C2
Hopping Av	7	310	B1	366	C1
Houseman Av	3	313	C6	359	A4
Houston La	2	301	A5	359	B4
Houston St	14	301	A5	359	B4
Howard Av	1	296	C1	359	B6
Howard Cir	1	296	A2	359	A6
Howard Ct	10	293	B5	359	A5
Howard Pl	B.C.	314	C1	352	C1
Howard Pl	J.C.	317	A4	353	A4
Howe St	10	294	A3	359	A5
Howell St	J.C.	320	B2	346	C1
Howton Av	8	303	C5	367	A5
Hoyt Av	1	290	C1	359	A5
Hudson Av	5	298	B2	360	B2
Hudson Av	G.T.	332	B3	347	A4
Hudson Av	U.C.	328	C2	346	B3
Hudson Av	W.T.	327	A4	346	B3
Hudson Av	W.N.Y.T.	329	A4	346	A3
Hudson Ct	B.C.	314	A3	352	B2
Hudson Pl	3	301	A4	358	A3
Hudson Pl	H.C.	323	C5	346	C3
Hudson Pl	W.T.	329	C4	346	B3
Hudson St	4	296	B3	359	B6
Hudson St	H.C.	323	B5	346	C3
Hudson St	J.C.	319	C5	353	A5
Hughes Av	14	300	B2	358	B2
Huguenot Av	12	307	B4	366	A3
Hull Av	6	304	A3	359	C5
Humbert St	5	295	C6	360	C2
Humphrey Av	B.C.	292	A2	359	A4
Hunt La	4	294	C3	359	B5
Hunter Av	6	304	A3	359	C6
Hunter Pl	1	290	C1	359	A5
Hunter St	4	295	C4	359	B6
Hunton St	4	295	C4	359	C6
Hurlbert St	5	305	A5	359	C6
Huron Av	J.C.	320	B3	346	C1
Huron Pl	1	295	A4	359	A5
Hurst St	10	292	C3	359	A4
Husson St	0	305	A4	359	C6
1-199	5	305	A4	359	C6
200-OUT	6	304	B3	359	C6
Hutton St	J.C.	322	A1	346	C2
Hyatt St	1	291	B5	359	A6
Hygeia Pl	4	296	A3	359	A6
Hylan Blvd	0	295	B6	360	B2
1-69	5	297	C6	360	B2
1970-3534	6	304	B3	359	C5
3535-4225	8	308	B3	367	B5
4226-5503	12	308	C1	367	B4
5504-6800	9	311	B4	366	C3
6801-OUT	7	310	C1	366	C2

Staten Island

Ibsen Av	12	302	C3	367	A4
Ida Ct	12	307	B5	367	B4
Idaho Av	9	306	C3	366	B2
Idlease Pl	6	305	B4	359	C6
Igros Ct	9	306	C3	366	B2
Ilion Pl	6	304	B1	367	A6
Ilyse Ct	6	303	C6	367	A5
Ilyssa Wy	12	302	C3	367	A4
Ina St	6	304	C3	367	Inset
Indale Av	9	311	B5	366	C3
Independence Av	14	303	B4	367	A4
Industrial Dr	J.C.	315	A4	352	B3
Industrial Lp	9	306	A1	366	B2
Industry Rd	14	300	B1	358	B2
Inez St	9	311	B5	366	C3
Ingham Av	B.C.	293	A4	359	A5
Ingram Av	14	301	B6	359	B4
Ingwersen Pl	J.C.	317	A4	353	A4
Innis St	0	313	C6	359	A4
1-134	2	313	C6	359	A4
135-OUT	3	313	C6	359	A4
Inwood Rd	1	295	B4	359	B6
Iona St	5	305	B5	359	C6
Ionia Av	0	307	B5	367	B4
1-796	12	307	B5	367	B4
797-OUT	9	306	B3	366	B3
Iorio Ct	J.C.	316	B2	352	A3
Iowa Pl	14	301	B6	359	B4
Iris Ct	9	306	A3	366	A2
Irma Pl	1	295	A4	359	B5
Iron Mine Dr	4	304	A3	359	C5
Ironwood St	8	303	C6	367	A5
Iroquois St	5	305	B5	359	C6
Irving Pl	4	296	C3	359	B6
Irving Pl	S.T.	324	A2	346	A2
Irving St	J.C.	326	C1	346	B2
Irvington St	12	307	C5	366	C3
Isabella Av	6	304	C2	367	A6
Isabella Av	B.C.	314	C2	352	C2
Isernia Av	6	304	C3	367	Inset
Island Blvd	S.T.	330	C1	346	A2
Islin Pl	2	292	C3	359	A4
Islington St	8	303	C5	367	A5
Ismay St	14	301	C5	359	C4
Isora Pl	6	304	C2	367	A6
Ithaca St	6	304	C2	367	A6
Ivy Ct	9	306	A3	366	B2
Ivy Pl	J.C.	317	A4	353	A4
Jackson Av	5	298	C1	360	C2
Jackson Av	J.C.	317	A4	353	A4
Jackson St	4	297	A4	359	A6
Jackson St	G.T.	332	B2	346	A3
Jackson St	H.C.	322	B3	346	C2
Jackson St	W.N.Y.T.	332	C1	346	A3
Jacob St	7	310	B2	366	C2
Jacques Av	6	304	B2	367	A6
Jaffe St	2	301	A5	359	B4
James Av	J.C.	320	B2	346	C1
James Ct	14	301	A4	358	B3
James La	12	308	B1	367	B4
James Pl	5	295	B6	360	B2
Jamie La	12	302	C3	367	A4
Jane St	N.B.T.	324	B4	346	B2
Jane St	W.T.	327	A4	346	B3
Jansen Ct	12	308	C1	367	A4
Jansen St	12	307	C5	366	C3
Jardine Av	14	300	B3	358	B3
Jarvis Av	12	307	C5	367	B4
Jasper St	14	301	C5	359	C4
Jay St	6	305	B4	367	Inset
Jeannette Av	12	308	B1	367	B4
Jeannette St	U.C.	328	C1	346	B3
Jefferson Av	6	304	A3	359	C5
Jefferson Av	J.C.	322	B1	346	C2
Jefferson Av	S.T.	324	B2	346	B2
Jefferson Blvd	12	307	A5	366	B3
Jefferson St	0	304	A3	359	C5
1-200	4	305	A4	359	C6
201-OUT	6	304	A3	359	C5
Jefferson St	H.C.	323	A4	346	C3
Jefferson St	W.T.	328	C3	346	B3
Jefferson St	W.N.Y.T.	332	C1	346	A3
Jeffrey Pl	7	310	B2	366	C2
Jenna La	4	304	A3	359	C5
Jennifer Ct	14	300	C3	358	C3
Jennifer La	6	304	C3	367	Inset
Jennifer Pl	14	301	B4	358	B3
Jerome Av	5	295	C6	359	C6
Jerome Rd	5	305	A5	359	C6
Jersey Av	J.C.	318	C2	353	A4
Jersey City Blvd	J.C.	317	B5	353	A4
Jersey St	1	290	A3	359	A6
Jessica Ct	12	308	A1	367	B4
Jessica La	9	306	B2	366	B2
Jewett Av	0	292	C3	359	A4
1-593	2	292	C3	359	A4
594-OUT	14	301	B6	359	B4
Jewett Av	J.C.	316	A3	352	A3
Jillian Ct	10	301	A6	359	B4
Joan Pl	14	301	B6	359	B4
Joan Reeter	B.C.	314	B2	352	C2
Joel Pl	6	304	B1	367	A6
Johanna La	9	307	C4	366	C3
John F Kennedy Blvd	B.C.	292	A1	359	A4
John F Kennedy Blvd	G.T.	332	B2	346	A3
John F Kennedy Blvd	J.C.	326	C1	346	B2
John F Kennedy Blvd	N.B.T.	332	A2	342	C2
John F Kennedy Blvd	U.C.	326	A2	346	B2
John F Kennedy Blvd	W.N.Y.T.	328	A3	346	A3
John F Kennedy Boulevard East Blvd	N.B.T.	333	B5	347	A4
John F Kennedy Boulevard East Blvd	W.T.	329	C4	346	B3
John F Kennedy Boulevard East Blvd	W.N.Y.T.	329	A5	347	B4
John St	2	313	C6	359	A4
John St	J.C.	316	B3	352	A3
John St	S.T.	324	A2	346	A2
Johnson Av	7	310	B1	366	C1
Johnson Pl	4	305	A4	359	C6
Johnson Pl	W.N.Y.T.	329	A5	347	A4
Johnson St	9	306	A1	366	A2
Johnston Av	J.C.	318	C1	353	A4
Johnston Ter	9	311	B5	366	C3
Joline Av	7	310	B2	366	C2
Joline La	7	310	C2	366	C2
Jones Pl	10	294	A3	359	A5
Jones St	14	300	B3	358	B3
Jones St	J.C.	320	B3	346	C1
Jordan Av	J.C.	317	A4	353	A4
Joseph Av	14	301	C6	359	C4
Joseph Ct	7	310	B2	366	C1
Joseph La	5	295	C6	360	B2
Josephine St	14	294	B2	359	B5
Journeay St	3	313	C4	358	A3

Joyce La	7	310	B2	366	C1
Joyce St	5	305	A4	359	C6
Jules Dr	14	300	A3	358	B3
Julie Ct	14	301	B6	359	B4
Julieann Ct	4	304	A3	359	C5
Juliette St	B.C.	292	A2	359	A4
Jumel St	8	303	C5	367	A5
Juni Ct	14	303	A5	358	C3
Juniper Pl	6	304	A3	359	C5
Juniper St	J.C.	316	B1	352	A2
Jupiter La	3	301	A4	358	A3
Justin Av	6	304	C1	367	A6
Kaltemeier La	5	297	C5	360	B2
Kalver Pl	3	313	C6	359	A4
Kamp Pl	N.B.T.	331	B5	342	C3
Karen Ct	10	301	A6	359	B4
Katan Av	0	308	A1	367	A4
1-479	8	308	A3	367	A4
480-OUT	12	308	A1	367	A4
Katan Lp	8	308	A3	367	A5
Kathleen Ct	7	310	B2	366	C2
Kathy Ct	12	303	C4	367	A4
Kathy Pl	14	303	B4	358	C3
Kay Pl	5	295	B6	359	B6
Kearney Av	J.C.	316	A3	352	A3
Keating Pl	14	303	A5	358	C3
Keating St	9	311	B5	366	C3
Keats St	8	309	C4	367	A5
Keegans La	8	309	C4	367	A5
Keeley St	5	297	C6	360	B2
Keiber Ct	14	301	B6	359	B4
Kell Av	14	301	B6	359	B4
Kelleys La	N.B.T.	332	B2	346	A3
Kellogg St	J.C.	316	A1	352	A2
Kelly Blvd	14	303	A5	358	C3
Kelly Pkwy	B.C.	292	A3	359	A4
Kelvin Av	6	309	A4	367	A6
Kemball Av	14	301	B6	359	B4
Kenilworth Av	12	302	C3	367	A4
Kenmore St	12	302	C3	367	A4
Kenneth Pl	9	311	B4	366	C2
Kennington St	8	303	C5	367	A5
Kenny Rd	9	310	B3	366	C2
Kensico St	6	303	B6	367	A5
Kensington Av	5	295	C6	359	C6
Kensington Av	J.C.	316	A3	352	A3
Kent St	6	304	B1	359	C4
Kenwood Av	12	308	C1	367	C4
Keppel Av	7	310	B2	366	C1
Kermit Av	5	295	C5	359	C6
Kerrigan Av	U.C.	326	A2	346	B2
Kerry La	7	310	B2	366	C2
Keune Ct	4	295	C4	359	B5
Kiesel Ter	N.B.T.	332	A2	342	C2
Kimberly La	4	297	C4	359	B6
King Av	W.T.	328	C3	346	B3
King St	0	308	B2	367	B5
1-209	8	308	B3	367	B5
210-OUT	12	308	B2	367	B5
Kingdom Av	12	307	C5	366	B3
Kinghorn St	12	308	C1	367	B4
Kingsbridge Av	14	300	B3	358	B3
Kingsland St	9	311	B5	366	C3
Kingsley Av	14	301	A6	359	B4
Kingsley Pl	1	290	C3	359	A6
Kingston Ct	W.N.Y.T.	329	A6	347	A4
Kingswood Rd	W.T.	327	A5	346	B3
Kinsey Pl	3	300	A3	358	A3
Kirby Ct	1	290	B2	359	A6
Kirshon Av	14	300	B3	358	B3
Kissam Av	6	304	C2	367	A6
Kissel Av	0	293	B6	359	A5
1-399	10	293	B6	359	A5
400-OUT	1	290	C1	359	A5
Kiswick St	6	305	B4	367	Inset
Klondike Av	14	303	A5	358	C3
Knapp St	14	300	C3	358	C3
Knauth Pl	5	298	B1	360	B2
Knesel St	9	306	A3	366	A2
Knollwood Ct	3	300	A3	358	B3
Knox Pl	14	294	B3	359	B5
Knox St	9	307	C4	366	C3
Koch Blvd	12	308	B2	367	B4
Koelle Blvd	S.T.	330	C1	346	A2
Korean War Memorial Pkwy	9	306	C3	366	B2
Korean War Memorial Pkwy	12	307	B4	366	B3
Kraft Pl	12	308	B1	367	B4
Kramer Av	9	306	B3	366	B2
Kramer Pl	2	301	A6	359	A4
Kramer St	5	295	C5	359	C6
Kreischer St	9	306	B1	366	B1
Kristen Ct	4	297	B4	359	B6
Kruser St	4	304	B2	359	C5
Kunath Av	9	306	A3	366	B2
Kyle Ct	12	302	C2	366	A3
La Forge Pl	2	292	C1	359	A4
La Grange Pl	2	301	A5	359	A4
Labau Av	1	294	B3	359	B5
Lacon St	6	303	C5	367	A5
Laconia Av	0	305	A4	359	C6
1-599	5	305	A4	359	C6
600-OUT	4	305	B4	359	C6
Ladd Av	12	302	C3	367	A4
Lafayette Av	1	290	A2	359	A6
Lafayette St	7	310	B1	366	C1
Lafayette St	J.C.	317	A4	353	A4
Laforge Av	2	292	C1	359	A4
Laguardia Av	14	294	C3	359	B5
Laguna La	3	313	C5	358	A3
Laidlaw Av	J.C.	322	C1	346	C2
Lake Av	3	313	C5	358	A3
Lake St	J.C.	320	B3	346	C2
Lake View Dr	J.C.	320	C1	346	C1
Lakeland Rd	14	294	B3	359	B5
Lakeside Pl	5	295	C5	359	C6
Lakeview Ter	5	295	C5	359	B6
Lakewood Rd	1	295	A4	359	A5
Lambert St	14	301	B4	358	B3
Lamberts La	14	300	B3	358	B3
Lamoka Av	0	308	A3	367	B5
1-331	8	308	A3	367	B5
332-OUT	12	308	A1	367	B4
Lamont Av	0	306	B3	366	B3
1-796	12	307	B4	367	B4
797-OUT	9	306	B3	366	B3
Lamped Lp	14	303	A4	358	C3
Lamport Blvd	5	295	C6	359	C6
Lander Av	14	300	B3	358	B3
Landings La	W.N.Y.T.	329	A6	347	A4
Landis Av	5	295	C6	360	B2
Lane	B.C.	314	C1	352	C1
Langere Pl	5	297	C5	360	B2
Lanni Av	J.C.	318	C1	353	A4

Lansing St	5	305	A6	360	C2
Larch Av	J.C.	320	B3	346	C1
Larch St	9	306	A3	366	A2
Laredo Av	12	308	A1	367	B4
Larkin St	2	292	B2	359	A4
Larrison Lp	14	301	C6	359	C4
Lasalle St	3	313	C6	359	A4
Latham Pl	9	306	B3	366	B3
Lathrop Av	0	301	A5	359	B4
1-300	14	301	A5	359	B4
301-OUT	2	301	A5	359	B4
Latimer Av	14	300	C2	358	C2
Latourette La	14	303	A6	359	C4
Latourette Pl	B.C.	314	C1	352	C1
Latourette St	9	306	C3	366	C3
Laurance Pl	W.T.	327	B4	346	B3
Laurel Av	4	296	B3	359	B6
Laurel Ct	J.C.	319	B4	353	A5
Laurie Ct	4	295	C4	359	C5
Law Pl	10	294	A3	359	A5
Lawn Av	6	304	B1	359	C4
Lawrence Av	10	294	A3	359	A5
Layton Av	1	291	B4	359	A6
Leason Pl	14	303	A5	358	C3
Ledyard Pl	5	295	C5	359	C6
Lee Av	7	310	B1	366	C1
Leeds St	6	304	C1	367	A6
Leewood Lp	4	295	B6	359	B6
Legate Av	12	307	A5	366	A3
Leggett Pl	14	301	B4	358	B3
Legion Pl	5	295	C6	359	C6
Leigh Av	14	300	B3	358	B3
Lembeck Av	J.C.	316	C2	352	B3
Lenevar Av	9	306	B3	366	B3
Lenhart St	7	310	B2	366	C1
Lennon Ct	6	303	C4	367	A4
Lenore Ct	14	301	B4	358	B3
Lenzie St	12	308	B2	367	B4
Leo St	14	301	A4	358	B3
Leona St	14	301	B4	358	B3
Leonard Av	0	301	A5	359	B4
1-330	14	301	B5	359	B4
331-OUT	2	301	A5	359	B4
Leonard St	J.C.	326	B1	346	B2
Leroy St	14	300	C1	358	C2
Leslie Av	5	295	C5	359	C6
Leslie La	12	308	B1	367	B4
Lester St	14	301	B6	359	B4
Leverett Av	0	303	C5	367	A5
1-546	8	303	C5	367	A5
547-OUT	12	308	A1	367	A4
Leverett Ct	8	303	C5	367	A5
Levit Av	14	301	B5	359	B4
Lewis Av	J.C.	320	B2	346	C1
Lewiston St	14	303	A5	358	C3
Lexa Pl	12	307	B5	366	B3
Lexington Av	2	301	A6	359	A4
Lexington Av	B.C.	292	A3	359	A4
Lexington Av	J.C.	316	A2	352	A3
Lexington La	8	303	C5	367	A5
Leyden Av	3	313	C4	358	A3
Liberty Av	0	304	A3	359	C5
1-149	4	304	A3	359	C5
150-OUT	5	305	A4	359	C6
Liberty Av	J.C.	321	A4	346	B2
Liberty Av	N.B.T.	332	B1	346	A3
Liberty Pl	W.T.	329	C4	346	B3
Library Ct	B.C.	314	C2	352	C2
Lienau Pl	J.C.	322	B1	346	C2
Lighthouse Av	6	303	B6	359	C4
Lighting Way	S.T.	330	C1	346	A2
Lightner Av	14	294	B3	359	B5
Lilac Ct	3	300	A3	358	A3
Lillian Pl	8	308	B3	367	B5
Lily Pond Av	5	298	B1	360	B2
Lincoln Av	6	304	B3	359	C5
Lincoln Av	S.T.	324	B2	346	B1
Lincoln Dr	J.C.	316	A3	352	A3
Lincoln North Dr	J.C.	316	A3	352	A3
Lincoln Pkwy	B.C.	314	A2	352	B2
Lincoln Pl	5	298	B1	360	B2
Lincoln Pl	W.T.	327	A4	346	B3
Lincoln Pl	W.N.Y.T.	333	C4	347	A4
Lincoln South Dr	J.C.	316	A3	352	A3
Lincoln St	14	294	C2	359	B4
Lincoln St	J.C.	322	A1	346	C2
Lincoln St	U.C.	328	B2	346	A3
Linda Av	5	298	C1	360	C2
Linda Ct	2	301	A5	359	A4
Lindbergh Av	6	304	C2	367	A6
Linden Av	3	313	C4	358	A3
Linden Av	J.C.	316	B2	352	A3
Linden Av E	J.C.	316	C2	352	B3
Linden Ct	J.C.	316	C2	352	B3
Linden Pl	5	297	C6	360	B2
Linden St	10	293	B6	359	A5
Linden St	B.C.	314	C1	352	C1
Lindenwood Av	8	308	A3	367	A5
Lindenwood Pl	8	308	A3	367	A5
Linder La	4	305	A4	359	C6
Linnet St	B.C.	314	C2	352	C2
Linton Pl	8	303	C5	367	A5
Linwood Av	5	295	C6	359	C6
Lion St	7	310	B2	366	C1
Lipsett Av	12	308	B1	367	B4
Lisa La	12	307	A4	366	A3
Lisa Pl	14	300	C3	358	B3
Lisbon Pl	6	304	B3	359	C5
Lisk Av	3	300	A3	358	B3
Liss St	12	308	B2	367	B4
Little Clove Rd	1	294	B3	359	B5
Littlefield Av	12	308	B3	367	B5
Livermore Av	0	301	B5	359	B4
1-99	2	301	A5	359	B4
100-OUT	14	301	B5	359	B4
Livingston Av	14	301	C6	359	B4
Livingston Ct	10	293	B6	359	A5
Llewellyn Pl	10	301	A6	359	A4
Lloyd Ct	10	294	A3	359	A5
Lockman Av	3	313	C4	358	A3
Lockman Lp	3	313	C4	358	A3
Lockwood Pl	14	301	A6	359	B4
Locust Av	6	304	B2	359	C5
Locust Ct	9	306	A3	366	B2
Locust Pl	8	308	A3	367	B5
Locust Pl	12	308	C1	367	B4
Locust St	J.C.	316	B1	352	A2
Logan Av	1	295	B4	359	B5
Logan Av	J.C.	320	C2	346	C1
Lois La	14	300	B2	358	B2
Lois Pl	1	290	B1	359	A5
Lombard Ct	12	307	A4	366	A3
London Ct	6	304	B1	359	C4
London Rd	6	303	B6	359	C4
Long Pond La	4	296	C3	359	B6

Long St	J.C.	316	C2	352	B3
Longdale St	14	300	B3	358	B3
Longfellow Av	1	295	C4	359	B5
Longview Rd	0	295	B4	359	B6
1-145	4	295	B4	359	B6
146-OUT	1	295	B4	359	B6
Lookout Dr	J.C.	320	C1	346	C1
Loop Rd	5	298	C2	360	C2
Lord Av	B.C.	292	A3	359	A4
Loret Ct	10	294	A3	359	A5
Loretto St	7	310	C2	366	C1
Loring Av	12	308	A1	367	A4
Lorraine Av	12	308	B1	367	B4
Lorraine Lp	9	306	A2	366	B2
Lortel Av	14	294	B3	359	B5
Lott La	14	303	B4	358	C3
Lott St	J.C.	320	C3	346	C2
Louis St	1	296	A2	359	A6
Louis St	S.T.	324	B2	346	B1
Louisa Pl	W.T.	329	B4	346	A3
Louise La	1	294	C3	359	B5
Louise St	12	307	C5	367	B4
Lovelace Av	12	308	A1	367	A4
Lovell Av	14	303	A5	358	C3
Lowell St	6	304	B1	359	C4
Lucille Av	9	306	A2	366	B2
Ludlow St	12	308	A1	367	A4
Ludlow St	J.C.	316	C2	352	B3
Ludwig La	3	301	A4	358	B3
Ludwig La	10	301	A6	359	B4
Ludwig St	10	294	B2	359	A5
Luigi Pl	6	304	B2	359	C5
Luis Munoz Marin Blvd	J.C.	319	C4	353	A5
Luke Ct	6	303	C6	367	A5
Luna Cir	12	308	C2	367	B4
Lundi Ct	14	303	A5	358	C3
Lundsten Rd	9	306	B1	366	B2
Lundys La	J.C.	321	A4	346	B2
Lurene Pl	N.B.T.	333	A5	342	C3
Luten Av	12	307	C5	366	B3
Lyle Ct	6	303	C6	367	A5
Lyman Av	5	298	B1	360	B2
Lyman Pl	4	295	C4	359	B6
Lynch St	12	308	C1	367	B4
Lyndale Av	12	308	B2	367	B4
Lyndale La	12	308	B2	367	B4
Lynhurst Av	5	297	C5	360	B2
Lynn Al	H.C.	322	B3	346	C2
Lynn Ct	14	301	A4	358	B3
Lynn St	6	304	C2	367	A6
Lynnhaven Pl	10	294	A3	359	A5
Lyon Pl	14	301	B5	359	B4
Mace St	6	303	C5	367	A5
Macon Av	12	303	C4	367	A4
Macon Av	12	307	A5	367	A4
Macormac Pl	3	312	C2	358	A3
Mada Av	10	293	C6	359	A5
Madera St	9	307	C4	366	B3
Madigan Pl	4	295	C4	359	B6
Madison Av	14	301	B4	358	B3
Madison Av	J.C.	317	A4	353	A4
Madison St	G.T.	332	B2	346	A3
Madison St	W.N.Y.T.	332	C2	346	A3
Madsen Av	9	306	C1	366	C2
Madson St	H.C.	322	B3	346	C2
Magnolia Av	5	305	A4	359	C6
Magnolia Av	J.C.	318	A1	346	C2
Maguire Av	9	306	C3	366	B2
Maguire Ct	9	306	C3	366	B2
Maiden Ct	7	310	B2	366	C1
Maiden La	J.C.	317	A4	353	A4
Main St	7	310	C1	366	C2
Maine Av	14	301	A5	359	B4
Majestic Av	9	306	A2	366	A2
Major Av	5	298	C1	360	C2
Malden Pl	6	304	C2	367	A6
Mall Dr E	J.C.	319	B4	353	A5
Mall Dr W	J.C.	319	A4	346	C2
Mallard La	9	306	B2	366	B2
Mallory Av	5	295	C6	359	C6
Mallory Av	J.C.	316	A2	352	A3
Mallow St	9	306	A3	366	B3
Malone Av	6	304	C1	367	A6
Manchester Dr	12	307	A4	366	A3
Mandy Ct	9	306	B2	366	B2
Manee Av	9	306	C3	366	B3
Manhattan Av	J.C.	322	B1	346	C2
Manhattan Av	U.C.	326	B3	346	B2
Manhattan St	7	310	C2	366	C1
Manila Av	6	304	C3	367	Inset
Manila Av	J.C.	319	B4	353	A5
Manila Pl	6	304	C3	367	Inset
Manley St	9	306	B1	366	B1
Mann Av	14	301	B6	359	B4
Mann Av S	14	301	B6	359	B4
Mannarville Ct	5	295	C6	359	B6
Manning Av	J.C.	318	C1	353	A4
Manor Ct	6	303	B6	359	C4
Manor Rd	0	301	A6	359	A4
1-200	10	301	A6	359	A4
201-OUT	14	294	B2	359	B5
Mansichewitz Plz	J.C.	319	B4	353	A5
Mansion Av	8	309	A4	367	B5
Manton Pl	4	295	B5	359	B6
Maple Av	2	292	B2	359	A4
Maple Ct	12	307	A4	366	A3
Maple Pkwy	3	313	C4	358	A3
Maple St	J.C.	318	C1	353	A4
Maple St	W.T.	327	A4	346	B3
Maple Ter	6	304	C3	367	Inset
Mapleton Av	6	305	B4	367	Inset
Maplewood Av	6	304	B1	367	A6
Maplewood Pl	6	304	B3	359	C5
Marble St	14	301	B5	359	B4
Marc St	14	301	A4	358	B3
Marcia Lp	5	297	C6	360	B2
Marcus St	J.C.	316	B3	352	A3
Marcy Av	12	307	B4	366	B3
Marcy Av	J.C.	316	A2	352	A3
Maretzek Ct	9	306	C3	366	B2
Margaret St	8	308	A3	367	A5
Margaret St	B.C.	314	C1	352	C1
Margaretta Ct	14	301	B6	359	B4
Marge St	S.T.	324	B2	346	B1
Margo Lp	1	291	C5	359	A6
Maria La	12	308	A2	367	B4
Marianne St	2	301	A5	359	A4
Marie Pl	4	295	C4	359	B6
Marie St	4	295	C5	359	B6
Marine Dr	9	311	B5	366	C3
Marine Rd	N.B.T.	333	B5	347	A4
Marine Wy	6	304	C3	367	Inset
Mariners La	3	313	C5	358	A3
Marion Av	4	296	A3	359	A6
Marion Ct	B.C.	292	A3	359	A4

Marion Pl	J.C.	320	C2	346	C1
Marion St	10	301	A6	359	A4
Marisa Cir	9	306	B3	366	B2
Marjorie St	9	306	B1	366	B2
Mark St	4	295	C4	359	C6
Market Pl	W.N.Y.T.	328	A3	346	A3
Market St	10	293	C5	359	A5
Markham Ct	10	293	B5	359	A5
Markham Dr	10	293	B5	359	A5
Markham La	10	293	B5	359	A5
Markham Pl	14	301	B6	359	B4
Markham Rd	10	293	B5	359	A5
Markham Wk	10	293	B5	359	A5
Marks Pl	N.B.T.	331	B5	342	C3
Marne Av	12	308	A1	367	A4
Marscher Pl	9	311	B5	366	C3
Marsh Av	14	303	B4	358	C3
Marshall Av	14	294	C2	359	B5
Marshall Rd	5	298	B1	360	B2
Marshall St	H.C.	322	B3	346	C2
Martha St	1	296	C1	359	B6
Martin Av	14	301	B5	359	B4
Martin Luther King Dr	J.C.	316	B2	352	A3
Martineau St	3	312	B2	358	A3
Martling Av	0	294	A2	359	B5
1-214	10	294	A2	359	B5
215-OUT	14	294	A2	359	B5
Marvin Rd	9	306	B3	366	B2
Marx St	1	294	B3	359	B5
Mary St	4	295	B5	359	B6
Maryland Av	5	297	C6	360	B2
Maryland La	5	295	B6	359	B6
Maryland Pl	14	301	A6	359	B4
Mason Av	0	305	A4	359	C6
1-532	5	305	A4	359	C6
533-OUT	6	305	B4	359	C6
Mason Blvd	9	306	B3	366	B2
Mason St	4	295	C4	359	C6
Massachusetts St	7	310	C1	366	C1
Mathews Av	10	294	A3	359	A5
Matthew Pl	3	301	A4	358	B3
Maxwell St	J.C.	318	B3	353	A5
May Av	14	300	B3	358	B3
May Pl	12	308	B1	367	B4
Mayberry Promenade	12	308	C2	367	B5
Maybury Av	8	309	A4	367	B5
Maybury Ct	6	309	A4	367	B5
Mazza Ct	12	302	C1	366	A3
Mazzoni Pl	N.B.T.	330	B3	342	C2
McAdoo Av	J.C.	316	B2	352	A3
McArthur Av	12	308	A1	367	A4
McBaine Av	9	306	B3	366	B2
McCall Pl	4	295	C5	359	B6
McClean Av	5	298	C1	359	C6
McCormick Pl	5	295	C5	359	C6
McCully Av	6	304	B1	359	C4
McDermott Av	5	305	A5	359	C6
McDivitt Av	14	303	A5	358	C3
McDonald St	14	301	C6	359	B4
McDougal St	J.C.	317	A4	353	A4
McFarland Av	5	298	C1	360	C2
McGinley Sq	J.C.	317	A4	353	A4
McGregor St	9	307	C4	366	C3
McKee Av	8	309	A4	367	B5
McKinley Av	6	303	C5	367	A5
Mckinley Pl	W.N.Y.T.	333	C4	347	A4
McLaughlin St	5	305	A6	360	C2
Mcpherson Pl	J.C.	318	A2	346	C2
McVeigh Av	14	303	A5	358	C3
Mead St	J.C.	320	C2	346	C1
Meade Lp	9	306	C2	366	C2
Meade St	9	306	C2	366	C2
Meadow Av	4	295	C4	359	B6
Meadow Av	N.B.T.	325	B4	346	B2
Meadow Ct	9	306	A3	366	B2
Meadow La	6	309	C4	367	A5
Meadow Pl	6	305	B4	359	C6
Meadow St	B.C.	314	C2	352	C2
Meadow St	J.C.	320	B2	346	C1
Meadowlands Pkwy	S.T.	324	A1	346	A1
Meadowview Av	N.B.T.	332	C1	346	A3
Mechanic St	B.C.	314	C2	352	C2
Medford Rd	4	295	C4	359	C5
Medina St	6	304	C2	367	A6
Meeker St	6	304	B1	359	C4
Meisner Av	6	304	B1	359	C4
Melba St	14	301	C5	359	B4
Melhorn Rd	14	294	B3	359	B5
Melissa St	14	301	A4	358	B3
Melrose Av	1	295	A4	359	B5
Melrose Pl	8	308	A3	367	B5
Melville St	9	311	B5	366	C3
Melvin Av	14	302	A2	358	C2
Melyn Pl	3	301	A4	358	B3
Memo St	9	311	B5	366	C3
Memphis Av	12	308	A1	367	B4
Mena St	6	303	C5	367	A5
Mendelsohn St	5	295	B6	360	B2
Mercer Loop	J.C.	318	B1	353	A4
Mercer Pl	8	308	B3	367	B5
Mercer St	J.C.	318	B2	353	A4
Mercury La	14	303	A5	358	C3
Meredith Av	14	300	C1	358	B2
Merkel Pl	9	309	A6	367	A6
Merle Pl	5	295	B6	360	B2
Merrick Av	1	294	C3	359	B5
Merrill Av	14	300	B3	358	B3
Merriman Av	14	301	A6	359	B4
Merritt St	J.C.	316	C1	352	B2
Merry Mount St	14	303	A4	358	C3
Merseles St	J.C.	318	B1	353	A4
Mersereau Av	3	312	C3	358	A3
Metcalfe St	4	296	C3	359	B6
Metro Wy	S.T.	324	B1	346	B1
Metropolitan Av	1	295	A4	359	B5
Meyer La	5	298	A1	360	B2
Michael Ct	8	303	C5	367	A5
Michael Dermott Pl (Pvt)	J.C.	320	A3	346	B1
Michele La	6	304	C3	367	Inset
Michelle Ct	3	301	A4	358	A3
Middle Loop Rd	8	308	A2	367	A4
Midland Av	6	304	B3	359	C5
Midland Ct	W.N.Y.T.	329	A6	347	A4
Midland Rd	8	308	A3	367	A5
Midway Pl	4	295	C4	359	C6
Milbank Rd	6	304	C3	367	Inset
Milburn St	6	304	B1	359	C4
Milden Av	1	295	B4	359	B5
Mildred Av	14	302	A2	358	C2
Miles Av	8	303	C5	367	A5
Milford Av	1	295	B4	359	B5
Milford Dr	1	295	B4	359	B5
Mill Ridge Rd	S.T.	330	B1	342	C1
Mill Rd	6	304	C2	367	A6

Staten Island

Staten Island

BRIDGES & TUNNELS